EXPLORERS
OF
ARABIA

EXPLORERS
OF
ARABIA

From the Renaissance to the End of the Victorian Era

ZAHRA FREETH
and
H. V. F. WINSTONE

HOLMES & MEIER PUBLISHERS, INC.

NEW YORK

First published in the United States of America by
Holmes & Meier Publishers, Inc.
101 Fifth Avenue
New York, NY 10003

© 1978 George Allen & Unwin (Publishers) Ltd.

Library of Congress Cataloging in Publication Data

Freeth, Zahra Dickson.
   Explorers of Arabia from the Renaissance to the End of
the Victorian Era.
   Bibliography: p.
   Includes index.
   1. Arabia—Discovery and exploration.
I. Winstone, Harry Victor Frederick, joint author.
II. Title.
DS204.5.F73 1978   953.03   77–15632
ISBN 0–8419–0354–9

PRINTED IN GREAT BRITAIN

Preface

A word of explanation is called for concerning the people chosen to represent the story of exploration and discovery in Arabia. We have selected travellers whose achievements seem to us praiseworthy or neglected, but in doing so we have inevitably made important omissions. A powerful case could be made for the inclusion of the Spaniard Ali Bey, the Swede George Wallin, the Strasburgian Charles Huber, and Germans Johann Wild, Baron Nolde and Ulrich Seetzen. All made notable journeys of discovery. We have brought them into our story wherever appropriate, but we do not pretend that our selection is without subjective preference. In our own century there have been remarkable explorers and outstanding personalities whose inclusion would have added considerably to the picture of Arabia as it built up in the Western mind over the centuries, culminating in the mapping of the last unexplored deserts of central Arabia, particularly the Rub al Khali or Empty Quarter, between the two Great Wars. Few who went before them achieved more by way of discovery, or contributed more to the sum of our knowledge of the lands and people of Arabia, than H. St John Philby and Captain W. H. I. Shakespear; but recent works on both men are readily available, as are the findings of travellers like Thomas and Thesiger. We had to draw the line somewhere and so we started at the Renaissance and finished with the later Victorians, choosing selectively, and sometimes painfully, along the way.

We are gratefully aware that good modern biographies exist of Burckhardt, Burton and Palgrave, and we are indebted to their authors for much background information. But there still seemed a need for more detailed accounts of their Arabian journeys, which were but episodes in full and vigorous lives; for of necessity a biography can deal with them only briefly, against a much broader backcloth. As for the travellers' own tales, most are out of print and of those that are available few make for easy reading. In Sir Richard Burton's case, for example, the account of the pilgrimage to Mecca and Madina is massively indigestible, with its forest of footnotes, its long and erudite conjectures and dissertations on race, religion and the basics of language. By condensing his own lengthy and discursive story we are able to separate some of the finest and most evocative travel prose ever written from the exhaustive detail that surrounds it. In telling Varthema's tale we have, wherever possible, used Eden's Elizabethan English rather than the later style of Winter Jones, the former being more consonant with the voyager's own period and manner.

As for the vexed question of the English spelling of Arabic names and places, we have followed no system save that of common sense. While trying to be consistent in our own text, we have let alternative spellings stand in quotations, except where they are unnecessarily confusing or irritating. But each case has been judged in isolation. Doughty, for instance, makes sublime use of Arabic word and phrase in his unique manner of telling a story and it would be folly to change his carefully judged transliteration. On the other hand, Palgrave and Guarmani used systems of translation which seem tiresomely obtrusive in a modern text and we have changed their spellings throughout. In the case of the wandering people of the desert we have in our own text avoided the Franco-Arabic *bedouin* in preference for the more correct *badu* (collective) and *badawi* or *badawin* (singular and plural). With most other commonly occurring words we have used customary forms.

A book such as this could not be written without the help of those libraries and institutions which keep an ordered record of the past. In particular, our thanks are due to the Royal Geographical Society, the Royal Asiatic Society, the India Office, the Public Record Office, the London Library and, as always when access is needed to rare and ancient books and manuscripts, the British Museum and its associated institution the British Library. Without the generous help of the keepers, librarians and archivists of these bodies, we could not have begun to cover so wide a field, for many of the accounts of early travels in Arabia have long been out of print, some for several centuries. For assistance in establishing some unrecorded facts about Joseph Pitts we would like to express our gratitude to the City Librarian of Exeter. As for illustrations of our subjects we have had to rely on existing and mostly well-known portraits for reference, and our thanks are due to Moira Buj for her fresh rendering of the originals. In the case of the three travellers of whom no known portraits exist – Varthema, Pitts and Guarmani – we have used title pages from early editions of their own works to introduce their chapters.

Finally, it would be churlish to forget the contribution of our publisher, whose guidance brought agreement and action whenever doubt and uncertainty threatened the enterprise, or of our families whose forthright opinions and long-practised forbearance are appreciated in equal measure.

Contents

Illustrations

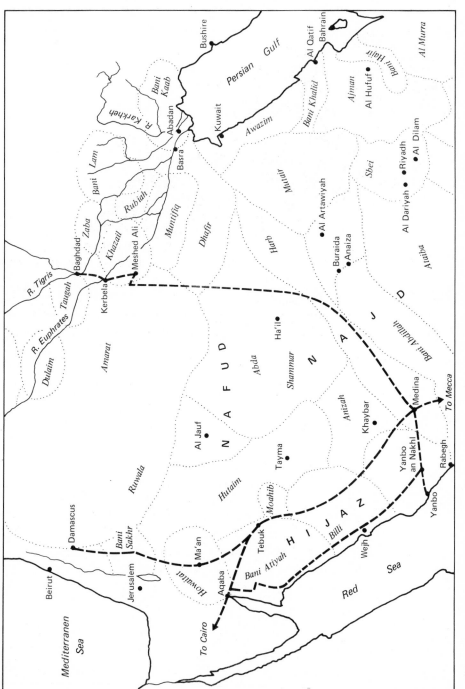

1 Principal features of Arabia – pilgrim routes, chief tribal regions and main places, derived from maps by the Blunts and H. R. P. Dickson

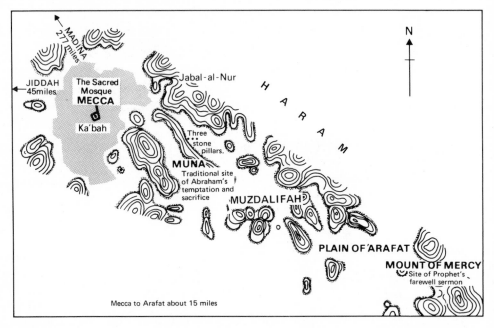

N

MADINA 277 miles

JIDDAH ←45miles

The Sacred Mosque
MECCA
Ka'bah

Jabal-al-Nur

H A R A M

Three stone pillars.

MUNA
Traditional site of Abraham's temptation and sacrifice

MUZDALIFAH

PLAIN OF 'ARAFAT

MOUNT OF MERCY
Site of Prophet's farewell sermon

Mecca to Arafat about 15 miles

2 Haram (sanctuary) and major places of pilgrimage at Mecca (*courtesy ARAMCO Magazine*)

Introduction

Places to which men and women would once journey in the expectation of discovery and adventure are today the easily accessible resorts of the tourist. Desert regions which no more than fifty years ago were the homelands of tribes still following an ancient way of life now house vast complexes of industry. In tracing the pioneering journeys of the explorers of Arabia we have to remember the world as it appeared to them, with its blank spaces, its uncertain delineation, its unknown hazards.

The ancient Greeks and Romans had skirted the coasts of Arabia and sailed through the Red Sea and the gulf that was sometimes called Arabian and sometimes Persian, but through the dark ages following the collapse of the Roman Empire Europeans no longer ventured to the East. The Crusades turned Europe's attention once again to the lands of the Arabs, but they were matters of political intervention and religious zeal that had little to do with exploration.

By the time Europeans began to look again towards the East with thoughts of trade and discovery, much that the ancient wayfarers discovered had been lost. The process of exploration had to begin afresh.

It was the Italians, the Portuguese and the Spaniards who took the initiative in voyaging eastwards once again, setting up new trade routes across lands and seas that were by now under the nominal control of the Tartar moguls and the Ottoman Turks. In the fourteenth century, following the voyages of Marco Polo and his successors, Arabia and the Levant, the Red Sea and the Persian Gulf became once more the highways and staging-posts of trade between Europe and the East. From Basra the commodities of the Orient were taken by land to Aleppo, Damascus and Beirut, where they were picked up by the galleys of Venice. The pilgrim caravans of Mecca began to carry the spices and drugs of the Indies back to Cairo and Damascus.

In the late fifteenth century King John of Portugal set out to find India by the land route. With his Arabic-speaking companions Pedro de Couillan and Alfonso de Payua, he went from Naples via Rhodes to Cairo and through the Red Sea to Aden. De Couillan became the first European since the last days of the Roman Empire to make a recorded visit to the Arabian mainland. The Portuguese went on to win command of the seas and to dot the coastlines of Arabia, the Indies and Africa with their fortresses and trading stations.

The Dutch stirred too. In the sixteenth and seventeenth centuries their fleets began to compete with Spaniards and Portuguese in the new mood of adventure and discovery. England, glorying in the strength of its navy, was still pleading with Elizabeth I for authority to join in the mercantile race but it was not until 1609 that the East India Company's ships were able to offer real opposition to the Portuguese and Dutch. When they did, the English quickly demonstrated their mastery of trade and diplomacy at the court of the Great Mogul, at Aleppo and Isfahan, Ormuz and Baghdad.

But though the ships and merchants of the West began to visit the harbours and towns of coastal Arabia, the interior long remained inviolate. The unwelcoming depths of Najd were to remain a mystery for many centuries to come. Here was a vast and intriguing question-mark on the map, and one which posed a challenge of a special kind.

David Hogarth, in his book *The Penetration of Arabia*, published in 1904, writes of the men who took up that challenge:

But short as the roll is, a reader might well wonder that it shows so many names as in fact it does, and among them an unusual tale of men of varied and great gifts – men like Niebuhr, Seetzen, Burck-hardt, Wallin, Burton, Palgrave, Halévy, Doughty, Blunt, Huber, Euting, Hurgronje, Glaser – men of too serious mind to have been tempted by mere love of adventure or the forbidden thing. Why did such as these hazard themselves in a land so naked that none covets it. . . . ?

And he answers his own question thus:

Had the Arabs propagated Islam only, had they only known that single period of marvellous expansion wherein they assimilated to their creed, speech and even physical type, more aliens than any other stock before or since ... even so the Arabs would still make a paramount claim on western interest. But when we remember that, not only as the head and fount of pure Semitism they originated Judaism, and largely determined its character and that of Christianity, but also that the expansion of the Arabian conception of the relation of man to God and man to man (the Arabian social system, in a word) is still proceeding faster and farther than any other propagandism, can we wonder that men of serious mind and imaginative temperament have braved so much to study this folk in its home?

Exploration usually demands the qualities of bravery, curiosity and organising ability. Arabia, by the time the East had been opened up by the mariners and the new merchantmen, demanded more of the voyager: linguistic ability of a high order, scholarship and, as Hogarth observed, imaginative temperament. It was always possible to explore the inner reaches of India, Africa and much of Asia without bothering even with the rudiments of language, as Speke and others were to demonstrate in the nineteenth century, and as countless occupying forces had shown from time immemorial. But when geographical enquiry and religious curiosity became the twin incentives to travel in Arabia it was necessary to speak the language with fluency. It was also necessary to pass as a native, if not of Arabia then of part of the Islamic world. There were special difficulties in store for the traveller who went as an unbeliever.

Inevitably, the holy cities of Mecca and Madina attracted would-be travellers from the Western world for centuries after the medieval awakening. It was not, in fact, until the nineteenth century, when geographical enquiry and the elaboration of existing maps became matters of urgent concern to Europe, that explorers began to turn their attention to the great central deserts, to Nafud and Najd, to the Empty Quarter and the Hadhramaut.

The early explorers faced untold dangers. Schisms among the faithful had caused great rivalry within Islam and even at Mecca there was seldom much amity between the Sunni, Shia and other factions. The pilgrim, and especially the Christian in disguise, who followed the established routes, the Darb al Hajj, to Mecca, was wise to learn the nature of a believer's faith before entering into too intimate a conversation.

Apart from differences inherent in the faith, tribal conflict tore at the heart of Arabia until, at the beginning of the eighteenth century, a new and cohesive religious zeal came to the desert under the guidance of the austere and puritanical Muhammad ibn Abdul Wahhab. The immensely powerful tribes of Najd were the first to fall under his spell and in 1745 Muhammad ibn Saud, chief of the Aridh province, became the first Wahhabi amir. Thus the House of Saud, hereditary rulers of the lands at the centre of Arabia, became associated for ever after with the name of the founder of the reformed faith. By the end of the century the Wahhabi state stretched from one end of the peninsula to the other, with its capital at Dariya under the leadership of the Sauds. It was not until 1818 that the Saudi army was halted in its march of conquest by the Ottoman power. Some of the most powerful tribes, with a truly badawin sense of self-preservation, deserted the cause of the Sauds and soon another source of desert conflict emerged from the ashes of Saudi defeat. A new dynasty arose in central Arabia, the House of Rashid based at Hail, capital of Jabal Shammar. The struggle for ascendancy which followed, with its history of tribal warfare and of murder and assassination among the princes of Hail, must rank as one of the most treacherous and bloody episodes of modern history.

It is within the framework of these religious and secular struggles, and of the hazards posed by the desert and its tribes, that our travellers set out to discover Arabia.

Of those who made the hard and testing journey into the depths of the peninsula some perished before they could tell their tale. A few wrote accounts of their own. Others left diaries and records from which their stories could be told at second hand. Among those travellers who went by camel and foot to face the searing day and the shivering night, none would have denied the truth of Lord Belhaven's observation: 'Arabia is a hard, barren mistress and those who serve her she pays in weariness, sickness of the body and distress of the mind.'

Chapter I

LODOVICO VARTHEMA

Gentleman of Rome

1503–1508

'If any man shall demand of me the cause of my voyage, certainly I can show no better reason than the ardent desire of knowledge, which has moved many a man to see the world and the miracles of God therein.'

Varthema

Title page of 1519 edition of Varthema's *Itinerary* published in Milan
(*courtesy British Library*)

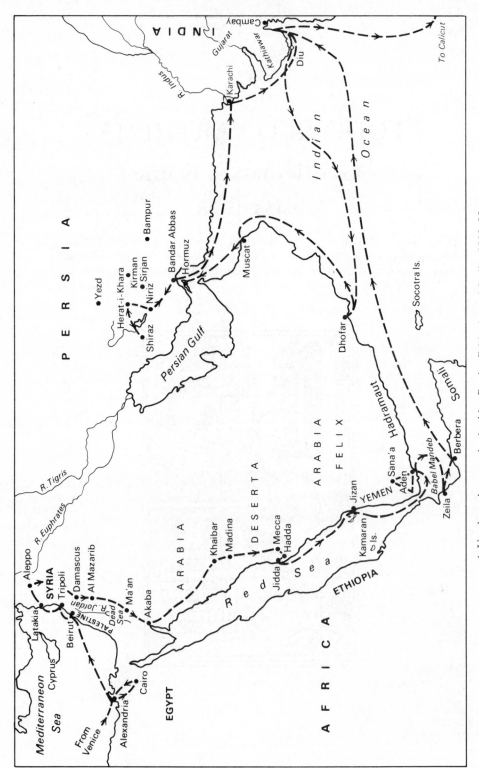

4 Varthema's routes in Arabia, Persia, Ethiopia and India, 1503–08

It was no more than four years after the opening up of the sea route to India by Vasco de Gama that Lodovico Varthema left his native Italy for the East.

His journey in the earliest years of the sixteenth century took him to Egypt and the Levant, to Arabia and across the Red Sea to the land of Prester John, to Persia, Syria and the Indies. He joined the Portuguese army and he took military service, along with the delights and dangers of exploration, in his eager stride. He learned new languages as he went, adopted foreign customs with cosmopolitan ease, and embraced loyalties and religious faiths as readily as he cast them aside. He helped himself to the fruits and the livestock of his hosts, and not infrequently to their womenfolk, and he observed many strange and hitherto unrecorded sights, 'keeping before me that the thing which a single eye-witness may set forth shall outweigh what ten men may declare on hearsay'.

There is no contemporary portrait, no extant description of Varthema. Yet from his own tale we have little difficulty in conjuring an image of the sixteenth-century pilgrim as he whoops his way through remote and unwelcoming lands, savouring their choicest commodities; sturdy of limb and swarthy of countenance, his manner composed of vagabond arrogance and easy charm, and guided by an irrepressible *joie de vivre*.

It is generally believed that he came from Bologna, but he preferred the designation 'Gentleman of Rome'. There is no record of his birth or death. His own account of his journey and a few circumstantial details are our only guide to the man and his achievement. '... what incommodities and troubles chanced me in these voyages, as hunger, thirst, cold, heat, wars, captivity, terrors and divers other dangers, I will declare by the way and in their due places'.

Thus he prefaced his own account of a long and eventful journey, cataloguing the tribulations that others who followed him to Arabia were to suffer in their turn, but never complaining.

Some time in 1503, he and his companions – he does not tell us their names or how many they were – took their leave of Rome. They made for Venice, whence they sailed with prosperous winds to Alexandria. They did not delay long at the Egyptian port but sailed straight away up the Nile to Cairo.

Varthema travelled with a mind at once receptive and alive with preconception and imagery. 'I marvelled more than I can say', he remarked of Cairo when he first caught a distant glimpse of it. He was disappointed on closer inspection. The place was more thickly populated than Rome and full of Muhammadans and Mamelukes, 'which are such Christians as have foresaken the faith to serve the Muhammadans and Turks'; a distinction which is neither accurate nor fair since the Circassian Muslims who were called by the Arabic name of *mamluk* or liberated slave, were reared in the faith.

The Italian left the swarming crowds of Cairo after a few days and took sail for Phoenicia and Syria, coming first to Beirut. He saw nothing of note in that town, remarking only that it was well victualled, but outside it he discovered the first of the landmarks of legend and biblical history that were to punctuate his journey – one of the several chapels of the Levant associated with St George, and the slaying of the dragon.

He was a curious explorer, imaginative and quick of wit, but vague as a chronicler. He seldom confides his goal, but we can be reasonably sure that Mecca was in his mind at this early stage of the journey. Its secrets, even its physical characteristics, had been mysteries to the Christian world for 900 years. Sketchy descriptions from the hands of Arab writers had found their way to the West but they gave no clear idea of the place or of the customs of worship which prevailed there. Varthema knew that he must master the Arab tongue if he was to pass among the people of the desert, much less gain access to their holy places, and he did not set out for Mecca directly.

Two days' sailing from Beirut brought him to Syrian Tripoli where he noted only that the soil was very fertile. 'For the great traffic of merchandise, the place abounds incredibly with all things.' Continuing northward, he and his companions reached Aleppo after another eight days. They looked in awe at the great staging-post of Syria, 'this goodly city', teeming with commerce and with goods brought in by caravans from all parts of Asia. Varthema went to the market-places where the merchants displayed their enticing wares and the caravans were loaded for their long journeys by way of Turkey, Arabia and Armenia, and inevitably he sampled the juicy fruits before turning south along the mountain road that led through Hama and Menin to Damascus. The Syrian capital was even more to his liking than Aleppo.

'It is incredible, and passes all belief, how fair the city of Damascus is, and how fertile is its soil.' Allured by the pleasures of the place, he was content to linger there while pilgrims in their thousands and even greater numbers of animals assembled for the trek to the holy cities of Madina and Mecca. Perhaps he parted from his fellow countrymen here, for there is no further mention of them, and he quickly decided to join the hajj caravan and thus make his way to the heart of Islam. He began to polish his Arabic among the Muhammadan inhabitants and Mameluke soldiery and to mix freely with both, as with the Christians of Damascus who lived, he said, 'after the manner of the Greeks'. There was a great deal of sightseeing to be done and Varthema went about it with breathless energy and no little credulity. The great citadel of the Bibar amïrs, the city's main fortification since 1262, caused him to seek out the history of the place and its rulers and he was told a strange story of the gift of Damascus to a Florentine convert who saved the Amir Malik from the effects of poison.

Each day more 'marvels' came to light. The streets were lined with red and white roses, 'the prettiest I have ever seen', and with orange and lemon groves, pomegranates and sweet apples. The market-places were filled with flesh and corn and fruit and vegetables. But the city was not entirely above criticism. Varthema, who was more often governed by his appetite than by intellectual curiosity, thought the peaches and pears unsavoury.

A fine clear river, the Abana, ran through the place and every-where fountains spilled cool water. There were many mosques, the finest of which, the great Omayyad masterpiece, he compared to St Peter's at Rome. He invariably compared the features of the places he visited with Rome, never with Bologna, which suggests that he may have left his reputed birthplace in early youth. He observed that the mosque of the Omayyads 'had no roof at its centre' but that it was otherwise vaulted in the Western tradition, and that it was supposed to contain the body of the prophet Zacharia.

Wandering around Damascus he found several houses once in-habited by Christians, their woodwork finely carved and embossed, now in ruins. He inspected the tower within the city wall where St Paul was let down in a basket by his friends, to escape the hostile Jews, and outside the gates the place of Christ's interrogatory 'Saule, Saule, cui me persequeris?' The excitement of a past unravelling before his eyes seemed to sharpen his pursuit of the present. He de-cided to take a closer look at the Mamelukes who swaggered in mili-tary manner through the streets of Damascus. 'They live licenciously in the city', he observed.

Yet they are very active and are brought up in learning and warlike discipline, until they come to great perfection. They receive a sti-pend of six pieces of gold a month, as well as meat and drink for themselves and servants and provision for their horses. They walk not singly but in twos or threes, for it is counted dishonourable for any of them to walk without company. They are valiant and if they chance to meet women (they tarry for them about such houses whither they know the women resort) licence is granted them to bring them into certain taverns, where they abuse them.... The women beautify and garnish themselves as much as any. They use silken apparell and cover them with cloth of gosampine, in manner as fine as silk. Their shoes are red and purple. They garnish their heads with many jewels and earrings, and wear rings and bracelets. They marry as often as they like. When they are weary of their first marriage they go to the chief priest (who they call the Kadhy) and request him to divorce them. This they call Talacare. A like liberty is also granted to husbands. Some think Muhammadans had five or six wives together, which I have not observed. As far as I could perceive they had but two or three.

From his observation of the lives of these settled people at the edge of the desert, Varthema was able to learn a good deal that would be helpful when he travelled into Arabia. While he waited for the caravan to depart he kept up his observation of life in Damascus.

He watched the milk-sellers at work. They drove their goats to the houses, he noted, and milked them inside the living quarters. The goats' ears were sometimes 'a span long', and they had many udders or paps and were very fruitful. He had the curious habit of enlarging the physical characteristics of the animals he met on his journey and of diminishing those of his human contacts. Even in describing the landscape he veered wildly between hyperbole and understatement, changing the size and shape of a mountain or a building to suit the mood of the moment.

The Italian cultivated the friendship of the despised Mamelukes. He may have had more of a taste for their ribaldry and merrymaking than he cared to admit. One in particular, the captain of the pilgrim caravan, the *amir al hajj*, became a close companion, although Varthema complains that he paid a great deal of money to be allowed to accompany him on the journey. Camels and pilgrims were gathered in numbers the like of which, if we are to believe the figures, have never since been approached on the *hajj* routes. Some 35,000 camels, 40,000 men and a goodly number of horses are said to have assembled for the journey. Varthema purchased a horse, dressed himself in Syrian clothing and adopted the name Yunis to see him through the pilgrimage. The caravan left Damascus on 8 April 1503 accompanied by a party of merchants.

Three days out, to the west of Jebel Hauran, they came to the small town of Muzairib where the merchants went about their business and the pilgrims replenished their provisions. Here they had their first sight of the badawin, members of a desert tribe said to be ruled by a shaikh called Zambei. He was apparently a man of great power, much feared by the sultans of the north. He had three brothers and four children and claimed 40,000 stallions, 10,000 mares and 4,000 camels. Such possessions would have represented riches indeed in the Arabia of the sixteenth century! 'The country where he keeps these beasts is large', says Varthema, 'and his power is so great that he maintains a constant state of war with the Sultan of Babylon, the Governor of Damascus and the Prince of Jerusalem, all at once.' At harvest time when the pickings were good this desert

warrior gave himself up entirely to robbing, 'deceiving his prey with
great cunning'. His mares are of such swiftness that 'they seem to
fly rather than to run'.

Varthema was quick to observe the dress and fighting habits of
the badu.

They ride on horses covered only with a loose cloth or mat, and
wearing nothing but a petticoat. For weapon they use a long dart
made of reed, of the length of ten or twelve cubites, tipped with
iron after the manner of javelins and fringed with silk. They march
in order and are despicable and of little stature, of colour between
yellow and black, which some call *olivastro*. They have the voices of
women and long black hair. They are of greater number than a man
would believe and are continually at strife and war among themselves.

From the Italian's description, the caravan seems to have been
passing through the stony desert of the Hauran, with the Syrian
mountains on their right, and the tribesmen of the Bani Sakhr to
harry them as they went. It was a time of great disorder among the
tribes of northern Arabia and Syria. Religious observance had fallen
from favour among the desert chiefs and their people. Lawlessness
was rife, pillaging and loose living were the fashion of the day.

However, the 'despicable' little men of the desert seem to have
allowed the caravan to proceed unmolested. They had left Muzairib
on 11 April, protected by their Mameluke guards. Each day they
marched for twenty-two hours, a vast array of men and beasts surging
wearily across the hot, uncomfortable desert. Mecca was a full forty
days from Damascus. They were perhaps six or seven days closer
by now, the pilgrims learning to sleep as they jogged and swayed
on their camels, even riding on horseback with their eyes closed, but
not for long; they had to keep watch for each other in case of attack
by thieves. The caravan contained many poor pilgrims from distant
lands; often such men and women were making the journey after
saving for a lifetime. Sometimes they had money enough only for
a one-way journey.

The caravan passed tents of the badawin, 'black and made of wool
and mostly filthy'. Otherwise they were alone on the well-trampled
road to the cities of the Prophet. After their twenty-two hours'
stretch, they were allowed to rest for the remaining two hours of the
day. The captain gave a trumpet call and commanded every man
to remain on the spot assigned to him, 'there to victual himself and
his animals'. Then he gave a second blast on the trumpet and the
replenished caravan moved off into the night. So they went on, day
after day. Every eighth day the camels were rested while the men,
or those of them fortunate enough to have two animals at their

command, took to their horses. The camels were laden with incredible burdens, each carrying twice the normal load of a mule. They were allowed to drink but once in three days and were fed on great raw barley loaves, five at a time. Every eighth day again, the pilgrims dug for water in the sand. When they came to established wells on the route there was usually a squabble with Arabs who gathered around. But there was seldom bloodshed, which Varthema attributed to their 'weak and feeble' nature. It might also have been the case that the Arabs were unarmed at these watering-places. The Mamelukes, brought up in the military arts, were formidable fighting men. Varthema took great delight in telling tales of their exploits which often resembled medieval European joustings.

A favourite sport was to place an apple on the head of a servant, stand some twelve or fourteen paces away and swish a long lance over the head of the terrified victim until the fruit was struck. Fortunately the Mamelukes seldom missed. Their horsemanship was exemplary. They would take a fast mare with saddle and halter, undress it at full gallop and ride on with the saddle on their own heads. And they replaced it at full gallop. They were gymnastic soldiers, and not too scrupulous about whom they fought or with what inequality of arms. There had already been a few skirmishes and one of the Mamelukes had been killed in a battle with an Arab force said to number some 40,000. 'No Arabs are to be compared to Mamelukes in strength or force of arms', Varthema observed.

Twelve days out from Damascus they struck another valley. The Italian surmised that it was the site of Sodom and Gomorrah and he saw all around him 'confirmation of holy scripture'. It was clear to see, he said, 'how the people of the place were destroyed by a miracle'. He affirmed that there were three cities and still the earth seemed mixed with red wax, three or four yards deep. 'It is easy to believe those men were infected with the most horrible vices, as the barren region testifies, utterly without water.' Unfortunately, he was on the wrong side of the Dead Sea, a good many miles from the biblical scene he so vividly reconstructed.

In fact, the caravan was probably in the desolate region between Tabuk and Madain Saleh on the road from Maan by now, according to Varthema's timetable. They seem to have been travelling a good way east of the road that became established in later centuries as the Darb al Hajj; a road which kept close to the hills along the Red Sea coastline for much of the way. Their present route was far from comfortable. Thirty or more of the company perished of thirst in the desert while others were buried in the soft sand and left to their fate 'not yet fully dead'. The fact is stated without remorse or comment, an event like any other to be borne with fortitude on a journey of many hardships. Farther on they found a small mountain with water at its foot where they rested. Next day a force of Arabs estimated to be 24,000 strong came to ask payment for the water the pilgrims had taken. 'We answered that we would pay nothing, for it was given to us by the goodness of God.' The two sides soon came to blows. The pilgrims and their Mameluke guards were gathered together on the side of the mountain, organised into a fighting unit consisting of a bulwark of camels with a soft core of pilgrims and merchants at their centre, flanked by the armed escort. The ensuing fight went on for two days until both sides collapsed for want of water. The Arabs, not to be deprived of their reward, surrounded the mountain and threatened to break in among the camels. The captain, hoping to bring the proceedings to a close, offered them gold. More generous with the pilgrims' and merchants' money than he might have been with his own, he offered them 1,200 pieces. The badawin took the money and promptly announced that 10,000 pieces would not compensate them for the amount of water that had been drawn. The belligerent captain needed no further prodding. He commanded the able-bodied to dismount from camels and horses and to prepare to fight on foot. Next morning the camels were assembled in massive array enclosing a battalion of 300 men. The Arab force was taken by surprise and routed. 'We lost only a man and a woman' while we slew 1,500 Arabs', says Varthema, always at his most matter-of-fact when he is stating the improbable. (It was the first mention of a woman being in the party, though what she was doing in the van of the fight is not clear.) He added: 'One should not marvel at the magnitude of the victory though, for they are poorly armed and, besides, almost naked.'

Eight days later they came to a place where the uplands fell away into a valley ten or twelve miles in girth, inhabited by Jews who, if we are to believe our traveller, were pigmies with small, womanish voices and black in colour. They were said to be 5,000 in number, some blacker than others, and to feed on nothing but mutton. All were circumcised and, says Varthema with customary phlegm, 'do not deny that they are Jews'. Small and effeminate they may have been, but these mountain people were also fierce, it seems. 'If by chance a Muhammadan came into their hands they flayed him alive.' The caravan must have arrived at Khaibar, a remote and ancient colony of Jews settled in an oasis in the lava fields. Travellers centuries later were to identify and describe the place, but by then the Jews, if ever they were there, had gone.

The pilgrims found a hole at the foot of a mountain that was full of rainwater. It was a precious commodity and they proceeded to fill their goatskins and load up their 16,000 camels. The Jews were greatly offended by the act but they were in some fear of the Mamelukes. Rather than take action they retired to the refuge of the

branching valleys around Khaibar. Before leaving, the pilgrims witnessed another unexpected sight, a pair of turtle doves in one of the
seven or eight thorn trees that grew at the base of the mountain.
They had not seen beast or fowl for fifteen days.

They were now in a region which, if it had been visited before
by outsiders, had gone unrecorded. Two days from the oasis of the
Jews, they sighted Madina, *Madinat al Nabi*, the city of the Prophet's
tomb. Four miles outside the city they halted at a well to wash and
refresh themselves and change their clothes. This was almost certainly the ritual cleansing of the pilgrims and donning of the *ihram*,
the simple outer garments in which the faithful enter the holy places.

Madina they found to be well peopled and to have surrounding
walls or bulwarks of earth. The houses were made of stone and brick.
The soil was utterly barren, 'cursed of God', except that at a short
distance from the city there was a cluster of date trees, the garden
of Kuba. A watercourse was nearby, the Ayn al-Zarka which flows
from the direction of Kuba, falling away to a lower plain to which
the pilgrims led their thirsty camels.

It was widely believed at this time that Muhammad was buried
at Mecca rather than Madina and that his tomb was suspended in
the air by the force of giant natural magnets of loadstone. 'I affirm
that neither is true nor has any likeness to the truth', says Varthema.
They stayed for three days to 'come to a true knowledge of these
things'. They were led by the hand to the burial-place of the Prophet
by a *muzowwar*, one of the countless guides who served the pilgrims
at Madina.

The Italian gives us this first eye-witness account of the great
mosque:

It is square and a hundred paces in length and fourscore in breadth.
The entry to it is by two gates. From the sides it is covered with
three vaults, and is borne up by four hundred pillars of white brick.
There are about three thousand hanging lamps. From the other
part of the temple is seen a tower of five paces circumference,
vaulted on all sides and covered with a cloth of silk, and is borne
up with a grate of copper, curiously wrought. It is seen, as it were,
through a lattice. Towards the left hand is the way of the tower
which must be entered through a narrow gate. On every side of
the door are seen books, on the one side twenty and the other
twenty-five, which contain the traditions of Muhammad and his
fellows. Within this gate is the sepulchre, a grave under the earth
where Muhammad is buried, along with his fellows.

Varthema then lists the Prophet's companions: Abu Bakr, Osman,
Omar and Fatimah. 'But Muhammad, a true Arab, was their chief

captain', he observes. He was wrong in his belief that Osman was buried in the mosque.

He goes on to examine the schisms of the faith.

All have their own books of facts and traditions. And hereof proceeds the great dissension and discord of religion and manners among this kind of filthy men, while some confirm one doctrine and some another by reason of their divers sects of patrons, doctors and saints, as they call them. By this means they are marvellously divided among themselves, and like beasts kill themselves for such quarrels of opinions. This also is the chief cause of war between the Sophie of Persia and the great Turk, being nevertheless both Muhammadans, they live in mortal hatred one against the other, for the maintenance of their sects, saints and apostles, while each of them thinks his own the best.

Coming from an emissary of sixteenth-century Europe, the doctrinal criticism was, perhaps, pusillanimous. All the same, Varthema's description was not only the earliest European account of the burial-place of the founder of one of the world's great religions, but also remarkably accurate in much of its detail. Neither for him nor for later Christian visitors was it easy to make measurements. The pilgrim was supposed to be there to pay homage, not to carry out a survey. To be found making notes would have been dangerous, if not fatal. Pacing the distance between one object and another must necessarily be a surreptitious act. His observations were to be corroborated, corrected and modified by later pilgrims; his record of the place has seldom been excelled for its colour and piquancy of observation.

'Now shall you understand', he says, 'with what craft they deceived our caravan.' There follows a strange story; the request they were about to make was one that no Muslim, Mameluke or otherwise, would entertain. 'The first evening that we came here, our captain sent for the chief Priest of the Temple to come to him, and asked to see the body of the Prophet, and for that he would give three thousand seraphins of gold.' The good captain assured the priest that he had no other motive than zeal of religion and the salvation of his soul, and was therefore greatly desirous to see the body of the Prophet.

The priest answered: 'Darest thou, with those eyes with which thou hast committed so many horrible sins, desire to see him by whose sight God hath created Heaven and Earth?'

'My Lord, you have said truly', the captain replied, 'but I pray that I may find favour with you, that I may see the Prophet, and when I have seen I will immediately thrust out my eyes.'

It was the request of a naïve or equivocal man of the faith, for he and the religious guide, the *muzowwar*, must have known that the body could not possibly be seen since it was hidden from view and sacrosanct.

Nevertheless, the so-called priest agreed to take the captain and his companions to the sepulchre, 'so that no man can deny that he died here who, if he would, might have died at Mecca, but to show in himself a token of humility, and thereby to give us example to follow him, was willing rather here than elsewhere to depart from this world, and was incontinent of angels, borne into Heaven, and abides in the presence of God'.

While in the mosque, the captain asked: 'Where is Jesus Christ, the son of Mary?'

'At the feet of Muhammad' was the reported reply. It is difficult to conceive that the reply was genuine. No Muslim believes that the body of Christ was left in this world, though a place is reserved for him in the *Hejrah*, the railed and curtained sepulchre within which lie the tombs of the Prophet and his lieutenants, at the second coming. But Varthema's account of Islam's holy cities precedes the Ottoman occupation of 1520. Custom and ritual changed a good deal from then on.

The captain ended the exchange with the words, 'Enough, enough, I will hear no more.'

That night a dozen or more Muslim elders came to the caravan which had pitched camp in an open space outside the built-up area, probably at Barr al-Manakhah where the Damascus caravan traditionally stays. The old men ran through the assembly of pilgrims and Mameluke guards like madmen, shouting 'Muhammad the messenger of God shall rise again. O Prophet, O God, have mercy on us.'

The caravan leader and his men took to their weapons, supposing the Arabs to be robbers. But the elders had come to ask the pilgrims if they had not seen the light that shone from the sepulchre of the Prophet, a question that was asked of many a subsequent pilgrim, for the superstition that a light shines from the tomb dies hard. Varthema suspected some kind of torch shone by the priests in the tower. The captain assured them that he and his companions had seen nothing. Unabashed, one of the old men expressed curiosity about the fair-skinned mercenaries, 'Are ye slaves, bought men?'

'We are indeed Mamelukes,' said the captain.

'You, my Lords, cannot see heavenly things for you are neophytes not yet confirmed in our religion', said the old man.

'I had thought to give you gold, you mad insensate beasts,' shouted the Mameluke chief, 'but now O dogs and progeny of dogs, I will give you nothing.' He was deeply offended by the suggestion of the

Hijazi that he and his kind were of an inferior breed of Muslim. The pilgrims decided that they had seen enough of Madina. Guided by a pilot with a mariner's box 'as used for sailing on the sea', they bent their path south, towards Mecca.

Soon they found a fountain flowing with water and were told by the inhabitants that St Mark was the author of this miracle, wrought when the region was burned with incredible dryness. Since the name St Mark is unknown to the Arab, we must again suspect invention by Varthema or the Mamelukes. After watering their animals they moved on into a 'sea of sand', where they experienced the desert *shimal*, the northerly wind which blows fine sand into swirling clouds that obscure the vision and make a journey unaided by compass difficult as well as uncomfortable. Perhaps their mariner's box did not serve them well and they wandered off course; perhaps, as has been suggested, a guide of the Hijaz would simply not have had a compass, though it is hard to imagine why Varthema would have invented such a device. One thing is certain; there is no 'sea of sand' between Madina and Mecca. Wherever the caravan was at this time, conditions were far from pleasant. Many of the pilgrims perished of thirst. Others died from drinking too much when they came to water. They found bodies, mummified by the fierce sun, whose dry flesh was thought by the nomads to be medicinal. As they fought their way out of this hot, windblown stretch of desert they saw badawin seated in their camel litters and wished that they had some protection.

To their left was a mountain against which the north-east wind was driven, probably Jabal Warkan on the sea road to Mecca. Thus they were back on the pilgrim way. Arabs believe this mountain to be an arm of Mount Sinai. Varthema noted that it had pillars, artificially wrought, which the Arabs called *ianuan*, and on its left side at the top of a ridge there was a den with an iron gate, said to be the place where the Prophet lived in contemplation. Horrible noises apparently issued from the mountain and they departed in fear of their lives.

Twice on their way through the desert they were attacked by hordes of Arab tribesmen, on one occasion amounting, in Varthema's rounded numbers, to 50,000. They avoided or fought off the dangers posed by men and nature and eventually arrived at Mecca, where 'all things were troubled by reason of the wars between two brothers, contending which of them should possess the lordship of the place'.

Varthema found the city on first acquaintance to be 'very fair', well inhabited and containing some 6,000 houses, as well constructed as those he was used to in his native Rome. The better residences were liable to cost 3–4,000 ducats of gold, a measure of the holy city's popularity among the rich in those early times. No wall surrounded the city, but mountains on all sides served as bulwarks. Our traveller noted four points of entry from the surrounding mountains. The Sultan, one of four brothers claiming descent from the Prophet, was subject to the Sultan of Cairo and was constantly at war with his contending brothers.

The caravan led by the captain and his men entered Mecca on 18 May 1503. Thus it had taken this pilgrim a mere five months from Venice to the major goal of his journey. He had mastered the language of the desert well enough to pass among the badawin and to converse with the guides and keepers of the religious sanctuaries of Islam. Such were the prerequisites of survival. Discovery of his pretence would have cut short his journey with a finality that he dared not contemplate. Yunis the convert of convenience was by now accustomed to his role. The first non-Muslim to look on the forbidden city and set down a description of it observed its features and recorded its legends in great detail.

> We entered into the city by the north side: then, by a declining way, we came to a plain. On the south side are two mountains, the one very near the other, divided only by a narrow valley, which is the way that leads to the Gate of Mecca. On the east side is an open place between two mountains, and this is the way to the mountain where they sacrifice to the patriarchs Abraham and Isaac. This is about eight or ten miles from the city and three stones' cast high. It is of stone as hard as marble, yet not of marble. At the top of the mountain is a maschita or temple made after their fashion, with three ways of entry. At its foot there are three cisterns which conserve water without corruption; of these, one is reserved for the caravan of Babylon or Cairo, the other for them of Damascus. It is rainwater, derived from far off.

Varthema was correct in describing the Muna valley as the open space on the way to Mount Arafat, though the sacrifice takes place not on the mountain but in the valley. He was, of course, wrong in his belief that Isaac was a patriarch of Islam. Ishmael is the progeny of Abraham to whom Muslim devotion is directed and from whom the blessing of the 'language of angels' stems.

Darting from place to place, observing acutely the artefacts of man and the effects of nature, Varthema was quick to find divine support for his own preconceptions. He found the city greatly cursed, a fact attested by its barrenness and the lack of fruit and corn. 'It is scorched with dryness for lack of water, and you cannot for four quarters buy as much water as will slake your thirst for a single day.' Most of the town's provisions came from Cairo, the rest from South Arabia, he noted.

On arrival at Mecca, the pilgrims found that the Cairo caravan had preceded them by eight days. Varthema departed on this occasion from his usual liking for round numbers and calculated that the Cairo contingent consisted of 4,060 camels and pilgrims and 100 Mamelukes – roughly one-tenth the strength of his own party!

In Mecca, the pilgrim guides take on the name of *mutowwaf*, as distinct from the *muzowwar* of Madina. Accompanied by their new guides, they found the place thronged with pilgrims from every quarter of Islam; from Syria, Persia, Ethiopia, the Indies. 'I never saw a place with a greater abundance of people, insofar as I could tell by tarrying there for twenty days.' These people, he said, came to Mecca for several reasons, some to observe their vow of pilgrimage, others to have pardon for their sins.

Varthema's own simple and precise description of the great mosque of Mecca deserves to be read as it stands.

In the middle of the city is a Temple, in fashion like the Colossus of Rome, the Amphitheatre I mean, like a stage yet not of marble or hewed stones, but of burnt bricks. For this Temple, like an Amphitheatre, has fourscore and ten or a hundred gates, and is vaulted. The entrance is by a descent of twelve stairs, and in the porch are sold jewels and precious stones. When you are past the entrance, it is enclosed above and the gilded walls shine on every side with incomparable splendour. In the lower part of the Temple (that is under the vaulted places) there is a marvellous multitude of men; for there are five or six thousand men that sell nothing other than sweet ointments, and especially a certain odoriferous and most sweet powder, with which dead bodies are embalmed. It passes belief to think of the exceeding sweetness of the savours, far surmounting the shops of the Apothecaries.

Using the language of Catholic Europe, Varthema called the *hajj* a 'pardon', which reasonably expresses the underlying Muslim idea of the pilgrimage. The 'pardon' began on the 23rd day of May, five days after Varthema's arrival. Of the Kaaba itself, the holiest shrine of Islam, he says: 'In the middle of the Temple was a turret, six paces in circuit, no higher than an average man and hung with silk tapestries. The sinners entered by a silver gate. On every side there were vessels filled with balm. Round, iron grates were fastened at every vault of the turret.'

Early on the morning of 22 May, pilgrims began to arrive in vast numbers, walking round the turret seven times, kissing every corner and sometimes feeling and handling its furnishings. About twelve paces from the turret was another building, like a chapel, with three or four entrances and a well at its centre, 'ten cubites deep, its water infected with saltpetre'. Here was the holy well of Zemzem. Eight men drew water from it for all the people who sought to be cleansed. As the pilgrims came to the well they touched its brim with reverence and asked for forgiveness. Then three buckets full of the holy water were poured over the head of each of the appellants, soaking him from head to foot. 'Then', says Varthema, 'the doting fools dream that they are cleansed of all their sins; that their sins are forgiven them,' forgetting that there are precedents in other religions for such ablutions.

In the light of subsequent accounts, Varthema's version of the events which make up the days of the hajj is confused in some respects, but his story is best told as he related it.

After their first circumambulations and while wet from the water of *Zemzem*, the worshippers make their way to Mount Arafat, where they remain for two days, sacrificing to Abraham their sheep, some two, some three, richer sinners as many as ten. In one day as many as thirty thousand sheep were offered up at sunrise. The place flowed with blood. The meat was given as a thanks offering to the poor who camped there by tens of thousands, roasting the carcasses on camel-dung fires.

Varthema's compassion for the poor of Mecca was intense. He observed their plight with deep feeling, 'these people, mostly African *takruri*, who fight over scraps of food, even parings of cucumber, when there is so much fodder to be had. I believe they come rather from hunger than for devotion.'

On the following day the *Kadhi* went up into the mountain to lead the prayers. Varthema listened and reported the supplications, but he cannot have heard well: 'O Abraham beloved of God, O Isaac chosen of God and His friend, pray to God for the people of the Prophet.' When the sermon was over the people lamented, but their devotions were interrupted by a rumour that an Arab army some 20,000 strong was approaching. Varthema and his companions fled with the rest for safety.

Hurtling towards Mecca they came to Muna with its wall where pilgrims normally stopped to stone the devil, as Varthema supposed. In fact, this ancient and confused ritual is supposed to commemorate the stoning of the *Rajim*, the lapidated one, by Abraham. Varthema speaks of Isaac taking up a stone and hurling it at the enemy of mankind. At any rate he and his fellow pilgrims stopped neither for theological speculation nor for the sport of stone throwing. They fled through the first opening they could find, only to be joined as they headed for the city by a flock of doves. They were greatly surprised. The birds, said Varthema, were supposed to be the progeny of the dove that spoke into the ear of the Prophet in the likeness of the Holy Ghost. 'To take them or kill them is esteemed worthy of death.' He did not put the matter to the test. He stayed long enough, however, to witness a final 'miracle': a unicorn or, more precisely, two unicorns.

On the other part of the Temple are enclosed parks, where are seen two unicorns, and are shown to the people for a wonder. One is much taller than the other, not unlike a colt of thirty months. In the forehead grows only one horn, in manner right forth. The other is younger and like a young colt. This beast is of the colour of a horse of weasel shade, and has a head like a hart, but no long neck, a thin mane hanging only on the one side. Their legs are thin and slender, like a faun's or hinde's. The hoofs of the forefeet are divided like a goat's. The beast tempers its fierceness with a certain comeliness.

A rare and precious gift, according to the Italian, they were given to the Sultan of Mecca by the Ethiopian King.

It is fitting that Varthema should end his account of the first recorded visit to the holy cities of the Hijaz with the story of the unicorns. They were probably no more than oryx seen through eyes conditioned by myth and fable to expect such things of the dark and mysterious East. He saw many remarkable and improbable things, as did many travellers of his time, prepared as they were for strange sights. Such men did not set out to deceive when they went to unknown places and wrote down their impressions. They simply realised the legends that were in their minds, like Othello's 'anthropophagi and men whose heads do grow beneath their shoulders'. Varthema, more importantly, witnessed much that was to stand the test of examination over more than four centuries.

As his days in Mecca drew to a close, he became anxious about his safety, a matter of rare concern to the Italian since discovery of his disguise would have been extremely dangerous. He began to plan his escape, and soon his fears were given substance when he was accosted in the bazaar by a Mameluke who obviously knew him to be a Christian. The man asked him in his own language: '*Inte mename?*' Whence art thou?'

'I am a Muhammadan!'

'Thou sayest not truly.'

'By the head of Muhammad I am a Muhammadan.'

Varthema had heard enough. The man invited him to his house and our traveller followed without argument. Then the man confided in him that they had met and that he knew Varthema to be an impostor. The Italian was persuaded and admitted that he was from Rome but had professed to the faith of Islam at Cairo where he had joined the Mamelukes. A friendly discussion ensued and soon Varthema summoned the courage to seek his new acquaintance's help in leaving Mecca. He pretended to be an artillery expert and said that he had told the Mamelukes that he wished to leave them so that he could fight against the enemies of Portugal in India. Soon a conspiracy was afoot to smuggle fifteen camels laden with spices from the city without paying duty to the Sultan.

'Praise be to the Prophet who sent thee hither to do him and his Moors good service', exclaimed the man, who then asked Varthema to remain in his house with his wife while he went away to make the necessary arrangements with the Mameluke captain, on whose co-operation the success of the smuggling operation depended. The husband thus joined the caravan while the Italian pilgrim made himself at home.

While I lay hidden in the Muhammadan house I cannot express how friendly this wife was to me. My entertainment in the house was also furthered by a fair young maid, the niece of the Muhammadan, who was greatly in love with me. But in the midst of all these troubles and fears, the fire of Venus was almost extinct within me, so that with dalliance of fair words and promises I kept myself in her favour.

A few days later he left for Jidda. Jews and Christians were forbidden entry to the port, though it teemed with every Islamic nationality. He merged with the thousands of poor people who crowded into the mosque on their way to their home countries. After fifteen days of sweltering heat and discomfort, Varthema found a sea captain willing to take him to Persia. Six days later they arrived at the port of Jizan in northern Yemen. It was richly endowed with the good things that never failed to fill the Italian with rapture. Five days more and he was in Aden, where he and the rest of the ship's company were stoned by the inhabitants as a token of the reception that awaited them. A full-scale fight ensued and Varthema and his new companions put to death twenty-four Yemenites and took hens and calves belonging to the Arabs aboard their ship. Not surprisingly, Varthema, who played a leading part in the escapade, was arrested. He was taken before the Sultan's lieutenant wearing Mameluke garb, escaping the death penalty by a hair's breadth. He was put into irons for fifty-five days, a comparatively light sentence in view of the offence, and accepted the punishment with what, for the fiery Italian, was good grace.

After his term of imprisonment, during which an angry crowd attacked the gaol demanding his blood, he was taken to Rada, a town south of Sana in the Yemen. He admitted to being a Roman who had apostasised at Cairo and said that he had visited Mecca and Madina to fulfil a vow. He proceeded to flatter the Sultan who, unmoved, asked him to pronounce the words of the true believer, *La ilaha il Allah Muhammad ar rasul Allah.* Varthema could not bring himself to utter them, 'either that it pleased not God, or that for fear and scruple I dared not'. The Sultan ordered his continued imprisonment. He was watched over constantly and 'denied the fruition of heaven', a glimpse of the open sky. Soon after his renewed imprisonment, however, the Sultan and his Ethiopian troops left to attack Sana, armed with slings and artillery of stones, leaving the Italian to the tender mercy of the Sultana. It was a fortunate turn of events.

Varthema decided to feign madness, and in his efforts to give conviction to the part he did some strange things. He pursued a fat sheep, trying to convert it to the faith. He allegedly killed an ass because it would not repeat the words that he himself eschewed when he was not pretending to be mad. Now, whenever he met an animal he muttered the words: 'There is but one God and Muhammad is his only Prophet.' Over and over again he intoned the sacred phrase of Islam. Doubtless the animals were as astonished as his fellow prisoners. He attacked a Jew who accosted him with the familiar curse of the East, 'Christian dog, progeny of dogs!', beating the unfortunate man until he was nearly dead. Varthema was not a model prisoner and even by the standards of his day he was capable of remarkable uncouthness. Some fifty children turned up to stone the mad prisoner. He collected their missiles and stoned them in return. Himyarites, holy men from the mountains, were summoned to pronounce on his sanity. 'I confirmed their worst suspicions by pissing into my hands and throwing it in their faces', commented the unrepentant prisoner. The Sultana was greatly amused by his antics and he found special comfort in her. 'She was much in love with me and liked white men', observed Varthema.

After a time she began to pay him regular nightly visits, armed with good things to eat, for she soon found the quickest route to the Italian's heart. Their dialogue was worthy of Boccaccio. She called him Yunis and they addressed each other in the tenderest terms.

'Come hither Yunis, thou art hungry.'
'I give thee my word sweet lady, I am hungry for the hunger to come, I am not mad now.'
'I know. Thou art the wisest man in the world.'
I held her well for two hours and she told me I was marvellously strong. Then she said:
'Thou art my husband, my sons and all my knights.'

She whispered as our bodies were joined that she would like to
have a son by me. Then, again:

'Come my Yunis, art thou not hungry?'

'No. No, madam.'

'Pray, let me take off your shirt.'

'I am not mad now, madam.'

'I know that thou art not mad, nor ever were. There has never
been a man like thee. O God, thou art white like the moon. O God,
O Prophet! Mine husband is black, mine son is black, and this man
is white. If it please God I shall have a white son with the help
of this man.'

Varthema was circumspect when it came to reporting his amorous
adventures. In his absence the Borgia pope he had left behind, Alexander VI, had died and the papal saviour Julius II was on the
throne. The ecclesiastical censorship was no less pronounced for the
new pope's enthusiastic patronage of the arts. When the voyager
came to write his story he knew that he had to be careful in matters
of religion and in relating his friendly encounters with Muslims.

He allegedly told the Sultana: 'I am already in chains. I do not
want to lose my head.' The lady, he said, wept bitterly, but she kept a
nightly vigil over her white man, and even offered him the services
of her damsels. Then the Sultan returned from battle, and it was
Varthema's turn to weep.

Varthema's journey to Yemen, 'Happy Arabia', even though most
of it was spent in prison, was as rumbustious and fearless as his earlier
sojourn in the north. As he was the first European to describe the
badawin of the stony desert of the Hamad, the first to find Khaibar
and the Mountain of the Jews in the eastern Hijaz (it was not until
three centuries later that his finding was confirmed), and the first
to describe the Hijaz and its holy cities, so he must also be allowed
priority as an explorer of inner Yemen.

When finally he escaped from captivity, with the connivance of
the Sultana who persuaded her husband to let him go to Aden on
the thin pretext that he wished to consult a holy man, he found a
sea captain willing to take him on to India by way of Persia. Before
taking ship, however, he wandered through the mountains of Yemen
to Sana, where one of the Amir's twelve sons 'by a natural tyranny
and madness delights to eat the flesh of men'. He travelled on
through the deserts and mountains and lush regions of the far south
of Arabia, coming upon monkeys, lions and brigands. Inevitably,
he joined some of the more doubtful nomadic bands who roamed
the area, hunting and raiding with the badu as if to the manner born.
When, finally, he took sail for Persia, the ship was blown off course
and he found himself in Ethiopia. Varthema maintained a custo-

mary calm. As might be expected, he saw many things in the place he called the land of Prester John. The animals and people, and their appendages, were always a good deal larger or smaller than life size. When he reached his ultimate goal, India, he found milk and honey and more trouble. He traversed the entire west coast of Portuguese India and enlisted in the Portuguese army. When in Calicut he told a Persian merchant, 'I should like to see them [the Portuguese] converted to our Muhammadan faith.' Yet he proudly insisted, 'I am a Roman.' He set his mast to the prevailing wind and sailed on.

When he returned to Europe in 1508, after five eventful years, he went first to Lisbon where, on the recommendation of the great navigator Tristan da Cunha, he received the Order of Chivalry for service to Portuguese India from Dom Manuel. From there he went briefly to Rome and then to Bologna. There is some evidence that he brought with him from his travels a young lady who was the niece of his Persian companion Khadjar Djauher, for according to Marino Sanuto in his *Diary*, published at Venice in 1882, she painted his portrait on his return to Italy, though there is no trace of the work. On 5 November 1508, Lodovico Varthema was admitted to the College of Venice where he gave a warmly applauded lecture on the people and customs of the Indies. He was paid twenty-five ducats. The first edition of his *Itinerario* was published in 1510. Back in Rome he was received into the exclusive circle of Cardinal Raphael Riario, through whose offices he was introduced to Agnesina Feltria Colonna, the Duchess of Tagliacozzo and Countess of Albi, daughter of the Duke of Urbino. She wrote an introduction to the edition of his work published in Milan in 1519. He, perhaps characteristically, faded from sight soon after his account of the journey was published. We do not know where, how or when he died.

It has been said of some explorers and travellers in the East that intellect obstructed vision. No such accusation could be levelled at Varthema. Perhaps more reliable witnesses were to tread the hajj routes to the holy cities of Arabia, and the desert paths of the badawin. Their observations were to discount some of the things he saw and recorded, and confirm and supplement others. None ever came back with a more vivid, robust or entertaining account.

Lodovico Varthema, Gentleman of Rome, was an uncomplaining traveller. If he was ever sick or weary or afraid, he never said so. He was a cavalier of desert exploration, irrepressible, sharp of wit, imprudent, and impudent.

His place in history is assured, for the quality of his account and for his achievement in becoming the first avowed Christian to enter the holy cities of Islam.

Chapter 2

JOSEPH PITTS

An Englishman at Mecca

c. 1687

'Persecution may, indeed, shake the resolution of the mind: but can never convince the judgement.' *The World Displayed*, 1774

A FAITHFUL
ACCOUNT
OF THE
Religion and Manners
OF THE
Mahometans.

In which is a particular
RELATION of their *Pilgrimage* to
Mecca, the Place of MAHOMET's
Birth; and a Defcription of *Medina*,
and of his Tomb there: As likewife
of *Algier*, and the Country adjacent;
and of *Alexandria*, *Grand Cairo*, &c.
With an Account of the Author's
being taken Captive; the *Turks* Cruelty to him; and of his Efcape. In
which are many Things never pub-
lifh'd by any Hiftorian before.

By *JOSEPH PITTS*, of *Exon*.

The THIRD EDITION, *Corrected, with Additions. To
this Edition is added a* Map *of* Mecca, *and a Cut of
the Geftures of the* Mahometans *in their Worfhip.*

LONDON,
Printed for J. Osborn *and* T. Longman, *at the Ship in*
Pater-nofter-row; *and* R. Hett, *at the Bible and*
Crown *in the* Poultry. M.DCC.XXXI.

Title page to third edition of Pitts' 'True and faithful Account', 1731
(courtesy British Library)

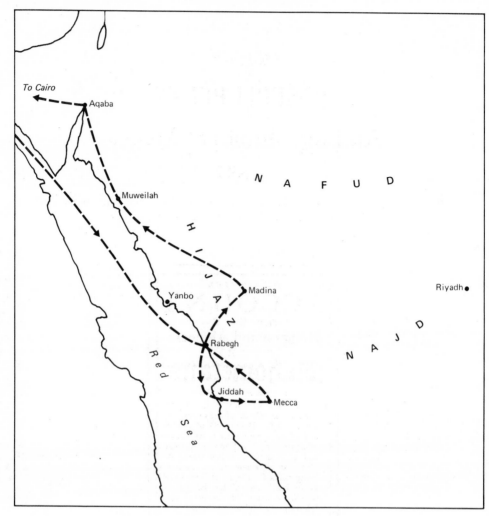

6 Pitts' route in Hijaz, c. 1687

For more than a century Varthema's journey through northern
Arabia and his description of the holy cities and the obscure regions
of the Yemen in the south remained a singular testimony to the
interest and curiosity of the outsider.

There is in the *Commentaries* of Alboquerque, the Portuguese explorer and chronicler, a reference to a certain Gregorio de Quandra
who was alleged to have visited Mecca in the company of a Moor
in 1513 and to have proclaimed himself there as a Christian. His
story is unsubstantiated, however, and it gives no detail which could
corroborate even his own observations, much less those of Varthema.
Since de Quandra claimed to have made a lone journey across north-

ern Arabia as far as the Euphrates after visiting Mecca, and since anyway our knowledge of him is at second hand, there is a temptation to assume that his story is largely, if not entirely, imaginary.

Another unsubstantiated sixteenth-century pilgrimage is that of Vincent Leblanc, a citizen of Marseilles, whose visit to Mecca in 1568 is referred to by Pierre Bergeron in his *Voyages Fameux*. 'Leblanc invokes the memory of Varthema', wrote Bergeron in a chapter devoted to the sacred features and curiosities of Mecca. But neither the traveller nor the historian tells enough to convince us of anything beyond the fact that the Frenchman had a rough knowledge of the Prophet's birthplace.

There is one other possible claimant to the distinction of having been the first to follow in Varthema's footsteps. Father Eugene Roger, in his *Description de la Terre-Sainte*, published in 1649, talks of an unnamed Venetian who was converted to Islam at the age of fifteen and sent to Mecca by the Governor of Cairo. His observations of Mecca and the Hijaz were inexact, but they contained enough substance to suggest that he made the pilgrimage. Roger was a faithful recorder and he claimed first-hand knowledge of the anonymous Venetian.

The first fully recorded visit of a non-Muslim to the Hijaz after Varthema was that of Johann Wild of Nuremberg. A conscript in the Austrian imperial army, he fought against the Turks and was taken prisoner in Hungary. Thus he found himself at Constantinople and from there was enlisted into the Mameluke escort of the Cairo hajj caravan. His journey to Mecca began almost exactly a century after that of the Gentleman of Rome, in 1604. Like Varthema, he escaped from the caravan on the return journey and sailed across the Red Sea to Abyssinia and thence to Yemen. He returned to Europe in 1611 and his account, remarkably accurate in much of its detail and hair-raising in its documentation of the hazards of Arabian travel, was published two years later in his native city. But Wild's account has been ignored or dismissed by historians until recent times. When Burton listed the accounts of the pilgrimage to Mecca as an appendix to his own more than two centuries later, even he had apparently not heard of the German.

It was not until the latter part of the seventeenth century that another involuntary traveller was able to hand down a well-documented description of Mecca and the religious observances of the pilgrims.

Joseph Pitts was born in Exeter, and like most Englishmen of the West Country he inherited a strong attachment to the sea. When he was fifteen years old he followed his inclination and joined the vessel *Speedwell*, whose master was Mr George Taylor. They left on a trading voyage to Newfoundland in the year 1678. Their return took them to Bilbao and the Canaries, and while sailing off the coast of Spain they ran foul of Algerian corsairs.

The entire company of the *Speedwell* was taken captive and sold into slavery at Algiers. Pitts was taken to the house of the ship's captain where he was given bread and water. Next day he and his companions were taken to the Dey of Algiers who chose an eighth part of the assembly for his own use, the rest being led off to the market-place where Christians were customarily auctioned.

> I was bought by a man who treated me with the utmost cruelty, and though it is most uncommon for Algerians to trouble themselves about the religion of the slaves my master was constantly beating me in order to force me to become a Muhammadan.

The plight of the young Englishman, still in his teens and far removed from home and family, was unenviable. But he had hardly begun to taste the rigours of persecution. His first master kept him for two or three months and then sent him to sea on a pirate ship. He went gladly, in the hope that a Christian vessel might reverse his fortunes by taking the Algerians captive. There was to be no such happy ending. 'My heart sank,' he wrote. 'We took one Portuguese ship in two months and then I returned to Algiers with foreboding.' He was sold to a new master who kept both Christian and negro slaves and who had two brothers in Algiers and one in Tunis. The young Pitts, it transpired, was to be given to the latter as a token of his brother's esteem. He was dressed handsomely 'to enhance my value as a present', and put on a ship for Tunis; after some twelve days at sea he arrived at his destination. His new patron's nephew was especially proud to have a Christian to wait on him and insisted that Pitts should walk with him in the town to enhance his prestige.

On one such journey through the fashionable quarter of Tunis, they came upon a well-dressed man who had the appearance of a Christian. He turned out to be the English Consul. The two young men were invited to his house, and Pitts was taken aside and questioned about his abilities at arithmetic and writing. He told the Consul that he could do both satisfactorily. To prove the point, or part of it, he wrote down the words 'The Lord be my guide, in him will I trust'. The Consul, impressed, assured the young Englishman that he would be welcome at his house at any time and that he would do his best to protect his interests while he remained captive. After thirty days in Tunis, Pitts was told that his most recent master had no further use of him.

There followed a frantic effort on the part of the Consul and two English merchants to buy the youngster's freedom. They offered 300 dollars for his redemption, a considerable sum in those days. The master, who had received him as a gift and who had no more need of him, insisted on 500. Pitts's fellow countrymen could not raise the necessary cash and he was returned to Algiers. He burst into tears when he learned that he was to go back to his old master, now a captain in a horse troop. There was small comfort in the parting words of the Consul that when he obtained his freedom and was able to return to England, he, the Consul, would prefer a petition to the King, commending the young man's behaviour in adversity.

The effort to convert Pitts to the Moslem faith which marked the first period of his captivity was now vigorously resumed. The younger brother of the master, also a cavalry officer, decided that his own debauchery and the various sins to which he admitted, including murder, could best be atoned for by making the Englishman a proselyte.

Upon this, my master, the elder brother, began to persuade and threaten me. One day when the barber came to the camp to shave him, he told me to kneel before him and ordered the barber to cut off my hair. I, mistrusting them, began to struggle; but by force they cut off my hair and then strove to shave my head, my patron all the while holding my hands. I kept shaking my head and he kept striking me in the face ... my patron would then have me take off my clothes and put on Turkish habit; but I plainly told him I would not: whereupon I was dragged along to another tent, where we kept our provisions, and there the cook and the steward stripped me and one of them held me while the other put on the Turkish garb. All the while I kept crying and told the patron that though he had changed my habit he could not change my heart.

The following night, the master entreated Pitts to renounce his religion. The Englishman replied that he was afraid of 'everlasting damnation', and pleaded with his master to sell him and find another boy who might more easily be converted.

'He told me he would pawn his soul for mine.'

At last the boy went to bed and prayed for guidance. But his patron was impatient. He woke him in the middle of the night so as to renew the debate. He asked Pitts to hold up his forefinger and utter the words of the Muhammadan creed. When he met with yet another rebuff, he called his servants and told them to tie the Englishman's feet to the tent post and beat his bare feet with a cudgel. Blows fell thick and fast.

I roared out with pain, but the more I cried the more furiously he laid on, threatening that he would bastinado me to death if I did not turn and stamping with his feet on my mouth to stop the noise of my crying. I begged my master to despatch me.

Joseph Pitts must have been close to insensibility or surrender. 'Having endured this merciless usage till I was ready to faint or die under it, and yet saw him as mad and implacable as ever, I begged him to forbear, and I would turn.'

The master asked Joseph to utter the words.

Again, he could not bring himself to do so. The beating began with renewed force. 'His cruelty was insatiable', said the young man. Finally, he submitted. 'Overcome with terror and pain I spoke the words, holding up the forefinger of my right hand.'

He was taken to a fire for warmth, his feet were bandaged and then he was put to bed. He could not stand for several days.

During the time of his own terror and conversion, Pitts had observed a more affable procedure for adopting a new faith. When conversion was compulsory, he noted, the requirement was simple. You simply uttered the words *La illah ilallah w'al Muhammad rasul allah. There is but one God and Muhammad is the Prophet of God.* But when the faith of Islam was adopted voluntarily, there was a great deal of ceremony. The convert went before the Dey to declare his intention. Then, seated on a fine horse, adorned with trappings and a turban on his head, he rode around Algiers with a staff clutched in his right hand. A guard of honour, twenty or thirty strong, accompanied him, naked swords in hand, while sightseers donated money to the volunteer, thanking God for his conversion. A few days later, the circumciser carried out his duties and a true believer entered the ranks of the faithful.

Pitts could hardly resist comparison with his own forced apostasy. The shame that stayed with him for the whole of his exile was not helped by a letter from his father soon after his involuntary conversion. A month or two after he was taken prisoner, Joseph had found a way of despatching a letter to his parents, in which he mentioned the efforts of his captors to convert him. The reply was tender and understanding. His father wrote:

Yet I cannot choose but call thee dear and loving son, although thou hast denied thy Redeemer ... especially, considering the tenderness of thy age, the cruelty of thy usage, and the strength of thy temptations.

Pitts replied in a mood of pathetic dejection:

Honoured, and dear Father and Mother,
It is not for want of duty or love which makes me negligent to write to you, but it is chiefly the consideration of the little comfort you

can take in hearing from me, having been a great grief and a heart-breaking to you. ... Dear father and mother, how often I have wished that I had departed this world when I hung upon your breasts, that I might not have been the bringer of your grey hairs with sorrow to the ground ... your grief, though great, is but little in comparison of mine. Put it to the worst, you have lost but a son; but I for my part, have lost a dear father and mother, brothers, relations, friends acquaintance, and all.

His life remained miserably confined and he was often tortured. A Christian in these parts did not become free by adopting the Islamic faith, he observed. His food consisted mainly of barley-bread and sour milk. Only if a sheep died was its flesh fed to Joseph Pitts and the other slaves. Sometimes his blood ran along the ground as he was beaten by his sadistic master. One advantage of the apostasy that weighed on him so heavily, however, was that it enabled him to gain access to the mosques of Algiers and so study the religious ceremonies of his masters and observe them in prayer and meditation. His command of Arabic and Turkish was by now accomplished and he took a great deal of pleasure in recording in detail the prayers of the faithful, the words of the preacher, the *imam*, the teaching of the Koranic scriptures, the responses of the congregation. His dedication to his own religion and the cruelty with which he was forced to disavow it, did not blind him to the images that he set out to observe and describe. If he did not like the culture or teaching of Islam, he at least tried to understand its tenets and to present them objectively.

His escape from Algiers was sudden and unexpected. His master was foolish enough to sponsor a rebellion against the Dey in the belief that he would succeed him. In the event he was executed for his pains. Pitts hoped that the mistress of the household would grant him his freedom. She proved as lacking in compassion as her late husband. She sold him to another master.

Fortunately for Pitts, his new owner was an old man of kindly disposition. He used the Englishman, who must by now have been in his eighteenth or nineteenth year, as a housemaid, and although the work was perhaps undignified for a strong and ambitious young man, it was more congenial than being beaten around the head and thrashed for his master's amusement. After a year of domesticity, Joseph was informed that his master intended to make the long-promised pilgrimage to Mecca and that he would accompany him on the journey. It was an opportunity not to be spurned, and they set off without a backward glance.

They got no further than Alexandria, however, before the old man was taken severely ill. Thinking his end had come, he took off his girdle and handed it to his companion who found in its purse a great deal of gold and a letter, which was to have been given him at Mecca, pronouncing his freedom. When the master recovered, Pitts found himself suspended betwixt a promised liberation and nominal servitude. He had handed back the letter, and the travellers went on their way as if nothing had happened.

From Alexandria they sailed for Rosetta, entered the Nile and continued up-river to Cairo, where they collected provisions for the next stage of the journey. There he observed the debauchery of the Turk and Egyptian. The men, especially the Turks, were 'much addicted to the cursed and unnatural sin of sodomy'. Their eating manners fascinated him.

They all sit down cross-legged, as Taylors do when they are at work on their shop-board; and they have a napkin that reaches all around to wipe with. The Victuals being put on the table, every one says his Grace (more, to my knowledge, than thousands of Christians do)....

They observed the Muslim ban on alcohol, he noted, except when the soldiers prepared for war, at which time they became both drunk and offensive,

insomuch that it is very dangerous for any woman to walk in the By-Place, but more dangerous for Boys, for they are extremely given to sodomy ... yet this horrible sin of sodomy is so far from being punished among them, that it is part of their Discourse to boast and brag of their detestable Actions of that kind.

He took careful note of the whores of the city plying their trade from doorways, and parading along the thoroughfares:

These Courtesans or Ladies of Pleasure, as well as other women, have broad velvet caps on their heads, beautiful with an abundance of pearls, and other costly and gaudy ornaments ... they wore their hair in tresses behind, reaching down to their very heels, with little bells, or some such things at the end, which swing against their heels and make a tinkling sound as they go.

From Cairo they travelled by camel to Suez and then took sail again to Rabegh, a small port between Yambo and Jidda. They were taking the easy route along the Red Sea coast, for the old man could not have been expected to survive the arduous hajj route across the desert – though pilgrim ships in these times were far from comfortable. Most of the pilgrims disembarked at Rabegh, changed into the *ihram*, the hajj dress of 'two light wraps', and sandals, and went inland on foot.

The traditions and myths of the Hijaz quickly impressed themselves on the travellers. 'The heat is intense and dry,' noted Pitts, 'and many of the pilgrims are blistered by the sun. However, when a man is in danger of losing his health by these austerities, he may lawfully put on his clothes, on condition that when he comes to Mecca he kills a sheep and gives it to the poor.'

Pitts and the old man returned to Rabegh and sailed on to Jidda, and from there made the rest of the journey by camel. Nothing is said of this last stage of the voyage, though Pitts's master must have been in some discomfort. On arrival at Mecca they found a *mutow-waf*, one of the guides of the holy city, and went with him to the fountains where they took the *wuzu*, the minor ablution, before entering the Great Mosque. Through the Bab-al-Salim, the gate of peace, a few steps forward, and their guide stopped and held out his hands towards the Kaaba, offering up a prayer. The pilgrims imitated his gestures and repeated his words. As they looked on the holy Kaaba the visitors melted into tears. Pitts was impressed by the simplicity of the place and the proceedings. Like Varthema more than 150 years before, he made the seven circumambulations and the *ruka'at*, two prayers accompanied by bows. Then came the running and sprinting with the guide from one part of the street to the other, 'about a bowshot distant': in fact the *sai*, ceremonial running between Safa and Marwah.

I confess I could not choose but admire those poor creatures, so extraordinarily devout and affectionate, when they were about these superstitions, and with what awe and trembling they were possessed; in so much that I could scarce forbear shedding tears to see their zeal, though blind and idolatrous.

He looked more closely at the Kaaba. It was, he said, about four and twenty paces square. At one corner was a black stone, fastened and framed in silver, the *Hajar Aswad*. Every time they came to that corner they kissed the stone, and having gone round several times performed the *ruka'at*. The legend and lore of Mecca inevitably coloured any attempt to describe the place with detachment. The stone, he was told, was formerly white when it was called the *Hajar As'ad*. But because of the sins of the multitude of people who kissed it, it became black and was called the *Hajar Aswad*, or black stone. It was not unusual in other religions for such legends to surround the objects of worship, and the fact that *Hajar As'ad* merely means blessed stone should not be held against those who propagated the belief that the sins of the faithful washed off on it, or against those who, knowing no better, listened.

'This place is so much frequented by people going round it, that the place of the *tawaf*, the circuit they make in going round it, is seldom void of people at any time of the day or night.' Joseph Pitts recognised the pleasure it gave to pilgrims that this should be so. Many had waited several weeks, even months, for the opportunity of joining the throng of worshippers; they had no wish to find the devotions at the end of their journey easy or uninhibited. 'They say', said Pitts, 'that if any person is blessed with such an opportunity, that for his or her zeal in keeping up with the honour of *tawaf*, let them petition what they will at the Kaaba, they will be answered.'

Many would walk round the shrine until they were weary. Old men and women, the infirm, all would take their places in the ambulating crowd, until they were too tired. Then they would rest before starting again, performing the customary *ruka'at* after every seventh revolution. 'Let them be never so far distant from it [the Kaaba], east, west, north or south, they will be sure to bow down towards it. Here was the object of their devotion, the idol which they adored.'

Pitts gives us the first detailed account through Western eyes of the observances of Mecca. Varthema, true to his character, had been too prone to make a quick assessment of numbers or to dismiss the devotions of the crowds in the Great Mosque as idolatrous humbug. Pitts reports simply and in great detail.

Sometimes there are several hundreds at *tawaf* at once, especially after the fourth service, which is after candle lighting, and these both men and women, but the women walk on the outside of the men, the men nearest the *Bet*. In so great a resort as this it must not be supposed that every individual can come to kiss the stone; therefore, in such a case, the lifting of the hands towards it, smoothing down their faces and using a short expression of devotion.

When women were at the stone he noticed that the men went discreetly past so that they could take their fill. It was considered rude and improper for men to go near them at this time and place.

Pitts numbered the gates to the temple of Mecca as forty-two. Varthema had estimated ninety to a hundred. Later pilgrims were to show that Pitts was much closer to the truth. Less surprising than their arithmetical differences, perhaps, is the contrast in their visual comparisons. Varthema likened the Great Mosque to the ampitheatre of the Colosseum. The Englishman might be expected to produce a more prosaic likeness. He found that it reminded him of the Royal Exchange in London, 'but near ten times bigger', not a comparison that would occur to many observers. He measured the Kaaba at twenty-four paces square, and about the same in height. Varthema, it will be recalled, measured six paces in circuit.

Mecca was not comfortable. It lay in hot country and people ran from one side of the street to the other to get into the shadow as the sun moved round. The inhabitants, especially the men, slept on the tops of houses for the cool air, or in front of their open doorways. Pitts slept in the open, without a bed covering; but he covered himself with a damp linen cloth at night.

Each day for two months Pitts and his wealthy master wandered round Mecca making a mental note of its buildings, its teeming populace, its religious observances. They lived in a house in relative comfort with enough provisions brought from Egypt to last them until they returned. There is no note of complaint in the young man's account of his sightseeing tour. His effort to record every detail of the place is almost frantic and, when he came to write it down, there was a suggestion of apology. He would jump from town to mosque and back again, repeating his description and challenging any man to doubt the accuracy of his findings.

'I shall now give you a more particular description of Mecca and the temple there.' His account is without method or discipline; without the preconception and imagery of Varthema before him or the awe-inspiring scholarship of some who came after. To that extent, his is the most valuable of the early descriptions of the citadel of Islam, painstaking and naïvely honest in its record of everything he saw or heard.

First, as to Mecca. It is a town situated in a barren place (about one day's journey from the Red Sea) in a valley, or rather in the midst of many little hills. It is a place of no force, wanting both walls and gates. Its buildings (as I said before) very ordinary, insomuch as it would be a place of no tolerable entertainment were it not for the anniversary resort of so many thousand of hajjis, on whose coming the whole dependence of the town (in a manner) is.

Of the people, he observes that 'they are poor, very thin, lean and swarthy'. Then he returns to the geography of the town. 'It is surrounded for several miles with little hills. I have been on top of some of them near Mecca, where I could see some miles about, yet was not able to see the farthest of the hills. They are all of stony rock and blackish.' He related the local tradition of the hills and rocks.

The people here have an odd and foolish sort of tradition concerning them: that when Abraham went about building the Bet-Allah, God by his wonderful providence did so order it, that every mountain in the world should contribute something to the building thereof;

and accordingly every one did send its proportion; though there is a mountain near Algier, which is called Corradog – the Black Mountain – and the reason of its blackness they say, is because it did not send any part of itself towards the building of the temple of Mecca.

He climbed Jabal Nur, which the local people called Hira, to the cave into which the Prophet was said to have retired for solitary contemplation and where the Archangel Gabriel conveyed to him a great part of the Koran. 'I have seen this cave, and observed that it is not at all beautified; at which I admired.'

About half a mile out of the town he found another steep hill, scene of the legend of the infant Muhammad who was supposed to have been carried there by the Angel so that his heart could be cleansed of mortal corruption.

He went with other pilgrims into the cupola on that hill and performed the customary prayer. Varthema, it will be recalled, heard such noises when passing the mountain containing the Prophet's cave that he and his companions fled for their lives.

Back in the mosque, Pitts has more to say of the rites and customs of worship. 'When any enter into the Bet [the Kaaba], all that they have to do is perform two prayers on each side ... and they are so reverent and devout about this that they will not suffer their eyes to wander and gaze about; for they account it very sinful to do so. Nay, they say one was smitten blind for gazing about. ...' Nevertheless, Pitts allowed his eyes to wander, 'and profess I found nothing worth seeing in it, only two wooded pillars in the midst, to keep up the roof and a bar of iron fastened on them, on which hanged three or four silver lamps, which are seldom if ever lighted.'

When the prayers of the pilgrims were over for the day, the Sultan of Mecca ('who is Sherrif, one of the race of Muhammad') came with his chosen companions to demonstrate that they were not too good to cleanse the shrine of Islam. They washed it first with the holy water of Zemzem, and after that with sweet water. The besoms used for the cleaning were afterwards broken into pieces and 'thrown amongst the mob'; anyone fortunate enough to collect a small twig or stick would keep it as a sacred relic.

The ground round the Kaaba was paved, Pitts said, with marble, though later observations showed it to be grey granite. Round the pavement stood pillars of brass fifteen feet high and twenty feet distant from each other. Iron bars were fastened from one to the other with glass lamps hanging from them to light the way of the nocturnal pilgrim. Every day the lamps were cleaned and replenished with cotton wicks and oil. About twelve paces from the Kaaba was the sepulchre of Abraham. Pitts describes it as 'like the tombstones which people of fashion have among us, but with a very handsome embroidered covering'. To the left was the well of Zemzem with its holy water. Our pilgrim was as scornful of superstitions of the West as of the East; 'the water thereof [Zemzem] they call holy water, and as superstitiously esteem it as the Papists do theirs.'

The well was in the middle of one of four little rooms, one at each quarter of the Place of God. Four men were employed to draw its water and dispense it to the multitude.

They do not only drink this water but oftentimes bathe themselves in it, at which time they take off their clothes, only covering their lower parts with a thin wrapper, and one of the drawers pours on each person's head five or six buckets of water. The person bathing may lawfully wash himself therewith above the middle, but not his lower parts, because they account they are not worthy. ... Yea, such an high esteem they have of it, that many hajjis carry it home to their respective countries in little latten or tin pots; and present it to their friends, half a spoonful maybe, to each, who receive it in the hollow of their hands with great care and abundance of thanks, sipping a little of it, and bestowing the rest on their faces and naked heads; at the same time holding up their hands, and desiring of God that they also may be so happy and prosperous as to go on pilgrimage to Mecca.

The Muslim belief that the well marks the place where Hagar laid down the infant Ishmael provided the substance of the story Pitts was told, the story recorded in the twenty-first chapter of Genesis. 'They say that in the very place where the child paddled with his feet, the water flowed out.'

Next he gives us an account of how, when and where the title of *Hajji* is conferred on those who make the costly and painful pilgrimage to Mecca. He details the dates of the Feast of Sacrifice and the events that follow: the Feast, two months and ten days after the fast of Ramadan; the change into the *ihram*, the mortifying habit; the journey to Al Arafat, the mountain of recognition, where according to Muslim belief Adam met Eve; the meeting of the faithful at the mountain. His detail is considerable and usually reliable. 'It is said by them that there meet no less than 70,000 souls every year, in the ninth day after the two months after Ramadan; and if it happen that in any year there be wanting some of that number, God, they say, will supply the deficiency by so many angels'. He did not think that on the occasion of his visit the number of pilgrims was as many as 70,000, though it was very great. Stones were arranged in the plain at the foot of the mountain, to delineate the sacred ground. There was a small cupola at the top of the hill. On the Day

of Arafat the pilgrims came to the sacred ground, performed their
ablutions in the early afternoon, and then went up into the hill to
hear the sermon, seeking pardon for their sins and the benediction
of the *imam*.

> It was a sight indeed, able to pierce one's heart, to behold so many
> thousands in their garments of humility and mortification with their
> naked heads and cheeks watered with tears; and to hear their griev-
> ous sighs and sobs, begging earnestly for the remission of their sins,
> promising newness of life, using a form of penitential expression,
> and thus continuing for a space of four or five hours until the time
> of the evening prayer which is to be performed about half an hour
> after sunset.

The effect on Pitts of the pilgrims' simple devotion must have been
considerable. Here was a man of little education who went to sea
at the age of fifteen, still living under the nominal if by now lightened
stigma of enslavement, who had been cruelly forced to abjure his
own faith; yet who at this moment could declare: 'It is a matter
of sorrowful reflection to compare the indifference of many
Christians with this zeal of these poor, blind Muhammadans; who
will, it is to be feared, rise up in judgement against them and con-
demn them.'

At the end of the day, the *imam* having conferred on those present
the title of *Hajji* which they would carry with them to their dying
day, the trumpet sounded and Pitts and his elderly companion joined
the other pilgrims on the journey of two miles or more to Muzdalifa,
where they rested the night.

Next day they moved on to Muna where Pitts's description of the
ritual and its religious background was no more instructive than that
of Varthema in the early years of the century before.

> ... the place, as they say, where Abraham went to offer up his son
> Isaac, and therefore in this place they sacrifice their sheep. I
> was here shown a stone, or little rock, which was parted in the
> middle. They told me that when Abraham was going to sacrifice
> his son, instead of striking him, Providence directed his hand to
> this stone, which he clave in two.

It is a different story from the earlier one, and merely adds to the
confusion of explanations for the ritual at Muna. Christian observers
could never quite bring themselves to understand that in the Koranic
version of the story it was Ishmael and not Isaac whom Abraham
was divinely instructed to sacrifice. When the pilgrims had pitched
their tents on the spacious plain below the mountain of knowledge,

they went and gathered seven small stones which they flung at the devil 'and them that please him'. Each day the stone-throwing ceremony was carried out with frenzied enthusiasm. As Pitts went to throw his stones at one of the pillars in their path, a facetious pilgrim told him that he could save his labour as that gentleman had already deprived the devil of his eyes.

After they had thrown their seven stones on the first day the pilgrims bought a sheep for the act of sacrifice, the meat of which was given to the poor, the very ragged poor, and to friends. What was left they ate themselves. They then had their heads shaven, threw off the *ihram*, and kissed each other with the greeting, 'The feast be a blessing to you'. The rest of the Three Days, the *Biram*, was spent in rejoicing, with the aid of illuminations and fireworks. 'They reckon that all their sins are now done away, and they shall, when they die, go directly to heaven, if they don't apostasise; and for the future, if they keep their vow and do well, God will set down for every good action ten; but if they do ill, God will likewise reckon every evil action ten.' During the Three Days, every fit pilgrim would take himself off to the Great Mosque, running most of the way. When they reached the Kaaba they burst into tears of joy and, after the customary circumambulations and prayers, they returned refreshed to Muna.

When the pilgrims finally went back to Mecca, the merchants and entrepreneurs of trade and entertainment had moved in. All kinds of goods from China and the East Indies had made their laborious way along the caravan routes and by the Red Sea from the Yemen and further east. As Pitts observed, the pilgrims could have bought the same things more cheaply in their home towns, but anything that could be bought in Mecca and dipped in the water of Zemzem helped to confirm the authenticity of the title they now proudly bore. All who could afford it bought the *kaffin*, the shroud of fine linen in which they would be buried. Whenever and wherever they travelled, they would be careful to carry the garment with them. A fair was in full cry. The joyful pilgrims made their last obligatory visit to the Kaaba, drank their fill of Zemzem, made their obeisances, walked backward through the Farewell Door and made their way to the distant places whence they had come.

Pitts set about finding camels and negotiated with the Amir al Hajj for a place with the Cairo caravan for himself and his companion, who by now, it seems, had recovered full health and vigour and was able to take the more arduous way home.

He gave, he said, as much for the hire of his camels as he would have paid for them as outright property, between £5 and £6 sterling, which was indeed a great deal of money in the seventeenth century. At first it was a straggling, disordered procession but it gradually took shape after a lot of fighting and quarrelling. They travelled four animals abreast, once they had assumed their proper places, all tied one after the other. The caravan was divided into several *kitar* or companies, each of which was given a name and consisted of several thousand camels. At the head of each company was 'some great gentleman or officer', carried in a litter borne by two camels, for and aft, and handsomely decorated with silks. They travelled mostly at night, carrying lights and listening to the musical sounds of the bells strung from the sumpter camels that carried the treasures of the Turkish gentry. The lights were held aloft on poles to direct the *hajjis* through the night, iron fitments giving off the glow of burning wood.

In the mornings they halted to pitch their tents and rest for a few hours, following the custom of the badawin who know the folly of travelling in the full heat of the sun. The camels were fed and watered at these stopping-places. They took coffee and then slept again until mid-afternoon, when the trumpeter would stir them to pack their tents and reassemble for the journey. After that they stopped only for prayer, punctually, the massive procession moving across the desert for some sixteen hours at a time. Many of the pilgrims were too poor to afford even water on the journey, and the badawin of the Stony Desert through which they passed demanded that water, and often passage, was paid for. Sometimes two or three pilgrims would hire the services of a poorer member of the party, discharging his expenses in return for attendance on them. There was an Irishman in the party who had been taken captive so young that he had lost not only his religion but his native language besides. He had endured thirty years' slavery in Spain and after that had served in the French galleys. Eventually he was redeemed and went to Algiers. He was accounted a zealot of the faith by the Muslims, retaining his loyalty to Islam in the face of the temptation to return to his native religion. Pitts had met him at Mecca and the man told him that God had delivered him out of hell upon earth and, at Mecca, had brought him into heaven.

Often on the journey home the 'skulkish, thievish' Arabs of the desert invaded the caravan. They would steal up in the darkness and pretend to be servants of the carriers or camel owners. When they found a *hajji* asleep on his camel they would untie the beast and lead it away, while a companion tied up the animal before and after, so that the train was unbroken and the line of camels went on as if nothing had happened. When they had secreted the unfortunate and unsuspecting pilgrim a safe distance from the caravan, they woke him and took everything including his clothes. He was usually allowed to return naked to his caravan, but sometimes he was despatched.

After ten days they came to Madina. Though Muslims from parts of the world distant from Arabia were not expected to embrace the place of the Prophet's burial in their pilgrimages, those from the nearer territories of the north were expected to call there.

Again, Pitts's description bears out most of Varthema's observations. The town he found small and poor but with a great mosque, though it was not as big as that of Mecca. In one corner was a place about fourteen or fifteen paces square with great windows fenced with brass plates. The roof was vaulted and in the middle of the temple was the tomb of Muhammad. For the first time in his account, Pitts gave vent to the prejudice of his own persuasion, and perhaps to the memory of his own forcible conversion. It was, he said, 'where the corpse of that bloody imposter is laid'. The tomb could not be seen by reason of the curtains round it, and the pilgrims were not allowed to enter there. They could simply thrust their hands at the windows, between the brass grates, and petition the dead Prophet with reverence and affection. The old man, Pitts's patron, had his silk handkerchief stolen as he played his own zealous part in the proceedings.

Pitts dismissed the idea of the Prophet's tomb being suspended by the force of loadstone magnets as emphatically as did Varthema, and he added properly that the idea came not from Islam, for he had never heard a Muslim suggest anything like it. Alongside Muhammad's tomb were the sepulchres of the followers, including that reserved for Jesus Christ, 'for they hold that Christ will come again in the flesh, forty years before the end of the world, to confirm the Muhammadan faith and say, likewise, that our saviour was not crucified in person, but in effigy, or one like him'.

They stayed three days in Madina and then set off towards Egypt. After another ten days' journey the caravan came to the Red Sea town of Al Mueyliha, where the pilgrims were met by a friendly crowd of Arabs who brought them fruit and a warm welcome. Fifteen days out from Cairo they were met by friends and relatives who brought them more presents and food. Together they climbed the steep incline to Aqaba, going gently with the camels which, having soft feet, found the climb difficult. When they reached the top of the slope they saw that there was no descent, just a vast plain sweeping ahead of them. They passed by Mount Sinai at night and so did not see it. More well-wishers joined them along the road to Cairo. They were in high spirits when they reached their destination, thirty-seven days' marching time and three days' tarrying after their departure from Mecca. 'In all this way there is scarce any green thing to be met with, nor beast nor fowl to be seen or heard; nothing but sand and stones, excepting one place which we passed through by night; I suppose it was a village, where were some trees, and, we thought, gardens.'

He made straight away for Alexandria, accompanied by his pilgrim companion, the Irish *renegado*. They saw an English ship in the
harbour and Pitts was encouraged to speak to one of the seamen
working on deck. Soon he was confiding his story to the stranger
and at its conclusion another sailor was called from below. He
remembered Pitts, for they had played together as boys in Exeter.
There was an impassioned embrace and the two men spent many
happy hours in conversation. This might have been the golden
opportunity for the exile to escape. But he realised that to desert
his companions and thus show his anxiety to get away would be disastrous. It would be better to take to sea with Algerian corsairs and
hope to be intercepted by a Christian vessel.

The old man had been as good as his word at Mecca and released
his young companion from bondage. But although he was free, it
would still be dangerous to demonstrate a wish to escape his former
masters. They now regarded him as one of them in spirit if not in
nationality. Pitts passed to the West Countryman aboard the ship
letters to his family, a Turkish pipe for his father and a silk purse
for his mother, and bade the Englishmen farewell.

He joined the Algerian army and resigned himself to another long
wait before escaping to England.

He had time once more to study the people and customs of Algiers.
He met another fellow West Countryman, James Grey, whose path
he had crossed before leaving for the holy cities. Grey, who came
from Weymouth, had decided to 'turn Turk'. Pitts the reluctant convert was suspicious of him and went in fear of the renegade, lest his
desire to escape should be exposed.

Wandering through the town, he turned his attention to the multitude as it went about its colourful and often macabre business. On
one occasion a pair of negro slaves, a Muslim and a Christian claiming Portuguese citizenship, were led past curious crowds to be
punished for robbing and murdering their patron. The former
suffered what Pitts described as 'a fair death'. He was taken to the
top of a high wall where a rope was tied to his neck at one end and
to the stone structure at the other. Then he was pushed off his perch.
The other prisoner was stripped naked, and his hands were tied and
drilled so that burning candles could be inserted into them. The same
operation was performed on both shoulders, and thus burdened the
man was paraded through the streets as an incendiary warning
to other wrongdoers. 'I thought they intended to have burnt him
alive and therefore went without the gate to see him executed, but
they cut off his head first, and then burnt his body to ashes,' said
Pitts. The young man of Exeter had suffered much remorse and
experienced great cruelty in captivity. He came to terms with both,
absorbing the lessons of life and observing and reporting with

simple honesty, without sentimentality or pity towards himself or others.

My generous master, who loved me as if I were his own son, freely gave me board and let me know that he proposed to leave me something considerable at his death: but notwithstanding this pleasing prospect, and all the gratitude I felt for his kindness, the hope of being retaken made me leave him and go to sea, but my wishes were not granted.

How long he served as a militiaman aboard the Algerian naval ships, we are not told. At length the Turkish Grand Sultan asked the Algerians for some armed ships and Pitts volunteered to go with them to Smyrna, 'flattering myself in hopes of making my escape there'. He went to Alexandria *en route*. The plague raged through the town and he was alarmed at the sudden appearance of massive carbuncles under his arm and in his groin. They were lanced, however, and he recovered. He also suffered an eye complaint and was attended by an Englishman who was said to understand physick and surgery. This amateur physician lived with a merchant, Mr Butler, and from him Pitts received a letter of commendation to the British consul at Algiers, Mr Baker, who was the brother of the consul at Tunis who had earlier tried to redeem him. He in turn gave Pitts a letter to the consul at Smyrna, a Mr William Ray. Thus, when he arrived at his destination, the Englishman was at last able to look to forces influential enough to effect his escape. He met there yet another West Countryman, a successful merchant by the name of Eliot who had been a fellow apprentice in their boyhood days.

Shortly, through the efforts of Ray and Eliot, he was put aboard a French ship bound for Leghorn. Pitts and his companions, dressed as 'gentlemen', swinging elegant canes, walked openly from the consul's residence, took drinks together aboard ship and parted the next morning. Eliot gave the captain £4 to ensure that his friend was safely delivered at Leghorn. When the ship finally sailed Pitts prostrated himself on the deck and kissed it, 'blessing God for this undeserved mercy'. He travelled through Italy and Germany and finally arrived in Holland where he boarded a ship bound for Harwich.

His homecoming, so long awaited, was far from auspicious. 'I had received many favours and much consideration from strangers on the road', he remarked, 'but on my first night in England I was impressed into the army.' He implored his new captors to let him go, telling them that he had been in exile from his own country for many years and that he had suffered greatly in slavery and captivity. For his pains, they put him in Colchester gaol. He wrote from there to his father and to Sir William Faulkner of the Smyrna Company in London, to whom he had been given a letter of introduction by the Consul Ray. Before his protests and calls for help reached their destinations, however, he was sent to HMS *Dreadnought*, one of the navy's most formidable men-of-war, to prepare to fight the French.

In the end, Faulkner worked what for the unfortunate Pitts was the ultimate miracle. He intervened with the Admiralty, and the young man of Exeter was allowed to go home. On his way he called on Sir William to thank him profusely and while in London he stopped to see a few of the sights of the capital. He danced for joy as he hastened to his native town. On arrival he was too overcome to go straight to his family. He went to a local tavern where he was immediately recognised by old friends. His father was sent for and he rejoined his son after their long separation. They embraced and left the hostelry with their arms round each other, followed by a noisy crowd of well-wishers. Pitts was grieved to learn that his mother had died a year before. He had been abroad for fifteen years, and had taken twelve months in effecting his escape to England. He was in his thirty-first year at his homecoming.

When he came to write his *True and faithful Account of the religion and manners of the Muhammadans etc.*, he applied himself to the task with characteristic humility. 'It may be thought presumptious of me to put forward this little book ...... I cannot pretend to abilities that are required in a person who writes such a history.' He added, though, that he possessed the most valuable of qualifications, a regard for truth. He dedicated his book, which was first published by the local printer in Exeter High Street in 1704, to the Consul William Ray. 'Honoured Sir, I humbly beg leave ..... Next to Almighty God I am in debt to you; who so readily ventured your life to procure my liberty.'

Nowhere in the narrative did Pitts give the dates of his wanderings, except for the departure from England in 1678. But his story suggests that his stay in Algeria after the journey to the holy cities was shorter than the period of his captivity before the pilgrimage. If his service with the Algerian army and fleet, and his final escape, occupied six years, the pilgrimage would be placed at 1687. Sir Richard Burton, in the account of his own journey to Mecca and Madina, suggested 1680, but such a date is much too early. More recent scholarship has suggested 1684, but even that date would indicate less than five years in captivity before setting out on the hajj, and an aftermath of nearly ten years in Algeria. It is unlikely that we shall ever know the exact date of the journey.

Chapter 3

CARSTEN NIEBUHR

Survivor
of a Tragic Expedition
1762

'. . . that intelligence and courage which first opened Arabia to Europe.'
W. G. Palgrave

Carsten Niebuhr has a specially honoured place among the earliest pioneers of Arabian exploration, even though the area he covered was not much more than a small triangle in the Yemen. His experiences produced the first European attempt at a complete account of Arabia, its people and their way of life, and such were the qualities of factual honesty in his *Travels in Arabia* that it became the natural source book for Edward Gibbon's chapters on the Arabs in the *Decline and Fall*, as well as for other European scholars of the eighteenth and nineteenth centuries.

Carsten Niebuhr was German-born, though he considered himself Danish from the time he entered the service of the Danish king. He came of humble but sturdy stock, and after leaving school early was driven by ambition to train as a surveyor. At twenty-two he enrolled at Hamburg University; two years later he moved to Göttingen to read mathematics under the celebrated Professor Kästner and soon won a scholarship to study astronomy.

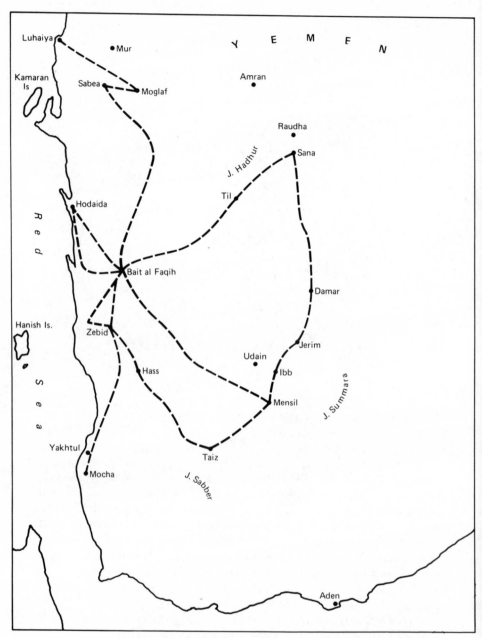

8 Niebuhr's route in Yemen, 1762–3

The following year, 1758, came the unexpected invitation to join an expedition to Arabia, an event which is described thus by Niebuhr's son in his biography of his father:

It was an afternoon in the summer of 1758. Professor Kästner had just been to a meeting at the Academy of Sciences, and he now entered my father's room. 'How would a trip to Arabia strike you?' he asked. 'Why not, if someone can be found to pay the expenses?' answered my father, who had no ties in his homeland and was possessed of a great urge to see the world.

So it was in a mood of 'Why not?' that Niebuhr made the decision to embark upon the greatest adventure of his long life. Others have been drawn to Arabia by a compulsive desire to pioneer the exploration of unknown deserts, by a love of danger and excitement, by intellectual enquiry or romantic curiosity. Niebuhr set out simply to do a job. He had neither read about Arabia nor felt any special attraction towards that land rather than another.

The idea had first been mooted by Professor Michaelis of Göttingen University, foremost orientalist of his time. Knowing that ships plied regularly between Denmark and its colony of Trankebar in south-east India, he suggested that a specially trained Danish party might sail with one of these ships and disembark in South Arabia to explore that land.

Bernstorff, the Foreign Minister, saw the project as one which would give Denmark a name in geographical research. He was able to persuade the king, Frederick V, to sponsor the expedition and finance it. In that age of eager intellectual activity, rulers were judged by their patronage of the arts and sciences. Here was an opportunity for King Frederick to earn prestige and distinction.

It was a time when the literal truth of the Bible was just beginning to be challenged by scholars. Michaelis himself was a deist and an empiricist, and it was through his enlightened attitude that the expedition was given the task of searching for knowledge which might lead to a more accurate understanding and interpretation of the Scriptures.

So far so good; but when, after many difficulties, the expedition's members were finally selected, the team was composed of men so different in character, motivation, and attainments that they were to find it almost impossible to work together. Professor Friedrich von Haven was a Danish philologist, a lazy dilettante full of his own self-importance but apprehensive about the possible dangers of Arabia. Georg Baurenfeind, a 32-year-old German artist and engraver, was to illustrate the discoveries made in Arabia, and Christian Kramer, a young and inexperienced doctor, was recruited as the party's medical officer. By far the most brilliant member of the group was Peter Forsskal, the Swedish scientist who at the age of twenty-nine already had behind him a formidable record of academic distinctions. At Uppsala University he had been for five years a pupil of Linnaeus; he had studied oriental philology under Michaelis at Göttingen, and his doctoral dissertation had earned him election as a Corresponding Member of the German Academy of Sciences at the unheard-of age of twenty-four. Along the way he had also acquired a respectable knowledge of theology, Hebrew, Latin, and Greek.

Finally there was Carsten Niebuhr himself, whose duty would be to survey and map the land they were to explore. In the two years which elapsed between the time he was recruited and the final preparations, he had continued to apply himself to the techniques of surveying; he had trained himself to repair his own instruments; he had conscientiously, if not very successfully, tackled the Arabic language, and had become thoroughly versed in astronomy under the distinguished Professor Mayer. Niebuhr promised his tutor that he would make all his calculations of longitude in accordance with a new theory developed by Mayer, and the professor repaid this enthusiasm by personally helping to calibrate the quadrant Niebuhr was to take to Arabia, the 'astrolabe' which figures frequently in the story of his travels.

Later, when Bernstorff was shown the astrolabe, he asked why Niebuhr had sent in no bill for the cost of the instrument; it was typical of the modest young surveyor that he had been prepared to pay for it himself. Bernstorff's suggestion that Niebuhr be given the title of professor to put him on a par with von Haven and Forsskal was met by embarrassed protests from Niebuhr. In the end it was agreed that he should have the rank of engineer-lieutenant.

Niebuhr was introduced to Forsskal in September 1760, but it is unlikely that his qualifications impressed the Swede. It was part of the tragedy of the expedition that the erudite Forsskal was not a man who mixed easily with others. Always ready to challenge the opinions of those in authority, he was by nature a sceptic, argumentative, proud, tactless and prickly.

In the preparations which took up the final months of 1760, Forsskal spread dissension in all directions. He suggested one of his own Swedish friends as doctor to the party, and there were stormy scenes between him and officialdom before he was forced to accept the appointment of Kramer. With total lack of tact he asked to be allowed to send natural history specimens back to his master Linnaeus. An official reprimand pointed out that since the Danish king was personally paying for the expedition, all material collected would naturally be returned only to Copenhagen.

A new quarrel broke out upon von Haven's arrival in Copenhagen. He had hoped to be leader of the party, considering himself senior in learning as well as age, but Forsskal insisted on equality of rank among the members. Disappointed of the leadership, von Haven expected at least to have charge of the group's finances, and was incensed to learn that Niebuhr had been made treasurer. When all the members of the group met together for the first time, von Haven protested vigorously at the decisions already made. Bernstorff refused to alter the arrangements, but we may imagine the feelings of the individual members after this acrimonious meeting: von Haven nursing a bitter grudge against Niebuhr and Forsskal; Forsskal angered at von Haven's assumption of intellectual superiority; Niebuhr and Kramer conscious that their participation in the project was not really welcomed by the two scholarly members. Only Baurenfeind the artist was not drawn into the general discord.

Such was the situation as the day of their departure drew near.

In the final orders received from King Frederick at the end of December there were forty-three paragraphs of detailed instructions for the group. Among them were the following points: once arrived in Arabia the party was to explore inland as well as along the coast; it was pointed out hopefully that the presence of a doctor would allow them without danger to visit places where deadly diseases were endemic. The party were at all times to behave with decorum towards the Muslims, not offending against their religion or customs, and showing particular respect to their women. All members were to keep diaries during their travels. They were instructed to look out for and buy oriental manuscripts on natural history, history and geography, as well as early biblical texts in Hebrew and Arabic, and to find out the answers to a list of questions drawn up by Professor Michaelis and other scholars. In specific instructions to individual members, Niebuhr was to map the areas they visited, and to record information on climate, antiquities, population, agriculture, and the economy of the country. Von Haven was to observe the customs of the Arabs in relation to the Scriptures, to research into pre-Islamic religion in Arabia, and to search for possible variant versions of the Bible among ancient manuscripts. Dr Kramer was to report on the diseases of the region, and Arab medical practices. Forsskal was to make collections of natural history specimens, in particular of things mentioned in the Bible.

On 4 January 1761 the five men, with their Swedish servant Berggren, embarked from Copenhagen to sail to Alexandria. Thus was launched a project whose noble aims raised high hopes among Europe's scholars. In the event, the expedition led to tragedy and death, and only Carsten Niebuhr, after more than six years of travel, was to see Copenhagen again.

Eighteen months after their departure the party had got no further than Suez. Tensions and jealousies continued to divide them, though by the time they left for Jidda in October 1762 they seem to have reached some measure of accord. Perhaps the prospect of Arabia and its unknown hazards looming close made them feel the need to close their ranks. After a lengthy stay in Egypt Forsskal and Niebuhr, and perhaps also von Haven, had acquired a good working knowledge of vernacular Arabic. All had adopted Egyptian clothes and were tanned and bearded.

Disembarking at Jidda, they set foot for the first time on Arabian soil, and were 'under strong apprehensions of ill-treatment from its inhabitants'. To their pleasant surprise the citizens were not unfriendly. The Danish party was able to rent a house, and during their six-week stay Niebuhr investigated the town's imports and exports, customs tariffs, and water supplies, and recorded all available useful information. He drew a plan of the city and did some surveying outside the town walls.

From Jidda they sailed down the Red Sea in a *tarrad*, a native open boat. Their intended destination was Mocha, but when the vessel put in at Luhaiya, the most northerly port of Yemen, they decided to go ashore in the hope of proceeding from there by land. It was 29 December 1762.

The Danish party received a warm welcome from Farhan, the negro amir or dowla of the town, who was not unfamiliar with Europeans, since he had met English merchants from India who sailed regularly to Yemen to buy coffee. But Farhan was surprised and intrigued when he understood that in this party there was a physician, an astronomer, and one who collected plants. Perhaps curiosity rather than natural hospitality made him encourage them to leave the boat and spend a few weeks in his town.

They had letters of introduction from Jidda to the amir and to a leading merchant named Mahsin, and both these gentlemen went out of their way to be helpful. The amir simplified their dealings with the boat captain, who now demanded full payment for their passage as far as Hodaida. He helped them to arrange for some heavy boxes containing specimens collected by Forsskal to continue by sea to Mocha, and even wrote to the dowla of that town asking him to store the boxes till their owners should arrive. Finally Farhan sent his own boat out to collect their other baggage from the *tarrad*. Mahsin the merchant was indisposed at the time of their arrival, and invited them to stay in one of his houses, as he was anxious to have the services of the Danish doctor. But when they preferred to stay on the beach with their baggage for their first night ashore, he sent an excellent meal from his own kitchen.

Of the amir Niebuhr says: 'We found him to possess the dignified politeness of a nobleman, the strict integrity, and the candid benevo-

lence of a true friend to mankind.' He added that the Arabs seemed
to be more civilised the further they proceeded from Egypt.

The next day the party opened their baggage at the customs house
and provided a diverting morning for the amir and his retinue.
Everybody was amazed to see a louse hugely magnified under
Forsskal's microscope. One of the servants commented that it must
be a European louse, since they had none in Arabia of that size. But
the most successful novelty was Niebuhr's astronomical telescope,
through which things were seen upside down. When the Arabs
looked through it at a woman walking 'they could not conceive how
it happened that although she appeared topsy turvy, yet her under-
garments did not turn about her ears, and exclaimed repeatedly
Allah Akbar, God is great'.

The inhabitants of Luhaiya were 'curious, intelligent, and
polished in their manners'. Naturally everyone was inquisitive about
the Europeans, and when the party installed themselves in a house
they were forced to hire a porter to keep away the gaping crowds.
Even so, people gained admission on the pretext of consulting the
doctor. The young and inexperienced Kramer had never known
such a demand for his professional services, and soon discovered
that the Arabs judged the quality of medicines by their drastic
results.

Mr Kramer had given a scribe a vomit which operated with
extreme violence. The Arabs being struck at its wonderful effects,
resolved all to take the same excellent remedy; and the reputation
of our friend's skill thus became very high among them. The Amir
Bahr, or inspector of the port, sent one day for him; and as he did
not go immediately the Amir soon after sent a saddled horse to our
gate. Mr Kramer, supposing that this horse was intended to bear
him to the Amir, was going to mount him, when he was told that
this was the patient he was to cure. We luckily found out another
physician in our party. Our Swedish servant had served among the
hussar troops in his native country, and in that service had learned
some knowledge of the diseases of horses. He offered to cure the
Amir's horse and succeeded. The cure rendered him famous: and
he was often sent for afterwards to human patients.

It was inevitable that before long their advice would be sought
on one of the perennial problems of the East. An elderly merchant
confided to them that his life had been made happy by the enjoyment
of nearly a hundred beautiful young slave-girls. 'He still had two
of these; and he would die content, he said, if he could only forget
the frailty of old age now and then in their company.' Another rich
man offered Kramer a hundred crowns if he could provide effective

medicine for his similar incapacity, but 'neither Mr Kramer's pre-
scription, nor yet those of some surgeons of some English ships whom
he had consulted, could restore him to his genial vigour'.

Their initial fears about the hostility of the Arabs had quickly
faded under the friendly protection of the Dowla Farhan, and they
enjoyed their days in Luhaiya. So relaxed and happy were they that
Niebuhr and Baurenfeind got out their violins and played duets
together in their spare time. When the music was heard from the
street it roused new interest among the inhabitants. They were summoned by a well-to-do citizen to come and play at his house, but
Niebuhr refused, believing that professional musicians were held low
in the social scale among Arabs, and he did not want to be thought
only a musician. However, when the citizen showed himself interested enough to ride round on his donkey and ask them to play, they
obliged him.

We played some solemn tunes, which are more to the taste of the
Orientals than our gayer music. He seemed to be pleased and
offered each of us half a crown at parting. The Arabs refuse no
presents, however small, and he was not a little surprised when we
declined accepting his money; especially as he could not conceive
what inducements any person could have to learn music if not to
gain by it.

The violins, in that remote corner of Arabia, sound a cheerful note
to us from two hundred years ago. But the 'solemn tunes' may also
be taken as an ominous symbol of the more serious preoccupations
which were to face the party before long. The violins are not
mentioned again in Niebuhr's story.

Between such moments of relaxation, the more conscientious
members of the group were busy with their appointed tasks. Forsskal,
indefatigable as usual, noted the units of weights and measures,
coins, and exchange rates, as well as writing an account of the legal
system. But most of his time was spent ranging through the countryside as far as the foothills of the mountains, searching for plants
among the fields of indigo, basil, and millet, and during this period
he collected more than 100 new specimens. Von Haven, by contrast,
found nothing to do. There were no ancient manuscripts to be seen
in Luhaiya, and growing ever more bored and moody he spent his
days complaining about the discomfort of their living conditions.
Niebuhr was busy with his cartography, and earnestly filling his
notebooks with facts. From his writings we gain the impression of
a good-natured and dutiful man, probably somewhat lacking in
humour, but genuinely interested in exploring an unknown land and
intent on carrying out his orders. In their early days in Arabia he

still felt that Forsskal and von Haven regarded him as their social
and intellectual inferior, and probably hoped by hard work to justify
himself and earn their appreciation.

After nearly two months they felt that the time had come for them
to move on, and they decided to make for Bait al Faqih, a trading-
post lying inland half-way to Sana, the capital. Bidding a friendly
farewell to the dowla, they presented him with a telescope and a
watch. The latter gift was something totally unfamiliar to him, but
a Cairo merchant who was present at the council of the leading men,
the *majlis*, promised Niebuhr that he would be responsible for winding the watch daily.

Having hired camels for their baggage, and asses for themselves,
they set out on 20 February 1763. At no time in or around Luhaiya
had they ever met with any hostility, so there was no need for them
to join a caravan. They travelled south-east across the bare, dry
Tihama plain which runs along Arabia's western coast between the
sea and the mountains, and every time they stopped for the night
at a village coffee-house they found their hosts had received orders
from the amir of Luhaiya to supply a sheep for their dinner.

On 25 February, when they arrived at Bait al Faqih, a letter from
Mahsin the helpful merchant of Luhaiya gained them a welcome
from a leading trader in the town, and they continued to enjoy
friendly co-operation from the people. The fact that the dowla here
took no particular interest in them was regarded by Niebuhr as an
advantage, since it left them freer to make their excursions into the
country unaccompanied by the escort which Farhan had always insisted on providing.

Bait al Faqih lay roughly equidistant from Luhaiya, Mocha, and
Sana, with the coffee-hills one day's journey inland to the east. It
had therefore become an important coffee-market, attracting merchants from Morocco, the Levant, Persia, Abyssinia, India, and often
also from Europe. It was an unwalled town with a number of stone-
built houses, but the commonest type of dwelling was the small one-
roomed hut, built of mud walls with a roof of straw thatch. The tall
minaret of the principal mosque rose from the centre of the town,
and a stoutly built citadel on the outskirts formed the chief defensive
feature.

The various members of the party had fallen into the habit of
occupying themselves each in his own way, and this they continued
to do from their new base. But von Haven and Kramer, finding little
of interest in Bait al Faqih, returned to the coast to Hodaida. They
paid their respects to the dowla there, and enjoyed a pleasant spell
in comparative comfort being entertained as his guests.

Niebuhr was now working systematically over the country to produce a map of the Yemen. Measuring distances by establishing how

far his donkey walked in half an hour, and with only a pocket compass to find his direction, he plotted the position of villages and landmarks. In the evenings he checked his notes with astronomical bearings. His map was one of the remarkable achievements of the Arabian expedition. For over a century it served as the only guide for those who followed.

Adapting himself to local ways, Niebuhr travelled light on his map-making excursions. 'I had for some time endeavoured to suit myself to the Arabian manner of living, and could now spare many conveniences to which I had been accustomed in Europe.' He rode his hired donkey, accompanied by only one attendant. He kept his eyes open for possible ancient sites or monuments, copying any inscription which seemed to be of interest. At Zebid, a once prosperous city which had fallen into decline, he saw mosques and a ruined aqueduct erected by the Ottomans during their occupation of the Yemen. The Wadi Zebid was an indigo-growing area, and he heard that outside the town there were more than 600 vats in which the dye was prepared. Whenever he was not actually travelling Niebuhr sought out learned men with whom he could talk about Arabia in general, and from such conversations acquired information for those chapters of his book which deal with territories and peoples of which he had no first-hand experience.

Forsskal meanwhile had found a botanist's paradise up in the coffee-hills. Not only was the country rich in plants but the climate was delightful and the scenery offered a pleasant change from the barren coastal plain. Forsskal's glowing description of the uplands decided Kramer and Baurenfeind to join him in an excursion there, and Niebuhr followed shortly after. Working his way with dogged perseverance through as much territory as he could, Niebuhr had been finding the heat of the plain daily more exhausting as spring turned to summer. A brief visit to the cool air of the mountains was a welcome relief.

Niebuhr joined his companions in the hillside gardens of a village called Bulgosa. He was enchanted by the scenery, the cascades of water, the lush groves of coffee-shrubs, and the 'exquisitely agreeable' perfume from their flowers. He noted that the mountains were composed of 'basaltic columns', a useful form of rock which could be easily separated to build the terrace walls of the fields.

They spent an agreeable evening in the village inn at Bulgosa. After the men of the village retired they had a visit from their hostess, 'with some young women accompanying her, who were all very desirous to see the Europeans. They seemed less shy than the women in the cities: their faces were unveiled; and they talked freely with us: as the air is fresher and cooler upon these hills, the women have here a finer and fairer complexion than in the plain.' Baurenfeind has left us a picture of one of the young women whose company they enjoyed on that pleasant evening.

But the idyllic interlude was brief. The next day the party returned to Bait al Faqih. Niebuhr now hoped to extend his map-making southwards to Taiz. Though they had so far travelled unmolested he feared that a lone stranger might not pass so easily among the highlanders, and since Forsskal had acquired a knowledge of the mountain dialect, Niebuhr asked the Swede to join him on his intended expedition. Till now the members of the party had shown little desire to work or travel together, but Forsskal liked the idea of a longer journey through the hills whose vegetation was of so much interest. He agreed, and the two men set out from Bait al Faqih on 26 March.

The preparations for our journey were easily made [wrote Niebuhr]. We hired two asses, and the owner attended us on foot as our guide, our servant, and occasionally our interpreter. We had already large beards in the Arab fashion; and these, with our long robes, gave us a very oriental appearance. To disguise ourselves still more each of us assumed an Arabic name; and under these pretensions our real condition was so perfectly concealed that even the owner of the asses thought us Christians of the East; and had no suspicion that we were Europeans.

Niebuhr assumed the name Shawash Abdullah. They travelled by little-frequented paths, through mountains formerly notorious as haunts of robbers, skirting round the villages as far as possible. But those whom they did meet greeted them with friendly interest.

The Arabs of Yemen, and especially the Highlanders, often stop strangers, to ask whence they come, and whither they are going. These questions are suggested merely by curiosity; and it would be indiscreet therefore to refuse to answer. We told them that we came from Esh Sham, the north; which led them to imagine that we were Turks from Syria. When asked whether we were Turks, we replied that we were Nassara; and they then supposed us Greeks or Armenians. We concealed our country lest we should have exposed ourselves still more to the impertinence of their curiosity. The mistress of the coffee-house supposed us to be Turkish clergymen, and recommended herself to our prayers.

In the bare little inns they ate coarse millet bread and drank camels' milk, for which they had no great taste. By contrast they found the mountain water delicious.

Having completed the week-long journey to Taiz, they did not wait to look round this mountain city, which they intended to visit again when they all went on to Sana. Without entering the city walls they turned immediately to make their way back to the coastal plain by a more westerly path. For Niebuhr the whole expedition had been useful but undramatic as he daily made his calculations of distance and direction, and recorded the names of new villages and districts. For Forsskal, on the other hand, the return from Taiz to Bait al Faqih yielded the greatest discovery he was to make.

One of the chief aims of the botanical side of his work was to discover the 'Mecca balsam tree'. This plant had become a thing of fable; by Muslim tradition the Queen of Sheba was supposed to have presented it to Solomon. Another story held that at the command of the Prophet it had sprung up in Hijaz from the blood of a martyr of Islam. Theophrastus and Dioscorides had described it. Cleopatra was supposed to have introduced it into Egypt. From the gum of the tree was produced the 'balm of Gilead', an extract to which were ascribed semi-magical qualities of healing.

Forsskal had already searched unsuccessfully in Egypt for this tree, about which European scientists were eager to know more. On 4 April 1763, travelling between Taiz and Hass, he found it. Niebuhr's account of the moment is somewhat prosaic.

In this desert tract, upon the confines of the Tihama, Mr Forsskal was much rejoiced to discover the tree which affords the balm of Mecca. The plant which he found was pretty large and in flower. Here was nothing to hinder my friend from examining and making a description of it. This tree grows in many places through Yemen. But the inhabitants, who call it Abu Scham, the sweet smelling tree, know no other use for it but to perfume their apartments, by burning the wood. Many branches of the specimen which we found had been torn off for this purpose.

Forsskal was ecstatic. Such was his excitement that, against all instructions, he reported his discovery to Linnaeus and sent him a piece of the tree. His letter said:

Now I know the genus Opobalsamum; the tree grows in the Yemen, but the population do not know how to collect balsam from it. I cannot report my discoveries in private letters, but this much I can say: it is not Pistaca, nor is it Lenticus, but one of Brown's genera.... This country is in truth a country that well deserves a botanical expedition. ... But if it is not granted to me to live until I can discuss my collection with you, then I and science will have lost more than one can possibly say.

The letter and the sprig of balsam were not to reach Uppsala till more than a year later.

As the two men descended from the mountains to the stifling air of the plain they felt well satisfied with their work. At least they, if not their companions, had already achieved much of what they had been commissioned to do. But now their luck changed. Between Hass and Zebid they stopped at an inn. Niebuhr, exhausted by the overpowering heat, was rash enough to sit and fall asleep in a cooling draught, and later reproached himself for his foolishness, for the next day he was seized by a violent fever. In spite of his illness they rode on to Bait al Faqih, where they rejoined their party on 6 April.

They found that von Haven had also fallen sick in their absence. He lay disconsolately in the house, 'weary of the mode of life to which we were here confined'. Niebuhr's illness continued unabated after their return, and it was a fortnight before he and von Haven were sufficiently recovered for the party to make their planned journey to Mocha. Though Niebuhr's account does not dwell unduly upon their illness, it was obviously a weakening and depressing experience. He attributed it in part to the bad water of the Tihama and the unsuitable food which they were eating. In fact the malady which had struck them both was malaria, of whose nature and seriousness they were totally ignorant.

As they planned to move on to Mocha they faced a dilemma known to successive generations of Arabian explorers. Arabs travel by night in the hot weather, resting and sleeping in the daytime. But the European who wishes to see and survey the country must expose himself to the full heat of the sun. In the end it was decided that Niebuhr and Forsskal, for the sake of their work, should travel by day, while the rest of the party with the baggage went by night.

It was a journey of fierce heat and great discomfort – 'we were overjoyed whenever we could shelter ourselves for a little in any paltry coffee-hut' – and when they arrived at Mocha at the end of three punishing days, the guards at the city gate told them that Europeans might not ride donkeys in the town, and they were forced to go on foot to find lodgings. This first rebuff, in sad contrast to earlier welcomes, heralded a series of misfortunes in Mocha.

Though they had their usual letters of introduction to the dowla, to a prominent merchant, and to an Indian who might be a useful contact, they hesitated to approach respectable citizens looking like vagrants in their travel-worn clothes. There was present in the city an English merchant from Bombay, a Mr Francis Scott, but they were also reluctant to visit him when they first arrived. Instead, Forsskal and Niebuhr went to the house of a certain Ismail Saleh, whom they had met on the boat from Jidda, and who had seemed well-disposed. They were later to find that he and his father were confidence tricksters who lived by defrauding foreign merchants. When these rogues were frustrated in their hopes of material gain from the Danish party, they retaliated by inciting customs officials and others against the visitors.

Soon after their arrival in Mocha Niebuhr and his companions went to the customs house, where the chests full of Forsskal's specimens which had gone on by sea from Luhaiya were waiting. They requested that their personal baggage should be cleared first by the customs, but the dowla, who was present in person, refused, and demanded that the chests be opened first. One of them contained Forsskal's collection of Red Sea fishes, preserved in a barrel of spirit. To the party's dismay the rough customs men forced open the barrel and poured the contents on the ground, and were then furious at the stench which filled their shed. Next they proceeded to rummage through a collection of sea-shells, unable to understand that anyone could seriously collect such things, and suspecting trickery. When they came upon a spirit jar in which some snakes were preserved, it was the last straw.

At first sight of this the Arabs were terrified. A person who was servant to the dowla observed that those Franks had come hither to poison the Mussulmans, and that it was in order to succeed in this, that one of them pretended to be a physician. The Dowla who was an old man, and till now did not seem to have conceived any prejudice against us, became suddenly in a passion when this idea was suggested, and swore, by God, that we should not remain a single night in the city.

The customs house was promptly shut with all their baggage inside and they were left facing an angry crowd of officials and bystanders. At the same time a messenger came to say that the house they had rented had been ransacked, their books and other belongings thrown out of the windows, and the door barred against them.

Most of the town was now set against them, and the outlook was bleak for the tired and dispirited party. But one kindly Arab agreed to take them to his house, and shortly afterwards Scott, the English merchant, came to their aid. 'He had heard of our difficulties and perplexity; and although we had not yet visited him, gave us an invitation to dinner, which we accepted with the greatest pleasure. He expressed a warm desire to serve us; and we now perceived how foolishly we had acted in not applying at first to him and his Banian interpreter.'

But there was still the problem of rescuing their belongings from the customs house. The officials there, suborned by Ismail Saleh, refused them access either to their baggage or to the dowla. They finally agreed to pay the governor fifty ducats to have their belongings released. Niebuhr was on his way to hand over the money when he heard that the dowla had accidentally shot himself in the foot. He turned back, hoping that the governor's need of a doctor would give them a bargaining counter which they could use to their advantage. Nothing happened. Kramer's services were not requested.

One can imagine the frustration, anger and despair of the party, and of Forsskal in particular, since he had had to watch the wanton destruction of his scientific specimens. In the end it was Forsskal who resolved the matter. He demanded an audience of the dowla.

We can only guess how the fiery-tempered Swede faced the governor of Mocha. All we know is that the audience was granted, and the subdued old dowla 'chid him for not applying directly to himself at the first. Next day ... he sent us a present of four lambs and two small bags of rice; and at the same time gave orders that our effects should be delivered to us, without being more particularly examined.' The situation had certainly improved.

The dowla, still suffering from his wound, was half-fearful of sending for Kramer, lest the doctor might take revenge for the ill-treatment the Danish party had suffered. But an enlightened *kadhi*, or local magistrate, spoke well of them to him.

These representations, and the alarming state of the wound, which was becoming worse ... induced the Dowla to send on the 4th of May, to enquire whether we were still angry with him, or if our physician would undertake to cure him. We were overjoyed to hear that the prejudices which the governor had conceived against us were so perfectly removed; and Mr Kramer gladly offered his services.

Once friendly relations had been established with the governor, the attitude of the people also improved. Niebuhr was able to make his usual investigations about Mocha, then the principal port of the Yemen. To the English of those days it was a place of such importance that it gave a new word to our language, a word that survives though the town itself is today all but forgotten.

According to Niebuhr, the town had about 700 inhabitants. An elegant mosque outside the walled precincts marked the tomb of Shaikh Shaedeli, a holy man who was supposed to have encouraged the visits of foreign ships which first brought prosperity to the place. We are also given an amusing account of a French bombardment of Mocha in 1738, as related to Niebuhr by the Arabs. Apparently the French East India Company, having difficulty in recovering a debt of 82,000 crowns owed them for goods bought by the local dowla, sent a man-of-war which fired upon the citadel and the governor's house. The population, after seeing a number of citizens killed, obliged their leader to make peace. 'Several of the Arabs still recollect this little affair with pleasure, and remember, with a degree of gaiety, those pots of fire, as they called them to me, which pursued their Dowla backwards and forwards wherever he went. Since that time the Arabs have entertained a high opinion of the military talents of the Europeans.'

During this attack by the French the people of Mocha apparently did not feel moved to vent their spite on the English and Dutch residents of the town, with whom they carried on a highly lucrative business. But by the time of the Danish party's visit trade with the West had slumped, and European buyers no longer lived in Mocha. Only the English were still buying coffee, but because of the town's unhealthy coastal climate their affairs there were left in the hands of Indian Banian agents. There was practically no market for coffee in India itself, and English ships bringing goods from India to Mocha had little return cargo, except for specie with which the Arab merchants entrusted them. The boat on which the Danes were finally to sail when they left Yemen was carrying 250,000 crowns in coin. 'These sums are almost always in European coins, Venetian ducats, or German coins.... The ships which sail from Basra to India are in the same manner freighted with money which has passed from Europe through Turkey.' But the coffee-trade remained the principal source of revenue for the Imam of the Yemen, who received a quarter of the sale price of every export load before it could be put aboard a ship.

After their return to favour with the dowla the Danish party felt reasonably at ease in Mocha, but only three or four weeks were to pass before illness struck them again. Niebuhr suffered from fifteen days of severe dysentery. Von Haven, who had not fully recovered from his earlier attack of malaria, now had a relapse. By 24 May he was in the throes of high fever and delirium, and the others could do nothing to help him. He died that night.

Von Haven and Niebuhr had had nothing in common, in background, interests, or character; but Niebuhr's published epitaph on his colleague is correct and courteous. 'He had paid more attention than any other of us, to oriental literature. The public have lost, by his death, some very interesting discoveries, and some curious collections of this sort, which he had made.' Many years later Niebuhr expressed to his son his true feelings about von Haven. He judged him idle, incompetent, and totally out of place on the expedition. In Yemen von Haven had thought only of getting home, and complained endlessly about their hardships.

Peter Forsskal, in his private diary, was characteristically blunt.

'Professor von Haven died here on 25th May, and by his demise made the expedition incomparably easier for the rest of us. He was of a very difficult disposition.'

The Danish party had to have a coffin specially made. It was impossible to buy one since Arabs are buried in shrouds only. With a bearer party of six sailors from Mr Scott's ship, they gave von Haven a decent burial, attended by all the English in Mocha. 'On this occasion,' remarks Niebuhr, 'the Arabs of the Yemen showed themselves reasonable and humane.' He was writing with the knowledge of later and sadder events, though at the time in Mocha he did not know that further tragedy lay ahead.

There were three English ships in Mocha during May, and some of the party wished to stay there and take passage to Bombay with the English coffee-merchants who were to sail at the beginning of August. But they had not yet visited Sana, the capital, one of the main objectives of the expedition. In the end those who wished to go to Sana – and there is little doubt that it was Niebuhr and Forsskal who were keenest to do so – imposed their will on the others. They hoped they might even get there and back before the English ships sailed. The Danish party had been in the Yemen five months, and their first pleasant impressions of the country had been modified by the harsh climate and the threat of mortal illness. Von Haven's death and Niebuhr's continuing ill-health made all the party anxious to finish their work and be gone.

When they made the decision to leave Mocha for Sana the dowla at first refused them permission to depart, since he still needed Kramer's attention for his wounded foot. Fortunately he was able to find another local 'surgeon' and before long agreed to let them go and rewarded Kramer for his services.

Niebuhr, as treasurer of the party, decided not to carry their money with them on the uncertain journey to the capital. Instead he banked it with the Indian interpreter who served the English merchants, and this Indian gave them bills of exchange upon fellow Indians in Taiz and Sana. It was the first time they had been able to make such financial arrangements, which worked very satisfactorily.

On 9 June 1763 they set out in oppressive heat. Across the plain they travelled at night, but once in the hills they found the rough stony paths too difficult to negotiate in the dark. It took them four days to reach Taiz, where their letter of introduction to the dowla brought them an immediate invitation to his residence, and an empty house was put at their disposal.

Taiz, which Niebuhr and Forsskal had previously reached incognito, was a heavily-walled mountain town with only two gates. In the years before their visit it had suffered from rival claimants to the governorship, and had been sacked in 1760. As a result of these feuds much of the city was in a ruinous state, though its latest rulers had built some impressive palaces.

At first all seemed to go well with them in Taiz, and they regained their strength somewhat in the cool, refreshing climate. But while Niebuhr was able to make notes on the history of the town, Forsskal was not so fortunate with his own researches. Taiz stood at the foot of a conspicuous hill called Sabber, which even along the Arabs was noted for the variety of its vegetation. 'Mr Forsskal had this mountain daily before his eyes; but to his infinite mortification, could not obtain permission to botanize upon it.' The semi-autonomous shaikhs in the surrounding territory were enemies of the Dowla of Taiz, whose inhabitants scarcely dared venture out into the mountains. Yet Niebuhr and Forsskal had travelled safely through those same regions when they had been alone and unknown to local officials.

The Dowla then began to be difficult in other ways. He claimed to have received a letter from the governor of Mocha ordering the foreigners to return there. In a personal interview granted to Forsskal (who doubtless hoped to repeat the success he had had in browbeating the governor of Mocha) the Dowla refused to listen to a request that they might be allowed to stay till the Imam, temporal and spiritual ruler of Yemen, sent them permission to go to Sana. Peremptorily the governor of Taiz ordered the Europeans out of his city.

But even as they reluctantly prepared to turn back, news came that the Imam in Sana was ready to receive them. In Taiz, the Dowla continued to insist that they must return to Mocha, but once again a kindly *kadhi* spoke up for them and persuaded the Dowla to change his mind. In addition the *kadhi* provided a letter of recommendation to the Imam's vizier; 'his probity and beneficence ... inspired us with the highest veneration for his character, and the liveliest gratitude for his favours'.

Their visit to Taiz had not been a happy one, and Forsskal had become more frustrated and irritable as the days passed. This moodiness probably marked the onset of the illness which was soon to strike him, but Niebuhr in retrospect saw it as a contributory cause of that illness.

They set out for Sana on 28 June, and for the first three or four days travelled on a good, paved road. It rained nearly every day, but at regular intervals they found large, well-built caravanserais where they could shelter and lodge at night. But though the travelling was easier, it soon became evident that Forsskal's health had broken down. Till now he had retained remarkable mental and physical energy, but by the sixth day out from Taiz his companions saw that he was nearing collapse and urgently needed rest. They were glad to find a comfortable caravanserai at the village of Mensil, but the camel-men said the place had no pasture for their beasts and suggested they move on to Jerim, a day's journey further. They promised that Forsskal could travel in a litter borne by men over the rough roads of Jabal Sumara. The party rested for a day, then agreed to move on. On 5 July Niebuhr set out before the others, wishing to travel in the cool of early morning. But when the others tried to arrange for Forsskal to be moved, the Arabs refused to take him in a litter, since they would not carry a Christian. Finally Forsskal's 'bed' – probably only the common type of cotton quilt used by the Arabs – was strapped to the back of a camel with the sick man upon it, and he had to endure a terrible march lying bent over the camel's hump, lurching giddily along the mountain paths. Not surprisingly, he was in 'a deplorable condition' by the end of the journey.

Niebuhr himself had a recurrence of his malaria during the same day. 'I soon felt myself affected with a severe rheum, vomitings, and excessive thirst, which I could not have quenched on that desert mountain if I had not fortunately met with a peasant who permitted me to drink out of his pitcher of water.'

When they reached Jerim they stopped first at the public inn, but here they were surrounded by crowds of curious and importunate Arabs, and realised they must find private lodgings where Forsskal might be nursed back to health. When they wanted to move the sick man to their new house the Arabs once again refused to help. The Europeans themselves carried their sick friend.

At this stage in their travels we can only marvel that Niebuhr, despite his own illness and that of Forsskal, could still make the effort to write notes for a chapter on 'The City of Jerim'. He mentions hearing that in ancient ruins about two miles outside Jerim there was a stone with an inscription that neither Jews nor Muslims could read. He guessed that this must be a 'Hamjarine' inscription, and at any other time such information would have sent him off eagerly to record this new discovery. As it was, he could not bring himself to move from Jerim, and only reports the existence of the stone as hearsay. This was, in fact, the first news which reached Europe of an extant Himyaritic inscription. More than seventy years were to pass before Lieutenant Charles Cruttenden of the *Palinurus* survey ship brought back from a journey to Sana copies of four such inscriptions, the first recorded in Yemen.

As well as describing the sights and customs of Jerim, Niebuhr has left a drawing of the town as he saw it from the room where the sick Forsskal lay, a melancholy reminder of how the four stronger members of the party must have watched over their friend.

For four days Peter Forsskal lay racked with fever and often delirious, till on the evening of 10 July,

> he sunk into a deep lethargy, in which state he continued till his death the next morning. We were deeply affected at his loss. In consequence of his botanical excursions, he had learned more than any of us, of the Arabic tongue, and its different dialects. Fatigue, or the want of conveniences, never discouraged him; he could accommodate himself to the manners of the people of the country, without doing which, indeed, no one can hope to travel with advantage through Arabia. In short, he seemed formed by nature for such an expedition as that in which we were engaged.

There is no doubt that in the adventures and hardships they had shared, the scientist and the surveyor had finally formed a strong friendship, in spite of their seeming incompatibility.

The party notified the officials at Jerim of their companion's death, and after some difficulty were told of a place where an infidel's body might be buried. Again the Arabs were unwilling to carry a Christian, and it was almost impossible to find anyone to take the body to the grave, even though liberal payment was promised. 'At last we prevailed with six men to convey it to the burying place at midnight. They performed the task, but ran and hid themselves in the best manner they could, all the way; so great is the aversion of those people to touch a Christian.'

Once more they had had a coffin specially made, but realised only afterwards that this had been a tragic mistake. After their arrival in Sana news came to them that robbers, believing that Europeans buried valuables in the coffin with the dead, had dug up Forsskal's grave, and that the body, bereft even of its shroud, had been left lying in the open till the dowla had ordered the Jews to bury it again.

Forsskal was thirty-one when he died. If he had returned to Europe and fulfilled the promise of his early achievements he would be remembered as one of the great scientists of the century. As it is, few men know of the brilliant scholar whose remains were buried without honour or memorial outside an obscure Yemeni village.

It is sad to record that even his zoological and botanical work in Arabia did not bring him recognition when his specimens were shipped home. Several chests of material and notes finally reached Copenhagen from India in 1766, but by then the Arabian expedition had been almost forgotten. The cases were left unopened, alcohol evaporated, specimens of birds and fishes rotted. Fortunately his 1,300 specimens of plants arrived intact, but even these had to wait five years before they were systematically studied, and in that time much of the collection suffered from bad storage. In the Forsskal

Herbarium today only about one-third of the original material survives. Forsskal's diary was not published by his contemporaries, and
the manuscript was lost during the nineteenth century. In 1920 it
turned up in the library of Kiel University, and it was finally published in 1950.

The party, now reduced to Niebuhr, Kramer, Baurenfeind, and
the servant Berggren, left Jerim on 13 July. They stopped the next
night at the town of Damar where stones were thrown through the
windows of their lodgings. When they wished to leave, Berggren was
ill and unable to travel. He agreed to remain behind alone, and when
he recovered he was able to rejoin them in Sana.

Reaching Seijan, they prepared to enter Sana the following day,
and changed from their travelling clothes into their best Turkish
outfits. Then on the morning of 16 July, halted a mile from Sana
on the 10,000-foot mountain plateau where the capital stands, they
sent their servant with the letter of introduction to the Imam's vizier.
But news of their coming had preceded them, and a secretary came
out to meet them. The Imam had provided them with a house in
the suburbs, but when they reached it they were disappointed, for
it had no furniture and no supply of provisions, and they had to go
without food till a servant could go shopping in the city. However,
next morning gifts from the Imam arrived, five sheep, wood, rice,
lamps, and spices. They were now able to make themselves quite
comfortable, but were told that they must stay inside till the Imam
could receive them, which would not be for another two days because
he was busy paying his mercenaries.

Finally on 19 July came the day which must have seemed the
culmination of all their weary travel and exertion. The vizier's secretary came to conduct them to the Imam's palace of Bustan el
Metwokkel. They expected a small private audience, and were taken
aback to see that the occasion was to be one of grand ceremonial.
The palace courtyard was so full of cavalry and officials that it
needed the master of the horse to clear a passage for the visitors.

The hall of audience was a spacious square chamber having an
arched roof. In the middle was a large bason, with some *jets d'eau*,
rising fourteen feet in height. Behind the bason and near the throne,
were two large benches, each a foot and a half high; upon the throne
was a space covered with silken stuff, on which, as well as on both
sides of it, lay large cushions. The Imam sat between the cushions,
with his legs crossed in the eastern fashion; his gown was of a bright
green colour, and had large sleeves. On each side of his breast was
a rich filleting of gold lace, and on his head he wore a great white
turban. His sons sat on his right hand, and his brothers on the left.
Opposite to them, upon the highest of the two benches, sat the

Vizier; and our place was on the lower bench. On the two sides
of the hall, sat many of the principal men about court.

We were first led up to the Imam, and were permitted to kiss
both the back and the palm of his hand, as well as the hem of his
robe. There was a solemn silence through the whole hall. As each
of us touched the Imam's hand, a herald still proclaimed: 'God pre-
serve the Imam!' All who were present repeated those words aloud
after him. I was thinking at the time how I should pay my compli-
ments in Arabic, and was not a little disturbed by this noisy ceremony; but I had afterwards time to recollect myself.

The language of the Sana court was different from that which they
had learned to speak in the Tihama, so they had to communicate
with the Imam through interpreters. In this way they told him that
they were travelling to the Danish East Indies, and that having heard
of 'the plenty and security which prevailed through the dominions
of the Imam' they had resolved to see his country with their own
eyes so that they might describe it to their countrymen. The Imam
expressed his welcome, and said they might stay as long as they
wished.

That afternoon the vizier invited them to his own house, and asked
them to bring their scientific apparatus to show him. Niebuhr did
not take any of his precious mathematical instruments lest the vizier
might ask to keep them. They were pleasantly surprised at the chief
minister's intelligent interest and his fair knowledge of science and
geography.

With the formal visits over, Niebuhr was able to explore Sana.
He inspected the markets and the artisans' quarters, and admired
the noble palaces with their fountains and orchards. He observed
the Jewish community, who lived outside the capital in a suburb
of their own, whence they came daily to work in Sana. The finest
artisans, especially potters and goldsmiths, were Jews, and they were
also responsible for striking the coinage. Vines grew freely everywhere, and there was a considerable industry in drying grapes for
export. The Jews were allowed to make a little wine, but were
severely punished if they sold it to the Arabs. Everywhere he went
Niebuhr was surrounded by inquisitive crowds who made it impossible for him to draw a town plan of Sana, but he saw and described
every feature of note.

One of the sights of Sana was the Imam's ceremonial procession
to and from the mosque on Friday, which took a long circuitous route
to show off the ruler's magnificence. The Imam and the royal princes
who led the procession had large parasols carried over them. Behind
them came at least 600 other dignitaries, all mounted on superb
horses. On each side of the Imam was borne a standard carrying

a small silver casket of amulets which were believed to render him invincible.

The leading citizens were friendly, and urged the Danes to spend a year in Sana, but after their various contretemps with the provincial governors the party had learned a measure of distrust. They felt goodwill might on the slightest pretext turn to enmity. None of them was in good health, and they did not find the climate of Sana salubrious, despite its coolness. Having seen two of their companions die they were haunted by the fear that they would all meet the same fate unless they could leave the country soon, and they still hoped to sail with the English ships from Mocha to India.

So on 23 July, after a week's stay, they paid their farewell visit to the Imam and were received in more informal audience. They showed the ruler their scientific 'curiosities' which he had specially asked to see, and he was suitably impressed, and asked many questions about the customs, trade and learning of Europe. Kramer's services were required to explain the uses of drugs contained in a small medicine-cabinet which had been a gift from an Englishman, and a secretary wrote down his instructions. In the middle of all this Niebuhr, who was suffering another bout of fever, felt so ill that he was obliged to excuse himself and go and sit in the courtyard. He managed to return to the Imam's hall for their final leave-taking. They were each presented with a full set of new clothes, the traditional gift from a shaikh to important visitors. The Yemeni garb of the time consisted of a long shirt worn over wide cotton trousers, an outer garment with narrow sleeves worn over the shirt, and a flowing cloak to cover all. The outfit was completed by a girdle into which was tucked the curved dagger worn by every Yemeni of standing.

In their anxiety to return to Mocha in time to catch the English ships, they had difficulty in deciding which road to take back to the coast. They already knew the route via Taiz; should they go back on their tracks or try the shorter, more precipitous way, cutting back through the mountains to Bait al Faqih, and thence to Mocha? Because of Niebuhr's desire to see and survey new areas of the country, it was decided to travel via Bait al Faqih.

They set out on 26 July, travelling south-west on a road which wound through the 12,000-foot mountain range, between rocky peaks on which small villages were dramatically perched. The track proved far worse than they had expected, 'the most rugged road I saw in all Yemen'. The hills were bleak and forbidding, and in the deep valleys lay only a few wretched hamlets. They could not believe the going could get any more difficult, but on the second day out they were almost forced to turn back. Round the side of a steep hill, where the track was only wide enough for a single camel, they found that heavy rain had washed away an eight-foot stretch of the path. Their Arab companions said there was nothing for it but to return to Sana and take the Taiz road instead. But the determined Danes, now probably feeling a desperate sense of urgency, considered that such a delay would lose them the chance of sailing with the English ships. Weak from ill-health, and ridiculed by their Arab guides, Niebuhr and his companions set about collecting stones to rebuild the wash-out on the track. When the Arabs saw the foreigners labouring with their own hands they consented to help, and after three hours of hard work the path was made passable.

Their journey continued slowly and often dangerously. More than a dozen times they had to ford a winding torrent which was running in spate. But Niebuhr always found something to interest him. In a coffee-house at a village called Til they met some pilgrims returning from Mecca. Among them was a man from Do'an, 'a city five and twenty days' journey east from Sana ... a country entirely unknown to Europeans: I was vexed at the short time of our interview.' [The Do'an is in fact one of the great wadis of the Hadhramaut.] Niebuhr never lost an opportunity to seek information even from such chance encounters.

To their relief the way became easier after Til, as they were now descending the western slopes of the coffee-hills. They finally reached Bait al Faqih on the evening of 1 August after pushing onwards by forced marches through five days of the hardest travelling they had yet experienced.

Down on the Tihama plain they were back in the torrid heat of midsummer, and they continued by night marches via Zebid to Mocha, where they arrived on 5 August to see the welcome sight of Francis Scott's ship still anchored offshore. But after the nightmare journey from Sana, Niebuhr fell sick again on the 8th, and shortly afterwards Kramer, Baurenfeind, and Berggren were all seriously ill. Scott was able to help them, and provided them with European food which at this point they felt did them more good than any medicines, though it was no cure for the malaria from which they were all suffering.

By good fortune, or perhaps owing to the compassionate interest of the Englishman, Scott's ship was detained on business in Mocha till 23 August. By that time Niebuhr was somewhat recovered, but his three companions remained very ill. Nevertheless they were all determined to sail: to the melancholy and dispirited party immediate escape by sea seemed their only hope.

It was a sad voyage to India. Baurenfeind died on 29 August, and Berggren the servant, who had followed them so cheerfully in all their adventures, on the following day. The two men were buried at sea.

Kramer and Niebuhr disembarked at Bombay on 13 September 1763, but Kramer never fully recovered and died in India a few months later. Niebuhr now remained alone, the most junior member of the expedition which had set out nearly three years before. Perhaps it was sheer dogged determination, part of the peasant character of his forebears, or perhaps a genuine and insatiable interest that made Niebuhr continue both in India and the Middle East to record all that he saw and heard. A lesser man might have decided to take the next ship back to Europe, but Niebuhr intended to follow his original instructions and return via Basra and Aleppo. To his diary he confided, 'I have only the smallest hope of ever seeing Europe again', but the importance of reporting what he had learned at such cost must have given him a strong incentive to survive. While in India he arranged for the shipment of the party's manuscript records to London by an English ship, so that their papers would reach Copenhagen, even if he himself never got back.

He busied himself for nearly a year in India, until 8 December 1764, when he embarked on a small East India Company warship for Muscat. Here he disembarked and pursued his usual tasks of mapping the city and observing its people and customs. At Muscat he saw Frenchmen working as sailors on Arab dhows. Such European *renegados* were mercenaries who had deserted from armies in India or Turkey, and many were to be found scattered through the East, where they professed Islam and gained the protection of Muslim rulers. At one time in Yemen the Danes had themselves employed a French *renegado*.

After a fortnight in Muscat Niebuhr sailed up the Gulf to Bushire, and his association with Arabia drew to an uneventful close.

For seven months in 1765 and 1766, disguised as a humble Arab, Niebuhr made his way through Iraq and Syria to Aleppo, where at last he reached the friendly hospitality of the Dutch consulate. Then for another year he travelled the Levant and Asia Minor before returning via Poland and Germany to Copenhagen where he arrived on 20 November 1767. He had been away nearly seven years.

In 1772 his first volume about his travels, *Beschreibung von Arabien*, was published. His diaries and papers later filled three more volumes. The fact that he lived to the age of eighty-two, despite the impairment of his health in Arabia, is proof of his remarkable toughness.

After the sickness, hardships and tragedies which beset the Danish expedition, Niebuhr's tenacity in returning home and publishing the story of their adventures gives him an honoured place in the history of travel and exploration. But his account of Arabia, though welcomed by scholars, did not achieve wide popular success. Its unliterary style and the sheer density of factual information in it made it dull for the average reader. Later generations, however, reversing the judgement of his times, have learned to value the *Travels in Arabia* for these very qualities. Because his writing is simple and unrhetorical, it serves to impart new knowledge with admirable clarity. And his unassuming modesty which never sought to impress anybody ensures that he never indulges in fanciful exaggeration or embellishment.

Much of Niebuhr's information about Arabia was based on the evidence of others, as he says himself: 'as ... I had time to travel over only a few of the provinces of that widely extended country, I sought information concerning the rest from different honest and intelligent Arabs'. But he distinguishes clearly between things observed personally and things learned from others. The latter are dealt with in a section of his book entitled 'Of Arabia in General'. Yet though his account moves into the realms of hearsay, where it is so easy for the traveller to pass from fact to fantasy, later investigation has proved the truth of a great deal of this material.

Among the subjects treated in the more general section of his book are the government of Arabia, Hijaz and the holy cities, Yemen and its history, the Hadhramaut, Oman, Hasa and Najd, the badawin, the Arabs' religion and character, their manners, customs, language, sciences and agriculture, and the natural history of Arabia.

His account of Najd, produced by his technique of cross-checking information from different sources, gives a most useful description of the heart of Arabia, at that time totally unknown to Europeans.

This province is of vast extent. It comprehends all the interior parts of Arabia. ... The soil is various; among the hills fertile, and bearing abundance of fruits, especially dates, but being bounded by arid tracts of country, its rivers are only short streams, which after passing through the valleys, have their waters absorbed in the sandy plains, before they can reach the ocean. Upon this account, the inhabitants are, in many places obliged to dig deep wells; and cultivation is there difficult or almost impossible.

The Bedouin inhabit a great part of this province. The remainder is mountainous, full of cities and villages, and parcelled out among so many petty sovereigns, that almost every little town has its own shaikh. ...

The inhabitants of this vast country resemble the other Arabs in their moral qualities; they are at once robbers and hospitable. ... I have however learned that the inhabitants of Najd carry on a considerable trade among themselves, and with their immediate neighbours; and it is therefore not improbable that an European might travel in safety even through this remote part of Arabia.

Niebuhr's chapters on the badawin are especially accurate. Though he saw no real badu in Yemen he had met people of this type in Sinai. Later, on his way home, his journey in disguise through Iraq gave him first-hand knowledge of the tribes there and in the Syrian desert. From this experience, and from his incessant process of enquiry, he pieces together a picture from which no essential feature is lacking. His notes on tribal structure and the badawin manner of electing their tribal shaikhs are excellent, and he lists many of the most important tribes, though notably omitting those of central Najd and the Persian Gulf coast.

Niebuhr was working in a field which was not only entirely new to himself, but also to the scholars of Europe, and if he occasionally goes astray we may be surprised at how much is correct, rather than carp at the little which is not.

Among the subjects Niebuhr had been specially required to investigate was the question of polygamy in Arabia. But if his readers turned hopefully to this chapter to find some racy account of shaikhs with harems full of scantily-clad beauties they were to be disappointed. His observations are, as always, drily factual. He points out, as all serious commentators have done since his time, that the average Arab does not usually take the four wives which his religion permits. 'None but rich voluptuaries marry so many wives, and their conduct is blamed by all sober men.' As for eunuchs, he says there were none to be found in Arabia, an impression which was to be contradicted by later travellers. He corrects the idea that Arab women are treated like slaves: 'The Arabian women enjoy a great deal of liberty, and often a great deal of power, in their families. They continue mistresses of their dowries and of the annual income which these afford, during their marriage; and in the case of divorce all their own property is reserved to them.'

The most valuable and important part of Niebuhr's information on social and political conditions in Arabia is his chapter on 'The new religion of a part of Najd'. This was the first intimation received in Europe about the Wahhabi movement, whose founder was still alive during Niebuhr's time in Arabia.

Some time since, a new religion sprang up in the district of Al Aridh. It has already produced a revolution in the government of Arabia, and will probably hereafter influence the state of this country still further.

The founder of this religion was one Abd al Wahhab, a native of Ayaina, a town in the district of Al Aridh. This man in his youth, first studied at home those sciences which are chiefly cultivated in Arabia; he afterwards spent some time at Basra, and made several journeys to Baghdad and through Persia.

After his return to his native place, he began to propagate his opinions among his countrymen, and succeeded in converting several independent Shaikhs, whose subjects consequently became followers of the new prophet.

These Shaikhs who had hitherto been almost constantly at war amongst themselves, were now reconciled by the mediation of Abd al Wahhab, and agreed to undertake nothing in future without consulting their apostle. By this association the balance of power in Najd was destroyed. Those petty Shaikhs who could maintain their independence against any of the members of the league separately, were unable to resist the whole acting together. Wars also became, from the same causes, more keen and frequent, religion now intermingling itself with other grounds of dispute.

Abd al Wahhab, having thus reduced great part of Aridh, the Shaikhs who were worsted, called in to their assistance Arar Shaikh of Al Hasa.

The Shaikh of Hasa was unsuccessful in opposing the Najdis, who were supported by Shaikh Macrami of Najran who marched across Arabia with a small army to attack the Hasa chief in 1764. Shaikh Macrami was also a theologian and religious reformer. The Arabs said of him that 'he sells paradise by the yard', since he was prepared to assign places in heaven to those who paid him for that privilege.

When Niebuhr was in Basra on his way home in 1765 he heard that various Arab chieftains who had not yet succumbed to the Wahhabis had appealed to the people of the Basra area for assistance against the Najdi fanatics. There were also many refugees from Najd who had settled at Zubair.

There is one important omission in Niebuhr's account of the growth of Wahhabism. He had not grasped the fact that the Al Saud family had allied themselves with Muhammad ibn Abd al Wahhab as leaders of the new and irresistible force which was sweeping through Najd. He speaks of a Muhammad who was chief of Aridh, but believes him to have been the son of the original Ibn Abdul Wahhab, when this was in fact Muhammad ibn Saud, founder of the Saudi dynasty.

On the subject of the Wahhabi teaching Niebuhr remarks diffidently that he 'can say nothing positive with respect to its tenets' because he did not personally meet any of its disciples. But he correctly grasped the basic principles and the mood which lay behind the movement. He learned from a man who had travelled through Najd of the superstitious practices which had grown up among the Sunni sect, contrary to the spirit of the Prophet's teaching, and that Wahhabism sought a return to the purity and simplicity of Islam. 'Experience will here show, whether a religion, so stripped of every thing that might serve to strike the senses, can maintain its ground among so rude and ignorant people as the Arabs.'

The reader is left with the final impression that it was Niebuhr's humility which enabled him to win the confidence of those he questioned, and to set down straight the information he received. His story is never 'dashed with a little of the marvellous' as he admits that Arab stories are prone to be. Nor was he ever condescending towards the Arabs. As a Dane he had none of those imperialist pre-conceptions which tended to bias the judgement of such nations as Britain and Portugal against native peoples.

> In Yemen, Oman, and Persia, an European is treated with as much civility as a Mahometan would find in Europe. Some travellers complain of the rude manners of the inhabitants of the East, but it must be allowed that the Europeans often involve themselves in embarrassments in these countries, by being the first to express contempt or aversion for the Mussulmans.

Such was the honesty and objectivity with which Niebuhr, writing in his homely, unpolished German, prepared the notes of his travels for publication. Later generations have cause to be grateful for the work of this shrewd and humane observer of the Arabian scene.

Chapter 4

JEAN LOUIS BURCKHARDT

A Swiss
in the Holy Cities
1814

'He is, as it were, a grammarian of exploration, a pedant turned explorer, a classicist in the wilderness. . . .'
                                                              Alan Moorhead

Jean Louis Burckhardt was a Swiss, born in Lausanne in 1784. He had early shown signs of a gifted intellect, and had studied at universities in Germany before he came to London in 1805 in an ill-judged attempt to find employment. During an unhappy year he remained out of work and short of money, but he was able to learn English, the language in which he later wrote his books.

The redeeming feature of his time in London was his acquaintance with Sir Joseph Banks, to whom he had a letter of introduction from one of his professors at Göttingen. Banks was active in the Association for Promoting the Discovery of Africa, and at his home Burckhardt

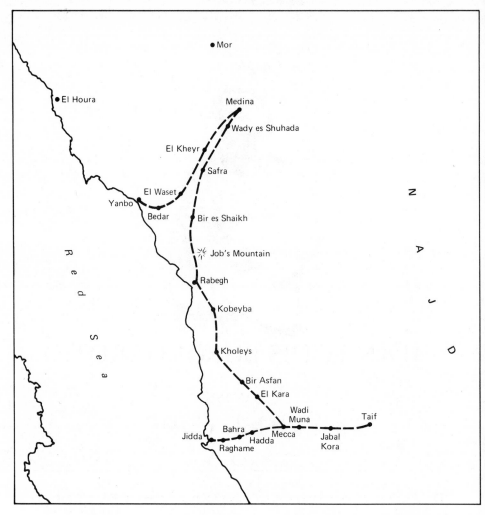

10 Burckhardt's route in Hijaz, 1811

met other men concerned with African exploration. He felt himself
drawn to Africa and the East, and offered his services to Banks. The
African Association allowed him a grant to go to Cambridge to study
in preparation for his travels, and for a year or so there he studied
Arabic as well as some chemistry, astronomy and medicine, all subjects which he believed provided a useful background for an explorer.
While at Cambridge he also spent periods training himself for the
physical hardships which lay ahead, practising walking barefoot in
the English countryside, sleeping rough and living on the most
meagre food.

In 1809, at the age of twenty-five, he left England for the Orient.

He was heading for Aleppo, where he intended to perfect his Arabic by 'losing himself in the crowds'. He so effectively learned to speak and live like an Arab that he was soon able to make long journeys to the Syrian interior, passing everywhere as a native Levantine. It was during this period that he re-discovered Petra for the modern world. He adopted the name of Shaikh Ibrahim ibn Abdullah, and though if questioned he would admit that he was a Frank, he claimed to be a convert to Islam, and allayed all suspicion by his scrupulous observance of Muslim religious duties. Since he had read much classical Arabic literature and learned most of the Koran by heart he could hold his own with any learned men he might meet.

Arriving in Cairo in 1812 he proceeded up the Nile, pioneering the exploration of the river between Aswan and Dongola. In this he was fulfilling his brief from the African Association, but it was evident that he had developed a deep interest in the Arabs, and there was much that he wished to see in Arabia. In May 1813 he wrote to the Association from the Upper Nile saying that he intended to go to Mecca. He hoped to fit this journey in before joining one of the infrequent caravans from Egypt to Fezzan in southern Libya.

To get to Arabia he joined a group of slave-traders on their regular route from Shendi down to Suakin on the Red Sea. Unfortunately his year on the Nile had already affected his health; during this time he suffered bouts of sickness and a severe attack of ophthalmia. It was to take him a year before he reached Jidda, and another year before he finally returned to Cairo having made the pilgrimage.

A description of Burckhardt's physical appearance at this time has been left by the English traveller J. S. Buckingham in his autobiography. Buckingham had sailed up the Nile to Esne in Upper Egypt, and he tells us that Burckhardt,

hearing of the arrival of a boat with an English traveller ... hastened down to the river bank, came on board, and introduced himself, speaking excellent English. He was dressed in the commonest garments, as an Arab peasant or small trader, with a blue cotton blouse covering a coarse shirt, loose white trousers, and a common calico turban ... he had a full dark beard, was without stockings, wearing only the slipshod slippers of the country, and looked so completely like an Arab of the north – a Syrian having a fairer complexion and lighter eyes than the Egyptians – that few would have suspected him to be a Swiss, as he really was....

It was July 1814 when he arrived in the damp, enervating heat of Jidda, dressed in rags after his travels from the Nile. The letter of credit which he brought to a merchant of the town was not honoured, since it was eighteen months old; Burckhardt was practically penniless. The merchant gave him hospitality for two nights, after which the Swiss had to move out to a khan or lodging-house. His small remaining amount of money was sewn up in an amulet on his arm. But he then developed a high fever, and in this illness his only help was a friendly Greek ship's captain. His little money was soon spent, and he was forced to raise more in a way for which he was later censured by Europeans. He had bought a young slave in Africa, and he now asked the Greek captain to take this slave to market and sell him. The Greek obtained forty-eight dollars for him, yielding Burckhardt a profit of thirty-two dollars.

At the time Muhammad Ali Pasha, the formidable Viceroy of Egypt, was in residence at Taif, the Hijazis' summer resort in the mountains east of Mecca. He had come to prepare a new campaign against the Wahhabis whose power still threatened the Ottomans in Arabia.

The militant religious movement led by the rulers of Najd had continued its conquests in Arabia after Niebuhr brought the first news of it to the outside world. In 1803 the Wahhabis reached the climax of their power when they overran Taif and captured the holy cities of Mecca and Madina. An expedition sent against them from Egypt in 1811 suffered an ignominious defeat, with great loss of prestige for the Ottoman power. A second expedition in 1812 was more successful; Madina was recaptured by Tousun Pasha, Muhammad Ali's son, and Jidda, Mecca, and Taif surrendered without bloodshed. Though Turkish control was now re-established over the holy cities, Muhammad Ali was determined to inflict a final defeat on the Wahhabis in their Najd stronghold, and in Taif had been working to win the support of badawin tribal leaders in preparation for a new attack.

When Burckhardt was in Jidda the hinterland was still dangerous for travellers because of bands of Wahhabi raiders. The Swiss felt that it would be impractical for him to travel as a beggar; instead he assumed the clothes and character of 'a reduced Egyptian gentleman'. The pilgrimage which he intended to join was to take place in November, in three and a half months' time, and before then he urgently needed money. Though he wrote to his bankers in Cairo he could hardly expect an answer in less than four months. In his difficult situation he decided to appeal to the great Muhammad Ali himself. He had met the Pasha in Cairo, and indeed had been helped financially in the Sudan by Ibrahim Pasha, Muhammad Ali's other son. 'Having therefore already had some money dealings with the Pasha, I thought that ... I might now endeavour to renew them in the Hijaz, and the more so, as I knew that he had formerly expressed rather a favourable opinion of my person and pursuits.'

Burckhardt wrote to the Pasha's Armenian physician Bosari, with whom he was acquainted, asking him to approach the Viceroy for a cash advance against a bill drawn on his Cairo banker, and resigned himself to wait for an answer. But news of Burckhardt's presence had already reached official circles in Jidda, and Yahya Effendi, personal physician to Tousun Pasha, the governor of Jidda, invited the Swiss to his house. When Yahya heard of Burckhardt's difficulties he proposed a different solution. He was intending to send his savings back to Egypt (about £100 in the currency of the day), and he now suggested that he paid this sum instead to Burckhardt, accepting for it Burckhardt's bill upon Cairo. Burckhardt was amazed at the trust which the doctor's offer implied, but Yahya Effendi told him that 'some of his friends had given me a flattering character while at Cairo, and that he could not, therefore, entertain the slightest doubt of my solvency and respectability'.

While Burckhardt was congratulating himself that he could now live comfortably for the next few months, assistance also came from Muhammad Ali, though not through Bosari's help, for the physician had not dared to ask the Pasha for favours for Burckhardt. The Pasha had heard independently that the Swiss traveller was in Jidda, walking about in rags, and he immediately sent orders that Burckhardt was to be provided with a suit of clothes and five hundred piastres. He also desired the Swiss to come to Taif, and his messenger had brought a spare dromedary for that purpose.

Burckhardt admits that he had an aversion to receiving a present rather than a loan from the Pasha, and that he had not intended to go to Taif at that time, but 'the invitation of a Turkish Pasha is a polite command'. He did not entirely trust the Pasha, and changed all the £100 (3,000 piastres) from Yahya into gold which he hid in his girdle. He thought he might need it either for a bribe, or to get away from Taif if the Pasha held him there.

Following his concept of the traveller's scholarly duty, Burckhardt provides a detailed account of Jidda, its outward appearance, its people, and its trade. He was a man for minutiae, and his pages are filled with the intricacies of mercantile practice and fluctuating commodity markets. To gain his information he must have sat for hours on end in the bazaars and coffee-shops, keeping his eyes and ears open, probably never asking a direct question but leading conversation round to the subjects about which he wanted to know more.

He noticed that all the Jidda merchants wore good European watches. It commonly happened that even well-to-do pilgrims found themselves short of cash in the Hijaz, and were forced to sell some of their belongings. 'The watch is always the first, then the pistols and the sabre, and lastly the fine pipe, and the best copy of the

Koran: all these articles are consequently very common in the auc-
tion markets of Jidda and Mecca.'

Jidda was the principal Turkish army depot of the Hijaz. Muhammad Ali had given strict orders that his soldiers were to behave correctly in Arabia, since he knew the Arabs were quick to take offence.
They had always disliked the Turks, whose inability to speak Arabic
and general ignorance of the country aroused Arab contempt. The
elaborate court ceremonial of the Pashas was also contrary to the
egalitarian traditions of a desert people. The Turks for their part
reciprocated the Arabs' dislike. For them Jidda was a place of exile,
and they hated the Arabs all the more because they could not use
their customary domineering manners against them, knowing this
would provoke retaliation.

On 24 August 1814 Burckhardt set out on his journey to Taif. It
was already Ramadhan, the Arab month of fasting, which would
end with three days of festival. He and his guide were accompanied
by twenty Bani Harb camel-men who were carrying money to Mecca
for the Pasha's treasury, but on the second day, after a night
march, Burckhardt decided he must rest, and at a place called
Hajalia he lay on the sand and slept through till daybreak with
only his escort beside him. The rest of the caravan went on its
way.

The Pasha had told his messenger to bring Burckhardt by the
northern route, bypassing Mecca. But the guide, never suspecting
that Burckhardt might not be a Muslim, queried the Pasha's instructions, and said it was shorter to go through Mecca. Burckhardt willingly agreed to take the more direct road, from which they obtained
a fine view of the holy city as they descended from the hills to skirt
the eastern side of the town.

Three days out from Jidda they started climbing the mountains
to ascend towards Taif. Burckhardt found Jabal Kora 'the most
beautiful spot in the Hijaz' with its refreshing air and gardens of
fruit-trees and vines.

The fields round Kora belonged to members of the Hudhail tribe,
whose small houses built of stones and mud stood in groups of four
or five together. It was in one of these that Burckhardt had spent
the night. 'These apartments receive no light but from the entrance;
they are very neat and clean, and contain Bedouin furniture, some
good carpets, woollen and leather sacks, a few bowls, earthen coffee-
pots, and a matchlock, of which great care is taken, it being generally
kept in a leathern case.'

After descending into the valley where Taif stands, they reached
the town at midday, and Burckhardt went straight to the house of
Bosari the physician. Since it was Ramadhan all the notables would
be asleep during the daytime, and he knew he could not expect to

see Muhammad Ali until after sunset. Meanwhile Bosari questioned Burckhardt closely about his purpose in coming to the Hijaz.

In the evening the doctor went to tell the Pasha of Burckhardt's arrival, and came back to say that Muhammad Ali was willing to receive him. He also reported that when the Pasha heard that the Swiss intended to visit Mecca and Madina he had commented, 'It is not the beard alone which proves a man to be a true Moslem.' The kadhi of Mecca who was sitting with the Pasha had observed that he did not believe that Burckhardt, knowing that only Muslims were permitted to see the holy cities, would declare himself to be one unless he really was.

But Burckhardt was not happy about the Pasha's attitude. 'I told Bosari that he might return alone to the Pasha; that my feelings had already been much hurt by the orders given to my guide not to carry me through Mecca; and that I certainly should not go to the Pasha's public audience if he would not receive me as a Turk.'

A stranger alone in an alien land cannot afford to be less than subservient to potentates on whose goodwill he depends, but Burckhardt's instinctive judgement allowed him to walk the tightrope between distasteful obsequiousness and offensive arrogance. His answer was that of an honest man with a clear conscience. But then he knew that Muhammad Ali, Viceroy of Egypt, was no ordinary ruler. The Pasha, a European Turk risen from humble origins to conquer and rule an empire, a man brilliantly resourceful in both military and civil affairs, was the most famous and powerful personality of his day in the eastern Mediterranean.

It was hardly surprising that Bosari was reluctant to carry Burckhardt's message back to the Pasha. In the world of court officials no one spoke to the Viceroy in such tones. Nevertheless, he finally returned to Muhammad Ali to report Burckhardt's words, upon which 'the Pasha smiled, and answered that I was welcome, whether Turk or not'.

About eight o'clock in the evening I repaired to the castle, a miserable, half-ruined habitation of Sherif Ghaleb, dressed in the new suit which I had received at Jidda by the Pasha's command. I found his highness seated in a large saloon, with the Kadhi on one hand, and Hassan Pasha, the chief of the Arnaut [Albanian] soldiers, on the other; thirty or forty of his principal officers formed a half-circle about the sofa on which they sat; and a number of Bedouin shaikhs were squatted in the midst of the semicircle. I went up to the Pasha, gave him the 'Salaam aleykum,' and kissed his hand.

Burckhardt did not speak Turkish, and for a few minutes the two men exchanged courtesies through an interpreter. Then the Pasha returned to discussing some business with the badawin chiefs, and when this was concluded ordered everyone to leave the hall except for the kadhi, Bosari and Burckhardt.

I expected now to be put to the proof, and I was fully prepared for it; but not a word was mentioned of my personal affairs.... As soon as we were alone the Pasha introduced the subject of politics. He had just received information of the entrance of the allies into Paris, and the departure of Bonaparte for Elba.... He seemed deeply interested in these important events, chiefly because he laboured under the impression that, after Bonaparte's downfall, England would probably seek for an augmentation of power in the Mediterranean, and consequently invade Egypt.

As they conversed for two or three hours, Burckhardt spoke either Arabic with the kadhi interpreting, or Italian through Bosari, and when the time came to leave, the Pasha said he would expect his visitor at the same hour the following evening.

Next day Burckhardt decided it would be prudent to pay a call on the kadhi, and to this senior religious official he expressed his pained surprise that the Pasha should doubt if he were a true Muslim, 'after I had now been a proselyte to that faith for so many years'. While he was with the kadhi sunset came, and the two men broke their fast together, and Burckhardt then joined his host for the evening prayer, 'when I took great care to chaunt as long a chapter of the Koran as my memory furnished at the moment'. After this they went again to call on the Pasha.

During his stay in Taif Burckhardt knew that he was being closely watched. He was never allowed to be alone for a moment, and Bosari was obviously reporting his every action back to the Pasha. He found he was in 'a sort of polite imprisonment' from which he was uncertain how to extricate himself. Although professing to be of the Muslim faith, Burckhardt told important officials he was an Englishman, 'because at that time none but the subjects of England and France enjoyed in the east any real security'. As a result, it seems that the Pasha thought him an English spy, sent to investigate affairs in the Hijaz and to report to the authorities in India. Because of its trade up the Persian Gulf, the East India Company was taking a lively interest in the imminent clash between the Ottoman power and the Wahhabis of Najd. Under the circumstances Burckhardt felt it was only the Pasha's respect for British power which made him so affable towards his visitor.

Though Burckhardt grew restless in Taif, he was reluctant to take his leave too hastily for fear of rousing more suspicion. Finally he contrived a situation where his host Bosari, rather than himself,

should suggest his departure. He began to disrupt the doctor's household with tiresome demands, ordering meals at inconvenient times,
installing himself in the best room and so on, knowing that by the
laws of eastern hospitality Bosari could not object, and yet determined to irritate his host into indicating that the time had come for
him to move on.

This little game went on for seven days, then, when Bosari asked
if he would be staying much longer, Burckhardt replied that he could
make no decision till he knew the Pasha's wishes concerning himself.
We may imagine that Bosari, who had the Pasha's ear, was not slow
to hint to his master that he would be glad to see the back of his
troublesome guest. At any rate, the same evening, during Burckhardt's customary visit to the Pasha, the great man suggested that
since the kadhi of Mecca was leaving on 7 September for the holy
city, it might be as well for Burckhardt to travel with his party.

Though Burckhardt requested a firman or passport from Muhammad Ali to facilitate his travels, the Pasha would not provide one,
while telling the Swiss that he might act as he pleased on his own
responsibility. He seemed more concerned with Burckhardt as a
potential spy than at the idea of his visiting the holy places. The
following year, after Burckhardt had made his pilgrimage, it was
being said openly in Cairo that he had managed to penetrate the
sanctuary at Mecca although he was a Christian. Muhammad Ali's
reaction to this was to tell the British Consul that it was out of friendship for England that he had allowed Burckhardt to go to Mecca.
Burckhardt comments: 'To Muhammad Ali it was of more consequence not to be thought a fool than a bad muselman.'

It was with relief that Burckhardt left Taif at the end of ten days.
He even managed to avoid travelling with the kadhi, who wished
to make the journey by night and agreed to let Burckhardt start
separately on the morning of the appointed day. Soon after leaving
the town Burckhardt fell in with three of the Pasha's Albanian irregu-
lars, who like himself were mounted on donkeys. They had been to
Taif to make a profit on money-changing, for there they could get
thirteen piastres for one Spanish dollar, whereas in Jidda the rate
was only eleven. They made the journey to take advantage of this
higher exchange whenever the road was safe. This time their pooled
resources had amounted to 1,000 dollars. 'They carried the money,
sewed in bags, upon their asses; and having forgotten perhaps, to
leave out any cash for travelling expenses, they joined me, finding
that my travelling sack was well stocked with provisions, and left
me to pay for our joint expenses on the road, whenever we stopped
at the coffee-huts.'

As the party made its way towards Mecca, Burckhardt began to
note in detail matters which earlier visitors had dealt with generally,

and often casually. Wadi Mohram is the point at which travellers approaching Mecca don the *ihram* or pilgrim garb, the two pieces of simple cloth which must have no seam or ornament. One of these pieces of cloth is wrapped around the loins, the other round the neck and shoulders. The head must remain bare, and so must the instep. Burckhardt duly changed into the prescribed garments when they reached the wadi, though the Turkish soldiers did not.

In the cool air of the highlands Burckhardt had recovered his health after his illness at Jidda, but he was constantly worried that in the scant covering of the *ihram* he would be vulnerable to chills. He did in fact have a mild recurrence of fever after being caught in a heavy shower at Jabal Kora.

At this point the kadhi's party caught up with him. Muhammad Ali had obviously thought it a good idea for his magistrate to keep an eye on the European. The kadhi, on the other hand, seems to have been unconcerned. As a sophisticated native of Constantinople he shared none of the true Arabian fanaticism about the holy places. So long as Burckhardt behaved outwardly as a good Muslim – which he unfailingly did – the kadhi had no complaints. So, though Burckhardt called at the kadhi's camp, the Turkish official did not insist that they should travel on together. Burckhardt set out again with the three soldiers, and was happy to be free of prying eyes and to make his journey at his own speed. He found his companions congenial fellow-travellers; they passed the hours telling amusing tales, and were generally such good company that he did not begrudge them the cost of their refreshment.

At one stage of the journey they found themselves in a valley between steep hills, and here they were caught in a violent storm which brought torrents of water pouring down the mountainsides. They tried to struggle on through swirling floods, but were finally forced to withdraw up a slope away from the water which had risen to a height of three feet in the valley bottom. It was three hours before the storm passed and the raging torrent abated, but even then they could not persuade their donkeys to go forward on the slippery ground. In the end they dismounted and drove the beasts before them. When night fell they found themselves in total darkness under heavy clouds. For three or four hours they stumbled blindly on, and came at last with relief to the coffee-houses of Arafat, only to find that the flood had run through here also, and there was scarcely a hut which had remained dry inside. Finally they found one which had proved more weatherproof than most, and here they were able to light a fire. Burckhardt, feeling miserably wet and cold, was glad to huddle over the flames and brew up some coffee.

Mecca was not far away, and they arrived there at noon next day. Every visitor entering the city from a journey of more than two days,

even outside the pilgrimage season, is expected to go at once to the
Great Mosque and perform the circumambulations of the Kaaba.
Burckhardt selected a *mutowwaf* outside the holy precincts and then
entered by the Bab as Salaam to perform the required rites.

Although it must have been a moment of crowning achievement,
Burckhardt does not record his reactions on arriving at Islam's holy
of holies. Like every place held sacred by millions, the Kaaba must
always stir the emotions of him who beholds it, whether Muslim or
not, but in Burckhardt's writing his intention was to impart information, and the description of his own feelings lay for the most part
outside his purpose.

There was no secret about the Great Mosque, the Kaaba, or the
rituals performed there, since by then several European and many
Arab and Turkish writers had described them, and Arabs have
always talked freely about them to non-Muslims. For a European
who gained access to the Haram (the Holy Place) at Mecca there
was only the sense of excitement at arriving where so few of his race
had been. Burckhardt did not even have the explorer's satisfaction
at being the first European to enter the Great Mosque. That distinction belonged to Lodovico Varthema. And in Burckhardt's own
century a Spaniard, Domingo Badia y Lieblich, travelling under the
name of Ali Bey al Abbasi, had made the Mecca pilgrimage in 1807.
Ulrich Jaspar Seetzen, a noted German orientalist, had also been
there in 1810.

Burckhardt wanted to see Mecca for himself, to satisfy that burning curiosity about exotic scenes and customs which was such a strong
part of his make-up. Then, by reporting with the factual honesty
of a scientist all that he observed, he hoped to make a genuine contribution to Western knowledge about the East.

He tells us that he felt no anxiety for his personal safety. He had
no fear of being denounced as an interloper, since in the crowds who
gather for the hajj there are men of so many types and races. But
he was handicapped by poor health, and on his own admission this
prevented him from seeing and doing all that he wished to in and
around the holy city. Later he wrote that 'the worst effect of ill-health
upon a traveller, is the pusillanimity which accompanies it, and the
apprehension with which it fills the mind. . . .' This is the only hint
he leaves that in Mecca there must have been times when he felt
depressed and unhappy, never knowing whether the malaria which
he carried in his bloodstream might strike again with fatal severity.

As well as the mandatory visit to the House of God, a visitor had
various other stipulated duties to perform in different parts of the
city. From the Great Mosque Burckhardt and his guide walked 100
yards to the hill of Safa to carry out the *sai* ritual, shuttling seven
times back and forth between the hills of Safa and Marwah; part of

the course, marked at either end by pillars, must be done at a run, in memory of Hagar's running in search of water when she was left in the wilderness with Ishmael, a ritual described by Varthema, Pitts and other pilgrims. Specified prayers had to be said at various points.

Burckhardt was exhausted by the time he had done the *sai* and did not at this time attempt the *umra* or 'little pilgrimage', another compulsory exercise which involved travelling three miles out of Mecca to a shrine to the north-east. Following custom he went to have his head partially shaved in one of the many barbers' shops, where he was able to linger awhile and recover from his exertions. When he asked the barber about lodgings in the town, he was told that Mecca was already full with crowds who came to spend the end of Ramadhan there, and that he would have difficulty in finding a place to stay.

Burckhardt had no friend or acquaintance in the city, he was physically weak, and had no place to sleep, but in the face of such setbacks he could draw upon great reserves of courage and determination. He later succeeded in renting a room from a pilgrim-guide, who not only overcharged him grossly, but also stole some of his clothing.

The sight which most impressed Burckhardt in his first few days in Mecca was the brilliance of the Great Mosque after dark, when all the lamps were lit, as was customary through Ramadhan. In the great court ringed with colonnades the whole male populace seemed to gather in the evening.

The hajjis ... assembled in large crowds in the mosque, for their evening devotions. Everyone then carried in his handkerchief a few dates, a little bread and cheese, or some grapes, which he placed before him, waiting for the moment of the call to evening prayers, to be allowed to break the fast. During this period of suspense they would politely offer to their neighbours a part of their meal, and receive as much in return. Some hajjis, to gain the reputation of peculiar charitableness, were going from man to man, and placing before each a few morsels of viands, followed by beggars, who, in their turn, received these morsels from those hajjis before whom they had been placed. As soon as the Imam on the top of Zemzem began his cry of 'Allahu akbar,' every one hastened to drink of the jar of Zemzem water placed before him, and to eat something, previous to joining in the prayer; after which they all returned home to supper, and again revisited the mosque for the celebration of the last evening orisons.

On 15 September, after the third day of the festival which ends Ramadhan, Burckhardt returned to Jidda to buy supplies. On the

way there he was nearly taken prisoner by 'a flying corps of Wahhabis'. He was forced to stay in Jidda for three weeks because of
ulcers which afflicted his legs, a common ailment in the humid
climate of the coast. Before returning to Mecca in mid-October he
bought himself a new slave, a boy who had been in the caravan to
Suakin with him. He also stocked up with a camel-load of flour,
biscuit, and butter, which cost him only a third of the prices obtaining at Mecca. Once back in the holy city he found that the pressure
of visitors for the Ramadhan feast was over, and he was able to hire
a pleasant apartment where he settled in to pass the few weeks till
the hajj season.

During this sojourn he gathered facts for an encyclopaedic description of life in Mecca. He calls it 'a handsome town', with streets
generally broader than in other places, and lofty stone houses looking
rather more European by reason of the windows facing on to the
streets. All the houses except those of the richest families were built
to accommodate lodgers, since every Meccawi counted on making
money out of the pilgrims in this or some other way. There were
no trees or gardens in the city, and the precinct of the Great Mosque
was the only public open space, which doubtless explained why it
had become the common meeting-place for the population.

Burckhardt describes his daily routine in Mecca:

I usually spent the early part of each morning, and the later part
of the evening, in walking about the town, and frequenting the coffee-houses in its extremities, where I might meet with Bedouins,
and, by treating them with a cup of coffee, soon engage them to
talk about their country and their nation. During the mid-day
hours I staid at home: the first part of the night I passed in the
great square of the mosque, where a cooling breeze always reigns.

He had made friends with a perfume-seller in one of the bazaars or
suqs, and daily passed an hour or two here, 'seated on a bench before
his shop, smoking my nargyle, and treating my friends with coffee.
Here I heard the news; whether any great hajji had arrived the pre-
ceding night; what law-suits had been carried before the Kadhi;
what was going forward in Muhammad Ali's army; or what great
commercial bargains had been concluded.' There was news of
Europe to be had, too, from pilgrims from Constantinople and
Greece. Among the subjects of bazaar discussion was a public execution which had been carried out in the main street. The offender
had robbed a Turkish pilgrim of money worth £200 in the value
of those days.

Of the Bait Allah, 'the House of God' as the Great Mosque is
known, his account is typically thorough. Indeed so exact are his

details on its dimensions, the numbers of pillars in its colonnades, the various features of the sanctuary, and so on, that Burton, who usually delighted to point out the mistakes of others, not only found no fault with the account, but in his own *Personal Narrative of a Pilgrimage to Al-Madinah and Meccah* quotes verbatim the whole of Burckhardt's description of the mosque: 'I will do homage to the memory of the accurate Burckhardt and extract from his pages a description which shall be illustrated by a few notes.' Homage indeed, from one who rarely found that others reached his own standard of observation or erudition.

Inevitably, in this goal of the Muslim pilgrimage, there were moving scenes of elation, ecstasy, or simply the joy of life-long wishes fulfilled. Burckhardt saw a pilgrim from the inland regions of Sudan arrive at the mosque on the last night of Ramadhan.

> After a long journey across barren and solitary deserts, on his entering the illuminated temple, he was so much struck with its appearance, and overawed by the black Kaaba, that he fell prostrate close by the place where I was sitting, and remained long in that posture of adoration. He then rose, burst into a flood of tears, and in the height of his emotion, instead of reciting the usual prayers of the visitor, only exclaimed 'O God, now take my soul, for this is Paradise!'

The water from the holy well of Zemzem was thought to cure all diseases, and Burckhardt tells of a fellow-lodger in his house who spent every evening in the mosque, drinking Zemzem water to the limit of his capacity. He then lay on the pavement near the Kaaba until he could drink some more. When this practice brought him 'to the verge of death', he protested that his illness had worsened only because he had been unable to drink as much of the water as he should have.

Dispassionate though he tries to be, Burckhardt has to admit that he found the sunset prayer in the Great Mosque a moving and impressive ceremony. 'The effect of the joint prostrations of six or eight thousand persons, added to the recollection of the distance and various quarters from whence they come, and for what purpose, cannot fail to impress the most cool-minded spectator with some degree of awe.' He describes the holy tradition that the mosque will contain any number of the faithful, even including the world's total Islamic population, since it is believed that the guardian angels of the place miraculously enable it to expand to accommodate all who wish to be there. Burckhardt himself estimated that it would hold 35,000 people.

As in other great mosques of the East, there was always noise and bustle within the precincts, though never at the times of prayer, when total silence reigned while the Imam led the devotions. Many poor pilgrims laid their mats under the colonnades and lived there for the whole of their stay in Mecca, and the diseased and disabled lay there in great numbers. Men of business met there to conduct their affairs, boys played in the great court, and porters carried their loads through if this was the most direct route from one part of the city to another. There were always corners where learned teachers lectured to the faithful, and in other parts boys' schools were held. But though Burckhardt was accustomed to busy worldly scenes in holy places, he expresses his disgust at the 'indecencies and criminal acts' which took place, apparently causing no great concern to the devout. We must suppose that he refers to homosexual acts, though he is not explicit. He also says that prostitutes were sometimes to be found soliciting in the mosque, where they mingled among the women who sold grain for pilgrims to feed the pigeons of the holy precincts.

Burckhardt was later to see and describe a much-changed scene after the hajj was over, when the great shrine presented a mournful spectacle.

Disease and mortality, which succeed to the fatigues endured on the journey, or are caused by the light covering of the ihram, the unhealthy lodgings at Mecca, the bad fare, and sometimes absolute want, fill the mosque with dead bodies, carried thither to receive the Imam's prayer, or with sick persons, many of whom, when their dissolution approaches, are brought to the colonnades, that they may either be cured by a sight of the Kaaba, or at least have the satisfaction of expiring within the sacred enclosure. Poor hajjis, worn out with disease and hunger, are seen dragging their emaciated bodies along the columns; and when no longer able to stretch forth their hand to ask the passenger for charity, they place a bowl to receive alms near the mat on which they lay themselves. When they feel their last moments approaching they cover themselves with their tattered garments; and often a whole day passes before it is discovered that they are dead.

Burckhardt himself, with the aid of a Greek *hajji*, was able to help one such dying pilgrim, a man from Morocco, who made signs that he wished to be sprinkled with Zemzem water. As Burckhardt and the Greek did him this last service, he died.

The duties of cleaning and maintaining order in the Great Mosque belonged to a corps of eunuchs led by a chief or Aga. These men – if such they may be called – were supplied by Ottoman potentates who sent them when young as gifts to the House of God. In

Burckhardt's day there were ten adult eunuchs and twenty boys, the latter living in a communal house until they grew up and completed their training. 'Extraordinary as it may appear, the grown-up eunuchs are all married to black slaves, and maintain several male and female slaves in their houses as servants.' The eunuchs enjoyed great prestige in Mecca, and many of the lower classes would kiss their hands on meeting them. They wore a distinctive Turkish uniform, and carried a staff, with which they would lay about them if the crowd became unruly. They enjoyed considerable affluence, receiving many donations from pilgrims in addition to their payment from the mosque. Having once been in the service of the Kaaba, a eunuch could perform no other work for the rest of his life.

Of the inhabitants of Mecca, Burckhardt tells us that they were mostly of mixed blood, descended from foreign fathers and local mothers.

In every hajj some of the pilgrims remain behind: the Muhamma-dan, whenever resident for any time in a town, takes a wife.... Hence most of the Meccawis are descendants of foreigners from distant parts of the globe, who have adopted Arabian manners, and by intermarrying, have produced a race which can no longer be distinguished from the indigenous Arabians.... The Meccawi is careful in preserving, by tradition, the knowledge of his original country. My Mutowwaf or guide traced his descent to an Usbek Tatar from the neighbourhood of Bokhara....

A native of Mecca or Jidda is marked by ritual scarring of the face. A male child when he is forty days old has three long cuts made down each cheek, and the Meccawis take pride in this distinction which prevents other inhabitants of the Hijaz from claiming the honour of having been born in the holy city or its access port.

Trade with the pilgrims provided the livelihood of most of the Mecca people, and in this they had a reputation for sharp practice known throughout the Muslim world. But many men followed the profession of *mutowwaf* or guide, since every stranger needed help in being shown the prescribed rituals not only at the Great Mosque, but also in all the lesser obligations at places round the city. Burck-hardt also describes the *muhallil*, a special class of guide who is available to contract a formal marriage with widowed or divorced women who wish to make the pilgrimage, since Muslim law does not permit those without husbands to do so. The marriage is understood to be purely nominal and the couple are divorced as soon as the pilgrimage is over.

Burckhardt enjoyed the cheerful gaiety of the Meccawis. He found them in general vivacious, shrewd, and possessing 'great suavity of manners'. But he was disappointed that Mecca was not a great centre of Islamic scholarship, though the reason for this was not hard to find: 'learning and science cannot be expected to flourish where every mind is occupied in the search of gain, or of paradise'.

By mid-November the opening day of the actual hajj season was drawing near. It was heralded by the colourful arrival in Mecca of the two great pilgrim caravans, one from Syria and one from Egypt, in which thousands of pilgrims travelled together for safety under the leadership of an Amir al Hajj. Each of these caravans was led by a camel bearing a *mahmal* or ceremonial litter, richly caparisoned and adorned, which came from Damascus and Cairo carrying gifts to God's House from the Turkish Sultan and the Egyptian Khedive, and which betokened Turkish sovereignty over the holy cities of the Hijaz.

The two caravans reached Mecca a day or two before the devotional season was due to open with the sermon at Arafat. At the same time Muhammad Ali Pasha arrived from Taif to make the hajj, and also to inspect the cavalry which had come with the Egyptian caravan; he hoped to use these soldiers in his campaign against the Wahhabis.

When the Egyptian contingent arrived all the hajjis already in Mecca put on the *ihram*. Two days later amid scenes of excitement and jubilation the two *mahmals* paraded through the city and led their caravans to Arafat.

For three dollars Burckhardt had hired two camels to take him to Arafat, but he chose to walk on the six-hour outward journey, an act by which a pilgrim acquires extra merit. He joined the great flood of humanity which choked the streets of Mecca on this, the first activity of the pilgrimage proper. Once outside the town the crowds were able to spread out and march more easily over the plain, but going through the valley of Muna the surging procession was bottled up into a densely-packed mass which pushed and shoved in frightened confusion.

About three hours after sunset Burckhardt reached the plain at the foot of Mount Arafat, where in a vast encampment hundreds of people were searching for companions lost on the road. The plain was lit by the flicker of countless camp-fires, and clusters of brilliant lamps marked the pavilions of Muhammad Ali, Sulaiman Pasha, and the Egyptian Amir al Hajj. Few people in the great concourse slept that night. Many sat up praying, while the less devout thronged the coffee-shops or sat in groups singing and clapping their hands in their own family parties.

The approaching dawn was heralded by the firing of a cannon by each of the two caravan leaders, signalling that the first day of pilgrimage had begun. It was 25 November.

With many others Burckhardt began his day by walking up to
the 200-foot summit of Arafat. Looking down from the top he
counted about 3,000 tents belonging to the notables. Most of the
ordinary people, like himself, were without tents, and he estimated
the crowd at something like 70,000 with about 25,000 camels.

The most magnificent tent of all was that of Muhammad Ali's wife,
who had lately arrived from Egypt. Five hundred camels had been
needed to carry her baggage from Jidda to Mecca.

Her tent was in fact an encampment consisting of a dozen tents
of different sizes, inhabited by her women; the whole enclosed by
a wall of linen cloth, eight hundred paces in circuit, the single entrance to which was guarded by eunuchs in splendid dresses....
The beautiful embroidery on the exterior of this linen palace, with
the various colours displayed in every part of it ... reminded me
of some descriptions in the Arabian Tales of the Thousand and One
nights.

The sermon, the *khutbat al wagifa*, for which the pilgrims had come
to Arafat, lasts from mid-afternoon till sunset, and is an occasion
at which attendance is compulsory for anyone who desires the title
of hajji. The preacher, according to custom, rode on a camel to a
platform on the lower slopes. Having dismounted, he read his sermon
from a book, adding emphasis from time to time by stretching his
arms to heaven and imploring God's blessing. The crowds filled the
air with the pilgrim's cry of *Labbaik!* ('Here am I, Lord'), and waved
the skirts of their *ihrams*, so that 'the side of the mountain, thickly
crowded as it was by the people in their white garments, had the
appearance of a cataract of water'.

But there were many in the crowd who showed no religious ecstasy
and not a great deal of interest. Turkish soldiers talked and joked,
other Arabs sat and smoked their *narghilehs*, and parties of coffee-
drinkers continued in their convivial gatherings.

When the sermon ended and the preacher shut his book, the
crowds turned and ran, all trying to leave Arafat as quickly as possible. This race, *ad dafa min Arafat*, is also considered meritorious, and
Burckhardt records that in previous years there had been great com-
petition between the Egyptian and Syrian caravans to see whose
mahmal would get away first, with 'bloody affrays' resulting as each
tried to impede the other. On this occasion a greater propriety prevailed, which he ascribed to the powerful authority of Muhammad
Ali.

The procession back to Muzdalifa, where they were to spend the
night, was marked with a wild gaiety; the two Pashas' military bands
played, Turkish officers set off colourful rockets, and the soldiery

fired their muskets. Burckhardt, like thousands of others, had lost his camels in the flight from Arafat, and after hours of fruitless searching lay down to sleep on the sand covered only by his *ihram*.

Setting out next day after pre-dawn prayers, the procession made the hour-long journey to Wadi Muna, where the famous stoning of the devil takes place. Three points along the wadi, two marked by pillars and one by a stone wall, symbolise the devil, and the pilgrim has to cast seven small stones at each of these markers. After this, every pilgrim who can afford it sacrifices a sheep or a goat. This is done in any part of the wadi, where, within the space of a quarter of an hour, between 6,000 and 8,000 sheep and goats were slaughtered on the day when Burckhardt was present.

The first stage of the pilgrims' duties was thus completed. Men went to the barbers' shops and had their heads shaved, resumed their ordinary clothes, and congratulated one another on having made the hajj thus far. Burckhardt had to stay in his pilgrim garb till after sunset, since only then did he find his servants with the camels. 'Fortunately,' he remarks, 'my purse, which I had hung about my neck ... enabled me to buy a sheep for sacrifice, and pay a barber.'

After remaining for two more festive days at Muna, when the ceremony of stoning is repeated twice, the pilgrims returned to Mecca on the afternoon of the third day. On re-entry to the city the faithful go to the Great Mosque and make the *tawaf* or seven circumambulations of the Kaaba, which in the meantime has been covered by the new black *kiswa* or cloth brought from Cairo. Next they perform the *sai* (which Burckhardt had completed when he first arrived), and resume the *ihram* to make the 'little pilgrimage' to other holy sites. Finally the *tawaf* and the *sai* are repeated once again, and the rituals of the hajj are over.

On 1 December Burckhardt left the seething streets of Mecca and returned to Jidda, which soon became just as crowded, with homeward-bound pilgrims thronging the port to take ship. 'Among the ships in the harbour, ready to take the hajji passengers on board, was a merchant vessel lately arrived from Bombay, ... commanded by an English captain, who had beat up to Jidda against the trade-winds, at this late season. I passed many agreeable hours in the company of Captain Boag, on board his ship, and regretted that my pursuits should call me away so soon.' Burckhardt had spent two years in disguise, adopting totally the habits of those amongst whom he lived; what a relief it must have been in the privacy of that ship's cabin to drop all pretence, without the fear that one false move might cause the ruin of all his hopes and plans.

Before Burckhardt left Jidda, Captain Boag presented him with a compass and allowed him to take a pocket volume of Milton's poems which he had chosen from the ship's library. A week or so later Burckhardt was back in Mecca.

Now he intended to see Madina, to complete his investigation of the holy cities. But he was forced to delay a further month in Mecca because it was impossible to hire camels. A rumour that Muhammad Ali was requisitioning beasts for his army had caused all the badawin cameleers to take to the hills.

Burckhardt's health deteriorated again during this time, and when not actually feverish he suffered from depression and a total lack of energy and appetite. But his delay in Mecca enabled him to leave a vivid account of the city after the great annual tide of pilgrims receded.

> Mecca appeared like a deserted town. Of its brilliant shops, one-fourth only remained; and in the streets, where a few weeks before it was necessary to force one's way through the crowd, not a single hajji was seen, except solitary beggars.... Rubbish and filth covered the streets, and nobody appeared disposed to remove it. The skirts of the town were crowded with the dead carcasses of camels, the smell from which rendered the air, even in the midst of the town, offensive, and certainly contributed to the many diseases now prevalent. Several hundred of these carcasses lay near the reservoirs of the Hajj, and the Arabs inhabiting that part of Mecca never walked out without stuffing into their nostrils small pieces of cotton, which they carried suspended by a thread round the neck.

The whole of the Hijaz was now in a state of suspense awaiting Muhammad Ali's decision to attack the Wahhabis. He finally led out his army in early January and four days later won a decisive victory against the enemy forces at Bissel near Taif. As a result the regular caravan traffic which had been suspended was now resumed, and Burckhardt was able to join a Madina-bound party on 15 January 1815.

He travelled by the route which skirts along the western slopes of the Hijaz mountains. With customary care he describes the terrain, the water supply, and the features of each place where they halted. His observations were helped by the compass that Captain Boag had given him, and he had bought a good watch which enabled him to record travelling-times.

At one point Burckhardt, who had walked on in front of the caravan, nearly fell victim to robbers, but his account of the incident is pitched in his usual low key, and he makes little of it. He was sitting alone, waiting for his companions to catch up with him, when five badawin who had stalked him behind some bushes suddenly burst upon him and grabbed his stick, his only weapon, which he had laid on the sand beside him. They accused him of being a deserter from the Turkish army, and therefore their lawful prize. Burckhardt offered no resistance, explaining calmly that he was a hajji, as they would see if they waited a little till his caravan drew up. The robbers hesitated; punishment for robbing pilgrims was severe. Uncomfortable minutes passed as Burckhardt waited for the rest of his party to appear. He had not realised they had halted for the evening prayer, and it was a long quarter of an hour before they came in sight. 'I expected every moment to be stripped, when, the tread of the camels being at last heard, the Bedouïns retreated as suddenly as they had approached.'

The group with whom he was travelling were mostly Malayan and Javanese, and Burckhardt was to form a low opinion of them. One of the poorer men who could not afford a camel had strayed in the night, and had been found by a party of Auf badawin. The Malay had offered them twenty piastres to guide him back to the caravan, and though he looked destitute, they agreed, expecting his companions to pay the reward. But the other Malays not only refused to pay, but denied all knowledge of the man, upon which the badu said they would hold him hostage until he could be ransomed by other Malays passing that way. Burckhardt could easily have paid the twenty piastres himself, but felt it was the duty of the man's fellow-countrymen to do so, and tried vainly to persuade them. The caravan was on the point of departure, the camels loaded, and the riders mounted, while the wretched hostage held by the badu was wailing loudly in fear and distress.

> I had waited for this moment. Relying on the respect I enjoyed in the caravan from being supposed a hajji in some measure attached to Muhammad Ali's army, and the good-will of our guides, ... I seized the leader's camel, made it couch down, and exclaimed that the caravan should not proceed till the man was released. I then went from load to load ... and I took from every one of their camels twenty paras (about three pence) and after a long contest made up the twenty piastres. This sum I carried to the Bedouins ... and representing to them his forlorn state, and appealing to the honour of their tribe, induced them to take ten piastres. According to true Turkish maxims, I should have pocketed the other ten, as a compensation for my trouble; I, however, gave them to the poor Malay, to the infinite mortification of his countrymen.

The incident throws a revealing light on the character of the Swiss. He was usually reluctant to draw attention to himself, but obviously felt strongly about the helpless Malay disowned by his countrymen.

They were proceeding by long night marches, sometimes thirteen hours without stopping, and at least once Burckhardt fell asleep on his camel and rode for eleven hours before he woke up at the next stop. The pace of the camels was only about 2¼ miles an hour. Having travelled along the plain for the first week, on 22 January they turned north-eastwards to enter the Hijaz mountains. Climbing up the Wadi Zugag they reached the top of the range and camped at the village of Safra. In the market here Burckhardt wanted to buy some *balesan*, the balm from the Mecca balsam tree which grew in this region, but he could not afford a whole sheepskin, and in the entire village no small bottle was to be found in which he might take a more modest quantity.

After they left Safra their route passed through the Wadi Jedaida, the scene of the Ottomans' defeat by the Wahhabis in 1811. It was a narrow defile offering easy opportunities for ambush, and for centuries the Harb bedu had pillaged the pilgrim trains here. In Burckhardt's day this tribe were allowed to levy a toll on hajj caravans, and there was a Turkish army post in the wadi to keep the peace. They continued over a plain and on into higher mountains where they endured intense cold and went in constant fear of robbers. On 27 January after a rest on the plain of Faraish they climbed up to the summit of the easternmost range, and from there had their first sight of Madina. But it was midnight when they arrived at the gate of the city, and they had to wait till daylight before it opened.

The whole party had been soaked to the skin by severe rain earlier in the day, and when the temperature dropped below freezing in the early hours of the morning as they sat huddled outside the gate, they all suffered acutely. Burckhardt had apparently been in good health during the twelve-day journey from Mecca, but this final night in dreadful conditions was before long to cause a new and severe breakdown in his health.

Immediately on arrival at Madina Burckhardt found himself lodgings, then visited the Prophet's tomb, the main shrine of the city. The necessary ceremonies there were completed in a quarter of an hour. Later, when he tried to buy provisions, he had some difficulty, since the tribesmen who normally brought in supplies had here too been frightened away by the possibility of having their camels commandeered for the Turkish army. With the help of his pilgrim-guide he was able to obtain some flour and butter, though 'not in the public market'.

He soon heard that Yahya Effendi, Tousun's doctor who had helped him in Jidda when he first arrived, was now in Madina with Tousun. Burckhardt, remembering his earlier kindness, went to visit him. Later Yahya returned Burckhardt's call, and in his lodgings noticed that the Swiss had half a pound of 'good bark' (quinine) in his medicine sack. Several prominent men at Tousun's court were ill, and the Pasha himself not in the best of health; Yahya had few medicines and had clearly been feeling somewhat inadequate in his professional ministrations. 'He begged of me the bark,' says Burckhardt, 'which I gave him, as I was then in good health, and thought myself already in the vicinity of Egypt, where I hoped to arrive in about two months.' It was a generous but rash gesture. Only two days were to pass before Burckhardt went down with a fresh attack of malaria, and when he requested some of his bark back from Yahya the Egyptian said he had already distributed it all, and could only give Burckhardt some stale gentiana powder which had lost its efficacy.

Burckhardt's lodgings were near a gate of the main mosque, through which corpses were habitually brought for prayers to be said over them, and from his sick-bed he could hear the pious exclamations accompanying such last rites – hardly a cheering sound for a sick man. Every day throughout his illness one or two funerals passed under his window, a fact which he mentions to show the extraordinarily high mortality rate in Madina, whose population he estimated at 16–20,000.

Grievously ill, Burckhardt lay alone in his rented room, sweating profusely and vomiting daily. Yahya Effendi proved to be a fair-weather friend; after the first days of Burckhardt's illness he did not come again, and in March left with Tousun Pasha for the Wahhabi war. After Burckhardt had tried all his remaining drugs without success, his sickness was left to take its course. At the end of a month he rallied briefly, but then the fever returned with renewed violence, and he was finally reduced to a state of helpless debility. 'I was now unable to rise from my carpet, without the assistance of my slave, a poor fellow, who by habit and nature was more fitted to take care of a camel than to nurse his drooping master.'

Burckhardt believed he was dying, and fell into a mood of deep depression; the ravages of the fever had this time defeated even his indomitable spirit. As the interminable days of his illness had dragged on he was particularly grateful for the small volume of Milton's poems he had obtained from the English ship, since he had neither friends to comfort him, nor other distractions to take his mind off his melancholy imaginings. His only human contacts were with his elderly and infirm landlady, who would call down from the balcony of a room above his own to converse for half an hour every evening, and with his *muzowwar* or guide, who paid him occasional visits, 'in order, as I strongly suspected, to seize upon part of my baggage in case of my death'.

Burckhardt had arrived in Madina on 28 January. It was the beginning of April before the malaria left him, and another fortnight before his wasted body regained strength to walk out of the house. By this time his one thought was to leave Madina, with its polluted water, unwholesome climate, and endemic disease. Abandoning earlier plans to visit Hajar where there were supposed to be ancient ruins, he decided to get away as soon as possible by making for the coast and embarking for Egypt. On 21 April he joined a group of badawin going to Yanbo, and shook the dust of Madina off his feet.

Having spent two months of his time in Madina prostrated by sickness, and the rest in a state of despondent convalescence, Burckhardt might well be forgiven if he did not provide his usual description of the surroundings in which he found himself. In fact he devotes four substantial chapters of his *Travels in Arabia* to the Prophet's city, its environs, and government, believing that Madina was totally unknown to Europeans.

Burckhardt's description of the city includes a town-plan which he made in the few days before he fell ill. The principal quarters are named and their features noted. He goes on to give a full account of the mosque where the Prophet Muhammad is buried, a place of veneration which makes Madina second only to Mecca in spiritual significance for Muslims. Burckhardt listed and named its gates, paced out its dimensions, counted its rows of columns, and described in detail the outward appearance of the Hujra, within which lie the tombs of Muhammad, Abu Bakr, and Omar. In this sanctuary there had formerly been a great treasure in the form of golden vessels and jewellery, but during the Wahhabi occupation Saud, the Najdi ruler, had himself entered the sanctuary and seized the treasure, carrying much of it back to Dariya. The most precious article he took was reputed to be a star of diamonds and pearls, which had been suspended directly over the Prophet's tomb. Other items were sold by the Wahhabis to the Sharif of Mecca, and later Tousun Pasha was able to buy back some gold cups and restore them to the shrine.

Of the *Raudha* or 'Garden', that part of the mosque where the congregation assembles, Burckhardt comments that although at first it gives an impression of splendour, with gilt inscriptions and glittering adornments, closer inspection proves this to be 'a display of tinsel decoration, and not of real riches'. He found that in general this mosque was treated with a greater sense of awe than its counterpart in Mecca, and was less infested with beggars and idlers. It was, however, full of vermin which lived in the thick pile of its woollen carpets, and which plagued all who visited it.

As at Mecca, the sanctuary at Madina was looked after by a band of eunuchs, who had great standing in the community and exercised considerable influence in civic affairs. The Shaikh al Haram, as their leader was called, was considered the most important personage in Madina, taking precedence even over Tousun Pasha, the governor.

Burckhardt himself saw Tousun kiss the Shaikh's hands whenever they met.

Burckhardt writes at length on agriculture round the town and the system of land-holding. Another chapter is devoted to places of *ziyara* or pious visitation, which in Madina include the main cemetery where many of the Prophet's family lie buried. There was also Jabal Ohod, not far outside the town, the site of a fierce battle where the Prophet defeated the Quraish. His uncle was killed in the battle, and lies buried there with seventy-five other martyrs; pilgrims go to recite special prayers at their tombs. The cupolas of the mosque at this and most other holy sites had been destroyed by the Wahhabis, but these puritan fanatics had not been able to harm the fine dome which rises over the tomb of the Prophet himself. Burckhardt had been told that two workmen sent up to start the destruction slipped and were killed, and the attempt was abandoned.

As in Mecca, the people of Madina were of mixed race, and only a few of the original ancient families remained. The general inhabitants were paler in complexion than the Meccawis, for here there was more Syrian blood, while in Mecca contact with Africa was closer. Unlike Mecca, Madina was not a great mercantile centre.

While Burckhardt was in Madina, Muhammad Ali's wife, whose extravagant pavilions he had already noted at Arafat, appeared there, both to complete her pilgrimage and to visit her son Tousun. On the Prophet's birthday, a festival especially honoured in this city, she passed the greater part of the night in the mosque. But Burckhardt was more astonished at an incident which occurred later. Tousun Pasha visited her in her rented house in town, and when he left in the evening 'he himself ordered a carpet to be spread in the middle of the street, and there slept at the threshold of his mother's dwelling; offering a testimony of respect and humility which does as much honour to the son as to the character of the mother who could inspire him with such sentiments'. But while admiring Tousun's filial devotion, Burckhardt comments: 'we must regret that he is as much inferior in intellect to his father and his brother Ibrahim, as he is superior to them in moral character.' In fact, he believed Tousun to be genuinely devout, while Muhammad Ali's religious observances were purely diplomatic.

Following these reflections on the ruling family Burckhardt indulges in a bitter condemnation of Turkish influence on the Arab way of life generally. Of the Turks he declares, 'they are wholly deficient in virtue, honour and justice; ... they have little true piety, and still less charity or forbearance; and honesty is only to be found in their paupers or idiots'.

In writing of his journey to the coast with the caravan which left for Yanbo on 21 April 1815, Burckhardt cannot help contrasting the eager traveller that he was when he arrived, 'in full health and spirits, and indulging the fond hopes of exploring unknown and interesting parts of the Desert', with the sad figure who now departed, 'worn down by lingering disease, dejected and desponding'.

They started out on the road by which he had entered Madina, but the camel-train was held up by floods in the wadis after heavy rain. There was another torrential storm on the 23rd, and though a Muscati merchant invited Burckhardt to shelter in his tent, the Swiss grew feverish again during their next nocturnal march. The caravan could not halt for him, and he was forced to go on, sweating and shivering, unable to change his sodden clothing.

At Safra, the village where they had halted on the incoming journey, the track to Yanbo turned off the route to Mecca. Arriving at midnight, the caravan now paused only to drink coffee before pressing on. The long marches of fourteen hours at a stretch were purgatory for Burckhardt in his weakened state, and when the guides made the travellers dismount to ease the camels' ascent of one particularly steep mountain, he was scarcely strong enough to reach the summit. They rested a day at Badr Hunain, site of another of the Prophet's battles, and then moved on almost due west. As his sickness grew worse, Burckhardt spent a night of appalling misery on 26 April. In a feverish daze he jogged through the long dark hours on camel-back, concentrating all his efforts on not falling off the swaying beast, and when day came he was racked with a violent fit of vomiting. They rested for a morning and set out again at midday. There followed another fifteen and a half hours' march through the afternoon and night which brought Burckhardt almost to the limits of his endurance. But fortunately the journey was over. Just after sunrise on 28 April they reached the town gate of Yanbo.

The port was full of hajjis waiting to embark and Turkish soldiers returning from the war. Though four ships were waiting to take Muhammad Ali's wife and her retinue back to Egypt, for lesser mortals there was no passage to be had.

During his first day in Yanbo Burckhardt saw a number of funeral processions, and the idea of a possible epidemic in the town filled him with horror. That night, in his small, hot room, the cries of mourners and his own fears kept him tossing sleepless through the dark hours. But when he enquired of the Arabs next day whether the bodies he saw were plague victims, he was reproved for even asking such a question, since according to Muslim belief 'the Almighty had forever excluded that disorder from the holy territory of the Hijaz'. Nevertheless his fears were confirmed when he spoke to some Greeks, who told him that plague had broken out in Yanbo about ten days previously. It had been raging at Cairo for several months, and was also at Suez, whence the infection had come across to Arabia.

Five days after his arrival the death rate had risen to forty or fifty a day. 'The inhabitants now felt a panic: little disposed to submit as patiently to the danger as the Turks do in every other part of the east, the greater part of them fled into the open country, and the town became deserted; but the disease followed the fugitives, who had encamped close together; and thus finding no remedy to the evil, many of them returned.' To excuse their flight the Arabs would say that though God sent the disease to call them to himself, they were unworthy of his grace and therefore preferred to leave the scene of danger. Burckhardt himself would have left the town if he had been in good health, but sick and feeble as he was he felt incapable of further exertion, and hoped that by shutting himself up in his room he could escape infection.

With calm objectivity he describes the scenes in the city during this period of acute distress. The main street was lined with dead and dying asking for charity, and he saw a victim die in his own khan. His own sensible precautions against the disease were nearly rendered useless by his slave, who disappeared for a few days and on returning told his master that he had joined in the pious work of washing the dead who were laid out on the seashore. These were indigent pilgrims who had no family or friends to perform for them the last ritual ablutions.

But the human mind has its own defences against a surfeit of tragedy, and after the first few days in Yanbo Burckhardt became hardened to the idea of being in a plague-ridden city. A natural optimism made him reflect upon the many who did not contract the disease, and he was cheered by the other foreigners who walked about the town seemingly unconcerned. But he admits that the disease seemed to be of the most virulent kind, and there were very few survivors among those who caught it.

Weeks later, sitting in the safety of his house in Cairo as he finished writing his diary, he felt a delayed-action shock at the memory of the horrors he had lived through. 'The sense of the danger which then threatened me is much greater, now that I find myself far removed from it, than I felt it at the time.'

Among the strange scenes he saw at Yanbo during those terrible days was a superstitious ritual by which the helpless inhabitants hoped to ward off the plague. A she-camel, decorated with feathers, bells, and other gaudy ornaments, was led in procession through the town to the cemetery and slaughtered there. It was believed that the camel's body gathered into itself the plague which afflicted the town, and that the disease disappeared as the camel's flesh was consumed by the stray dogs and vultures.

True to his principles, Burckhardt tells us as much as he could learn about Yanbo. The natives of the town were pure Arab, unlike the racial mixture to be found in the pilgrimage centres. There was good anchorage in the deep protected bay, and the Yanbawis lived chiefly by trade and navigation. They had become daring smugglers to avoid the Turkish customs officials: 'no ship of theirs enters the harbour without a considerable part of its cargo being sent on shore by stealth, to elude the heavy duties'.

The town had a good water supply, due to the forethought of earlier generations of affluent citizens who had built several large subterranean reservoirs outside the city walls. This water was sold to the public, and Burckhardt considered it more wholesome than any he had yet found in the Hijaz. Although he saw Yanbo in the most unfavourable circumstances, he thought it a tolerably pleasant place. Its one drawback was that flies swarmed in the town in vast numbers. 'No person walks out without a straw fan in his hand to drive off these vermin; and it is utterly impossible to eat, without swallowing some of them, which enter the mouth the moment it is opened. Clouds of them are seen passing over the town; they settle even upon the ships that sail out of the harbour.'

As the days passed and Burckhardt watched the densely-packed boats leaving for Egypt he was glad he was not among the crowds of diseased soldiers. In the end, he booked a passage on a small sail-ing-craft which was going to Cosseir on the opposite shore of the Red Sea, thinking this might be a safer way of escaping. Though he was glad to leave after eighteen days in the plague-stricken city, conditions on the *sambuk* on which he sailed fell sadly short of his expectations. The captain had told him there would be only twelve Arab passengers aboard, and Burckhardt had paid three dollars above the normal fare for a special place behind the steering-wheel. But he had been deceived; there were at least thirty passengers in addition to ten crew members. And the space which Burckhardt hoped to have reserved for himself was occupied by the captain and his cronies.

Worse was to follow. Once they had set sail Burckhardt learned that in the hold were half a dozen very sick people. One of these died on the second day out and was thrown overboard. Making the best of the unhappy situation, Burckhardt tried to isolate himself from his fellow-passengers behind a protective barrier built of his own baggage.

For twenty days in the increasing heat of early summer the boat crept up the Arabian coast. Craft of this type rarely braved the open sea, and although they passed the latitude of Cosseir on the western shore, the boat was heading for the northern extremity of the Red Sea whence it would follow the coast southwards again. Burckhardt soon tired of this long-drawn-out voyage, and when they anchored off Ras Abu Muhammad at the southern tip of the Sinai peninsula, he asked to be put ashore. He knew the badawin of these parts would escort travellers to Tor, further along the coast, or to Suez. In any case, at this point he was much nearer to Cairo than he would be if he completed the voyage to Cosseir.

It was 5 June when he landed in the harbour of Sharm at the mouth of the Gulf of Aqaba, and the same evening he was able to join a group of badawin heading for Cairo. But he went with them only as far as Tor; news from Suez and Cairo indicated that plague was still rife in both places. He hoped by delaying for a fortnight to give the epidemic time to wane, and he was able to escape the heat of the coast by going inland to a pleasant village in the hills. The inhabitants treated him hospitably, and his health improved rapidly in the cool and restful gardens of Al Wadi. When he felt strong enough to be on his way again he was able to make the long, hot journey to the capital in six days. From Suez onwards he joined the caravan of Muhammad Ali's wife, whose path he had been crossing and re-crossing, and this gave him security through the final stretch of Egyptian desert.

So at last he reached Cairo again after an absence of nearly two and a half years. After the hardships, the debilitating sickness, and the weariness of long journeys in great heat, the traveller had come back to friends and civilised comforts. His health was sadly undermined, and he needed a long period of recovery.

The joy I felt at my safe return to Cairo was considerably increased by flattering and encouraging letters from England; but my state of health was too low to admit of fully indulging in the pleasures of success. The physicians of Cairo are of the same set of European quacks so frequently found in other parts of the Levant: they made me swallow pounds of bark, and thus rendered my disease worse; and it was not till two months after that I regained my perfect health at Alexandria.

After spending the summer in Alexandria, Burckhardt returned to Cairo and took a house in the Turkish quarter, setting to work to complete his accounts of his Nubian journey and his Arabian travels. During this time he expected to be off again soon to Central Africa, the original objective for which his preliminary journeys were regarded as preparation and training. One of his letters to his mother reveals how he now lived for travelling: 'This career of mine is wonderful, far better than my wildest hopes suggested. To return with the job half done would reduce my standing with my superiors, with the public and, I am sure, with you too.'

But the hoped-for chance of a caravan to the Fezzan seemed interminably delayed. Two years went by, during which he lived unostentatiously, enjoying the company of European travellers when the

opportunity offered, but content most of the time to be with his Turkish neighbours among whom he became an honoured and respected
figure. Then, in October 1817, he had a recurrence of dysentery.
The doctor of the British Consulate could do little to help, and Burckhardt's strength ebbed slowly away. On 15 October his friend Henry
Salt, the British Consul, was called to his bedside, and to him Burckhardt expressed his last wishes about the disposal of his property in
Cairo. Among his possessions were a large number of valuable oriental manuscripts which he bequeathed to Cambridge University. He
asked Salt to let the Turks bury him in their own cemetery in their
own way.

He died that night, aged only thirty-two, just when he felt himself
prepared by experience and maturity to undertake a new journey
which would be the climax of his achievements. The funeral
arranged for him by his Muslim friends accorded with his status as
a hajji and a scholar. He was buried in the great cemetery outside
the Bab al Nasr.

The question of whether Burckhardt was a sincere convert to the
Muslim faith has never been fully resolved. In the early years of the
nineteenth century an apostate was regarded with opprobrium, and
to pretend to adopt Islam for the purpose of travelling to Mecca
was almost as bad. Today, in a more liberal religious climate, the
question seems largely irrelevant. Certainly Burckhardt was a professed Christian before starting his travels, but after living the part
of a Muslim for several years it may be that he found himself
genuinely drawn to Islam. He would not have been alone among
travellers in eastern lands if he had felt that the Muslim faith was
peculiarly suited to Arabia and its people and therefore easily acceptable to one who was to spend his life in those regions.

Before his death Burckhardt had managed to send to London his
manuscripts on his African and Arabian travels, as well as his *Notes
on the Bedouins and the Wahabis*, and his collection of *Arabic Proverbs*.
He apologised for their unpolished state, explaining that his eyesight
was troubling him again and he had found it hard to put the finishing
touches to his writings. By the time his papers reached the African
Association Burckhardt was dead. His *Travels in Arabia* was prepared
for publication by Sir William Ouseley and appeared in 1829. For
more than half a century it was the standard authority on the holy
cities of the Hijaz, valued for its encyclopaedic detail and factual
reporting. D. G. Hogarth, the twentieth-century scholar, places
Burckhardt among the foremost of those who have written about
Arabia, and so he will remain to all whose own knowledge of the
East recognises in his modest and undramatic writings the unmistak-
able stamp of truth.

Chapter 5

BURTON
The Pilgrim
1853

'.... before middle age he had compressed into his life more of study, more of hardship, and more successful enterprise and adventure, than would have sufficed to fill up the existence of half a dozen ordinary men.' *Lord Derby*

By Victorian times central Arabia had taken the place of the holy cities of the Hijaz in the thoughts and ambitions of prospective voyagers. Who, after all, could follow Burckhardt along the pilgrim routes and hope to add appreciably to the volume or exactness of his findings, or to the profoundly objective manner in which those findings were presented?

It was more profitable by far to take up the challenge of the little-known regions of Arabia Deserta, of the Nafud and Najd. Even after the hearsay of Niebuhr and Burckhardt and the expeditions of Captain George Sadleir who went from Gulf to Red Sea as the emissary of the British Government in 1818, and of the great Swedish scholar-explorer Dr G. A. Wallin who made some remarkable journeys between 1845 and 1848, relatively little was recorded of these vast areas. Few place-names were marked on the map; tribal loyalties and conflicts had been revealed only fleetingly to the West. Wahhabism,

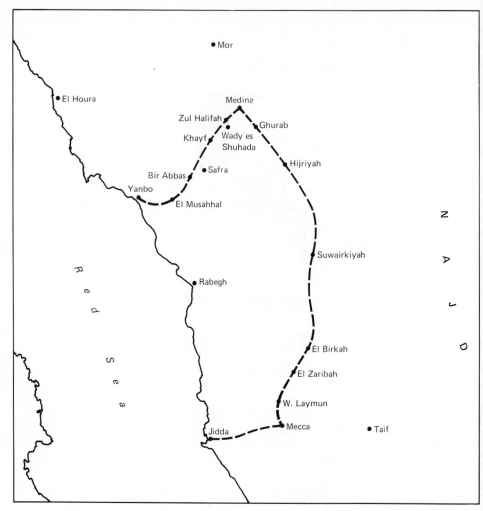

12 Burton's route in Hijaz

the religious movement that swept across the desert in the eighteenth century and finally conquered the citadels of Islam, was still
the source of power and the weapon of authority in its birthplace,
Najd, though as Burckhardt had noted its hold over the tribes had
weakened. New power struggles were beginning to emerge. There
was much yet to be assessed by a traveller of courage and tenacity,
armed with fluency of language and a lively curiosity in matters of
religion, politics, people and places.

Such a man awaited precisely that kind of challenge in the mid-
nineteenth century: Lieutenant Richard Burton of the Indian Army.

Even among his vastly talented contemporaries Burton stood out as a man of parts. As a traveller and explorer he had every imaginable advantage. Strong, physically imposing, capable of commanding any language or dialect with apparent ease, a master of disguise and dissimulation, he could play almost any part with conviction. Translator, linguist, ethnologist, anthropologist, geographer, philosopher, writer; he achieved a mastery of almost any subject he set his mind to. Yet, as a brief and disastrous sojourn at Oxford had demonstrated, he was not amenable to the established processes of learning. He taught himself with an ease that verged on the haughty, and he used his knowledge as a battering ram, dismissing opposition and contrary opinion with contumely and a wry contortion of his scarred and handsomely moustached face. Unlike almost all the other early travellers in Arabia, Burton achieved immediate fame through his writings. His prejudices, his social outrages and preoccupation with sexual customs and deviations only added to the dark and profitable eminence. He was the great eccentric of nineteenth-century exploration and literature: the outsider, eschewing religious, political and social conformity yet seeking approval and recognition from those people and institutions he most openly despised.

Characteristically, his proposed journey, in which he hoped to cross Arabia from the Hijaz to Muscat, met with official opposition before it could take definite shape, so the plan was changed to a second-best excursion. The 'huge white blot' on the maps of his time which negatively marked the central and southern regions of the peninsula, and which occupied his mind when he offered his services to the Royal Geographical Society in 1852, was to remain a blank for some time to come. The chairman of the Court of Directors of the Honourable East India Company, to whom he applied for three years' leave of absence, refused his request on the grounds that too many soldier-travellers in the East had fallen by the wayside in recent years. He was granted a compensatory furlough of a year in order to advance his Arabic studies, and decided to make for Al-Hijaz. Since army discipline had never weighed heavily with him, he kept in mind the possibility of an unofficial extension of his leave and itinerary should circumstances permit. If he could not add greatly to the sum of knowledge amassed by those who had gone before, he would demonstrate that 'what might be perilous to other travellers was safe to me'.

His own account of the journey, *Pilgrimage to Al-Medinah and Meccah*, was first published in 1855, dashed off in a matter of a few months after his return.

When he had finished writing he hurried from London to assuage a new bout of wanderlust, handing his manuscript to the Egyptologist Sir Gardner Wilkinson who tidied it up for the general reader. The indelicate references to sexual customs and aberrations which ran through the text and footnotes were simply not publishable in Victorian times, though 'Ruffian Dick' found delight in relating his discoveries and theories in such company as was most likely to be horrified by them. Even Sir Gardner talked of rejecting 'an amount of unpleasant garbage', though retaining some 'pornographic' footnotes which Burton had put into Latin to spare the blushes of all but the most educated of his readers.

His capacity for observing traits of human behaviour was that of an actor studying a part. Look, for instance, at the Indian Muslim drinking a glass of water.

With us the operation is simple enough, but his performance includes no fewer than five novelties. In the first place he clutches his tumbler as though it were the throat of a foe; secondly, he ejaculates, 'In the name of Allah the Compassionate, the Merciful!' before wetting his lips; thirdly, he imbibes the contents, swallowing them, not sipping them as he ought to do, and ending with a satisfied grunt; fourthly, before setting down the cup, he sighs forth 'Praise be to Allah!' – of which you will understand the full meaning in the desert; and fifthly, he replies, 'May Allah make it pleasant to thee!' in answer to his friend's polite 'Pleasurably and health!'

He boarded the new P & O steamer *Bengal* on the evening of 3 April 1853. He was in his thirty-third year. They had hardly put to sea before he began to address his thoughts to the places and prominences that came into view and to the origins of their names. 'The sight of glorious Trafalgar excited none of the sentiments with which a tedious sail used to invest it.' And the inevitable etymological footnote: 'Trafalgar is nothing but a corruption of Tarf al-Gharb – the side skirt of the West; it being the most occidental point then reached by Arab conquest.' Throughout his journey, he noted the minutest details of terrain, speech, dress and custom, a glittering commentary that came of a mastery of heaven knows how many languages.

They passed along the North African coast and soon they were embraced by the stillness of the East, 'the soft night breeze wandering through starlit skies and tufted trees, with a voice of melancholy meaning'.

And this is the Arab's *Kayf*. The savouring of animal existence; the passive enjoyment of mere sense; the pleasant languor, the dreamy tranquillity, the airy castle-building, which in Asia stand in lieu of the vigorous, intensive, passionate life of Europe. It is the result of a lively, impressible, excitable nature, and exquisite sensibility of nerve; it argues a facility for voluptuousness unknown to northern regions, where happiness is placed in the exertion of mental and physical powers; where *Ernst is das Leben*; where niggard earth commands ceaseless sweat of face, and damp chill air demands perpetual excitement, exercise, or change, or adventure, or dispassion, for want of something better. In the East man wants but rest and shade: upon the banks of a bubbling stream or under the cool shelter of a perfumed tree, he is perfectly happy, smoking a pipe, or sipping a cup of coffee or drinking a glass of sherbet, but above all things deranging body and mind as little as possible; the trouble of conversations, the displeasures of memory, and the vanity of thought being the most unpleasant interruptions to his *Kayf*. No wonder that 'Kayf' is a word untranslatable in our mother tongue.

Burton, the sceptic of the West, had an instinctive understanding of the oriental mind and manner.

He arrived in Egypt in the character of a Persian *darwaysh* or dervish, with the title of Mirza, having at some time been admitted to the order of Kadiriyah with the imposing name of Bismillah-Shah, King in the name of Allah. The part suited him well. 'The more haughty and offensive he is to the people the more they respect him; a decided advantage to the traveller of choleric temperament.' All the same, Persians are not generally liked in Arabia and he changed his identity to that of Abdullah, an Indian Pathan of Afghan origin, a name frequently adopted by Arab Christians since its meaning, servant of Allah, is acceptable to all sides of Islamic doctrine. He adopted the commonest of roles among Arabian travellers, that of a physician.

In Egypt he soon began to rub up against authority and the meddlesome interference of both native and British officials, revealing something of the residual Victorian imperialist among the many facets of his make-up. Egypt was becoming civilised, but 'nothing could be more uncomfortable than its present middle state, between barbarism and the reverse'. That acts of punishment like flogging your peasant, which in the good old days of the Mamelukes would have led to a beyship, were now likely to result in deportation, he found beyond comprehension or reason. 'When you curse your boatman, he complains to your consul; the dragomans afflict you with strange wild notions about honesty; a Government order prevents you from using vituperative language to the "natives" in general; and the very donkey boys are becoming cognisant of the right of a man to remain unbastinadoed.' As for the business of having to carry a passport, his indignation boiled:

I had neglected to provide myself with a passport in England, and it was not without much difficulty, involving much unclean dressing and an unlimited expenditure of broken English, that I

obtained from H.B.M's Consul at Alexandria a certificate declaring
me to be an Indo-British subject named Abdullah, by profession
a doctor. ... For this I disbursed a dollar. And here let me record
the indignation with which I did it. That mighty Britain – the mistress of the seas – the ruler of one-sixth of mankind – should charge
five shillings to pay for the shadow of her protecting wing! ... O
the meanness of our magnificence! the littleness of our greatness!

Armed with that offensive document, to which the signature of
an Egyptian vizier was added after several days of skirmishing with
officialdom, he took a Nile steamer to Cairo. He arrived at Cairo
in time for Ramadhan and so stayed put in a guest house. When
he was able to move on after the fast he took camel to Suez.

As he made the slow camel trek across the Egyptian desert he
began to reflect on the way in which human faculties are stimulated
by the vast emptiness of the wastelands.

It is strange how the mind can be amused by scenery that presents
so few objects to occupy it. But in such a country every slight modifi-
cation of form or colour rivets observation: the senses are shar-
pened, and the perceptive faculties, prone to sleep over a confused
mass of natural objects, act vigorously when excited by the capa-
bility of embracing each detail. Moreover, Desert views are
eminently suggestive; they appeal to the Future, not to the Past:
they arouse because they are by no means memorial. To the solitary
wayfarer there is an interest in the Wilderness unknown to Cape
seas and Alpine glaciers, and even to the rolling Prairie, – the effect
of continued excitement on the mind, stimulating its powers to their
pitch. Above, through a sky terrible in its stainless beauty, and the
splendours of a pitiless blinding glare, the Samun caresses you like
a lion with flaming breath. Around lie drifted sand-heaps, upon
which each puff of wind leaves its trace in solid waves, flayed rocks,
the very skeletons of mountains, and hard unbroken plains, over
which he who rides is spurred by the idea that the bursting of a
water-skin, or the pricking of a camel's hoof, would be a certain
death of torture, – a haggard land infested with wild beasts, and
wilder men, – a region whose very fountains murmur the warning
words 'Drink and away!' What can be more exciting? What more
sublime?

And a little later:

... believe me, when once your tastes have conformed to the tranquillity of such travel, you will suffer real pain in returning to the
turmoil of civilisation. You will anticipate the bustle and the con-

fusion of artificial life, its luxuries and its false pleasures, with repugnance. Depressed in spirits, you will for a time after your return feel incapable of mental or bodily exertion. The air of cities will suffocate you, and the care-worn and cadaverous countenances of citizens will haunt you like a vision of judgement.

Burton entered Suez in the company of a young Meccan, Muhammad al-Basyuni, who energetically sought the friendship of the older man, though he clearly regarded him as at best a heretic.

Burton always seemed to gravitate to the ruffian element of a gathering, and he enjoyed a brawl. In Cairo he had fallen in with a particularly aggressive Albanian soldier and the pair of them quickly came to blows. Burton felled the Albanian with a 'cross-buttock' throw. Soon they were the best of friends, drinking coffee in the hot Cairo evening. Now he was happily involved in the 'confusion at the eventful hour of departure', re-united with his fellow roughnecks, crowded aboard with a yelling mob of Africans, the *Maghrabin*. Burton could not resist the temptation to trace that word through forty lines of footnote:

Men of Maghrab, or Western Africa; the vulgar plural is Maghrabin, generally written 'Mogrebyn'. May not the singular form of this word have given rise to the Latin 'Maurus' by elision of the Ghayn, to Italians an unpronounceable consonant? From Maurus comes the Portuguese Moro and our Moor ... it has been my fate to hear, at a meeting of a learned society in London, a gentleman declare that in East Africa he found a people calling *themselves* Moors. Maghrabin – Westerns – then would be opposed to Sharkiyin, Easterns, the origin of our 'Saracen'.

They eventually set sail on 6 July but stayed their course at sunset, still within sight of Suez.

Their vessel was called the Silk al-Zahab, the *Golden Wire*, a sambuk of fifty tons displacement with two masts, narrow wedge bows and sharp keel. There was only a poop deck, the rest being undecked hold in which the passengers had to retain whatever foothold or seating position they were lucky enough to secure.

'Bakhshish' was the first word Burton heard when he entered Egypt. It was the last he heard as the ship pulled away from its mooring off Suez. The rapacious owner of the *Golden Wire* had said that he would put sixty passengers into the hold, but when it sailed ninety-seven pushed and shoved for space, while the outer ring of pilgrims bent over the sides in agonised postures. Burton and his cronies had placed themselves on the poop deck along with the piles of goods and bags that filled every available niche and a number of pilgrims

who had not paid the requisite fare. One of the Englishman's
favourite companions, a merchant known to the company as Saad
the Demon, appeared on the scene dressed as a seaman and together
with Burton and his new-found friends threw the unfortunate in-
truders and their baggage into the seething pit below. The Englishman then paid a dollar for the only bed available and settled down
to observe the 'pugnacity' with which the poor wretches around him
fought for survival with elbows, curses and occasionally daggers.
Many a bloody blow was struck with stave and knife in violent
quarrels between Maghrabis, Turks, Anatolians, Armenians,
Syrians, and the Englishman and his belligerent companions, before
the *Golden Wire* made its first port of call, a tongue of sand a little
way from the 'enchanted land' of the Arabs.

Each night they drew in to some sheltered bay, sailing through
the pirate-infested waters of the Red Sea only by day. Often they
went ashore to renew the battles between the rival factions of their
party, to sleep in the soft, comforting sand and to fill their water-
skins. And for Burton to note his impressions: 'The horizon is all
darkness, and the sea reflects the white visage of the night-sun as
in a mirror of steel. ... You are bound by the *bond of Orion*. Hesperus
bears with him a thousand things.'

Step by step on the journey to the holy land of Islam, Burton the
ruffian and Burton the poet marched cheek by jowl, never for a
moment conceding the disparity between one and the other. In com-
munion with Orion and Hesperus and with 'one look at a certain
little Star in the north, under which lies all that makes life worth
living through', he went contentedly to sleep, and awoke to the strife
and uproar of the pilgrim ship. Sometimes, though, the predictable
routine of savagery was broken by an act of kindness. 'Whenever
one of the party drew forth a little delicacy – a few dates or a
pomegranate – they gave away a share of it to the children, and most
of them took turns to nurse the baby. This was genuine politeness –
kindness of heart.'

They picked up Persian pilgrims from another vessel on the way,
and they called at Al-Wejh among the coral reefs along the coast –
which recalled Forsskal's exclamation *luxus lususque naturae* – and at
Marsa Mahar where they found half-naked Arabs lying in the shade
with nothing remarkable about them save their 'villainous countenances'.

They arrived at Yanbo twelve days after their departure from
Suez, and bade 'an eternal adieu to the vile *Golden Wire*'. The place
abounded with cafés, dirty and fly-infested. Here in the mid-nine-
teenth century the Sultan's dominion was supposed to begin and that
of the Pasha of Egypt to cease. In fact, the place seemed to be governed by an Arab Sharif and his negro police. The people were over-

armed and over-dressed, 'one of the most bigoted and quarrelsome races in Al-Hijaz'. Burton's party was soon bargaining with the natives for camels and provisions to take them to Madina, and since both sides were capable of spending several hours in fighting over a farthing, the negotiations were protracted and violent. In the end Burton, who naturally assumed the leadership of the group, insisted that he should have the best dromedary which he would share with his servant, Shaikh Nur, while the impudent young Muhammad and his baggage were borne by an inferior beast. The rest of the party, hearing that the Hazimi tribe was on the rampage between them and Madina, lost all interest in camels and loudly protested that they should stay where they were. Burton told them to hold their tongues. Saad the Demon entertained friends and strangers with endless anecdotes, whispering confidences as he went from one admiring group to another, consuming chunks of mutton and handfuls of rice on the way.

They were warned to wear Arab dress and not on any account to speak any language but Arabic, even to servants, within the hearing of villagers. They left Yanbo after evening prayer on 19 July.

So that he could make notes surreptitiously on the journey, Burton hired a *shugduf*, admitting that it was a device appropriate to women, children, the infirm and effeminate. Notes were more easily taken in it than on a dromedary's back, and the excuse of lameness (he had cut his feet on the rocks wading ashore) saved his dignity. Nevertheless, he was careful when entering any populous place to hire or borrow a saddled beast.

The notes he made on this part of the Hijaz and its people represent one of the most detailed and accurate accounts ever given of Arab dress, habit and adornment. The travelling costume of the shaikh, the *lisam* or veiling of the face in war or blood feud, the wearing of the silver-hilted *jambiyah* or curved dagger, the slung sword and matchlock, the *mizrak* or short javelin carried in the right hand, the *mashab* or crooked stick for guiding the camel; the dress of the lesser men of the desert, of the Arab woman, of the pilgrim – all had been described before by other travellers, but never in so much detail or to the accompaniment of such expert sketches, for drawing was another of Burton's many accomplishments.

The Englishman used one item of Arab dress to advantage. Many pilgrims, especially the Turkish variety, carried a pocket Koran in a crimson velvet or red morocco case, slung by silk cords over the left shoulder and hanging down by the right side. For this insignia of the pilgrim's holy errand, the *humail*, Burton substituted a similar device containing a watch, compass, penknife, pencils, slips of paper and ready money. The notes and observations he was thus able to make, by concealing small slips of paper in the palm of his hand

and writing and drawing with a pencil stub, were transferred at convenient moments into his diary, always taking care to ensure that
he was not caught in the act by badawin who would be quick to
suspect the spy, sorcerer or infidel at work.

They made their way towards Bir Abbas, savouring the sweet air
of the desert, under a dazzling moon, singing as Arabs will on such
occasions, and keeping a wary eye open for brigands.

His notes as he traversed the road to Madina ranged wide over
the character and manners of the desert. Of the Ottoman suzerain
he observed: 'They affect superiority over Arabs, hate them and are
despised by them'. Of the badawin he spoke sometimes with sympathy and liking, at others with anger. He advocated sterner
measures and harsher punishments to bring them under control, an
action that was easier to propose than implement, though more than
half a century later Ibn Saud was to bring his own children to heel
by the methods Burton advocated. Of his camel-man: 'like the lowest
orders of Orientals, he required to be ill-treated; gentleness and con-
descension he seemed to consider proof of cowardice and imbecility.
I began with kindness, but was soon compelled to use hard words
... then threats, which, though he heard them with frowns and
mutterings, produced manifest symptoms of improvement'.

They passed through the battlefield where Tousun and his 8,000
Turks had been defeated by a band of Wahhabi badu a third as
strong in number, and on 22 July reached Bir Abbas where they
camped. Here, in fact, they had their first sight of true badawin.

> They were Harb, dignified old men in the picturesque Arab cos-
> tume, with erect forms, fierce thin features, and white beards, well
> armed and mounted upon high-bred and handsomely equipped
> dromedaries from Al-Shark. Preceded by their half-naked
> clansmen, carrying spears twelve or thirteen feet long, garnished
> with single or double tufts of ostrich feathers, and ponderous match-
> locks, which were discharged on approaching the fort, they were
> not without a kind of barbaric pomp.

Burton's warnings about the difficulties of establishing place-
names or translating too literally the Arabic descriptions of natural
features provided salutary lessons for later travellers. One map of
the time showed a village on the Euphrates as M'adri, 'don't know'.
As for the protuberances of the desert which Arabs called *jabal*, whatever their size, he cautioned the traveller to understand that
although the word may refer to a mountain it may just as well signify
a small mound.

While camped at Bir Abbas, they were treated to a martial display
by Albanian Ottoman troops. 'There was a gallant reckless look

about the fellows which prepossessed me strongly in their favour!.'
Despite their ragged clothes, ill-assorted arms and sorry-looking
nags, Burton was impressed as he usually was by military efficiency
and expertise. These ragged warriors, delighting in the noise of
musketry, gave rise to another of those provocative and far-seeing
observations for which the author was renowned:

> When fighting, they often adopt the excellent plan – excellent when
> rifles are not procurable – of driving a long iron nail through the
> bullet, and fixing its head into the cartridge. Thus the cartridge
> is strengthened, the bullet is rifled, and the wound which it inflicts
> is death. Round balls are apt to pass into and out of savages, and
> many an Afghan, after being shot or run through the body, has
> mortally wounded his English adversary before falling.... I venture
> to hope that the reader will not charge these sentiments with
> cruelty. He who renders warfare fatal to all engaged in it will be
> the greatest benefactor the world has yet known.

As they moved on towards Madina, the travellers' mounting ill-
humour was stimulated by sun, sand and the furious Samun. The
'poison wind' that envelopes the desert traveller in a swirling, biting
cloud of sand had not so far inconvenienced the indomitable Burton,
but now he was compelled to tie his head-dress, the *kaffiya*, badawin-
fashion across his lower face. Soon, another hazard came into view.
As they passed through the gorge called Shuab al-Hajj, the Pilgrim
Pass, which had proved the undoing of many a voyager to and
from Madina, they spotted badawin swarming like hornets in the
hills above. 'They took up comfortable places on the cut-throat
eminence, and began firing upon us with perfect convenience to
themselves.' The party was reluctant to return the fire, knowing that
a dead Arab might bring hordes of badawin into the battle, and in
any case the desert warriors were in an invulnerable position. Burton's party lost twelve men and a good many animals before they
put up a smokescreen by blazing away with their guns and emerged
from its cover into the Wadi Sayyalah towards Shuhada, the place
of the Martyrs, where forty of the Prophet's men who fell in battle
are supposed to be buried.
  On past Bir al-Hindi, where a long-forgotten Indian voyager had
dug a well, through sickening heat to a resting-place of gravel,
covered with thorn trees and surrounded by unwelcoming rocks.
Suwaykah lived up to its reputation as one of the most rugged plains
of Arabia and the scene of many an Islamic battle. It derives its
name, as Burton noted, from a battle between Muhammad and Abu
Sufiyan who was accompanied by some 200 men, in the third year
of the Hegira. In order to escape the Prophet's wrath, the infidels

lightened their burden by emptying their bags of Sawik, or green grain mixed with dates: thus *Sawikah* or *Suwaykah*. On they went, Burton and Saad the Demon arguing fiercely and very nearly coming to blows, across the Mudarraj steps, cut in black basalt from the ridge of the Harratain, from the top of which they could see Madina. Their camel trek had taken them eight days. A good dromedary could have done the journey in two days, an average camel in four, said Burton. Theirs were patently inferior beasts. They arrived on 25 July at the first major goal of the journey.

The joy of the travellers was great.

O Allah! this is the Haram of Thy Apostle; make it to us a protection from Hell Fire, and a Refuge from Eternal Punishment! O open the gates of Thy Mercy, and let us pass through them to the Land of Joy!

The pilgrim band with Burton, Shaikh Hamid and Saad at its head changed its tune as it entered the city of the Prophet's tomb. Only the night before the quiet of the desert had been blasted by the imprecations and curses of the quarrelsome brotherhood as they lamented the exhaustion of Burton's tobacco supply and gave voice to various other grievances by calling each other owls, oxen, beggars, cut-off ones, Sons of Flight, goats of Akhfash, and sundry other names which provided Burton with an excuse to make up a directory of Arabic abuse.

'As we looked Eastward, the sun arose out of the horizon of a low hill, blurred and dotted with small tufted trees, which gained from the morning mists a giant stature, and the earth was stained with purple and gold.' So began Burton's portrait of Madina. He proceeded to describe the town in vivid architectural and sociological detail. Of those who went there before him, from Varthema, three and a half centuries earlier to the year, to Burckhardt who was sick and weak on arrival some forty years previously, none combined his power and accuracy of observation with anything like the same ability to evoke atmosphere.

From the *harra*, the volcanic ridge west of the town, Burton and his associates were able to gain a bird's-eye view along the tortuous road that led to the Ambari gate, and beyond to the dense grey mass of buildings pierced here and there by whitewashed rectilinear forms. To the left of the gateway, as he briefly sketched the outlines of Madina, was a pretty Turkish building, a Takiyah, erected by Muhammad Ali for the reception of dervishes. To the right, the barracks, white and garnished with ugly square windows. Among the clustered palm trees to the north were the ruins of a public fountain and between it and the town proper, the governor's palace, a conspicuous building in the Turkish pavilion style. At the north-west angle of the town wall, partly supported by an outcrop of rock, the fortress presented a European face to the sightseer, though its history was of oriental conflict, as Burckhardt had noted, between the nobility of the castle and of the town. At Al-Manakhah, 'the kneeling place of camels', stood the five mosques, their carefully cleaned domes and minarets gleaming against the sombre background. Behind them four substantial towers and a green dome flashing in the sunlight announced the gem of Madina, the mosque in which lay the Prophet's remains and those of his principal companions. Burton paused to quote Sir John Mandeville who, in the fourteenth century, had said that 'Machomet lyeth in the Cytee of Methone', and to admonish 'respectable authors' in the West who still believed that Sir John's Methone was Mecca. Partly concealed by buildings and palm groves were white specks on a green surface, the tomb-stones of the cemetery of Al-Bakia.

Burton rode into Madina by camel in his customary Arab manner, legs crossed, a man of arrogant style; an Elizabethan, as he said of himself, born out of his time. His companions of the caravan preferred to walk, affectionately embracing and kissing friends and relatives who came to greet them. Shaikh Hamid, the caravan leader, had preceded the main party into the town, having offered the Englishman the hospitality of his house. After Burton had been kept waiting for some five minutes at his porch, a transformed Hamid came to greet him, his ragged clothes replaced by a resplendent caftan, delicately edged pantaloons, silk and cotton garments on head and body, and reformed manners to match his dress. His other travelling companions, when they appeared, had effected the same changes. 'As men of sense they appeared in tatters where they were, or when they wished to be, unknown, and in fine linen where and when the world judged their prosperity by their attire.' Most of the men carried tobacco pouches about them and pipes, which showed how thoroughly the Wahhabi influence had been eradicated by this time in the holy land of Islam.

Talk of war filled the coffee-houses, and Burton listened while he sipped the delicious-smelling brew. The Sultan had, it seemed, ordered the Tsar of Russia to become a Muslim. The Tsar responded mildly, offering tribute and fealty. But, so the pundits of the coffee-houses and the *majlis* of the richer houses would have it, 'Allah smites the faces of infidels'. Moscow would be occupied and then it would be the turn of all remaining idolators, beginning with the English, French and Greeks. Burton held his tongue, or when forced to make an observation took care to ensure that it did not affront the popular mood. He took a more serious interest in a suggestion that the bada-win tribes of central Arabia, looking with some pleasure at the chance of dividing the spoils of Europe, intended to provide a contingent for the proposed Jihad or holy war. He still had it in mind to make the journey to Muscat, despite the opposition of his military superiors. An intervening desert teeming with warriors anxious to spread the message in Europe lessened his enthusiasm.

The pious do not delay their first visit to the Haram. First, however, the visitor insisted on sleep and an opportunity to bring his notes up to date. He took his leave of his host's unruly children – he did not see a woman in the house apart from a slave-girl – and settled down to the comfort of a meal, a bed and the water-pipe which the attentive Shaikh Hamid had prepared for him.

After resting, Burton was rejoined by the boy Muhammad, whose sad spirit at being so poor and badly dressed in the holy city was revived by the loan of a gaudy embroidered coat of Hamid's, and by Shaikh Nur his servant who had brushed his tarbush and borrowed some clothes from Burton so as to pass as a respectable slave. Burton himself dressed in white after taking the greater ablution and, because of his still sore foot, was mounted on a donkey, 'a pathetic creature'. They presented a colourful picture as they set out to make the *ziyarat*, the pious visitation.

The mosque was surrounded by 'ignoble' buildings, some touching the holy precincts. The Prophet's resting-place had no prospect from any direction. 'As a building', said Burton, 'it had neither beauty nor dignity', a situation which was not righted until the building of the Hijaz railway nearly fifty years later when a vista was made from the main square to the Haram. The interior was no improvement on the outside. The ceremony should begin at Bab al-Salam, but to avoid the intense sunlight Burton and his fellow pilgrims entered by Bab al-Rahmah, the Gate of Pity, and he was astonished at the 'mean and tawdry' sight that greeted him. 'The longer I looked at it, the more it suggested the resemblance of a museum of second-rate art, an old Curiosity-shop, full of ornaments that are not accessories, and decorated with pauper splendour.'

Already well read in the Muslim divines, Burton had no difficulty in following the ritual. The pilgrim at Madina is called *zair* while at Mecca he becomes hajji. The naming of the ceremonies and the acts of faith demanded of the pilgrim are precisely determined. The visitor here was supposed to use the mosque for five daily prayers and to spend time in it reading the Koran. Pilgrim dress is not worn and the *towaf*, the act of circumambulation obligatory at Mecca, must not be performed at the Prophet's tomb. The tomb must not be touched or kissed as the holy stone in the Kaaba is caressed and adored. Indians, ignorant of the correct ritual, prostrated themselves before the sepulchre at Madina, and they were despised for the act. To sit upon any part of the mosque or to commit any act of contempt is equally a sin. The Wahhabi invaders of Hijaz had held the Prophet's tomb to be unimportant and worship there to verge on idolatry. They plundered the mosque but did not destroy it. All in all, Madina is held by Islam to be more sacred as a town than Mecca, but the shrine of the latter, the Bait Allah, is the very heart of the creed, the obligatory crux of the pilgrimage. Burton, characteristically, describes the acts of devotion and the physical features of the Masjid al-Nabi with a sophisticated understanding of Koranic scholarship and a keen eye for architectural detail. He prayed, observed and paced and by the time he had finished with Madina he was able to draw an exact plan of the mosque, accurately dimensioned, each feature defined and described.

Adopting the ritual position of the hands, and setting off as was proper with the right foot, he and his *muzowwar* paced forward, parallel to the south wall from Bab al-Salam, along the Muwajihat al-Sharifah, the Illustrious Fronting, for the preliminary prayer. Burton apologised for 'the barbarous fidelity' of his translation:

In the name of Allah and in the faith of Allah's Apostle! O Lord, cause me to enter the Entering of Truth, and cause me to issue forth the Issuing of Truth, and permit me to draw near to Thee and make me a Sultan Victorious!

Between prayers and obeisances, Burton filled in the detail of the place and of the sects of Islam in a flurry of observations that were to occupy more space as footnotes than the narrative itself when he came to write them down, though others had given perfectly adequate accounts of such matters before him.

A dwarf wall to the left of the Muwajihat al-Sharifah was painted with arabesques and pierced by four doors leading to small prayer booths or niches. The western door led to an indoor area known as the garden or *Raudha*, after the saying of the Prophet 'Between my Tomb and my Pulpit is a Garden of the Gardens of Paradise'. That saying caused Burton to remark of Islamic traditions posterior to the Prophet's: 'so important are the variations that I only admire how Al-Islam does not follow Wahhabi example, and summarily consign them to oblivion . . .'. On entering the Raudha he was facing towards Mecca with his right shoulder opposite to, and about twenty feet distant from, the dexter pillar of the Apostle's pulpit, the Mambar. He said his afternoon prayer, performed the customary two bows and recited the 109th and 112th chapters of the Koran, the latter, the Declaration of Unity or *Kul, Huw' Allah*, taking a brief and simple form:

Say, He is the one God!
The eternal God!

He begets not, nor is He begot!
And unto Him the like is not.

Near by was the Mihrab al-Nabi, supposed to have been one of
the Prophet's favourite stations of prayer, commonly called the
Musalla Hanafi because it had been appropriated by that school.
His commentary on the *Raudha* was less than enthusiastic.

The *Garden* is the most elaborate part of the Mosque. Little can
be said in its praise by day, when it bears the same relation to a
second-rate church in Rome as an English chapel-of-ease to West-
minster Abbey. It is a space of about eighty feet in length, tawdrily
decorated so as to resemble a garden. The carpets are flowered,
and the pediments of the columns are cased with bright green tiles,
and adorned to the height of a man with gaudy and unnatural
vegetation in arabesque. It is disfigured by handsome branch can-
delabras of cut crystal, the work, I believe, of a London house, and
presented to the shrine by the late Abbas Pasha of Egypt.

The Hujrah, or Chamber of the Mausoleum, gave rise to a formidable account of the Koranic view of prayer and idolatry. The
chamber itself was the room of Ayesha, the Prophet's favourite wife,
an irregular square of 50–55 feet, isolated in the corner of the building. Its isolation was explained by a saying of Muhammad's: 'O
Allah, cause not my Tomb to be an Object of Idolatrous adoration!
May Allah's wrath fall heavily upon the People who make the Tombs
of their Prophets places of Prayer!' But the Prophet also enjoined
his followers: 'Visit graves; of a verity they shall make you think
of futurity.'

Burton took issue with Burckhardt over the spelling of Hujrah.
The Swiss had written the word 'Hedjra', which means 'flight', a
matter of transliteration involving the pronunciation of the first
vowel in Arabic.

As for the chamber itself, a railing surrounded it and only officials
in charge of its treasures and eunuchs who swept the floor were
allowed through its doors. The Hujrah is capped by the green dome
visible from the outskirts of Madina, with an outer crescent of gilt
springing from a series of globes. Muslims believe that a pillar of
heavenly light crowns the building. A special prayer is offered facing
the Hujrah, while most visitors to the Mausoleum recite *fatihahs*
(opening verses of the Koran) at the three windows marking the
tombs of Muhammad, Abu Bakr and Omar. Then, led by Hamid,
Burton visited the sepulchre of the lady Fatimah (usually called
Zahra in Muslim prayer) in the abode she shared with Ali, separated
by a thin wall from the Hujrah. Among the prayers offered here,

he liked especially the poetic tetrastich uttered at the Prophet's window:

> O Mustafa! Verily, I stand at Thy door,
> A man, weak and fearful, by reason of my sins:
> If Thou aid me not, O Apostle of Allah!
> I die – for in the world there is none generous as Thou art!

As others had observed before, there is according to Islamic authorities a space between the tombs of Omar and Fatimah that is reserved for Isa, Jesus Christ, at his second coming, but Burton was unable to find agreement among divines or the lesser mortals who had visited the Mosque as to the real dispositions of the bodies said to be incarcerated or anticipated there.

By straining his eyes through the window and standing on tiptoe, he could see the curtain or hangings described by Burckhardt on which were inscriptions in gold, informing the curious that behind lay Allah's Apostle and the first two Caliphs. The exact place of Muhammad's tomb was distinguished by a jewelled rosary, Kaukab-al-Durri, the brilliant star which the faithful look upon with awe. 'To me it greatly resembled the round glass stoppers used for the humbler sort of decanters', said Burton. 'But I thought the same of the Koh-i-Nor', he added.

Prayer at the eastern wall of the table gave rise to another of those knowledgeable and instructive footnotes scattered through writings of this learned, rough-cast man.

The act of blessing the Prophet is one of peculiar efficacy. . . . Cases are quoted of sinners being actually snatched from hell by a glorious figure, the personification of the blessings which had been called down by them upon Muhammad's head. This most poetical idea is borrowed, I believe, from the ancient Guebres, who fabled that a man's good works assumed a beautiful female shape, which stood to meet his soul when winding its way to judgement. Also when a Moslem blesses Muhammad at Al-Medina, his sins are not written down for three days – thus allowing ample margin for repentance – by the recording angel. Al-Malakayn (the two Angels) or Kiram al-Katibin (the Generous Writers), are mere personifications of the good principle and the evil principle of man's nature; they are fabled to occupy each a shoulder, and to keep a list of words and deeds. This is certainly borrowed from a more ancient faith. In Hermas II (command 6) we are told that 'every man has two angels, one of godliness, the other of iniquity' . . . a superstition seemingly founded upon the dualism of the old Persians. Mediaeval Europe, which borrowed so much from the East at the time of the

Crusades, degraded these angels into good and bad fairies for children's stories.

Ritual duties over, Burton and Hamid received the eunuch's salutation, *ziyaratak mubarak*, blessed be your visit, and the Englishman responded with his usual lack of enthusiasm to the demand for fees. 'Anyone with a high opinion of himself is forced to pay generously to Eunuchs and beggars', he remarked. Anyone but Burton. Female beggars at the mosque restricted themselves to the area outside Fatimah's window, where presumably they hoped that their pecuniary claims would be smiled on by the virgin daughter of the Apostle.

Now, with the duties of the good *zair* completed, they could circulate at leisure, visiting the Gate of Salvation, the Bab al-Salam, handsomely encrusted with marble and glazed tiles, observing the minarets rising from the perimeter wall, noting the historic associations of the pillars of the mosque and ruminating on the history and life of the Prophet and his burial-place. Burton doubted that the Prophet's body remained in the tomb which allegedly marked the spot in Ayesha's chamber where he died and was buried beneath his bed by his companions, Ali and the two sons of Abbas. The mosque or, more correctly, the six mosques that had been built in stages over the 1,300 years of Islamic history, had been burned and pillaged. For a long period Persian Shi'a were in charge of the chamber, and if they treated the tomb of the Prophet with respect it is unlikely that they would have extended the same concern to the resting-places of his successors. One thing is certain: few men, if any, have ever seen beyond the curtain that hides the tombs from the eyes of the world.

Madina was hot and dry in July, though the nights and early mornings were cool and dewy. The people slept on house-tops or along the pathways. Smallpox, endemic in the Hijaz, provided Burton with an excuse to air his medical opinions and to discuss suitable cures for it and other diseases. Ophthalmia, naturally enough a common affliction in desert regions, gave rise to a footnote of a length more appropriate to a medical journal. He noted the effectiveness of 'air, exercise and simple living' in treating most sicknesses. The population of the town he estimated at about 16,000. Sadleir before him had suggested 18,000. Unlike Burckhardt, he found the water sweet.

After drawing a detailed ground plan of Madina and examining even more closely the architectural detail of the mosque – the minarets, despite their admitted beauty and grandeur, he found 'bizarre and misplaced', the famous pillars 'architecturally lawless and without a redeeming feature' – he went on to three places of pious visitation outside the town, the mosque of Kuba, the cemetery of Al-Bakia and the tomb of the martyr Hamzah, the Prophet's uncle. The road to Kuba, with the *harra* ridge now to his west, he found among the most refreshing stages of the entire journey. The earth was sweet and was the source of excellent gugglets, his word for pottery water jugs.

Presently the Nakhil, or palm plantations, began. Nothing lovelier to the eye, weary with hot red glare, than the rich green waving crops and the cool shade, the 'food of vision', as the Arabs call it, and 'pure water to the parched throat'. For hours I could have sat and looked at it. The air was soft and balmy; a perfumed breeze, strange luxury in Al-Hijaz, wandered amongst the date fronds; there were fresh flowers and bright foliage; in fact at Midsummer, every beautiful feature of Spring. Nothing more delightful to the ear than the warbling of the small birds, that sweet familiar sound; the splashing of tiny cascades from the wells into the wooden troughs, and the musical song of the water wheels.

Kuba was the place where Muhammad dismounted from his camel in the flight from Mecca, its mosque built on the spot where she was supposed to have lain, refusing to move for Abu Bakr and Omar but willing to rise when Ali mounted her. The village was a 'confused heap of huts and dwelling houses, chapels and towers with trees between and foul lanes, heaps of rubbish and barking dogs'. It was, he believed, three miles from Madina, though Arab authorities made it two. The mosque was originally a small square, its first brick laid by the Prophet, its perimeter walls marking the footsteps of the she-camel. Osman had enlarged it. In Burton's time it was not the mean and decayed building reported by Burckhardt, though it had no pretensions to grandeur. It looked more like a place of defence than one of prayer. More prayers, more Islamic history and Koranic dogma, more philology and attacks on hypocrites and ill-informed travellers and writers; a row with 'young Machiavelli', his travelling companion Muhammad, who 'preached parsimony to me solely that I might have more money to spend at Mecca under his auspices'; and on to Hamzah's tomb. It was late August.

The tomb stood at the base of Mount Ohod or Uhud in whose shadow Madina stood. It was hung with the usual furniture of oil lamps, which provided no more than a fitful glimmer, and ostrich eggs. Other tombs had appeared since Burckhardt's visit. All were the scenes of much superstition, but Burton was tolerant of the quirks of the East, knowing that Europe could compete with most of them.

Of the holy hill which rose up at the rear of the tombs, the Prophet had said: 'Ohod is a Mountain which loves Us and which We love;

it is upon the Gate of heaven.' And of its neighbour, Jabal Ayr: 'And Ayr is a place which hates Us and which we hate: it is upon the Gate of Hell.' The former had sheltered Muhammad in a time of danger. The latter refused him water when he thirsted. It would be cast incontinently into Jahannam.

Burton was accompanied on this excursion by most of his fellow travellers. Even Saad the Demon, who had disappeared for much of the time spent at Madina, offered to join them and appeared in the best of humour. Hamid, the boy Muhammad and the slave Shaikh Nur all came along on their donkeys, armed with pistols and knives. As they examined the tombs and looked at the wells and mountains, Burton quietly made notes of the ceremonies and superstitions that abounded there.

Moslem divines, be it observed, ascribe to Muhammad miraculous authority over animals, vegetables and minerals, as well as over men, angels and jinnis. Hence the speaking of wolf, the weeping post (one of the pillars of the Medina Mosque), the oil-stone, and the love and hate of these two mountains.

Here, on the holy hill, on Saturday 11 Shawwal in the third year of the Hegira (AD 625), Muhammad and his 700 men fought 3,000 infidels led by Abu Sufiyan. The Prophet lost his uncle, the Lord of the Martyrs, for whom the devout pray on Thursday mornings. Burton left his mark amongst the graffiti in the tomb known as the Dome of Teeth and returned to Madina to join up with the Damascus caravan.

The caravan arrived in the last days of August. 'In one night had sprung up a town of tents of every size colour and shape; round, square and oblong; open and closed – from the shawl-lined and gilt-topped pavilion of the Pasha, with all the luxurious appurtenances of the Harim, to its neighbour the little dirty green "rowtie" of the tobacco seller. . . .' There were altogether 7,000 souls in the Hajj al-Shami, the Damascus pilgrimage. As he negotiated to join this immense, assorted party of pilgrims, Burton heard sounds of gunfire. The badawin of the Bani Harb tribe were engaged in battle, and there was talk of conflict in the desert regions of the Hijaz and westward in Nafud and Najd. He gave up the idea of going to Muscat and concentrated instead on Mecca, pleased that his disguise had held good so far and knowing that if trouble occurred at the other holy city, he could seek the sanctuary of the British Consulate at Jidda. There was the third and last place of visitation, the Bakia cemetery, to be accounted for while he awaited the caravan's departure.

All who die in Madina have a special sanctity. Some believe that

Fatimah was buried in the cemetery rather than in the separate tomb ascribed to her in the mosque. 'There is a tradition that seventy thousand, or according to others a hundred thousand saints, all with faces like full moons, shall cleave on the last day the yawning bosom of Al-Bakia.' About 10,000 of the Ashab, the Prophet's companions, are said to be buried there. The first of the flesh to arise would be Muhammad, after him Abu Bakr, then Omar and then the occupants of Al-Bakia, among whom was Osman, the fourth Caliph, buried within sight of the Prophet's living-quarter. The place was 'full of odour and sanctity', its earlier inhabitants in unmarked graves, though those buried in more recent times were commemorated by tombstones.

They were given twenty-four hours' notice of departure by the Amir al-Hajj, whom Burton calls the Pasha, and thus the pilgrims set about essential preparations. Burton patched the waterskins which had been gnawed by rats. Shaikh Masud of the Bani Harb tribe agreed to provide camels and to accompany them on the journey.

The night before departure they paid off their remaining debts. Shaikh Hamid and his brothers, having treated Burton hospitably, were given money with which to discharge their small commitments. Four routes were open to them: the coast road; Tarik al Ghabir, a mountain path too rugged for caravans; Wadi al Kura, the dromedary caravan road; and Zubaida's Darb al Sharki, the eastern road. They took the latter on the last day of August 1853, having been awakened by gunshot at 1 a.m.

Their path led across the *harra* desert of Madina, the lava-beds reported but not visited by Burckhardt, who took the coast road. Rolling hills were cut by fiumaras passing through the higher ground, the basins marked by ridges and flats of basalt and greenstone. Surrounding the barren plain were the mountains of the Hijaz, their landward sides sloping towards the lower ridges, perpendicular on their seaward sides.

Nowhere had I seen a land in which Earth's anatomy lies so barren, or one richer in volcanic and primary formations. Especially towards the South, the hills were abrupt and highly vertical, with black and barren flanks, ribbed with furrows and fissures, with wide and formidable precipices and castellated summits like the work of man.

Conscious that he was describing the area for the first time and recording features and place-names foreign to the geographers of Europe, he made careful notes on terrain and positions. 'Mahattah Ghurab, or the Raven's Station, lies 10° south-west from Ja al-Sharifah, in the irregular masses of hill on the frontier of Al-Hijaz, where

the highlands of Nejd begin.' On the road and at resting-places Burton observed the characters, habits and wiles of his companions, taking special delight in talking to the old badawin who had joined them
at Madina, Shaikh Masud. He was thin and scarred like most tribesmen, with a white beard and a firm eye. Before going to sleep Burton
would engage him in idle chat, though the rest of the party were
contemptuous of the Master at times like these when he ceased to be
the devilish leader of their band and instead asked endless questions
on such pointless matters as the disposition of places, the weather,
the genealogy of tribesmen. The old man defended him. 'Let the
father of Moustachios ask and learn', he said. The Father of Moustachios needed no encouragement, though the jeers continued merrily,
for the others recalled that Saud the Wahhabi, whom the people of
Hijaz had cause to remember, was known by the same nickname.

His account of the physiognomy of the desert race was laced with
references to the sexual habits, inbreeding and virility rites which
are held in common with, or differ from, those of African tribes. Thus
his footnotes revert to Latin and where the disguise is insufficient for
his Victorian readers he represents the occasional word in Greek.

Since Burckhardt had failed to give us a racial portrait, he provided one.

> The Badawin of Al-Hijaz are short men, about the height of In-
> dians near Bombay, but weighing on average a stone more. As usual
> in this stage of society, stature varies little; you rarely see a giant,
> and scarcely ever a dwarf. Deformity is checked by the Spartan
> restraint upon population, and no weakly infant can live through
> a Badawi life. The figure, though spare, is square and well-knit;
> fulness of limb seldom appears but about Spring, when milk
> abounds: I have seen two or three muscular figures but never a
> fat man. The neck is sinewy, the chest broad the flank thin and
> the stomach in-drawn; the legs though fleshless, are well made,
> especially when the knee and ankle are not bowed by too easy rid-
> ing. The shins do not bend, cucumber-like to the front as in the
> African race. The arms are thin, with muscles like whipcords, and
> the hands and feet are, in point of size and delicacy, a link between
> Europe and India. As in the Celt, the Arab thumb is remarkably
> long ... a perfect prehensile instrument; the palm also is fleshless,
> small-boned, and elastic.

The footnotes to his anthropological observations become wildly
conjectural, the anatomical detail as expert-sounding as it is often
wide of the mark. But his generalisations are remarkable for their
perception. Of face, expression and countenance:

The Badawi of the Hijaz, and indeed the race generally, has a small eye, round, restless, deep-set and fiery, denoting keen inspection with an ardent temperament and an impassioned character. Its colour is dark brown or green brown and the pupil is often speckled ... the narrow space between the orbits impresses the countenance in repose with an intelligence not destitute of cunning. As a general rule, however, the expression of the Badawi face is rather dignity than that cunning for which the Semitic race is celebrated ... the ears are like those of Arab horses, small, well-cut, 'castey', and elaborate.... The nose is pronounced, generally aquiline, but sometimes straight like those Greek statues which have been treated as prodigious exaggerations of the facial angle.

Of the women:

The Hijazi woman's eyes are fierce, her features harsh and her face haggard; like all people of the south, she soon fades, and in old age her appearance is truly witch-like. Withered crones abound in the camps, where old men are seldom seen.

Of the manners of badawin man:

[They] are free and simple: vulgarity and affectation, awkwardness and embarrassment, are weeds of civilised growth, unknown to the People of the Desert. Yet their manners are sometimes dashed with strange ceremoniousness. When two friends meet, they either embrace or both extend the right hands, clapping palm to palm; their foreheads are either pressed together, or their heads are moved from side to side whilst for minutes together mutual inquiries are made and answered. ... The best character of the Badawi is a truly noble compound of determination, gentleness, and generosity. Usually they are a mixture of worldly cunning and great simplicity, sensitive to touchiness, good-tempered souls, solemn and dignified withal, fond of jest, yet of a grave turn of mind, easily managed by a laugh and a soft word, and placable after passion, though madly revengeful after injury.

Then, demonstrating Burton's taste for the sexual ritual of the East, comes a description of *al salkh*, the flaying of the genitals of young men in proof of manliness, a pagan hangover practised in parts of the Hijaz but forbidden in Wahhabi Arabia.

.... this custom seems to be a way of showing virility and spirit. The friends and the father proceed forth, and stand around the young man who sits. ... The 'cutter' takes his dagger then ... peels the skin from penis and testicles by severing the prepuce, beginning at the navel or a little below, and stripping the stomach down to the thighs. The young man ... cries out with a loud voice, 'Cut away and don't be afraid!' Woe to the cutter if he hesitates, or if his hand trembles. If his son cries out in pain, the father often kills him. When the operation is over, the young man gets up and says 'Allahu akbar' ... often, overcome with pain, he lies on the ground. The remedy is salt, and turmeric; his food, camel's milk. The widespread suppuration kills some, but eight out of ten of the excoriated usually survive....

As Burton had already demonstrated in his writings on Sind, nothing was sacred, nothing taboo in his descriptions of the people and places he visited.

On the way to Mecca, he makes a mental excursion through the history and language of the badu digressing into the realms of poetry, intermarriage and incest, medicine, and theology, drawing comparisons with classical Greece and Rome; discussing the idea of passion becoming love under the influence of Christianity and the concept of the Virgin Mother, and dismissing the notion on the grounds that noble tribes of savages display the same principles; looking into the harem with approval, detailing the merits of polygamy and posing the Muslim's question 'Is monogamy open to no objections?'; praising Labid the warrior-bard of Arabia; supplementing his observations with a torrent of footnotes, and emerging every now and again from obscure and often far-fetched argument into impassioned and beautiful prose.

The warrior-bard returns from afar. He looks upon the traces of hearth and home still furrowing the Desert ground. In bitterness of spirit he checks himself from calling aloud upon his lovers and his friends. He melts at the remembrance of their departure, and long indulges in the absorbing theme. Then he strengthens himself by the thought of Nawara's inconstancy, how she left him and never thought of him again. He impatiently dwells upon the charms of the places which detain her, advocates flight from the changing lover and false friend, and, in the exultation with which he feels his swift dromedary start under him upon her rapid course, he seems to seek and finds some consolation for women's perfidy and forgetfulness.

In his summary of this famous example from pre-Islamic 'Suspended Poems', we see the felicity of interpretation that would eventually produce Burton's most celebrated work, the translation of *A Thousand Nights and One Night*, and to some of the finest of all English versions of the legends of the East.

For the present, he was more concerned to advise those who might follow in his footsteps:

The traveller will find no difficulty in living amongst the Hijazi badawin. Trust to their honour, and you are safe, as was said of the Crow Indians, to their honesty and they will steal the hair off your head. . . . But the wanderer must adopt the wild man's motto, *omnia mea mecum porto*; he must have good nerves, be capable of fatigue and hardship, possess some knowledge of drugs, shoot and ride well, speak Arabic and Turkish, know the customs by reading, and avoid offending against local prejudices. . . . There is no objection to carrying a copper watch and a pocket compass, and a Koran could be fitted with secret pockets for notes and pencil. Strangers should especially avoid handsome weapons; these tempt the Badawin's cupidity more than gold. The other extreme, defencelessness, is equally objectionable. . . . He should be careful in questioning, and rather lead up to information than ask directly.

Mirrored in the badu were some of Burton's own most pronounced features, and though he frequently compared them to the American Indians, he painted a recognisable self-portrait in describing them. Wild chivalry, a fiery sense of honour, immersion in the blood feud and the vendetta, gravity and caution in demeanour, formality of manner, love of plundering carried out to the strict rules of the desert; powerfully eloquent, dry of humour, satirical and whimsical, fond of boasting and of pithy proverbs; and with languages 'wondrous in their complexity'. Much of the author was contained in his portrayal of his subject.

The traveller, deep in conjecture, did not stop to describe the great caravan as it made its way across the desert, neither did he give us more than an occasional direct glimpse of himself. It is not hard to imagine the scene, though, as endless lines of camels surged across gravel and rock and sand, proceeding now across the black plain with its mountain-dotted perimeter, tired as the human burden they carried; and Burton, Abdullah the Physician, as imperious as any Prince of the Desert as he surveys the argumentative and weary multitude from the shade of his protective *shugduf*, calmly making notes amid the clamour and turning from his labour now and again to answer the imprecations and pay back tenfold the curses of his fellow travellers.

The caravan wound its way to Al Suwairkiyah, where a fortress of stone on a basalt hill rose above a small township, and beyond to the meeting-point with the hajj caravan from Baghdad. It was a smaller assembly than their own, some 2,000 strong, mostly

Persians and Kurds and a few Wahhabis. There was tension in the air
as the disparate pilgrims met on the road. Soon they were in country
destitute of the hills that had bounded the horizon so far. The camels
climbed up a precipitous ridge and then descended into a broad plain
... 'a desert peopled only with echoes, – a place of death for what
little there is to die in it, – a wilderness where, to use my companion's
phrase, there is nothing but *He*'. Allah follows the man of the desert
everywhere, the causative and expiatory agent in all things, under
whose guiding hand bitter extremes of suffering and cruelty can be
both excused and endured. 'Nature scalped, flayed, discovered all
her skeleton to the gazer's eye. The horizon was a sea of mirage;
gigantic sand-columns whirled over the plain; and on both sides of
our road there were huge piles of bare rock, standing detached upon
the surface of sand and clay.'

Again each stage of the journey is marked off in time and distance,
the topography minutely described.

Marching at night across rough ground covered with thickets they
made slow progress. When they came to a particularly bad ridge,
old Masud would seize the camel halter and while his son and
nephew went ahead with lanterns, he would encourage the animals
with gestures and loud admonitions. It was a strange and wild scene,
'the huge and doubtful forms of spongy-footed camels with silent
tread, looming like phantoms in the midnight air; the hot wind
moaned and whirled from the torches flakes and sheets of flame and
fiery smoke ...'

By now the combined caravans must have constituted some 8–
10,000 pilgrims and a like number of animals.

Burton met another agreeable and knowledgeable companion on
this stage of the journey, a citizen of Mecca called Shaikh Abdullah,
and they and old Masud formed a separate party, wandering off the
hajj road when they felt inclined and rejoining the caravan when
the badawin-infested by-ways became too dangerous. At last they
came to Al-Zaribah, the place of the *ihram*. After dressing, the pilgrims made the two-bow obeisance, prayed and uttered the *Labbaik*,
and went on along the Jidda road. From this point on, the pilgrim
is forbidden to kill animal or plant, quarrel, use bad language,
commit an immoral act or wash or cut his hair. It was no easy regime
for Burton's unruly party to follow, especially in the face of the provocation which soon presented itself. As they entered a deep wadi
a shot rang out from the hills and a camel dropped in its tracks.
The Ataiba tribe were on the attack. Panic struck the caravan, but
the Wahhabis of Najd who had joined them from the Baghdad
caravan needed no further provocation. They stormed up the hill
and quickly silenced the gunmen. Burton, handicapped by his disguise and his recently taken vow, could not join the fight. To demon-

strate his coolness and bravery while all around lost their heads, however, he called for supper.

As they turned northwards into the Wadi Laymun, the Valley
of Limes, they sighted the green-and-gold state pavilion of the Sharif
of Mecca. Burton, against his natural inclination, does not delay to
describe the Sharif, remarking merely that he 'must be a fanatic,
bigoted man', who like the Pope claimed both spiritual and temporal
dominion, though Ahmad Pasha of Al-Hijaz ruled politically in the
name of the Sultan of Turkey. Proceeding under the ordinance of
the *muharramat* by which even the act of killing lice on the body called
for atonement by the sacrifice of one sheep, Burton mischievously
persuaded Shaikh Masud to break a twig from the first shrub they
encountered. His companions roared with laughter, and the
astonished Masud stood condemned and must seek atonement. It
happened to be a Balsamon tree, celebrated in pagan, Christian and
Islamic literature.

In the distance, to their left, arose the blue mountains of Taif.
Soon there were cries of 'Mecca! Mecca!' and 'The Sanctuary! O
the Sanctuary!' and the pilgrims sobbed and burst into loud cries
of *Labbaik*. They passed the Sharif's whitewashed town palace, the
holy cemetery Jannat al-Ma'ala, into the Sulaymaniyah or Afghan
quarter. They turned away across the height of the Jabal Hindi with
its white fort and narrow lanes, and finally arrived at the boy
Muhammad's front door in the Syrian quarter at 2 a.m. on the morning of Sunday, 7 Zu'l Hijjah; 11 September 1853. Burton's distance
from Madina was 248 miles, though projected on Burckhardt's map
there was a disagreement of some ten miles between the travellers.

Unlike Madina, Mecca did not offer Burton a great deal of scope
for his diverse talents. Burckhardt, whose illness had deprived him
of both time and enthusiasm at the former city, had been able to
describe Mecca with all his zeal and power of understanding. Ali
Bey, the Spaniard, had also described it as, of course, had Islamic
authorities whose works were now available in England. To improve
on Varthema, whose detail was sketchy, and Pitts, who was more
thorough but simple, and sometimes naïve, was one thing. To
improve on Burckhardt another. Still, he allowed no obstacle to
stand in the way of full-blooded enjoyment and exposition.

He had become the guest of the taciturn boy Muhammad and
they were greeted by the shrill female cry which welcomes the Arab
wanderer to his home, the *zaghritah*, corrupted by Egyptian usage
from the classical Arabic *tahlil*, as Burton observed with inevitable
precision. He describes the vibrations and rolling of the tongue
involved in producing this ululation, expressing 'now joy, now
grief'.

'Scarcely had the first smile of morning beamed upon the rugged head of the eastern hill, Abu Kubays, when we arose, bathed, and proceeded in our pilgrim-garb to the Sanctuary.'

The journey to the Kaaba, through the Bab Benu Shaybah, the Gate of the Sons of the Old Woman, the prayers, the *Labbai,* the supplications as they approached the place of worship; all were by now well-known aspects of Muslim ritual at this most sacred place, to even the moderately interested European observer. Articles in illustrated magazines of the time described the Kaaba and the ceremonies of the pilgrimage with at least a semblance of accuracy. Yet Burton's account of his first sight of the shrine was to become famous in its day, and to remain for ever after a monument to the descriptive power of its author.

There at last it lay, the bourn of my long and weary Pilgrimage, realising the plans and hopes of many and many a year. The mirage medium of Fancy invested the huge catafalque and its gloomy pall with peculiar charms. There were no giant fragments of hoary antiquity as in Egypt, no remains of graceful and harmonious beauty as in Greece and Italy, no barbarous gorgeousness as in the buildings of India; yet the view was strange, unique – and how few have looked upon the celebrated shrine! I may truly say that, of all the worshippers who clung weeping to the curtain, or who pressed their beating hearts to the stone, none felt for the moment a deeper emotion than did the Hajji from the far-north. It was as if the poetical legends of the Arabs spoke truth, and that the waving wings of angels, not the sweet breeze of morning, were agitating and swelling the black coverings of the shrine. But, to confess humbling truth, theirs was the high feeling of religious enthusiasm, mine was the ecstasy of gratified pride.

He could not, after that passage, resist the hunt for the origin of the word Zemzem.

Some derive it from Zam Zam, or the murmuring of its waters, others from *Zam! Zam!* (fill! fill!) (ie. the bottle), Hagar's impatient exclamation when she saw the stream. Sale translates it stay! stay! and says that Hagar called out in the Egyptian language, to prevent her son wandering. The Hukama, or rationalists of Al-Islam, who invariably connect their faith with the worship of Venus, especially, and the heavenly bodies generally, derive Zemzem from the Persian, and make it signify the great luminary.

Whatever the provenance of its name, the water of Zemzem was found by Burton to cause diarrhoea and boils. And he agreed with those who said that it much resembled the infusion of a large dose of Epsom salts in tepid water. Turks and other irreverent visitors collected rainwater and drank it instead of the holy potion, to the Englishman's taunts and amusement.

After the obligatory *tawaf* he approached the sacred stone, helped through the praying throng by young Muhammad, and kissed it, rubbing his hands and forehead against it in order to form an idea of its mineral structure. By 2 a.m., the crowds of worshippers had thinned out sufficiently for him to pace out the sanctuary as a preliminary to sketching it, while admitting that it had been fully described by his predecessors.

On the second day of the pilgrimage they went out past Jabal Nur to Muna, about three miles from the city, and thence to Muzdalifa with its solitary tower, three miles farther on. Turning northward, they marched to the foot of Arafat, twelve miles due east from Mecca. On the way they saw five men lying by the wayside, dead from the rigours of the pilgrimage. He estimated a crowd of 5,000 at the ceremonies of Yom Arafat, the second day. The badu preferred to stand on the hillside to await the sermon. At 3.15 in the afternoon the Sharif's procession arrived, and the two *mahmals*, litters sent by the Sultan of Turkey and the Khedive of Egypt with gifts for God's House, took their places. The Sharif took his stance above them, with his retinue and standard-bearers. At the top of Arafat a small chapel was once in evidence but this was demolished by the Wahhabis at the time that Ali Bey was there. Burton, thorough as ever, describes the Wahhabi's manner of making the pilgrimage as it was told to him by a prince of central Arabia, Khalid Bey:

The Wahhabi (who, it must be borne in mind, calls himself a Muwahhid, or Unitarian, in opposition to Mushrik-Polytheist and other sects but his own) at Mecca follows out his two principal tenets, public prayer for men daily, for women on Fridays, and rejection of the Prophet's mediation. Imitating Muhammad, he spends the first night on pilgrimage at Muna, stands upon the hill Arafat, and, returning to Muna, passes three whole days there. He derides other Moslems, abridges and simplifies the Kaaba ceremonies, and, if possible, is guided in his devotions by one of his own sect.

Back on Arafat, Burton was distracted from his theological observations by a young girl. She was tall and about eighteen years, of the 'higher classes', with a graceful figure and beautiful eyes surmounted by symmetrical brows. As they listened to the *khutbat al wagifa*, the Sermon of the Standing, Burton was conspicuous in a red shawl which his young companion had spread over his shoulders. She glanced at him and the desire to report the sermon deserted him.

Flirtilla fixed a glance of admiration upon my cashmere. I directed a reply with interest at her eyes. She then by the usual coquettish gesture, threw back an inch or two of head-veil, disclosing broad bands of jetty hair, crowning a lovely oval. My palpable admiration of the new charm was rewarded by a partial removal of the Yashmak, when a dimpled mouth and a rounded chin stood out from the envious muslin. Seeing that my companions were safely employed, I entered upon the dangerous ground of raising hand to forehead. She smiled almost imperceptibly, and turned away. The pilgrim was in ecstasy.

The sermon lasts until nearly sunset, some three hours. By the time Burton took his eyes off Flirtilla, it was half over. Loud shrieks and verbal volleys exploded at intervals as the faithful responded to the Imam's word. Even Burton's shabby companions deemed it proper to shed a tear or two, or, if they were unable to do so, to bury their heads so that the lack of emotion was not apparent to other pilgrims. Then came the race from Arafat as the badawin came helter-skelter along the valley on their camels, urging the animals on as hard as they could, while tents and people, women, children and old men, were trampled underfoot. It was a chaotic scene, described almost as vividly more than three hundred years before by Varthema, though the Italian, being the first to describe the event, was muddled in his account of where he and his companions were and the significance of what they did. As for the rest, Burckhardt's description of Mecca and the ritual of the hajj was definitive, and much that Burton wrote had been said before by his Swiss predecessor. He paid the willing Shaikh Masud to follow the pretty Meccan girl and not let her out of sight, while he sketched the receding holy hill. Later in the day they went on to the ceremonies of lapidation and sacrifice.

The pilgrim, said Burton, was wisely dissuaded from staying on too long after the event, for 'reaction might make the marvel stale'. There was time for dinner with the old Zemzemi, Ali bin Yasin, whose company Burton had so reluctantly borne on the road to and from Muna and for whom he now entertained a high regard. Time, too, to list the places of secondary importance in Mecca, for if he had not time to visit them all he was thorough enough to enquire about them.

He distributed small presents, gave his young host Muhammad a 'just reward' for his companionship and services and made a leisurely way by ass to Jidda, immediately after the Muslim Holy Week. When he arrived at the Red Sea port he had only tenpence of borrowed coin to his name. The British Consul, he was told, was too ill to see him. The war with officialdom, which was to dog Burton throughout his life, erupted whenever he approached civilisation.

He eventually cashed a draft from the Royal Geographical Society, however, which saw him to Cairo and finally to London. He embarked, 'worn out with fatigue and the fatal, fiery heat', aboard the *Dwarka* on 26 Septem'~er 1853. Even at the last his domineering manner caused confusion. He was mistaken in Jidda for the Pasha of Al-Madina. 'I have been diffuse', he wrote, 'in relating this little adventure, which is characteristic, showing what bravado can do in Arabia.'

Perhaps his attitude to life and work, his love of the East, and his inability to accept the comforts and stultifying complacency of life in Victorian England, was best expressed, as so many of his thoughts are best expressed, in a footnote:

Thus in England, where law leaves men comparatively free, they are slaves to a grinding despotism of conventionalities, unknown in the land of tyrannical rule. This explains why many men, accustomed to live under despotic governments, feel fettered and enslaved in the so-called free countries.

As the personal narrative of the pilgrimage won converts in growing number to the author's robust and didactic approach to life and travel, so his zest for adventure grew more intense, his enjoyment of fame more pronounced, his brushes with authority more vigorous and, in the long run, more disastrous. By the time the *Pilgrimage to Al-Medinah and Meccah* was published, in 1855, he was off to Africa, to a lone incursion into Harar, the Somali capital where no white man had been before. There followed the bitter journey with Speke in pursuit of the Nile's source. Books flowed from his fertile pen, bringing to the literature of travel a breadth of knowledge, a command of language, a liberality of thought and a daring prurience that it had not known before. By the time he returned from the Hijaz, his connection with the Indian army was virtually severed. *First Footsteps in East Africa* (1856), his report to the Royal Geographical Society and *The Lake Regions of Equatorial Africa* (1860) added to a renown which now encompassed the English-speaking world. A brief journey to America gave rise to the *City of Saints* (1861).

The Foreign Office took note of his qualifications for public service but the other side of Burton, the social impropriety, the savage criticism of those he disagreed with, especially in official circles, the bluntness and lack of charm (which could be counted literary as well as personal shortcomings), militated against his diplomatic career. The sardonic humour, the intellectual arrogance were all very well in the company of Swinburne and other Bohemian friends, but were no great asset to Britain's foreign relations. As with other able men before and after him, imagination and independence of mind were to prove handicaps rather than assets in matters of preferment; for government service like any other depends on the stability of temperament of average and pliable men.

Burton was made consul at Fernando Po in 1861. He served his country afterwards at Santos in Brazil, at Damascus and Trieste. He was not a signal success as a politician or diplomat, but each new appointment presented opportunities to move among new people, to extend his remarkable command of languages and to produce more books. At his last post, Trieste, he completed his greatest literary work, the translation of the *Arabian Nights*. For a man so given to impulsive and intemperate writing, it was a labour of immense care and scholarship. Open to criticism for the harshness and complexity of its style in parts, it is yet a marvellous example of exactness in conveying the meaning and richness of words from one language to another. It is, even more than the account of the journey to Islam's holy cities, a monument to his knowledge of Arabic language and thought. He was knighted in 1868.

As successive editions of the *Pilgrimage* came from the presses, Burton added notes and comments which showed that he lost none of his vigour as he grew older. In the preface to the third edition of 1879 he took several writers on Arabia to task with all his capacity for disdain and contempt. Dr John Wilson, 'that learned and amiable philanthropist', author of *Lands of the Bible*, attacked the Spaniard Badia, alias Ali Bey al-Abbasi, for disguising himself as a Muslim pilgrim. Other well-meaning Christians, including the late Government Chaplain at Bombay and distinguished Arabic scholar, George Percy Badger, attacked Varthema and subsequent travellers for their dissimulation and, worse, their apostasy. Burton contemptuously dismissed their 'truculent' opinions, arguing that it would be impossible to enter the holy cities of Islam without disguise.

For several years after his own pilgrimage it was widely believed that he was the first Englishman to have entered Mecca. Even as late as 1910 Professor Lane-Poole was giving public expression to that fiction, but no blame can be laid at Burton's door for perpetuating it.

The last salient facts were stated by his wife Isabel in her famous introduction to the Memorial edition; and the final fanfare sounded:

Sir Richard Burton died at the age of 70, on the 20th October, 1890. During the last 48 years of his life, he lived only for the benefit and for the welfare of England and his countrymen, and of the Human Race at large. Let us reverently raise up this 'Monument', *aere perennius*, to his everlasting memory.

Chapter 6

PALGRAVE
Through
Central and Eastern Arabia
1862

'... the men of the land, rather than the land of the men, were my main object of research and principal study.' *Palgrave*

No other nineteenth-century Arabian explorer matched Burton's particular brand of wild and colourful genius, but in 1862 central Arabia was penetrated by another Englishman of exceptional talent: an Arabic scholar, a man of cultivated and sensitive intelligence, a writer of splendidly evocative prose, with a special gift for analysing and describing the human character. Yet William Gifford Palgrave's achievements in Arabia were regarded coolly by many of his contemporaries, and his book, *The Personal Narrative of a Year's Journey through Central and Eastern Arabia*, aroused controversy in academic circles and never received the acclaim which it deserves.

In England scholars were avid for precise geographical information and scientific facts, and expected any traveller in unmapped regions to return with exact observations on terrain, and, more important still, with carefully-noted place-names checked by compass bearings. Palgrave was not by nature a scientist. He was the imaginative poetic observer, more interested in spectacular views than in compass bearings, and more readily involved with men and their cities than with watersheds and continental drainage.

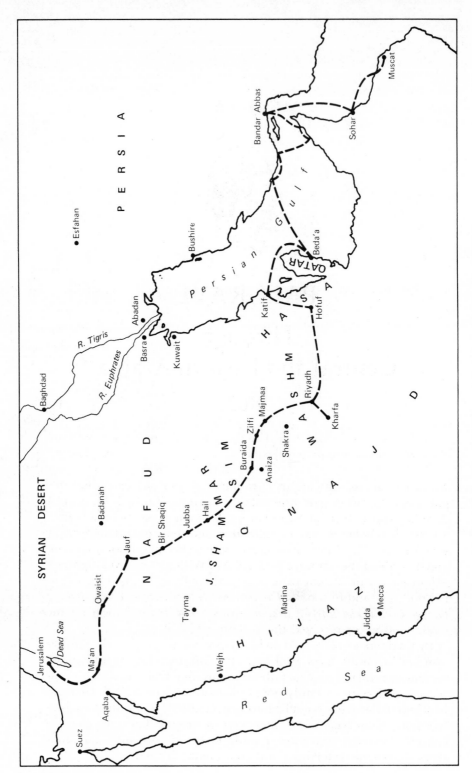

14 Palgrave's route through central and eastern Arabia, 1862–3

To anyone who does not want the technical details so dear to the geographer, Palgrave's book is a superbly readable adventure story of the period, containing some of the most perceptive comments ever written on the Arab mind and the Arab approach to life. He is guilty of inaccuracy, and often of wild exaggeration, and he sometimes improved a good story with the aid of his imagination; but today these faults are not serious enough to outweigh the great merits of the book and they cannot detract from the courage of its author. Palgrave went in disguise to the very heart of fanatical Wahhabi territory, where to be discovered as an impostor meant certain death, and lived for six weeks in Riyadh where Burton eight years before had not dared to go.

William Gifford Palgrave came of a gifted and artistic family. His father, Sir Francis Palgrave, founder of the Public Record Office, had been born with the surname of Cohen, but he took the name of Palgrave when he married a girl whose mother had borne that name. Gifford himself confused the matter of his name by using several different versions at various times of his life. He was reared in the Church of England, and in his early years the Jewish religion of his grandparents was not a fact of any significance, but a study of his life suggests that he inherited from the Jewish strain in the family some of that race's deep spiritual feeling, and perhaps also an intuitive affinity with eastern peoples.

Palgrave's three brothers all won success and recognition in life; the best remembered is Francis Turner Palgrave who compiled *The Golden Treasury*. Gifford himself in his years at Oxford had shown the most promise of all, and yet the distinction which his brothers achieved was to elude him in later life. There was in his character an erratic and indecisive streak; in spite of his brilliant scholarly mind he had a propensity for impractical dreams which faded in the harsh light of experience. The first forty years of his life were to pass before he found what might have been his true *métier*, the Diplomatic Service, if officialdom had not then failed dismally to exploit his talents.

His character was complex, and there is no simple answer to the question, 'What brought him to Arabia?' He was neither an extrovert adventurer like Burton, nor an eager pioneer explorer. He certainly felt a longing to travel in Arabia, but it was a vague romantic longing, which was finally channelled into action only when higher authority commissioned him to carry out a secret mission with political motives.

In 1846 while still at Oxford Palgrave made up his mind to join the Indian Army. His parents were totally dismayed. He came down with a first in Greats and a second in mathematics, achieved together in less than three years, and his family thought he was throwing away the chance of a brilliant career in public service. But Palgrave had set his mind on the East. He had eagerly started on a course of Sanskrit, and was taking lessons in riding and fencing. Before he left London he had begun to learn Urdu.

He duly sailed for India in January 1847 and reached Bombay in March. But for the rest of that year and on through 1848 he had recurring attacks of illness, and his experience of soldiering – he had been posted to the 8th Bombay Native Infantry – was confined to short spells of better health between sickness.

He had been little more than a year in India when his parents received a fresh disappointment. He had become a convert to Roman Catholicism. But worse was yet to come. In March 1849 he resigned from the army to join the Society of Jesus and train as a priest. So ended the first of his false starts.

His family were at a loss to understand his decision. They only knew that during his second year in India his letters home had indicated that he was feeling 'pulled down' by constant fevers and was in a listless and dispirited mood. Jesuit priests were always at hand in India; perhaps the Oxford intellectual, finding few kindred spirits among the young English extroverts in the army, had met among the European Jesuits a friend whose interests matched his own, one with whom he could converse in French or Italian and share his love of literature.

In April 1848 he became Frère William Gifford Palgrave, a novice at a Jesuit College in the Madras presidency, and there he passed the next four years. In 1853 he moved to Rome to finish his studies. He cherished the idea of joining the Jesuit missions in Syria, and was soon hard at work learning Arabic. He was now calling himself Father Michel Sohail, because he believed his activities as a Jesuit might cast reflections on his family if news of him should filter back to the English press. The establishment at that time was prejudiced against Catholics, and the Palgraves were prominent in public life. He did not want them to be hurt.

When he arrived in Syria (a country which then included what is today the Lebanon), he was based at a Jesuit house at Ghazir in the Lebanese hills. Having mastered literary Arabic in Rome he quickly began to learn the speech of the common people as he toured the country villages to preach and try to convert.

His final ordination as a priest came in 1856, after eight years in the order. He was now M. l'Abbé Michel Sohail. During the next four years he was given increasing responsibility in and around Beirut establishing schools and missions. It was a time of gathering tension between the different religious groups of Syria: Muslims, Christians and Druses. Between the last two groups, particularly, feeling was beginning to run high.

The tension finally exploded in the Syrian massacres of 1860, when Druses attacked the Maronite Christian villages around Beirut and slaughtered their inhabitants. The Turkish authorities did nothing to help the Christians, and news of fresh atrocities came in daily. In Zahleh four Jesuits were murdered by the Druses, and Palgrave, who was in Sidon when a Druse mob entered the town to burn and kill, narrowly escaped with his own life.

Europe reacted with shock and indignation at the news of the massacres, and France sent troops to protect the Syrian Christians. In the midst of diplomatic and political activity between the great powers and Turkey, Gifford Palgrave was sent home to tell Europe the facts and appeal for funds. After lecture tours in England and Ireland he returned to Paris, where he proposed to his Jesuit superiors that he make an expedition to Arabia for the Society of Jesus. During his time in the Levant he must have developed an interest in the vast territories which swept away to the south-east. His curiosity must have been aroused by badawin from the Jabal Shammar and the Qasim who often frequented the suqs of Damascus. Among the merchants he would have heard talk about the desert princedoms to which their trading caravans regularly plied. And once a year all Muslim thoughts turned to the Hijaz as the great colourful pilgrim-train set out from Damascus for the hajj.

To his superiors and his family he gave as his reason that he wished 'to ascertain how far missionary enterprise was possible among pure Arabs'. But he had had ample opportunity to hear about the Wahhabis, whose lands were hardly a promising field for Christian mission. It seems more likely that he was captivated by the romantic aura which at that time surrounded the idea of Arabia, but the only way he could satisfy his personal longing to travel in those regions was with the permission and financial backing of his order. The Jesuits, well-accustomed to mixing religion with politics when the occasion demanded, must have seen political advantages in Palgrave's Arabian project. In any case they did not delay in sounding out the French government about the Abbé Palgrave's idea.

The immediate result was that Palgrave was summoned to an audience with Napoleon III. The Emperor had a shrewd appreciation of the importance of the Levant: the construction of the Suez Canal had been started the previous year, with heavy French investment. To have first-hand knowledge of the lands bordering on Egypt and Syria seemed essential for the security of the Canal. Only just over fifty years before, a militant force had erupted from central Arabia and had come north to threaten Damascus. In spite of the Turkish campaigns into Najd in 1814–18 the politicians of Europe were uneasily aware that the embers of Wahhabism had continued to smoulder, and Faisal al Saud had revived the movement to restore

power and dignity to his country after its humiliation by the Ottoman forces. Those who watched Eastern affairs knew also that since
1847 the princes of the Jabal Shammar had grown in power to
counterbalance the central authority. It was important to know the
relative strength of these two political forces; the difficulty was to
obtain reliable information from a land which Europeans could enter
only in peril of their lives. When Palgrave presented himself before
Napoleon III, ready and willing to undertake a secret mission into
the centre of Arabia, it must have seemed the answer to an Emperor's
prayer.

H. St J. B. Philby, the great modern authority on Arabia, believed
that the Jabal Shammar was the area Palgrave was commissioned
specifically to investigate, for the extent of Ibn Rashid's power was
at that time the crucial unknown quantity in the Arabian scene.
Philby was violently prejudiced and considered much of Palgrave's
Arabian story to be pure fiction, but he was probably right in this
particular judgement.

It did not take long for the Emperor to make up his mind. He
agreed to subsidise Palgrave's expedition to Arabia to the tune of
10,000 francs. The Jesuits also made their contribution to his funds.
In Rome the Jesuit leaders were less enthusiastic about the project,
but Palgrave eventually gained their approval, was granted an
audience by Pope Pius IX, and went through the leave-taking ceremonies which were customary for missionaries going to convert the
heathen. In spite of the heady pleasure of receiving recognition and
instructions from the Emperor himself, it seems that Palgrave still
felt a sincere if misplaced missionary zeal. He was now thirty-four,
but had not outgrown the obsessive enthusiasms of a young man,
dreaming up ambitious schemes which did not allow him to rest till
he had worked them through to the limits of possibility.

He left Rome in June 1861 to sail to Alexandria. Proceeding to
Cairo he carried out the first part of his secret instructions from the
French Emperor. He met Halim Pasha, a son of the Ottoman Viceroy
Ibrahim Pasha, and suggested to him that if Egypt put herself under
French rule Halim could be the French Viceroy of the province. In
a letter to Gladstone many years later Palgrave was to write: 'I was
of course in possession of the whole plan, which had very wide ramifications, and which had indeed been in the main elaborated between
the emperor and myself.' One can detect, even long after the events,
a boyish relish in this cloak-and-dagger work, as well as a smug satisfaction in being able to link his name with that of the Emperor as
co-author of the plot.

But the *démarche* in Cairo proved abortive, and Palgrave sailed on
to Lebanon, where he spent the autumn of 1861 in general advance
planning for his journey. He made a practice-run with Sebaa bada-

win into north-east Syria, visiting Palmyra and crossing the desert
to the Euphrates. But Jesuits were not allowed to travel with laymen,
and on his return to Damascus he was reprimanded and told that
for his Arabian journey he must be accompanied by another priest.
Palgrave remembered a young Greek seminarist named Geraigiri
whom he had known at Ghazir, who was by this time a school-master
at Zahleh. This was the companion he wanted, and he requested
the bishop to accept him for ordination. Palgrave spent the winter
of 1861–2 working as a priest at Zahleh until Geraigiri was duly
ordained in February. There was nothing now to stop them making
final arrangements for the Arabian expedition.

Palgrave had decided to assume the guise of a Syrian doctor, calling himself Saleem Abou Mahmood al Eys, and in the succeeding
weeks equipped himself with all the materials of his trade, as well
as some Arabic treatises on medicine and whatever else would add
authenticity to the character. Geraigiri, now to be called Barakat-
esh-Shamee (Barakat 'of Damascus') was to act as his assistant and
also to be an itinerant trader. It was not part of Palgrave's plan
to pretend to be a Muslim. He and Barakat were both to be Syrian
Christians, not drawing attention to their religion, but not denying
it. He realised that among primitive people wary of strangers a
traveller's best protection is a thorough knowledge of the language,
customs, and religion of the country. His years in Syria had given
him a deep understanding of the Arabs, and it was this, rather than
any show of authority or force, that brought him unscathed through
a journey which was at times beset by great dangers.

Palgrave and Barakat set out from Maan, south-east of the Dead
Sea, at nightfall on 16 June 1862, with an escort of three local badawin. They were dressed like 'ordinary middle-class travellers of inner
Syria', wearing 'a long stout blouse of Egyptian hemp, under which,
unlike our badawin fellow-travellers, we indulged in the luxury of
the loose cotton drawers common in the East, while our coloured
head-kerchiefs, though simple enough, were girt by *akkals* or head-
bands of some pretension to elegance; the loose red leather boots
of the country completed our toilet'. But packed in his saddle-bags
Palgrave had some finer and more expensive clothes which he intended to put on when the need arose, to give himself greater status
in his professed capacity of physician.

The small camel-borne party headed slightly north of west to cross
the stretch of harsh, bleak desert lying between them and the Wadi
Sirhan, where they would hit the well-used trail from Damascus to
Jauf. It was high summer, not the season which anyone would normally choose to cross barren deserts, but after earlier delays Palgrave
was eager to get away.

On the seventh day of their hard, exhausting trek from Maan they

reached the Wadi Sirhan, the 'Valley of the Wolf', and were glad
to see numerous tents in this area of more plentiful wells.

His badawin guides had told Palgrave that once in this wadi they
could travel unmolested, since here they were in the dominion of
Tallal ibn Rashid, who ruled with a rod of iron. Though from contacts in Syria Palgrave must have learned something of the ruler of
Jabal Shammar, he professes almost total ignorance about him at
this stage of the journey.

> We could ... obtain but little exact information about the personal
> history or the political position of this prince. Whether he was of
> supreme or subaltern power, whether founder of his kingdom, or
> heir, what might be the extent or character of the kingdom itself,
> and much else, we would fain have learnt.... All that we could
> for the moment know with certainty, was that this chief resided
> in a town called Hail, situated in Jabal Shammar, somewhere to
> the south-east; that he was very powerful; that in his dominions
> neither plunder nor other violation of public order was permitted;
> and that from Wadi Sirhan, south and east, his word was law.

They continued on down the valley, and at the wells of Magu'a
they acquired a new *rafiq*, a desert guide, to lead them to Jauf. Next
day, in the approaches to this oasis they had to pass through a narrow
defile between rocky hills. It had been a long exhausting stage, and
the heat in the gorge was terrible as noon approached. Palgrave's
camel fell several times, but finally they turned a craggy projection
in the cliff and saw palm-trees clustering in a broad, deep valley.
They had arrived at Jauf, northernmost oasis of Arabia proper, and
gateway to the Jabal Shammar.

As they descended the slope to the town they were welcomed by
two horsemen, who produced dates and fresh water for the weary
travellers. It turned out that these two were Ghafil al Habub, chief
of a prominent Jauf family, and one of his kinsmen. With true Arab
hospitality Ghafil led Palgrave and Barakat to his house, where he
invited them into the *kahwa* or reception-room where coffee is served.
As Palgrave remarks, the description of one such room will suffice
for all others, since all follow practically the same style and arrange-
ment.

> The Kahwa was a large oblong hall ... the walls were coloured
> in a rudely decorative manner with brown and white wash, and
> sunk here and there into small triangular recesses, destined to the
> reception of books ... lamps and other such like objects. The roof
> of timber, and flat; the floor was strewed with fine clean sand, and
> garnished all round alongside of the walls with long strips of carpet,
> upon which cushions, covered with faded silk, were disposed at suit-

able intervals. In one corner, namely that furthest removed from the door, stood a small fireplace, or to speak more exactly, furnace, formed of a large square block of granite; ... this is hollowed inwardly into a deep funnel, open above and communicating below with a small pipe-hole, through which air passes, bellows-driven, to the lighted charcoal piled up on a grating about half-way inside the cone.

This type of furnace was peculiar to the Jabal Shammar where charcoal was the general fuel. Further south in Najd, where firewood was more abundant, the furnace was replaced by an open fireplace hollowed in the floor.

The description that follows, of the ritual salutations proper upon entering a coffee-room, and indeed of the whole coffee-making procedure, is an example of Palgrave at his best. Here he is speaking of something that he knows well, and his remarks are accurate, illuminating, and to the point. (There are times, when he draws comparisons with scenes in Europe, quotes poetry, and indulges in other literary artifices, when one cannot avoid the impression that he is covering up a lack of exact information.)

Palgrave gives a detailed account of Jauf, describing its characteristic houses with their round watch-towers, its gardens of vegetables and fruit trees, its palm-groves and its surrounding villages. He estimated the population of Jauf and its environs, including Sakaka, to be about 33–34,000. Such an estimate had to be almost entirely guesswork, and Palgrave usually erred wildly on the generous side. A third or a quarter of that figure might have been nearer the mark.

When he is describing the typical Jauf inhabitants he comes into his own again. His comments on people are always done with great flair, and vividly convey both appearance and general character. They were, he says, 'tall, well-proportioned, of a tolerably fair complexion, set off by long curling locks of jet-black hair, with features for the most part regular and intelligent, and of a dignified carriage.... Their large-developed forms and open countenance contrast strongly with the somewhat dwarfish stature and suspicious underglance of the Bedouin.'

The people of Jauf were liberal in their hospitality. 'Nowhere else, even in Arabia, is the guest, so at least he be not murdered before admittance, better treated, or more cordially invited to become in every way one of themselves.' Ghafil pressed Palgrave and Barakat to stay in his house – he wanted first choice of the goods they had to sell – but Palgrave insisted on separate lodgings, and the following day a small house was put at their disposal. Here they unloaded the stock of coffee, cloth, and other common wares which they had brought to sell if their medical services were not required. From the first their courtyard was crowded with curious visitors and haggling customers. 'Handkerchief after handkerchief, yard after yard of cloth, beads for the women, knives, combs, looking-glasses, and what not ... were soon sold off, some for ready money, others on credit; and it is but justice to say that all debts so contracted were soon paid in very honestly.'

During their days in Jauf they rose before sunrise and went out to some solitary spot in the gardens where they could spend a quiet hour discussing privately their plans for the day. When they returned they breakfasted with neighbours, and afterwards found their house besieged by customers who occupied their time till noon. Lunch was also provided by hospitable well-wishers, and they resumed business for three or four hours during the afternoon.

They visited the castle, a building whose lower tiers contained huge squared stones of some antiquity, to call on Hamud, Tallal's governor in the town. When Palgrave had presented him with a gift of fine coffee the governor offered his services if they should be needed. 'We replied that we stood in need of nothing save his long life, this being the Arab formula for rejoinder to such fair speeches; and, next in order, of means to get safe on to Hail so soon as our business in the Jauf should permit. ... In this he promised to aid us, and he kept his word.'

In Hamud's coffee-room they met three men from the Hail area. 'This was the first time that we heard the genuine Arabic of the interior spoken, and we were both of us much struck by its extreme elegance of enunciation; it is in fact the language of the Koran, neither more nor less. ...'

After a fortnight in Jauf, Palgrave began to grow impatient and not a little worried as to how they were to continue their journey. Between them and Hail lay the formidable sand-desert of the Great Nafud, and in the searing heat of July no one travelled across the Nafud without good reason. All his enquiries about obtaining camels for this next stage met with the response, 'Wait till the dates be ripe', which meant early September.

As it happened, chance gave them their opportunity. A dozen chiefs of a sub-clan of the Sherarat arrived at Jauf on their way to Hail to pay their allegiance to Ibn Rashid, who had recently forced their tribe into submission. Palgrave was able to hire two camels from a member of the group, and engaged their master as guide and companion. The Jauf people expressed their puzzlement that the two travellers should wish to move on so hastily – especially since the figs were in season, and figs were a delicacy that no one in his senses would forgo. But the Arab has always found foreigners a little mad, and they finally put down Palgrave's behaviour to the known contrariness of Syrians.

Their new guide summoned them to depart in mid-afternoon on 18 July, but that day, in accordance with Arab custom when starting a journey, they got no further than the outer edge of the gardens round the town. On the second morning they filled their waterskins at Bir Shakik, the last water-supply until they reached Jubba four or five days' march away. Then, under incandescent skies they faced the waterless Nafud.

Palgrave allows full rein to his powers of imaginative description in telling of their crossing of this terrible desert:

We were now traversing an immense ocean of loose reddish sand, unlimited to the eye, and heaped up in enormous ridges running parallel to each other from north to south, undulation after undulation, each swell two or three hundred feet in average height, with slant sides and rounded crests furrowed in every direction by the capricious gales of the desert. In the depths between the traveller finds himself as it were imprisoned in a suffocating sand-pit, hemmed in by burning walls on every side; while at other times, while labouring up the slope he overlooks what seems a vast sea of fire, swelling under a heavy monsoon wind, and ruffled by a cross-blast into little red-hot waves. Neither shelter nor rest for eye or limb amid torrents of light and heat poured from above on an answering glare.

To Palgrave the Italian scholar, the Nafud brought to mind a passage from Dante's *Inferno*, where one of the circles of hell is conceived as a plain of burning sand. His whole picture is vividly melodramatic, but it would be hard to exaggerate the heat, the glare, the sense of desolation to be found in the Nafud in midsummer. It was a courageous journey into the unknown for Palgrave and Barakat, who had to trust their badawin guides, knowing that often the badu can be feckless and treacherous; Palgrave learned later that some of his guides had suggested pillaging the foreigners and leaving them to die in the desert, but had been dissuaded by others who knew the ferocity of Tallal's justice.

The Nafud crossing 'proved worse than aught heard or imagined', and Palgrave conveys all the weariness and exhaustion that they suffered. But he was wise in allowing his badawin to make the decisions and set the pace. He did not argue with them when they pushed on far into the night when he was longing för rest. And having finally tumbled off his camel and fallen into blessed sleep, he did not protest at the call which aroused them only one hour later to resume the march.

With the water-skins flapping empty on the camels' flanks they came at last within sight of Jubba, and beasts and men summoned their last reserves of energy to reach the oasis. Too tired for elation, they found shelter and water once again: the Nafud was behind them.

After a day's rest they continued on the final stage towards the 'purple sierra' of Jabal Shammar, now visible before them, and reached the range's outer rocky fringes by evening. In the heart of the mountains lay the capital of the Rashid princes, and the way there wound through steep-sided gorges and fertile areas of cultivation. It was, as Palgrave noted, a location which provided excellent natural defences against an enemy.

The party of travellers finally emerged into an expansive plain, several miles broad and long, surrounded by mountains. In the middle of this plain stood Hail the capital, enclosed by high crenellated mud walls in which towers and gates were set at intervals. Palgrave's estimate of about 20,000 for the population of Hail has been modified by later observers to the more realistic figure of around 4,000. Even so, the city was imposing from outside. The lofty tower of Ibn Rashid's palace could be seen rising above the walls, and Palgrave later found that the royal residence and its gardens occupied about a tenth of the city's area.

Upon entering Hail they followed custom and couched their camels in the Meshab, the open square in front of the *qasr* or palace, then seated themselves on a stone bench along the wall facing the palace's main gate. The square was full of 'the better sort of citizens' come to chat and take the evening air, and around the palace gate was a group of richly-dressed officials, some carrying long silver-tipped wands, and others, more numerous, wearing silver-hilted swords.

The new arrivals were greeted by those near them with the customary badawin courtesies, then gradually the idlers of the town square gathered to gaze until Palgrave and Barakat found themselves encircled by a dense throng. At this point they were approached by one of the wand-bearers, who turned out to be Saif, the court chamberlain, whose special duty was the reception of guests. All proceeded well as they introduced themselves. Then comes one of those episodes which make the reader feel that Palgrave cannot let his story stand on its own merits. Not for the first time, he found himself in a tight situation when a former acquaintance, a merchant from Damascus, recognised him and came up to great him cheerfully, asking what he was doing in Hail. Upon this a second bystander, and then a third, all said that they had met him elsewhere, and it was only because he could vehemently and truthfully deny ever having seen the third man that the chamberlain seemed ready to overlook this strange series of recognitions. But did it happen? The hair's-breadth escapes from disaster crop up just too frequently as Palgrave's story unfolds, and the reader cannot help but wonder.

Saif led them into the *kahwa* of the palace. In this large hall with a row of six columns down the centre (later travellers, perhaps more accurate, say five), all Tallal's guests were received and given coffee.

Palgrave and his companion had explained that they were physicians who wished to stay awhile at Hail to practise their profession, and Saif now told them that they could pay their respects to Tallal when he came back from his evening stroll in the garden. They were also told that lodgings and an evening meal would be provided.

When they returned to the square with Saif they were in time to see a crowd of armed men on foot entering the space from the market end. In the middle of this party were three figures 'whose dress and deportment, together with the respectful distance observed by the rest, announced superior rank'. The middle figure was Tallal ibn Rashid, prince of the Jabal Shammar.

Short of stature, broad-shouldered, and strongly-built, of a very dusky complexion, with long black hair, dark and piercing eyes, and a countenance rather severe than open. ... His step was measured, his demeanour grave and somewhat haughty. His dress, a long robe of cachemire shawl, covered the white Arab shirt, and over all he wore a delicately worked cloak of camel's hair from Oman. ... A gold-mounted sword hung by his side and his dress was perfumed with musk in a degree better adapted to Arab than to European nostrils.

One of the companions of Tallal's evening stroll was Zamil, his treasurer and prime minister. The other was Abdul Mahsin, the prince's confidant and friend, who was to be the go-between in Tallal's dealings with the 'Syrian doctors'. He was a man whom Palgrave came to like and respect.

The assembled citizens stood up as the prince approached, and Saif led Palgrave and Barakat towards him. The prince held a whispered colloquy with his chamberlain before he condescended to cast a friendly glance their way. They touched his hand, giving him the salutation of 'Peace be with you. O the Protected of God'. He returned their greeting, and passed on and through the palace gate.

Their evening meal was served in one of the palace courtyards, where they were kept company by two ostriches, and afterwards they were led to the lodgings which had been prepared for them in a small room across the square. As the chamberlain left them for the night and the door closed behind him, Palgrave and Barakat were able to relax once more. For a while they discussed their future plans, but soon weariness overcame them and they lay down and slept soundly. Here, under the protection of Tallal, they could do so without thought of danger.

Next morning they were visited by Abdul Mahsin. This courtier, whom Palgrave found to have 'a cultivated intellect', was a native of Buraida and had taken refuge with Tallal when his family had been killed by Faisal ibn Saud. He had been ten years in Hail, and had won the friendship and affection of Tallal for 'his gaiety, his natural elegance, and his extensive knowledge of Arab history and anecdote'. But he was also a wise counsellor whose political shrewdness was highly valued by the prince.

Abdul Mahsin engaged Palgrave and Barakat in conversation, asking in the politest possible manner how and whence they had come, and seeking to discover their intentions and purpose. He had clearly been sent by Tallal to glean information before the visitors appeared at the royal audience which they had been promised later.

At this point in his story Palgrave sums up for his readers the rise of the Rashid family, historical information which he acquired only slowly in the course of his stay in the city.

During the first Wahhabi empire (1745–1818) Hail had been ruled by its own local princes of the Bait Ali family, who acknowledged the suzerainty of the Saudis in Najd. These local rulers were opposed by a young Shammar chieftain, Abdullah ibn Rashid, who made an unsuccessful attempt to seize power and was exiled to the northern deserts about 1820. During his exile in the Wadi Sirhan he and his followers were attacked by Anaiza badawin, who left the Shammaris, as they believed, all dead on the battlefield. The Anaiza, as was their practice, had cut the throats of all the wounded, including Abdullah ibn Rashid, to make sure that none survived. There follows a strange, poetic story, one of those minglings of legend and truth which grow about a family or personality of such stature and reputation that it seems specially favoured by providence.

> The destined possessor of a throne was not thus to perish before his time. While he lay senseless, his blood fast ebbing from the gaping gash, the locusts of the desert . . . surrounded the chief, and with their wings and feet cast the hot sand into his wounds, till this rude styptic stayed the life-stream in its flow. Meanwhile a flock of Kata, a partridge-like bird . . . hovered over him to protect him from the burning sun.

Thus helped by the desert creatures, Abdullah lived to fight another day. In due course he went to Najd, offering his services to Turki ibn Saud (a cousin of the Wahhabi ruler deposed by the Turks in 1818), who was trying to rally the Najdis after the disastrous Ottoman invasion which had destroyed the capital at Dariya. During a time of inter-family strife among the Al Saud, Turki was murdered and succeeded as amir by his son Faisal. In gratitude for

Abdullah ibn Rashid's services, Faisal made him Amir of Hail, and helped him to oust the Bait Ali and establish his rule in the Jabal Shammar. Abdullah, during his lifetime, regarded himself as Viceroy of the Saud family at Hail, and proclaimed the Wahhabi religion of his sponsors. But after his death in about 1845, his son Tallal, loyally supported by the Shammar, began to consider himself ruler in his own right, not subject to the Najdis. He consolidated his power by military excursions against such outlying areas as Jauf and Taima, which had not readily submitted to his authority. In the Jabal Shammar Tallal was highly popular:

> The young sovereign possessed in fact, all that Arab ideas require to ensure good government and lasting popularity. Affable towards the common people, reserved and haughty with the aristocracy, courageous and skilful in war, a lover of commerce and building in time of peace, liberal even to profusion, yet always careful to maintain and augment the state revenue, neither over-strict nor yet scandalously lax in religion, secret in his designs, but never known to break a promise once given, or violate a plighted faith; severe in administration, yet averse to bloodshed, he offered the very type of what an Arab prince should be.

He had improved the city of Hail, dug wells, and laid out gardens; and 'Tallal's peace' reigned on the trade routes which brought prosperity to Hail's merchant community.

The strict Wahhabi religion which Tallal's father had brought to Hail was relaxed – though Tallal's uncle Ubaid, a powerful personality in Hail, remained faithful to the Wahhabi creed and led a faction which was opposed to the new easier ways. The province of the Qasim to the south, where the Najdis had imposed their religion and rule, preferred the less ascetic régime which they saw established in Hail, and the northern part of the territory had gone over to Ibn Rashid. Faisal ibn Saud, still nominal overlord of Jabal Shammar, protested periodically, but 'judicious presents despatched from time to time to the Najd, and an alliance brought about with one of Faisal's numerous daughters, went far to appease the Wahhabi'.

Palgrave takes up his own story again with an account of Tallal's twice-daily audience in the main square, which was such a notable feature of life in Hail. Each session lasted about half an hour, during which time the prince was accessible to any of his subjects, and gave judgement in quarrels and complaints brought before him. On the first occasion at which Palgrave was present, the Sherarat chiefs who had escorted him across the Nafud made their submission 'much like runaway hounds crouching before their whipper-in'.

The two 'Syrian doctors' had been told that they would be received in private after the majlis, and when Tallal left the crowd
Palgrave approached him and offered the customary salutations. He
then gave Tallal the letter of recommendation which the governor
of Jauf had provided. This piece of paper was at once passed to
Zamil, the prime minister, since Tallal was almost illiterate. 'Then,'
Palgrave continues, 'laying aside all his wonted gravity and assuming
a good-humoured smile, he takes my hand in his right, and my
companion's in his left, and thus walks on with us through the court,
past the mosque, and down the market-place, while his attendants
form a moving wall behind and on either side.'

Tallal, it seems, readily accepted their own story that they were
Syrians, but not unnaturally suspected that aside from Palgrave's
activity as a travelling doctor he had other secret motives for coming
to Hail. Curiously, he believed that their true purpose was nothing
more sinister than horse-buying.

The prince interviewed them as they all strolled together towards
the coffee-room of Hassan the merchant, which stood at the market
end of the square. Then for an hour over coffee he questioned them
on a dozen different subjects, medicine and horses, Syria, Egypt, and
the state of the tribes bordering on his lands. In private, Palgrave
tells us, the prince would normally relax his grave official
demeanour. '[He] laughs, jokes, chats, enjoys poetry and tales, and
smokes, but only in presence of his more intimate friends.' During
this first audience with the foreigners his manner was courteous and
amicable, though still formal, and he offered them his 'favour and
patronage'.

Before evening the chamberlain, on Tallal's instructions, had
found a suitable house where Palgrave and Barakat might set up in
practice, and had offered them the hospitality of the palace for all
their meals. 'Our present lodgings were entirely at the king's cost,
whose guests we were accordingly to consider ourselves, however
long our stay might prove.'

The next morning found the 'doctor' and his assistant ready to
receive patients. 'The inner room on the left of the court had been
decently carpeted, and there I sat in cross-legged state, with a pair
of scales before me, a brass mortar, a glass ditto, and fifty or sixty
boxes of drugs, with a small flanking line of bottles.' They had put
on their best clothes which had been brought in readiness for just
this occasion, they had laid in bread, dates, watermelons and other
refreshments, and Barakat, 'who did his best to look like a doctor's
serving-man', positioned himself outside the door to receive clients
and to admit them one by one to the doctor's presence.

As in any small town, anything new immediately attracted the
attention of the people of Hail. The Syrian physician's arrival was

by now common knowledge, and their courtyard was soon crowded with people, some with genuine medical enquiries, but many calling out of politeness or curiosity. For the most part these people were friendly and without suspicion. Hail was a city on which the personality of the ruler left its mark, and Tallal's patronage was enough to make the newcomers acceptable to the citizens in general.

With the aid of some English and French medical books which were kept out of sight of his patients, Palgrave genuinely tried to help the sick, and his successful treatment of minor disorders gave the Arabs confidence in his skill. As a result he was able to gain friends in all sections of the population.

Among the succession of people who came to see him were rich and poor, princes, palace officials, humble artisans and badawin, and his vivid and often humorous descriptions give us a lively picture of the Hail community. There is, for example, the poor cultivator from one of the outlying villages. It appears the man has rheumatic pains, and Palgrave questions him further.

'What was the cause of your first illness?'

'I say, doctor, its cause was God,' replies the patient.

'No doubt of that,' say I, 'all things are caused by God: but what was the particular and immediate occasion?'

'Doctor, its cause was God, and secondly that I ate camel's flesh when I was cold,' rejoins my scientific friend.

'But was there nothing else?' I suggest, not quite satisfied with the lucid explanation just given.

'Then too, I drank camel's milk; but it was all, I say, from God, doctor,' answers he. . . . Next comes the grand question of payment, which must be agreed on beforehand, and rendered conditional on success; else no fees for the doctor, not at Hail only, but throughout Arabia. [The man offers a fat camel, butter, dates, and so on, all of which Palgrave refuses.] All ends by his behaving reasonably enough: he follows my prescriptions with the ordinary docility, gets better, and gives me for my pains an eighteen penny fee.

One day Abdul Mahsin brought the two elder children of Tallal himself, Badr and Bandar, so that Palgrave might examine them and see if they required any doctoring. Palgrave explains that this was a transparent ploy on the part of the prince to show publicly his confidence in the Syrian physician, and to help Palgrave in establishing his practice in Hail, 'for though by no means himself persuaded of the reality of our doctoral title, he understands the expediency of saving appearances before the public'. There was nothing wrong with the two lads, and they all knew it, but Palgrave duly examined them with the gravity their status demanded, and prescribed a draught of cinnamon water and sugar which Barakat prepared and which the boys drank with delight, 'thinking that if this be medicine, they will do their best to be ill for it every day'.

Palgrave was led to see a sick boy in the artisans' quarter; the house where he was taken turned out to be a smithy. After doing what he could for the lad, Palgrave was entertained by the family. They were from the Qasim, and in their house, which was a meeting-place for Qasim men, Palgrave learned much of affairs in that area. The chief subject of conversation at the time was the siege of Anaiza, their principal town, and the Englishman also heard much useful discussion of Najdi politics and of the bigotry and tyranny of the Wahhabis, to which they reacted with 'oft-recurring and cordial detestation'.

Anaiza was a great commercial centre, but its people also boasted a brave, independent character which made them disinclined to submit to the yoke of the Wahhabi regime in Riyadh. At the time of Palgrave's visit the ruler of the town was Zamil al Sulaim – known by the affectionate diminutive of Zuaimil – who was 'adored by his fellow-citizens and subjects for his gentleness and liberality in peace and his daring in war'. It was Zamil who was now holding out against the besieging forces of the Wahhabis.

By way of contrast to the family at the smithy, Palgrave introduces us to a certain Dohay, one of Hail's more affluent citizens.

This merchant, a tall and stately man of between fifty and sixty years of age, and whose thin features were lighted up by a lustre of more than ordinary intelligence, was a thorough Hayelite of the old caste, hating Wahhabis from the bottom of his heart, eager for information of cause and effect, on lands and governments, and holding commerce and social life for the main props if not the ends of civil and national organisation.... The rest of the family were in keeping with the elder members, and seldom have I seen more dutiful children.... The eldest son, himself a middle-aged man, would never venture into his father's presence without unbuckling his sword and leaving it in the vestibule, nor on any account presume to sit on a level with him or by his side on the divan.

Palgrave was particularly happy in the company of this congenial family. He saw them as the finest type of Arab of the Jabal Shammar, and comments that while in their company he was 'straining the eye of forethought to discern through the misty curtain of the future by what outlet their now unfruitful because solitary good may be brought into fertilising contact with that of other more advanced nations, to the mutual benefit of each and all.' In this tortuous sentence which seems to match the tortuous thinking behind his political mission we get one of the very few remarks which remind us that his journey was undertaken for something more than a simple love of adventure. For the most part Palgrave tells his story without obtruding his own European beliefs and principles. It needs real effort of the imagination to recall that it is a Jesuit priest who is writing with such sympathetic insight about the lives and customs of the Arabs. Not once does he disparage Islam, as distinct from the excesses of the Wahhabis, or judge it from a Christian point of view. In this he differs strikingly from one of his greatest successors in Arabia, Doughty, who allows his explicit dislike of the Muslim faith to colour his own narrative in *Arabia Deserta*.

Even his detractors allow that Palgrave has left us a picture of Hail unsurpassed in the literature of Arabian travel. Avoiding the dry, factual manner of Burckhardt, he managed not only to inform but to evoke in poetic prose the very spirit of the place. He noticed through the day the changing colours of the craggy mountains which surround the capital. He observed the manifold activities of the market which came to bustling life shortly after sunrise. He told how the palace dominated the city, a symbol of the power which gave the citizens the twin blessings of security and confidence. And during his visits to patients' homes he was able to explore the town and describe the houses and the home-life of people of different types and social classes.

But, all the time, Palgrave was aware that he and his companion were being watched by the spies of Ubaid, the Amir's strongly pro-Wahhabi uncle, and indeed by agents of Faisal of Najd. Having been six weeks in Hail, he felt that to delay their departure any longer would strengthen the suspicions of those who already mistrusted them. He requested an audience of Tallal to obtain from him the passport which was necessary for anyone who wished to cross the boundary into Najd. Tallal, who had remained friendly throughout their stay, readily provided a document which stated that the bearer and his associate were itinerant physicians and travelled under his protection.

The prospect of the dangers which lay before them gave Palgrave some anxious thoughts, and he admits that he was tempted to go no further. But determination prevailed; 'we had already got so far that to turn back from what was yet to traverse, be it what it might, would have been an unpardonable want of heart'.

The day before their last audience with Tallal they had, with the rest of Hail, gone outside the city to see the departure of the formidable Ubaid on a military expedition against some of the tribes. Amid a splendidly colourful scene, where the cavalry and camel-borne troops entertained the crowd with sham manoeuvres across the parade-ground, Ubaid's eye fell on Palgrave, and he cantered over

to speak to him. 'I have heard that you intend going to Riyadh'
he said; 'there you will meet with Abdullah the eldest son of Faisal;
he is my particular friend; I should much desire to see you high in
his good graces, and to that end I have written him a letter on your
behalf, of which you yourselves are to be the bearers; you will find
it in my house, where I have left it for you with one of my servants.'

Palgrave was not deceived by Ubaid's protestations of friendship,
knowing that he was a dangerous man, and no friend of Tallal.
Although Ubaid had made an outward show of cordiality, Palgrave
had regarded this as a 'profound dissimulation' of his true feelings.
So when from Ubaid's steward he later collected the letter, a small
tightly-folded packet secured by three seals, he carefully undid the
seals to read 'the royal knavery'. Palgrave's suspicions were justified.
The letter to Abdullah al Saud introduced the bearers as workers
in magic, and magic practices were rigorously forbidden by the Wahhabi faith. Needless to say, the letter was never delivered.

After their audience with Tallal they had asked Zamil the prime
minister to arrange for their escort for the onward journey. The same
evening three guides presented themselves at Palgrave's lodgings. He
bargained with them for the hire of two camels to carry themselves
and their baggage, and was pleased to find the men affable and good-
humoured.

On the evening before their departure a stream of friends came
to say good-bye and wish them well. Among them were Muhammad,
Tallal's brother, Dohay the merchant, Duhaim and his family from
the smithy, Saif the chamberlain, and Zamil the prime minister. But
of all those whose friendship they had enjoyed, it was Abdul Mahsin
the courtier, who called with young Badr ibn Tallal, whom Palgrave
was most sorry to leave.

> All along he had been our daily and welcome companion, and his
> cultivated and well-stored mind, set off by ready eloquence, had
> done much to charm our stay and to take off the loneliness that
> even in the midst of a crowd is apt to weigh on strangers in a foreign
> land. ... Abdul Mahsin assured us, in Tallal's name and his own,
> that we carried with us the goodwill of all the court, and we sat
> thus together till sunset, staving off the necessity of separating by
> word and answer that had no meaning, except that we could not
> make up our minds to part.

In the simple sincerity of this passage we can feel Palgrave's deep
and genuine love of the Arab. Beneath all the planning and scheming
for the Society of Jesus and the French Emperor, it may be that Palgrave's true motivation in going to Arabia was to meet and share
in the lives of men like Abdul Mahsin, and his narrative implies that

it was in such friendships as this that he himself found his reward
for the dangers and uncertainties of the whole adventure.

The following morning, 8 September, they were on their way,
travelling with a caravan of about twenty-seven people and heading
south-eastwards for Buraida. This section of Palgrave's story clearly
demonstrates his lack of interest in geography. Instead of being given
a detailed itinerary we are diverted with word-pictures of his companions, comments on the horse-trade, the inevitable description of
a threatened attack by Harb raiders, comments on Arab justice, and
a discussion of Arab poetry – the latter a charming interlude for
which many readers must surely be grateful. Where he does attempt
a general description of the conformation of eastern Arabia, as in
his estimate that from the Jabal Tuwaiq, the 'backbone' of Arabia
proper, the land slopes away on either side to the Red Sea and the
Persian Gulf, he guessed wrong, from imperfect knowledge.

So they travelled, 'while men of Qasim chatted and laughed, the
merchants conversed, the Meccans quarrelled, the Bedouins, who
sympathise little with the inhabitants of towns, nor overmuch with
each other, rode in general each alone and at some distance; . . . and
the women, wrapped up from head to foot in their large indigo blue
dresses, looked extremely like inanimate bundles to be taken to market somewhere; nobody talked to them and they of course talked
to nobody'. Their course lay sometimes across high steppe lands,
sometimes across sandy valleys where in winter there would be
sudden torrents; water occurred at easy intervals, and firewood was
plentiful along the way, so there was no need to hurry, and they
progressed at the steady five miles an hour which Palgrave estimated – rather optimistically – as the ordinary pace of a riding-
camel.

After six days they had crossed the boundary of Tallal's territory;
then after passing a few low hills they found themselves on the lip
of an escarpment from which they had a wide view of the Southern
Qasim.

As Palgrave and his party descended towards the oasis of Uyun,
lying a few miles distant in the valley, they saw something which
he rightly regarded as remarkable.

We saw before us several huge stones, like enormous boulders,
placed endways perpendicularly on the soil, while some of them
yet upheld similar masses laid transversely over their summit. They
were arranged in a curve, once forming part, it would appear, of
a large circle. . . . Two, at about ten or twelve feet apart one from
the other, and resembling huge gate-posts, yet bore their horizontal
lintel, a long block laid across them; a few were deprived of their
upper traverse, the rest supported each its head-piece in defiance

of time. . . . So nicely balanced did one of these cross-bars appear, that in hope it might prove a rocking-stone, I guided my camel right under it, and then stretching up my riding-stick at arm's length could just manage to touch and push it, but it did not stir. Meanwhile the respective heights of camel, rider, and stick taken together would place the stone in question full fifteen feet from the ground.

Palgrave could hardly avoid the obvious comparison with Stone-henge, and conjectured that the Arabian monument might have the same kind of planetary symbolism as was attributed to Stonehenge. His companions told him that a second stone circle existed at Rass, far along the wadi to the south-west.

Philby, writing in 1920, found the whole of Palgrave's description of the Qasim impossible to accept. Of the ecstatic passage which tells of the teeming settlements of the valley Philby comments: 'Is this indeed the testimony of the eye-witness of that desolate scene, a far-flung wilderness with nothing far and wide to break its monotony except a single oasis settlement – for that is all that he could have seen from that point or anywhere in its neighbourhood – the village of Uyun?'

He then expresses his doubts about the megalithic circle. Philby had not himself visited Uyun at the time of writing, but says that 'Leachman, who alone, I believe, of Europeans since Palgrave's time has visited the spot, failed to notice that monument'. Philby's bada-win companions expressed complete ignorance about such a stone circle, and Philby was prepared at first to leave the question open; but he later learned that the Alsasian Huber had also been to Uyun, without recording the stones, and added in a footnote, 'Huber, an explorer of exceptional capacity and a most careful observer, also visited this oasis and failed to notice the existence of the wonderful phenomenon here referred to. His silence is to my mind convincing evidence that it does not exist.'

For Philby, the existence or otherwise of the Arabian Stonehenge was crucial to establishing whether Palgrave in fact ever travelled south of Hail. 'If it is found not to exist, the chances are that Palgrave never saw it and never saw Uyun; if on the other hand, its existence can be established, there is every reason to believe that he did visit the locality and in all probability Buraida as well.' Philby continues by saying that if Palgrave is right about the stones, in spite of his 'wildly fanciful' description of the Qasim, then his later flights of imaginative description need not invalidate the story of his visit to Riyadh.

For more than twenty years Philby remained unhappy about the circle at Uyun. Then in 1947 when he was the acknowledged doyen of Arabian explorers, he arranged to fly over Uyun to scan the region from the air, still looking for Palgrave's stones. He saw no trace of them, and later a day spent searching at ground level yielded no greater success. He finally declared that the stones were not there.

But a recent biographer of Palgrave, Mea Allan, has come to Palgrave's defence with new evidence. An aerial survey by archaeologists in Saudi Arabia in 1966 revealed that at Sakaka, not far from Jauf, there existed a megalithic circle, dating possibly from the fifteenth century BC. Miss Allan goes on to quote Dr Abdullah Wohaibi of the University of Riyadh, who wrote to her: 'The paragraph concerning the stone circle near al Uyun is correct.... The circles at Rass and near Henakeeyah are also still there, although with their appearance marred year after year because of ignorant amateurs who do not know how to respect such valuables.'

The party took a midday rest under the shade of the great stones, before going down to the village of Uyun. After supper and a brief four hours' sleep they were on their way again, and, to quote the ever-sceptical Philby, 'the next stage in his journey is the non-existent oasis of Ghat, whose gardens and fields it took him, nevertheless, a full hour to pass'. Palgrave, in one of his numerous geographical errors, confused a village north of Buraida with Ghat, which is in fact south-east of the town. He was unhappily conscious of his lapses of memory, for, speaking of other villages seen in the distance, he remarks in the next sentence, 'I heard, but soon forgot their names. Inability to note down at once similar details was a great annoyance to me; but the sight of a pencil and pocket-book would have been just then particularly out of place, and I was obliged to trust to memory, which on this as on too many other occasions, played me false.'

A march of about twelve hours brought them to a hilltop from which they could see Buraida, standing within its oval fortification upon the plain. A tall watch-tower was the dominant feature of the town, rising above 'a mass of bastioned walls' outside which were gardens and groves of palms. Buraida had the reputation of being ruled in the strictest Wahhabi manner. Its governor, a certain Muhanna, was 'the most wicked and heartless' of Faisal's vice-rulers in the Najd, having been appointed here specially to break the spirit of the independent-minded Qasim.

As the guides who had brought them from Hail finished their duty at Buraida, they had to find companions for the next stage to Riyadh. After two days of enquiries they then realised this was going to be more difficult than they had expected.

For three days more we questioned and cross-questioned, sought high and low, loitered in the streets and by the gates, addressed

ourselves to townsmen and Bedouins, but in vain. At last we began
to understand the true condition of affairs, and what were the
obstacles which choked our way.

The central provinces of Najd, the genuine Wahhabi country,
is to the rest of Arabia a sort of lion's den, on which few venture
and fewer return.... Its mountains once the fastnesses of robbers
and assassins, are at the present day equally or even more formidable as the stronghold of fanatics who consider every one save themselves an infidel or a heretic, and who regard the slaughter of an
infidel or a heretic as a duty, at least a merit.

The continuing siege of Anaiza added to the general mood of unrest
in Buraida, since despite Muhanna's presence and propaganda the
town was really in sympathy with its sister town against the Najdis,
and although it had a force of Wahhabis camped outside its walls,
was on the verge of rebellion. Nobody from Buraida would go to
Riyadh except for most urgent reasons, and they were certainly unwilling to escort two foreigners to that citadel of xenophobia.

By the best construction that could be put on us ourselves and our
doings, we were certainly strangers, come from a land stigmatised
by the Wahhabis as a hotbed of idolatry and polytheism, subjects
too of a hostile and infidel government. To be held for spies of the
Ottoman was but a degree better here than to be considered spies
of Christian or European governments.

Palgrave and Barakat made the customary call on Muhanna, but
found him preoccupied with his dealings with the Persian hajj
caravan, which was encamped outside the town walls. The pilgrims
had been held up at Buraida by the extortionate demands for tribute
made by the governor. Later Palgrave felt that it was just as well
that he had shown no great interest in them: 'had Muhanna brought
his cunning and rapacity to bear on us...there would have been
little likelihood of our reaching Riyadh'.

They spent five days in Buraida trying to solve the problem of
guides for their onward journey, but meanwhile there was plenty
to divert them in the Persian camp. Palgrave describes with relish
the colour and bustle of the great pilgrim train, and the personalities
to be met among the crowds.

On their sixth day in Buraida, Palgrave, alone in his lodgings,
was consoling himself with the poetry of Ibn al Farid, when Barakat
entered suddenly with a cheerful grin which betokened good news.
He had found a guide who would take them to Riyadh. It turned
out that in a stroll through the Persian camp he had come across
another Syrian, a man named Abu Isa who was originally from

Aleppo but was now employed by the Najdi amir as a guide on the Persian hajj. He had finished his duty with the caravan and was due to go home to his family in Hufuf. When he recognised Barakat as a fellow-Syrian, and heard that he was looking for an escort to Riyadh, Abu Isa readily agreed to help. Barakat believed that he and Palgrave would be safe in his company, since Abu Isa was known to the Wahhabis, and the final good news was that their new friend's price for the hire of camels was extremely modest.

Once these immediate practical problems had been solved, Palgrave was free to observe the special features of Buraida. The towns of the Qasim differed most noticeably from those of Jabal Shammar in the fact that no gardens were enclosed within the town wall; the houses were in consequence more densely crowded together. 'Space within the walls becomes in proportion more valuable; hence the courtyards are smaller and the rooms narrow; a second storey too, is common here, whereas at Hail it is a rare exception.'

In spite of the apparently busy market, the puritan creed of the ruling power had had a deadening effect on Buraida.

> The whole town has an aspect of old but declining prosperity. There are few new houses, but many falling into ruin. The faces, too, of most we meet are serious, and their voices in an undertone. Silk dresses are forbidden by the dominant faction, and tobacco can only be smoked within doors and by stealth. Every now and then zealous Wahhabi missionaries from Riyadh pay a visit of reform and preaching to unwilling auditors, and disobedience to the customs of the Najdean sect is noticed and punished, often severely.

But Palgrave is objective enough in his judgments to admit that there are some advantages in Wahhabi rule.

> Bad though it certainly is, it was preceded ... by utter anarchy, by the feuds of local chieftains, by civil wars among townsmen and the unrestrained insolence of the Bedouins. Robber and spoiler too the Najdean ruler is, yet with this redeeming feature, that he reserves all the robbing and spoiling to himself.

For a fortnight Palgrave and Barakat waited for Abu Isa to indicate that he was ready to start for Riyadh. The reason for the delay was that he was negotiating with the Na'ib or headman of the Persian caravan who also wanted to go to Riyadh. While the main pilgrim-train went north, the Na'ib wished to go and complain personally to Faisal al Saud about the treatment he had received from Muhanna at Buraida. Faisal had apparently agreed to receive him, for the Persian caravan brought trade and profit to his country.

After an enforced stay of more than three weeks they finally got away early in October. In addition to themselves and Abu Isa, their party consisted of the Na'ib and three companions, a young merchant from Basra, and two travellers from Mecca. There was also an escort of four men armed with flintlocks, who on Muhanna's orders were to accompany the Na'ib to the frontier of the Qasim.

It is unnecessary to follow in detail the progress of Palgrave's journey onwards from Buraida. They decided to go via Zilfi (Zulphah) to the province of Sudair, since this road, though more circuitous, avoided the area of military operations against Anaiza. In general terms it seems that they made their way mostly along the foot of Jabal Tuwaiq, but sometimes climbed the escarpment and travelled along the plateau. Palgrave's topographical information is typically muddled, and causes Philby to remark derisively that he 'makes Wadi Hanifa run backward and accomplishes the astonishing feat of tracking in its whole length the mythical and, needless to say, non-existent valley of Wadi Aftan'.

But Palgrave's sympathetic account of people disarms criticism of his geography. On the long journey from Buraida to the capital his comments on the men they meet are lively and perceptive, in contrast to descriptions of villages and scenery in which it is obvious that imagination rather than memory too often supplies details. On their eighth day the party reached Huraimila, the birthplace of the founder of Wahhabiism. Here Palgrave was surprised by the sight of a large castle 'announcing in its symmetrical construction a degree of architectural and defensive science unusual in these countries'. The matter was made clear when he learned that the castle was one of several built by Ibrahim Pasha during his occupation of Najd. A little further on at Ayaina they saw more signs of the Ottoman invasion. 'For half a league or more the ground was intersected by broken walls, and heaps once towers and palaces, amid headless palm-trees, ranges of ithel marking where gardens had been, dry wells and cisterns choked with dust.'

Two days later, and ten days after leaving Buraida, they stood before Riyadh, 'the capital of Najd and half Arabia, its very heart of hearts'. So this was the secret city of the Wahhabis, which they had come so far to see:

large and square, crowned by high towers and strong walls of defence, a mass of roofs and terraces, where overtopping all frowned the huge but irregular pile of Faisal's royal castle. . . . All around for full three miles over the surrounding plain . . . waved a sea of palm-trees above green fields and well-matured gardens; while the singing droning sound of the water-wheels reached us even where we had halted, at a quarter of a mile or more from the nearest town walls.

After a few minutes' pause to take in the view, and to gather their courage to enter this 'lion's den', they went forward again, skirting the palm-groves which surround the town.

At the town gate Abu Isa's answer satisfied the challenge of the guards; they went through, and found themselves in a broad street which ran straight to the castle. The houses on either side were mostly of two storeys; mosques were numerous. They passed on the right the large new palace of the prince Abdullah, and on the left that of Jiluwi, Faisal's brother. At the end the street opened into a great square, whose southern side was formed entirely by the huge royal residence. 'In front of us, and consequently to the west a long covered passage, upborne high on a clumsy colonnade, crossed the breadth of the square and reached from the palace to the great mosque, which it thus joins directly with the interior of the castle, and affords old Faisal a private and unseen passage at will from his own apartments to his official post at the Friday prayers, without exposing him on his way to vulgar curiosity, or perhaps to the danger of treachery.' Faisal's father and great-uncle had both been assassinated while at worship in the mosque.

Behind the colonnade were shops and warehouses, which formed the north side of the square. Under the palace walls sat women with goods laid on the ground for sale, and the usual crowds of loiterers, camels, and piles of merchandise filled the rest of the area.

Understandably, at this point Palgrave's thoughts were not on the sights and sounds of the market-place. As they were about to enter the palace, the very citadel of Wahhabi fanaticism, he felt some apprehension. The great doorway was in itself forbidding.

Deep sunk between the bastions, with massive folding-doors iron-bound, though thrown open at this hour of the day, and giving entrance into a dark passage, one might easily have taken it for the vestibule of a prison; while the number of guards, some black, some white, but all sword-girt, who almost choked the way, did not seem very inviting to those without, especially to foreigners. Long earth-seats lined the adjoining walls, and afforded a convenient waiting-place for visitors; and here we took up our rest at a little distance from the palace gate; but Abu Isa entered at once to announce our arrival and the approach of the Na'ib.

For half an hour Palgrave and Barakat waited. No one spoke to them. Finally they were approached by a certain Abdul Aziz, the minister in charge of receiving foreign guests. Palgrave was to come to know him better, and says of him, 'His personal qualities are those which distinguish the majority of old Riyadh families. . . . A reserved and equable exterior, a smooth tongue, a courteous though grave manner, and beneath this, hatred, envy, rapacity, and licentiousness enough to make his intimacy dangerous, his enmity mortal, and his friendship suspected.' These, he declares, were the characteristics of the people from the Aridh district, who formed the hard core of the Wahhabi movement.

The usual invitation to coffee followed and Palgrave and Barakat were led into the palace. Abdul Aziz, with a smiling show of welcome, promised them a chance to speak to the king himself later.

Inside its high walls the palace was a sprawling conglomeration of inter-connecting households. In one block, a kind of 'palace within a palace', Faisal had his own private rooms, in addition to those of the harem, and there were also special quarters for his fifty-year-old unmarried daughter who acted as her father's confidential secretary. These parts were of three storeys, standing about sixty feet high. A glacis on the outside, adding to the thickness of the walls, confirmed the impression that this was a fortified keep within the castle itself.

Other parts of the palace were taken up by public reception rooms, a prison, kitchens, a private mosque, a section of workshops for the exclusive service of the royal family, and an arsenal and powder-magazine. In ever-extending ramifications there were quarters for Abdul Aziz, the man who had received them, Mahbub, the prime minister, Jauhar, the state treasurer, and other officials, with about seventy servants and their families. There was also a secret gate from the castle allowing for emergency escape. The rulers of Riyadh did not lie easy in their beds. In this labyrinthine castle, with its air of suspicion and watchfulness, informers and spies were everywhere, and intrigue flourished.

Palgrave came to know all the details of the palace later. For the moment, he and Barakat saw only the *kahwa*, where they took coffee among a group of other visitors who hardly dared speak for fear of Faisal's spies. Here they waited from early morning till noon, when finally a slave invited them to go upstairs and eat. When they had finished a rather modest meal, the Na'ib, who had arrived later than themselves, was also shown in, protesting indignantly because he could not obtain an immediate audience with Faisal.

Temporary quarters had been allotted to Palgrave and Barakat in Jiluwi's palace, and here they were later taken by Abdul Aziz. They had asked him on their first meeting if they might practise medicine in Riyadh, and now they tried to find out if the king had granted his permission, but Abdul Aziz parried their questions with vague assurances. In fact, as they later heard, Faisal, now old and blind and fearing enemies round every corner, had been thrown into a state of senile panic at the news of the arrival of Syrians and Persians in the capital. He had therefore left the castle by the secret gate and taken refuge in a secluded palm-garden on the other side of the town.

Here the old king hoped that he might escape 'the contaminations of polytheism and the perils of assassination, spells, and evil eyes'.

Unaware of all this, Palgrave and Barakat were unpacking in their rooms, and snatching the opportunity to enjoy the forbidden solace of tobacco. But the Wahhabi spy system was already in operation, and a knock on the door caused them to put out their pipes hurriedly. For a minute they delayed to give the smoke time to disperse, and then admitted their visitor. He was dressed in the manner of Afghanistan, and introduced himself as Abdul Hamid, a prince of north-west India. He was resident in Faisal's palace where he claimed to be a student of religion. Later Palgrave discovered that he was no prince but a murderer on the run from Peshawar; Faisal employed him as his chief spy, since Abdul Hamid, with his obvious foreign origins, was able to put strangers off their guard and encourage them to speak openly.

No sooner had their caller sat down than he

commenced cross-questioning and throwing out hints like angling-hooks, in hopes to fish up truth from the bottom of the well. ... Abdul Hamid tried me with Hindustani, Persian, and even a few words of broken English, but all in vain, and ended by inwardly concluding that the matter was far from satisfactory. Then he rose in a rather abrupt manner, and left us to give his report to those who had sent him. That this report was highly unfavourable I afterwards learnt.

Not long after the spy's departure they had a visitor of a different kind. He was a *Meddeyyi*, which Palgrave translates as 'Zelator', one of the secret council of the Riyadh government. When a cholera epidemic had ravaged the city in the 1850s, the Wahhabis had seen it as God's retribution for the general laxity in dress and manners which had crept into Najdi life following the Egyptian occupation. Believing that only a return to the original strictness of the faith would save them from the disease, the elders of the city had formed the band of Zelators, twenty-two in number, to purge Riyadh of its evil ways. They were chosen from the most exemplary of the inhabitants, and had absolute power to denounce offenders and to punish by beatings and fines. The list of offences which they were to eradicate was lengthy, and included smoking tobacco, wearing rich clothes, playing musical instruments, allowing children to play street games, talking or burning a light in the house after evening prayers, neglecting any of the stipulated prayer-times, and swearing by any name save that of the Almighty.

Palgrave describes the way they went about their duties. 'Pacing from street to street, or unexpectedly entering the houses to see if there is anything incorrect going on there, they do not hesitate to inflict at once and without any preliminary form of trial or judgment, the penalty of stripes on the detected culprit.' The prying and punishment of the Zelators was not confined to the poorer citizens. 'Rank itself was no protection, high birth no shelter.... Jiluwi, Faisal's own brother, was beaten with rods at the door of the king's own palace for a whiff of tobacco smoke; and his royal kinsman could not or would not save him.'

The activities of the Zelators had become a little less severe since their first institution, but their numbers were kept up, and they provided a powerful force ready at Faisal's command. The people of Riyadh treated them in public with great respect, while cordially hating them behind their backs.

The representative of this powerful body who called on Palgrave was typical of his kind, simply dressed, carrying his staff of office, and walking with the downcast eyes and grave manner which distinguished the Zelator from the ordinary people.

In conversation with the visitor, Palgrave's profound Arabic scholarship stood him in good stead. The Zelator naturally spoke of religious affairs, 'but he had luckily encountered his match; for every citation of the Koran we replied with two', says Palgrave, and he was able to hold his own in the ensuing discussion of learned theological commentaries until the Zelator relaxed and became 'half a friend'.

It was obvious from the start that to arrange a stay in Riyadh was not going to be as easy as it had been at Hail. Before Palgrave had time to find a private lodging from which he could do his doctoring, Abdul Aziz told them that the king did not consider Riyadh a suitable place for them to practise medicine. He suggested that Abu Isa should take them straight on to Hufuf, saying that Faisal was ready to give them each a camel, a new suit of clothes, and money, if they departed.

'Our own position was now an awkward one', writes Palgrave. 'We were thoroughly determined not to quit Riyadh till after fully satisfying our curiosity relative to its government, people, and whatever else it contained; yet how to prolong our stay?' In the end it was Abu Isa who suggested that a well-chosen gift in the right quarter might prove effective. That evening he went out to buy sandalwood, or *ood*, a luxury much loved by Najdis, and in the name of the doctor and his assistant left a packet of the precious commodity at the doors of Mahbub and Abdul Aziz. He believed that Faisal would be influenced by the opinion of his ministers.

Abu Isa's estimate of the situation proved quite correct. Next morning he was summoned to the king, who said that on reflection he had decided that Riyadh did stand in need of a doctor, and that the two Syrians were permitted to remain in that capacity, and might freely exercise their profession under Faisal's own patronage. This was the news they most wished to hear, and they now went ahead and established themselves in a small house which Abu Isa had found for them in a part of the town some distance from the palace.

Before telling us of their further adventures, Palgrave gives an exhaustive and often entertaining account of the intricate web of life in the city, with digressions on all manner of related subjects: the badawin, mosque architecture, camels, the abundance of game in the desert, slavery, agriculture, and the Najdi character. Done with a seeming artlessness, these detailed and wide-ranging observations build up into a comprehensive and valuable picture of Riyadh under Faisal's rule. Palgrave knew well that his penetration of the Wahhabi capital was his most important achievement and would be his chief claim to fame when he returned to Europe. He was the first European to see Riyadh. G. F. Sadleir, who had preceded him into Najd in 1819 on a mission from the East India Company, was there before Riyadh had become the capital city. He had seen only Dariya, the former capital, by now lying in ruins after the Egyptian attack.

Through the energetic propaganda of Abu Isa, who was well known at court, several important Wahhabi officials came for medical advice as soon as Palgrave and Barakat had set up in business. One of their first patients was Jauhar, the treasurer, a tall, handsome negro, splendidly dressed and wearing a gold-hilted sword. (In the Wahhabi casuistry a sword was not part of the dress, therefore gold was permissible on it.) Then there was Abdul Rahman, the 'palace chaplain', and Abdul Latif, the kadhi of Riyadh.

As the days passed, Palgrave came to know, by reputation if not personally, the royal family in Riyadh. Of the information he gathered much was totally new to Europe. Faisal, the once-great king, now in his old age was leaving his eldest son Abdullah to direct affairs. He had become a frightened recluse to whom only the Zelators and Mahbub the prime minister had unlimited access. Abdullah hated his half-brother Saud, who was made governor of Yamama and Hariq to get him out of Riyadh. Palgrave foresaw war between them when their father died, and indeed their rivalry was to last many years. Muhammad, Faisal's third son, was at that time in command of the forces besieging Anaiza. Of the fourth son, Abdul Rahman, Palgrave says he was 'a heavy-looking boy, who as yet inhabits his father's harem. He appeared to me to be between ten and twelve years old.' (This boy, when grown to manhood, became the father of King Abdul Aziz Ibn Saud, founder of today's state of Saudi Arabia.)

Having given an estimate of the strength of Wahhabi feeling in the various provinces of the country, Palgrave draws the following conclusions:

> To sum up, we may say that the Wahhabi empire is a compact and well-organised government, where centralisation is fully understood and effectually carried out, and whose mainsprings and connecting-links are force and fanaticism. There exist no constitutional checks either on the king or on his subordinates, save what the necessity of circumstance imposes or the Koran prescribes. Its atmosphere, to speak metaphorically, is sheer despotism, moral, intellectual, religious, and physical. This empire is capable of frontier extension, and hence is dangerous to its neighbours, some of whom it is even now swallowing up, and will certainly swallow more if not otherwise prevented. Incapable of true internal progress, hostile to commerce, unfavourable to arts and even to agriculture, and in the highest degree intolerant and aggressive, it can neither better itself nor benefit others.

In the peculiar circumstances of life in Riyadh they did not request an audience of the king, nor were they too eager to meet his son Abdullah. But they were not for long allowed to go about their business before a messenger arrived to say that Abdullah needed a doctor's services. In fact this was merely an excuse to bring Palgrave and Barakat to his palace so that he might satisfy his curiosity about them. After a long conversation he ordered them to visit him again on the morrow, and thus began a series of almost daily visits which continued for three weeks. During this time Palgrave felt that they had almost succeeded in winning Abdullah's confidence, and even the palace servants gave them a cheerful greeting when they arrived for their regular audience.

One result of this friendship was that Palgrave was asked to visit the royal stables to cure a mare which had developed a festering wound after a bite from another horse. Palgrave treated her as best he could. He writes at length about the stables and the horses there – 'never had I seen or imagined so lovely a collection' – and his remarks on the Najdi horse became celebrated in his day, till the more knowledgeable Blunts were to dismiss them as absurd.

Seeing the foreigners established in Abdullah's good graces caused a yet more powerful man to pay them a visit. This was Mahbub, the prime minister. Though Palgrave had heard much about him, he admits to being utterly startled on seeing him for the first time. Mahbub was 'so very boyish, so un-Najdean, so un-Arab in appearance'. The reason for this was that his mother was a Georgian slave woman; his father, though no one said so openly, was Faisal himself.

The youth is clever, of that there could be no doubt; that he is daring is equally certain. ... But vanity, imprudence, overbearing pride, despotic cruelty, and a levity of manner strangely contrasting with the gravity customary at Riyadh, are equally the share of Mahbub, nor any wonder, considering his origin and palace education. These faults are however in a measure veiled, ... by a manly independence of thought and manner, an outspoken tone, and a hearty cheerfulness at times, ... qualities certainly due to his mother rather than to his father. Last, not least perhaps, he is remarkably handsome, almost beautiful, a thorough Georgian.... Thus endowed in mind and body, this half-caste Caucasian stripling ... leads by the nose the old tyrant of Najd, browbeats his terrible son [Abdullah], commands the servility of courtiers, chiefs and Zelators, and wields almost alone the destinies of more than half the Arabian Peninsula.

'The graceful but blood-stained Mahbub' was only about twenty-five at the time, and Palgrave could hardly believe that his was the real power behind the throne. Nevertheless on Abu Isa's advice he was prudent enough to treat him with a healthy respect, and on the day following Mahbub's social visit Palgrave returned his call. Palgrave feared that the prime minister thought him an Egyptian spy, but Mahbub invited him back to his quarters in the palace for further visits after the courtesy calls. Palgrave was excited to find that the young minister owned the finest library he had yet seen in Arabia.

Mahbub was outwardly friendly; he arranged that Palgrave should be supplied with meat and coffee from the palace. He also gave the 'doctor' a handsome sum of money, 'which I accepted in the hopes of thereby lessening his preconceived suspicions. But his eye was always on me with the restless unsatisfied expression of one who pries into deep water for something at the bottom and cannot quite distinguish it.'

During their stay in the city plans were being made for a new and decisive attack against Anaiza, to be led by Abdullah. Saud, the ruler's second son, had been summoned from Hariq with troops to reinforce the army. His arrival in Riyadh provided the only occasion when Palgrave saw the king himself appear in public at his palace gate.

There sat the blind old tyrant, corpulent, decrepit, yet imposing, with his large broad forehead, white beard, and thoughtful air, clad in all the simplicity of a Wahhabi; the gold-hafted sword at his side his only ornament or distinction.... Up came Saud with the bearing of a hussar officer, richly clad in Cachemire shawls and a gold wrought mantle, while man by man followed his red dressed cavaliers, their spears over their shoulders and their swords hanging down.

The whole square filled up with armed men, forming an impressive spectacle; then, when all were drawn up before the king, Saud dismounted and bowed to kiss his father's hand.

With Saud's presence in the capital, the known hatred between himself and his brother Abdullah caused an atmosphere of heightened tension. Only with difficulty did Faisal persuade his sons to meet each other and avoid a public scandal. 'Intrigues, treasons, violence itself were hatching beneath the palace walls, and assassination, whether by the dagger or the bowl, I had better said the coffeecup, would have been quite in keeping.'

Although Palgrave and Barakat had never been able to relax in Riyadh as they had in Hail, they were justified in feeling that things had gone tolerably well for them during the month or more that they had managed to stay in the city. But now, in the already charged atmosphere, Palgrave knew that he had incurred Abdullah's disfavour. The truth was that he had grown impatient with Abdullah's importunate demands, and had on one or two occasions allowed his irritation to get the better of him.

There were two ways in which a dangerous foreign visitor could be rendered harmless. He could be killed, or prevented from ever leaving. Abdullah now proceeded to use the second technique on Palgrave by offering him a house and a wife, declaring 'that he could not think of letting Riyadh lose so valuable a physician'. Although Palgrave expressed his refusal as diplomatically as possible, Abdullah was obviously displeased.

Then came a more serious cause of trouble between them. In treating one of his patients Palgrave had effected a cure with a judicious use of strychnine, and the news of this particular case had spread through the town. Abdullah, after his offer of a house had been rejected, called Palgrave to the palace and requested from him some of his medicines, in particular some of the strychnine. There was no doubt that Abdullah knew the poisonous properties of this drug, and Palgrave felt certain that he wished to use it against his brother Saud. After the 'doctor' had firmly but politely refused, Abdullah renewed his demands the next day.

When a flat denial on my part had been met by an equally flat rejection and a fresh demand, I turned right towards him, lifted up the edge of his head-dress, and said in his ear, 'Abdullah, I know well what you want the poison for, and I have no mind to be an accomplice in your crimes. You shall never have it.'

Abdullah's face grew black with rage. It was an awkward moment, but the prince controlled himself, and a few minutes later left the coffee-room.

After this it was obvious that the two foreigners could no longer stay in Riyadh and they began to discuss plans for leaving as soon as possible. But the same evening, 21 November, Palgrave was again summoned to the palace and shown into a room where Abdullah sat with some of the most powerful men in the city. There were Abdul Latif the kadhi, some of the Zelators, and Mahbub, looking unusually serious.

When Palgrave entered none of them returned his salutation. He was signalled to sit down.

After an interval of silence, Abdullah turned half round towards me, and with his blackest look and a deep voice said, 'I now know perfectly well what you are; you are no doctors, you are Christians, spies and revolutionists ('mufsideen') come hither to ruin our religion and state in behalf of those who sent you. The penalty for such as you is death, that you know, and I am determined to inflict it without delay.'

Palgrave remained remarkably cool. Looking Abdullah straight in the face he replied, '*Istaghfir Allah* – ask pardon of God!' – a phrase commonly used to someone who has said something extremely out of place.

There followed a courageous speech by the threatened Englishman. ' "Christians", be it so', he replied, 'but "spies", "revolutionists", – as if we were not known by everybody in your town for quiet doctors, neither more nor less!' And he went on to point out that for a month and more he had been Faisal's guest, and therefore under the Arab laws of hospitality it would be impossible for Abdullah to harm him.

Abdullah threatened that he could have Palgrave killed secretly, and none would know, but Palgrave raised his voice and called on all present to bear witness that if any harm befell him it would be Abdullah's doing. At this an ominous silence filled the room.

Suddenly, Abdullah called for coffee, and a slave appeared bearing the coffee-pot. But there was only one cup in his right hand into which he poured, presenting it to Palgrave. The thought immediately ran through Palgrave's head that the cup was poisoned, but quickly assessing his chances he remembered that Abdullah would probably not have asked him for poison if he already had some on hand. 'So I said "*Bismillah*," took the cup, looked very hard at Abdullah, drank it off, and then said to the slave, "Pour me out a second." This he did; I swallowed it, and said, "Now you may take the cup away." '

It was a brave, dramatic gesture, and it had the effect of defusing the threats of the Wahhabi prince. After a little more general conversation Palgrave was able to take his leave. It was nearly midnight as he walked home through the dark and deserted streets, where he suddenly felt a 'feeling of lonely dread,' a kind of delayed shock after the events of the evening. Discussing the situation with Barakat, Palgrave decided that they should delay a day or two longer lest too hasty a flight should imply fear. Fortunately everyone at the palace was occupied with the departure of the troops for Anaiza.

On 24 November they packed and loaded three camels supplied by Abu Isa. Then, at the time of evening prayer when every man in the city was at the mosque, they crept stealthily from their lodgings, accompanied by Abu Isa and a servant, Mubayrik, and left Riyadh by the small northern gate, which for the moment was unattended. They headed rapidly south-east, making for cover behind a range of low hillocks. Here they stopped and waited till nightfall, but once it was dark they lit a camp-fire, and laughed with relief at having escaped from Abdullah's clutches. To save Abu Isa from incurring any blame on their account they decided that he should return to Riyadh, setting out again later with a merchant caravan which was due to leave in a few days for Hasa. Meantime he was to show himself openly in the palace and deny all knowledge of the foreigners' departure.

Abu Isa agreed to meet them in due course in the Wadi Sulai, on the way to Hasa, and they now made their way there guided by Mubayrik. They passed three days hiding in a sandy hollow, out of sight of the beaten track. Then, when they were beginning to grow anxious, Abu Isa reappeared. He had told Abdullah and Mahbub that the 'doctors' had taken the road northwards to Zubair, and he believed they were all now safe. The party proceeded to catch up with the large Hasa caravan with whom they were going to make their way to Hufuf.

The whole story of the confrontation with Abdullah and the escape from Riyadh makes racy reading – so much so that Palgrave has been accused of creating an adventure story worthy of the *Boy's Own Paper*. But the details are convincing, and once one accepts the extraordinary fact that Palgrave managed to survive six weeks in the Wahhabi capital, there is nothing unlikely about the manner of his escape. It would have been perhaps more surprising if this Englishman in disguise had not at some point in his six-week stay aroused Wahhabi suspicions and threats.

They marched on with the caravan for two days, and on the third watered at the wells of Uwaisit, the last water-supply before the sand-belt of the Dahana. The same evening they entered the rolling dune-country before stopping for the night. Palgrave's description of their surroundings when they stopped in the sands after dark has a magical quality. 'Around us loomed high ridges, shutting us in before and behind with their white ghost-like outlines; below our feet the lifeless sand, and everywhere a silence that seemed to belong to some strange and dreamy world where man might not venture.'

The following day they fell in with a band of Al Murra badawin, the most savage and primitive-looking of all the tribesmen that Palgrave had seen. Later they passed the Hasa army making its way to join Abdullah's campaign, dragging two heavy guns which had been sent from Qatif to help batter the walls of Anaiza.

That night they left the sand-belt, and stopped to rest on a gravel plain. Two more monotonous days of marching brought them down to the level of the Hasa coast. Knowing that they were now only fifteen miles from their destination, they decided to continue through the night. They might have reached Hufuf by dawn if they had not come across locusts in the night. The swarms were visible as large black patches on the white moonlit sand, and all the Arabs of the caravan had to stop to catch them. Palgrave, Barakat and Abu Isa left them to it and pushed on again. As day dawned next morning they could distinguish the dark streak of the palm-trees of Hufuf lying before them on the plain, and in due course arrived to enter the town by the southern gate. A few streets further and they found themselves at Abu Isa's house. Their journey from the Wadi Sulai had taken five days.

Abu Isa's wife gave her husband a joyful welcome, and after a bite of food the party lay down and enjoyed the luxury of untroubled sleep.

Palgrave provides us with the first description by an Englishman of the extensive Hasa oasis. Hufuf, standing in the midst of palm-groves and gardens, was a great mercantile centre, accustomed to trading with Iraq, Persia, India, and Oman, and to seeing foreign traders within its walls. Though it lay about fifty miles inland, its inhabitants were a coastal people, and had the liberal and outward-looking attitudes of their kind – totally different from the shut-in society of Riyadh. Hufuf merchants enjoyed great wealth, and had little liking for the Wahhabis whose vassals they had reluctantly become, for the killjoy beliefs of the Najdi fanatics had checked the flourishing trade in such luxuries as gold-embroidered cloaks, fine cloth, and tobacco, which had made Hufuf prosperous. Palgrave found that tobacco was still plentiful in the town, and the habit of smoking widespread, though of necessity practised in private.

While in Hufuf Palgrave and Barakat lived quietly, anxious not to draw attention to themselves, but continued to practise medicine in a modest way to earn their keep. After their first week there, two Wahhabis, obviously spies of the government, had come to see them, but Palgrave disarmed them by his lavish praises of Faisal, by his apt quotations from the Koran, and by his apparently learned talk of medical matters. The men went away suitably impressed.

It was now December, but down on the coastal plain the days were still warm and the skies cloudless. When he could, Palgrave made excursions into the coolness of the surrounding gardens, where he and Barakat bathed in the hot springs, picknicked under the trees and enjoyed other pleasant diversions. They deserved their hours of relaxation. They had made a truly remarkable journey, right down the centre of the Arabian peninsula, from the Mediterranean to the Persian Gulf. In terms of distance covered it was an achievement equalled in Arabia in the nineteenth century only by Doughty and Huber.

During the three weeks that they enjoyed Abu Isa's hospitality in Hufuf, their host told Palgrave how the charms of Oman exceeded even those of Hasa, and persuaded the Englishman to visit that region. Barakat, more practical than Palgrave, knew that he had had enough of strange lands, and wanted to return to Syria by the most direct route. They decided that when the time came for them to leave Hasa they would head for Bahrain; from there their ways would divide and Palgrave would indulge his wish to go on down the Gulf to Oman, while Barakat headed the opposite way to Bushire.

The first part of their onward journey took them to the small port of Qatif, a mouldering malarial spot on the Hasa coast from which they took ship to Bahrain. Abu Isa was not travelling with them, but had promised to meet them in Bahrain, where he had business in connection with the pilgrim traffic.

At the end of January 1863 Palgrave bade farewell to Barakat and Abu Isa and sailed for Qatar. Transferring there into another sailing-ship, he hoped to go to Oman and the Batina coast, but it was the season of storms in the Gulf, and his voyage ended up as a zigzag odyssey. They were blown across to the Persian shore before they could reach Sharja, and on setting out again were driven by a gale to Hormuz where they sheltered till the storms were over. A month had passed before they rounded Ras Musandam and sailed along the Batina coast in fairer weather.

Palgrave and a companion named Yusuf left the boat at Sohar, intending to go overland to Muscat, but on meeting another Arab captain who said he was bound for that port, they were rash enough to embark again. Two days later, as they sailed off Barka, they ran into yet another violent storm in the night; their ship foundered and Palgrave had to jump overboard and swim for it. Six men went down with the boat. Palgrave and some others were able to make for the ship's dinghy which had been cut loose as their boat sank, and later he was able to pull Yusuf out of the sea also.

The maritime adventures grow more and more dramatic, until the reader's credulity is stretched to its limits. We are back once more in the atmosphere of the *Boy's Own Paper* as we come to the final episode in the series of the hair's-breadth escapes which mar the plausibility of his story. Palgrave, now in the ship's boat, virtually took command. Tossed on mountainous seas, the dinghy filled with water and threatened to sink. Four men jumped overboard again and the rest were then able to row till they saw in the darkness a line of breakers and a sandy beach. Palgrave forced the sailors to steer away from some rocks and towards the pounding surf, where a large wave caught and overturned the dinghy. Then with Yusuf and the exhausted crewmen he had to swim for his life through the huge breakers and by great efforts finally gained the shore.

The wet and shivering men sheltered behind some bushes till dawn. Then they made their way along a track leading inland to the palace of the Sultan Thuwaini near Sib. In the disaster of the shipwreck Palgrave lost all his possessions, including his money and his later notes. (An earlier lot had been entrusted to Barakat.)

They were hospitably received by the Sultan and provided with clothes and a small sum of money, but once again danger threatened. Palgrave's nationality was suspected by two Ottoman soldiers at the palace, and next day he and Yusuf set off hurriedly for Muscat, which they reached two days later.

After a week in Muscat Palgrave was suffering from acute weariness and depression, which was in fact the onset of an attack of typhoid. All urge to explore further had left him, and he was thankful to sail on 23 March on a Kuwaiti ship bound for Bushire. On the voyage the full force of his fever struck him, and at Bushire he was carried ashore by the crew and taken to Abu Isa's house. Barakat had already left for Syria. His days in Bushire were spent in a state of semi-delirium until he was put on board the Indian mail steamer for Basra, where at last he was able to obtain medical treatment. Once restored to health in Basra he travelled via Kirkuk and Aleppo back to Syria.

He had come through a year and ten months of living in disguise. He had survived strenuous physical hardships, and psychological pressures which the modern reader can only guess at. He could look back on it all with a justifiable sense of triumph. But a study of his life seems to show that after these experiences he was never the same again.

In March 1864 he retreated to a monastery in Germany to write his book on his travels. During the period that he was occupied with this task he learned that the Jesuits were not prepared to follow up any schemes for expansion in the Middle East, and by the time his book was finished he had begun to feel that there was no future for him in the Jesuit order. In June 1865 in Berlin he publicly renounced his Roman Catholic faith. A few weeks later he was off to Abyssinia on a mission for the Foreign Office, and spent the rest of his life in the Consular and Diplomatic Services. He died on 30 September 1888, in Montevideo, where he was British Minister.

Chapter 7

CARLO GUARMANI
The Italian Horse-Coper
1864

'Inured to fatigue and hardships, thoroughly conversant with local usages, dressed as a badawin and mounted on horse-back he penetrates far into the desert. There he spends long days in a tent, studying the Arab horse....'

Dr Ansalda Feletti, Preface to 'El Kamsa'.

IL NEGED
SETTENTRIONALE

—

ITINERARIO DA GERUSALEMME A ANEIZEH

NEL CASSIM

DI

CARLO GUARMANI

DI LIVORNO

GERUSALEMME
TIPOGRAFIA DEI PP. FRANCESCANI
1866.

Title page of first edition of Guarmani's *Journey in Northern Najd*, published by the Press of the Franciscan Fathers, Jerusalem, 1866

(courtesy Royal Geographical Society)

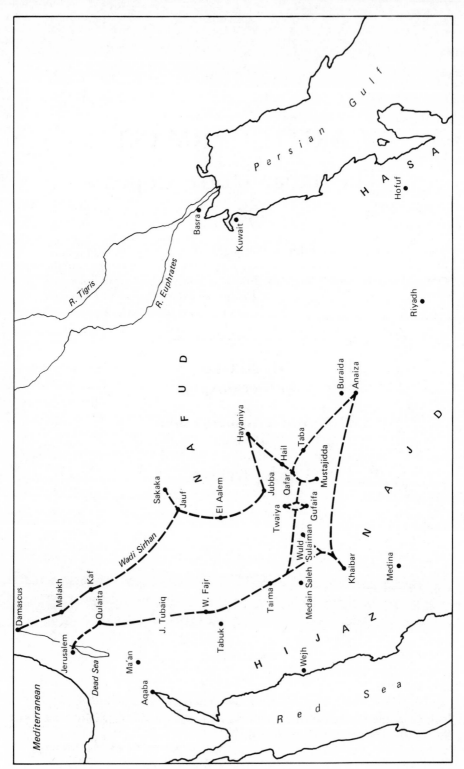

16 Guarmani's route in northern and central Arabia

In 1864 a book called *El Kamsa*, 'The Five', was published in Italy. It dealt with the five famous strains of the thoroughbred Arab horse, and its author was Carlo Guarmani, an Italian resident in the Levant.

Guarmani had come to Beirut from Leghorn when he was twenty-two, and his love of horses had soon taken him out into the Syrian desert where he had acquired a taste for living and travelling among the badawin while he sought out fine stallions to buy. He became known in Syria as one of the few Europeans who could wander in desert territory without risk, and as a result of this reputation he was called to Paris in September 1863 to meet the Director General of Napoleon III's Imperial Stud. Interest in Arab horses had been growing among European breeders since the beginning of the century. Abbas Pasha I, one of the Khedives of Egypt, was known to have formed an excellent stud by buying direct from Najd where his agents had been active after the Egyptian conquest of the Wahhabis in 1818. The sale of this famous stud in 1860 drew buyers from many European countries, and further stimulated interest in the type of horse which was believed to be available in central Arabia.

Thus it was that Guarmani's services were sought by breeders who were interested in improving their stock with new Arab blood from the strains which were justly famed for their stamina and speed. From Paris the Italian was invited by King Victor Emmanuel II to go to Italy, and in due course returned to Jerusalem in December with orders to buy Arab stallions for both Italy and France.

Was it only horses that Guarmani was commissioned to look for when he met his exalted patrons in Europe? Palgrave had made his Arabian journey the year before; perhaps the French and Italian rulers saw in Guarmani another who might glean intelligence for them in Arabia, and whose reputation as a buyer of horses would give him a valid cover if he travelled in the Jabal Shammar or even Najd. But if he was engaged in anything more devious than his ostensible purpose Guarmani was too shrewd to leave any evidence of it. The question remains open.

The Italian's journey into Arabia took him first to Taima, where only Wallin among Europeans had been before (in 1845), and on to Khaibar which he was the first Westerner to enter since Varthema. During his wanderings between Khaibar, Anaiza, and Hail, and back to Taima, before he left by the northern route across the Nafud, he covered much unmapped territory. After four months he returned with four stallions; it would have been five except that one was shot in a skirmish with tribesmen at the very end of his journey, an encounter which nearly cost Guarmani his own life.

The story of this expedition is told in his book *Il Neged Settentrionale,*

'Northern Najd'. The full Italian text was published by the Franciscan fathers in Jerusalem in 1866, but the Prussian Consul in Jerusalem had brought out an abridged German version of Guarmani's story in Germany in 1865.

In 1864 the heart of Arabia was still practically unknown to Europe, although the Egyptian expeditions against the Wahhabis had shed light on a limited belt of territory right across the peninsula. It is true that Sadleir and Palgrave had penetrated to central Najd, but the former, on an official mission, had been unable to make scientific observations or thorough notes. Only Palgrave, travelling with the leisure made possible by effective disguise, gave the outside world a comprehensive account of Hail, Riyadh, and Hasa, though the merits of his narrative, published the year after Guarmani's journey, were not fully appreciated at the time.

Guarmani was well qualified in temperament and ability for a pioneering exploit. We know his Arabic was fluent after fourteen years in the Levant, and with the characteristic dark hair and olive skin of the Italian he would have passed easily as an Arab. He seems to have been a natural extrovert, optimistic, talkative, good company. He adapted happily to badawin ways, taking in his stride all discomforts and difficulties, and showing a quick resourcefulness in moments of danger. His story is the direct and unpretentious narrative of one who relished adventure, and he gives as one reason for his travels his desire to add an Italian name to the list of those who had explored Arabia. Obviously he did not know about Varthema.

Whether or not he had additional political commissions, there is no doubt that Guarmani was genuinely in search of horses, which had always been his foremost interest. Already familiar with the horses of the Syrian tribes, he hoped there might be finer animals further south, and therefore planned to go to the Qasim and possibly deeper into Najd in the hope of buying in the oasis markets, or even from the amirs of Hail or Riyadh if the opportunity occurred. Since the amirs were in the habit of appropriating to themselves any fine examples of horseflesh to be found among their own tribes, they would be the most likely owners of the kind of animal Guarmani sought. Whether they would be willing to sell was another matter. He would have to wait and see.

In preparation for his journey he dressed in Arab clothing and armed himself well. Then on 26 January 1864, in bitterly cold weather, he set out from Jerusalem with his Arab servant Muhammad al Jazzawi. He collected an escort of four Palestinian Taamri badu, spending the night with them in their camp on the bank of the Jordan. Though he slept only fitfully, he says this did not worry him, 'for I had been able to learn the dozing habits of watchdogs and wild animals'.

During the next five days the Taamri took him on to a group of Bani Hamida, who in turn conducted him to an encampment of the Bani Sakhr at Qulaita in the mountains east of the Dead Sea. Guarmani writes of the badu in the matter-of-fact manner of one fully acquainted with their ways. No European before him had recorded so fully the tribes and sub-tribes of north-west Arabia, with their various chiefs and their tribal diras. But to add local colour for his European readers he gives us also more revealing personal details, such as his description of the kiss of farewell of the Taamri shaikh: 'he kissed every part of my face without actually touching me, and made the sound of a kiss in my ears', with which we may compare the different custom of the Bani Hamida who 'salute their relations with repeated kisses on the mouth; the first being given quickly, without removing their lips, and the later ones singly, one by one, lasting two or three seconds each'.

He is, of course, specially observant whenever horses appear, and adds some pleasing touches about badawin horsemanship. A warrior of the Bani Sakhr had a stylish way of mounting his horse: 'placing his left hand on the mane of his mare ... and resting his lance on the ground held in his right hand, [he] vaulted vigorously on to the back of the animal'. This tribal leader used no bit, only a halter. Guarmani points out that the badawin horse can breathe more freely and travel faster without a bit, and is normally bridled only for fighting.

The large encampment of Bani Sakhr at Qulaita consisted of the households of Shaikh Fendi al Faizi and his kinsmen, and we are told of the handsome four- and five-pole tents, outside each of which were planted the lances of the men who dwelt there. Guarmani was welcomed by the Sukhur with typical badawin hospitality, and embraced in the manner of that tribe; 'the Sukhur imprint a kiss on the face, whereas the Taamri do it in the air'.

His attention was caught at once by the fifty mares he saw near the encampment, and he gives details of badawin methods of hobbling the animals which are put out to pasture, and of how each mare will respond to the particular cry of its owner when they are called in at night.

During his three-day stay in the Bani Sakhr camp, Guarmani was able to accompany the men on a leopard hunt. They had discovered tracks the evening before, and set out on horseback to follow them, finally coming upon the leopard in its den. As the beast tried to escape it was transfixed through the neck by one of the badu with a lance, then, not yet dead, it was slung on bars to be carried back to the camp. There, wounded and powerless, it served 'as a plaything for the children and a subject of curiosity for the women' for several hours before it was finally despatched.

In preparation for his departure into the real wilderness Guarmani exchanged a pair of revolvers for a fine riding-camel, and bought a second camel for Muhammad. Then from the household of Fendi al Faizi he chose 'a fine young man, quick and intelligent, named Al Draibi, to serve me as guide and rafiq'.

At this point Guarmani observes that 'being accustomed to the fatigues and chances of the desert and being known to nearly all the principal chiefs of the Arab-Syrian nomadic tribes, I did not consider it an imprudence to do without the expensive escorts of Anaiza and Shammar rafiqs, although these would be absolutely necessary for any other traveller'. But by taking Al Draibi with him he hoped to give the impression that he travelled under the protection of the Bani Sakhr. From their Shaikh Fendi, Guarmani obtained a letter addressed to other tribes and allies of the Bani Sakhr, which introduced him as Khalil Aga, an agent of the Ottoman government commissioned to buy horses. He had also obtained a letter from Tallal ibn Faisal ash Shaalan of the Ruwala, to the shaikh of the Ruuqa section of the Ataiba.

On the night before they left the Qulaita camp there was a torrential rainstorm, with wind so strong that there was danger of the tent being blown down. Guarmani tells how the women and slaves went out into the darkness of the storm to tighten the cords and strengthen the poles, while the men of the camp never moved. Details such as this, confirmed by the experience of all who have ever camped with the badawin, give a ring of authenticity to Guarmani's narrative.

Next morning, 3 February, Guarmani set out for Taima accompanied by his servant Muhammad and the new rafiq, Al Draibi. 'We departed like true badawin, in old clothes without even an extra shirt, so as not to excite envy or attract attention.'

The path he took was not one of the highways of desert travel. He left to westward the Syrian hajj route which goes down via Tebuk and Madayin Salah, and chose instead a track not previously explored by Europeans, which followed an almost direct line for the 350 miles between Qulaita and Taima. Since he gives his date of arrival at Taima as 11 February, the small party must have travelled at almost unbelievable speed – one of several points which caused later critics to question the Italian's veracity. But his time is not impossible when one bears in mind the badawin habit of stopping for only short night rests and travelling many hours through darkness, and his account of the journey is convincingly detailed. Guarmani had a prismatic compass and surveyed the route as he went.

Since he was writing for those who might follow in his footsteps he tells us that this was an area frequented by roaming bands of raiders. On the second night, stopping in the Wadi Shumari west of Maan, they saw what they feared might be such a band, but when they withdrew up one side of the valley they saw that the supposed raiders had taken similar evasive action up the opposite slope. The two groups eyed each other for a while from their respective vantage-points, then Guarmani and his two men went down again to be met by three badawin from the other party. Once within gunshot range they stopped to parley. Al Draibi then discovered that they were Sherarat, allies of the Bani Sakhr, so there was nothing to fear, and the two groups camped together, joined by the women and remaining menfolk from the hillside.

Despite their abject poverty the Sherarat insisted that Guarmani and his companions shared their supper, a pathetically meagre meal of *samh* flour and *tarthuth*, an edible desert root, washed down with camel's milk. Meanwhile, the old man of the family, an extempore poet like many of his tribe, played his *rababa*, the one-stringed bada-win fiddle, and improvised a long poem, 'stimulating thus our appetite with the harsh sound of the instrument and the monotonous cadence of his verses. The final word of each was like a refrain, repeated by the empty mouths of his family, and by my companions between their mouthfuls.'

For the next four days they marched south-east under a light but steady rain, through a landscape which offered no shelter. They protected themselves by putting their fur coats over their heads, and Guarmani found this provided useful cover under which to write up his notes on the journey.

On the fifth day, when the rain had stopped, they found themselves in the valley of Fajr, and here they came to the tent of the Sherarat shaikh, Salim al Khawi. His henchmen were among the very poorest of badu, and though their shaikh wore a gown and desert cloak or *abba*, most of the others were naked except for a leather belt from which thongs of plaited leather fell over their loins. Here Guarmani and his companions were once again entertained to a poetry recital by an elderly relative of the shaikh. Al Draibi, not to be outdone, responded with a *qasida* of his own which was so lacking in expertise that it provoked much laughter from the women of the company.

From Salim al Khawi the Italian heard news of Najd which was 'as bad as it could be'. Faisal ibn Saud, ruler of Najd, was at war with the Ataiba, the large and powerful tribe of north-west Arabia. And the news from Hail, the other centre of power in the heart of the peninsula, was that Tallal ibn Rashid had sent his uncle Ubaid on a desert raid, a *ghazzu* against the Ruwala, and intended to join the campaign himself when spring came. Because of this disturbed state of affairs and the presence of hostile Shuwaimat badawin, Salim al Khawi would neither accompany Guarmani to Taima nor provide an escort. But since the Shuwaimat were friendly with the Bani

Sakhr, Guarmani's party were confident that the presence of Al
Draibi would give them protection if they should encounter the other
tribe, and they resumed their journey the following day.

Two days later they were in Taima. It was a town of 2,000 inhabitants, lying amidst thick groves of palms, the whole oasis ringed
about by an enclosing wall. As Guarmani arrived, his camels took
fright at the sight of the turrets above the gate in the wall, and nothing would make them approach the gate or go through it. Finally
the obliging inhabitants brought out ten camels to meet them, and
their own beasts, mingling with the local ones, were willing to follow
the camels of Taima through the gate without protest. Inside, Guarmani found that the settlement divided into three distinct quarters,
separated by internal walls. Some of the luxuriant groves of palms,
vines, figs and other fruits were watered from wells in their own
gardens, but many derived their water from a huge communal well
which was a prominent feature of the town. 'This well is about forty
metres in circumference and is very deep; forty-eight camels draw
water from it continuously....'

Guarmani went at once to call on the Amir Rumman, 'a little
man of sixty with a red face and a stomach very unlike a badawin's',
who accepted him as a Turkish official and gave him more information about the state of affairs in Najd. (In Guarmani's text this word
always includes the Qasim area, while other writers restrict it to an
area further south.) Guarmani explained his immediate objective
as the encampments of the Alaidan (otherwise called the Walad Ali),
the Walad Sulaiman and the Shammar. He was gratified when the
amir gave him a letter of commendation to Ibn Rashid; the more
official documents he had the more plausible would his mission seem
to the powerful shaikhs he expected to meet.

When he left Taima a badawin of the Walad Ali was his sole companion. Not wishing to risk carrying money into unknown territory,
he left his valuables with his servant Muhammad, who was to stay
at Taima with Al Draibi. Once again he was to follow a route unknown to Europeans: he planned to go to the lands of the Bani Tayi
(in the region which Doughty later identified as Yatruha), then cross
part of the great lava-field of the Harrat Khaibar to find the Ataiba,
and finally to enter Najd from the western Qasim. This part of his
narrative was called in question by scholars when it was first
published. One reason for their doubts is that the careful itinerary
which Guarmani provided for the earlier stages of his expedition is
not continued after Taima. But as Douglas Carruthers justly
remarks, 'Once entangled in the feuds and intrigues of rival tribes,
his difficulties became greater, his life endangered, and consequently
his geographical notes became negligible.... But it must be
remembered that the Khaibar trip was no more than it was intended

to be – a venture, from which he might be turned back at any moment.'

Guarmani was led by his Walad Ali guide to visit Shaikh Rajjia of that tribe, whose camp was situated three days' journey away on the northern edge of the *harra*. Here he was received somewhat warily, and he sensed that the shaikh believed him to be a Turkish spy. Rajjia belonged to a family well known as past opponents of the Wahhabis, though now acknowledging their rule, and the new-comer was treated to an endless stream of complaints about the Saudis. But when the Italian raised the subject of horses his questions were politely deflected. Rajjia boasted that his stallions were the best in his tribe, but requests to see them received the answer that they were scattered at pasture in the desert, and to round them up would take much time. It was the classic badawin technique of warding off unwelcome prying by inquisitive strangers.

Guarmani and his escort moved on towards Jauf Walad Sulaiman. Turning east among the hills of this region they came by chance upon large numbers of grazing horses. It turned out that these were the prized herds of the Alaidan, which the wily Shaikh Rajjia had not been willing to show him. In the same area were Walad Sulaiman horses also. Finding the Alaidan herdsmen friendly, the traveller and his guide spent several nights with them sleeping in the open and looking at the Alaidan horses. Some of the stallions he saw were very fine, but not, he comments, of the type he wanted. 'Nor would they have been appreciated in Europe on account of their small size. In Europe they have not faith enough in the regenerative power of the thoroughbred.' Guarmani understood that an Arab horse owned by badawin often presents a miserable appearance by European stan-dards, thin, unkempt, dirty. It is only the expert judge of horseflesh who can see in these conditions the elegant bone-structure, the poten-tial power and speed, which are so valuable when incorporated into other stock.

After inspecting the horses the Italian and his companion decided to return to the place where Rajjia had camped. They found the site empty; Rajjia had moved on. Tired and out of humour, since they carried no food and were counting on the shaikh's hospitality for their evening meal, they settled wearily to sleep in the shelter of a basalt grotto.

The following day, 29 February, eleven hours' march across the sharp ridges and boulders of the black *harra* brought them to the outskirts of Khaibar, the oasis situated in a wide, steep-sided valley which drops dramatically from the plateau of the lava-field. Guar-mani's reticence as a writer allows him no expression of satisfaction at beholding this strange community hidden in one of the most in-hospitable tracts of Arabia. He was not a traveller who was trying to score a 'first visit'. Perhaps his own rather prosaic account is to blame for the fact that European geographers doubted whether he had ever reached it. Even Doughty, entering the town thirteen years later, believed himself to be the first Westerner to set foot there. Later travellers have been more ready to believe Guarmani, and indeed his basic account of the town is such as one might expect from one who spent a brief two days there, during which time he was almost fully occupied with preparations for his onward journey.

He describes the oasis as divided into seven sections, each in a separate fold of the hills. The most notable feature of the place was the fact that its population was all black, consisting of 'Moors and Abyssinians', descendants of slaves once owned by the Alaidan and the Walad Sulaiman. 'These slaves stayed on there when their masters, some centuries ago, were killed off in great numbers by smallpox.' In his day Arab tribesmen would not settle at Khaibar, believing the water to be fatal to their kind, but went regularly to collect supplies of dates at harvest-time. Guarmani thought the dates were 'tribute', but Doughty was later to investigate more fully the system of co-ownership between nomads and settlers.

When Guarmani and his Walad Ali companion approached the town, the shaikhs of Khaibar, vassals of ibn Rashid, saw them coming down the rough path of the cliff and came out to meet them. The visitors were received by the Abyssinian governor of the town, Shaikh Hamad ibn Shamsi, who lived in a large tower on the plain, near the great natural rock outcrop which formed the ancient citadel of Khaibar. On the top of this rock stood the ruins of the old Jewish fort, the Qasr al Yahud. There was an ancient history of Jewish settlement at Khaibar, dating from pre-Islamic times. The early Caliphs had expelled the Jews but they were back by the twelfth century, and Varthema had found them there in 1503. They were driven out again at some later date, and Burckhardt and Burton heard that they had totally disappeared in the early nineteenth century.

The Italian now dispensed with the services of his Alaidan guide, and with the help of the governor found two Hutaim men for the next stage of his journey. They belonged to a low-class tribe, and were 'thieves by profession', but had the advantage of being well known to the Ataiba, towards whose tribal homeland or *dira* Guarmani was now heading. By the evening of 2 March they had reached a sandy valley to the south of the *harra*, on the Persian pilgrim road to Madina. Guarmani could have reached the pilgrim-route quicker by a direct path across the *harra* from Khaibar, but he deliberately chose a circuitous goat-trail round the side of the plateau, having experienced the painfully difficult passage across the lava-field during his approach to Khaibar.

Twenty-two hours' march now took him to a point which he calls

Jabal Tayi, but which has been fixed by Philby as almost certainly
Jabal Alam, lying between the *harra* plateau and the Wadi Rummah.
Guarmani says he was now in the Hutaim country, and Carruthers
regards this simple statement as an important proof of his veracity.
'He would not ... have met with the Hutaim before this, but on
the eastern flank of the Khaibar Harra he was unequivocally in
Hutaim territory. He could not have gathered this fact from any
previous writer.'

The traveller spent three days at Jabal Alam in a Hutaim
encampment. In the same region he found that large numbers of
the Ruuqa clan of the Ataiba had gathered with one of their shaikhs,
Maflak ibn Sfuk, creating the impressive spectacle of a thousand
badawin tents dotted over the plain. They were here because Abdullah ibn Saud, son of the Amir Faisal of Riyadh, had driven them from
the edge of the Qasim and now with his badawin army held a van-
tage-point between Anaiza and Mecca, preventing the Ataiba from
joining their allies in the south.

To begin with, Guarmani decided not to visit the Ataiba; the tribe
were watchful and nervous, and it must have seemed a bad moment
for a stranger to introduce himself on a horse-buying mission. But
he did have the letter to them from the shaikh of the Ruwala, and
he was reluctant to abandon his plans of going to the Qasim. He
finally resolved to approach the Ataiba and throw in his lot with
them in the risks which lay ahead in their inevitable confrontation
with Abdullah ibn Saud. On 8 March he arrived at the tent of
Maflak ibn Sfuk, and explained that he wished to join them until
he could go on his eastward way. Maflak, after attempting to dis-
suade him, agreed so long as Guarmani's Hutaim companions also
stayed. This the two guides were willing to do, and Guarmani
showed his appreciation to the Ataiba shaikh by having a sheep killed
and providing a meal to seal the bargain. He told the Ataiba that
they would not be held responsible if, in the course of their dispute
with the Al Saud, he were to be killed.

Before evening the shaikh of the Hutaim arrived on camel-back
at Maflak's tent. He brought a warning from Abdullah ibn Saud
that Maflak and his people must move out of the Jabal area before
dawn the following morning. Guarmani, who was more worried by
the prospect of being besieged for months in the mountain gorges
than he was by the idea of battle and adventure, welcomed this new
development. The camp was packed up in the night, and when they
were ready to trek, 200 horsemen headed the marching column, followed by the women and children with the flocks and the baggage,
while the rearguard was formed of 700 riflemen on camels.

For four days the whole tribe marched day and night, resting only
at intervals without pitching their tents. It was a wild and colourful

migration, as the hundreds of animals, with the frightened women-folk and uncertain leaders, attempted to escape involvement with the Najdi forces. But even as they marched they were harried continually by Abdullah's horsemen and by raiders from the Bani Qahtan. It seems it had never been the Saudi leader's intention to let them pass unmolested. The Ataiba warriors attempted at several points to break through the Saudi ranks, but without success. By the evening of 12 March they had been robbed of all their flocks, had 60 dead and 200 wounded, and found themselves forced back to the position from which they had originally set out. The Saudi army was encamped in the plain to the south-west.

Attempting to find a protected position from which his tribe could face the next attack, Maflak led his people that night into a deep gorge. This was a landscape of rugged hills and volcanic outcrops, which offered protection such as they would not have found in more open desert. The steep sides of this gorge enclosed them completely except to the south-west, and at this narrow opening Maflak placed his cavalry. His riflemen scrambled up the rocky sides to vantage-points among the boulders.

The following morning Maflak refused to be drawn into an engagement when Bani Qahtan horsemen galloped round the entrance to their stronghold, firing their rifles and challenging the Ataiba to combat. On 14 March the Saudis made an attack and were beaten off, and next day Abdullah personally led a more determined assault by all his forces, numbering about 10,000 men. Battle raged throughout the day, and it was only two hours after sunset, says Guarmani, that the Najdis finally retired, 'without having either dislodged us from our eagles' nests or having broken our brave cavalry'.

As the Saudi badawin rested that night after the day of strife, they were awakened at midnight by the Ataiba war-cry. Shaikh Sultan ibn Rubayan, the paramount chief of the Ataiba, with 400 horsemen and 5,000 camel-borne riflemen, had come to the assistance of his people and had taken the Najdis by surprise in the night. The blood-curdling cries of the attacking Ataiba spread terror among the battle-weary Saudi forces who were being mercilessly slaughtered. When the Ruuqa who had been guarding Maflak's stronghold realised that their kinsmen had arrived they came in to attack once again, and there was confusion and carnage in the Saudi camp until daybreak. With the dawn Abdullah saw that the Bani Qahtan had abandoned him in the fight, and he led his men in headlong retreat towards the Qasim. The Ataiba, exulting in their victory, did not follow. The two leaders, Sultan ibn Rubayan and Maflak ibn Sfuk, embraced on the battlefield, congratulating each other on a night's work well done.

Guarmani's account here turns from the vivid events of the fighting to a more personal note. He admits disarmingly that, throughout the heat of battle,

> my post was in the safest hiding-place in the gorge, with the wounded, the women and the baggage. At the most I was permitted from time to time to wander round amongst the horses tethered to the bushes by their fetlocks; and was thus enabled to study them at leisure, not minding the spent bullets which whizzed over my head or fell harmlessly at my feet. My observations were most interesting, for the Ataiba horses are by far the strongest in the desert. At times I was distracted by the groans of the wounded who were brought in to be dressed and by the cries of the women who received them with joy, and encouraged them to return to the fight as soon as possible, as soon, that is to say, as the dust and charcoal had staunched the blood streaming from their wounds, or as their cuts had been bound up.

Guarmani's two Hutaim guides had stayed by his side through the battle. By the badawin laws relating to rafiqs and travelling companions they were bound to protect him personally if at any moment he had been in real danger from the Saudis.

After the slaughter and action of the night, it may seem strange that Ibn Rubayan was ready the following day to discuss the sale of horses with Guarmani. But the victory had been theirs, and the mood of the Ataiba was one of elation and success. At any rate, Guarmani was able to buy from the shaikh three stallions 'in their prime', two dark bay and one bay with black markings. Ibn Rubayan would not name a price, but accepted Guarmani's offer of 100 camels for the three. The Italian believed he had made a good bargain, but once again later commentators have been critical. According to Doughty, the best brood mares, which were never sold, were valued at twenty-five camels, and a stallion would therefore be priced somewhat lower. The Blunts record that Ibn Rashid sold stallions to India for £100 each, equivalent to about sixteen camels at the time, but these would not be the finest breeding specimens. The fact remains that Guarmani, no fool when it came to horses, and one who knew the badu well enough not to be taken in, was more than happy with the deal, believing he had paid only a third of the animals' true value. He put his good fortune down to the fact that Ibn Rubayan had heard badu speak well of him, and also to the good offices of Shaikh Maflak who wished to see his guest safely on his way.

There follows an incident which shows that Maflak's mood towards the Italian was certainly favourable.

In the division of last night's spoils, some of the shaikhs quarrelled over a light bay horse with a star in front and two white stockings on the hind legs. Shaikh Maflak acted as mediator and persuaded them to give me the animal in question, for having helped to nurse the wounded while imprisoned in the gorge, saying he did not think I ought to be sent away with empty hands. I accepted with thanks.

Guarmani could not pay for the horses at the time, and Ibn Rubayan arranged that the two Hutaim guides should go off separately with the animals to Gufaifa west of Jabal Shammar. This would give the Italian time to collect the cash he had left at Taima. Under the badawin code, the Hutaim could be trusted not to hand the horses over to Guarmani till full payment had been made. If this were not done, they were to return the animals to the Ataiba through the Bani Harb, an associated tribe.

Having concluded his bargain, Guarmani went to inspect the battlefield. From the fact that he saw not a single Bani Qahtan casualty, either dead or wounded, he concluded that this tribe, in spite of their nominal alliance with the Najdis, had had no intention of harming the Ataiba, a powerful clan whose enmity was not to be incurred lightly. The Hutaim and the Bani Harb were in a similar ambiguous position, having declared their loyalty to the Saudis, yet not being prepared to join an attack on the Ataiba. In comments such as this Guarmani shows himself well versed in Arabian tribal divisions and their complex alliances.

His purchase of the three stallions was, for Guarmani, the end of the business for which he had come to Arabia, and at this point he seemed to drop his idea of penetrating south to central Najd. Perhaps his experience of the battle, vivid proof of the high temper of tribal feuds and the ferocity of the Saudis, went some way to make him feel he had done enough. 'Having gained my object,' he says, 'it would have been madness to go farther without a very good reason; all the same I seriously hoped to be able to return on some future occasion.'

A great feast celebrated the Ataiba victory. Fifty camels were killed, and Guarmani sat down with the shaikhs to a *tel al laham*, or 'mountain of meat', a camel roasted whole and served up on an enormous platter of savoury rice. This huge meal was soon reduced to bare bones. Afterwards the Italian parted company with his hosts.

The Ataiba departed an hour after sunset. I nearly wept when Maflak embraced me in the Sakhur manner, and I was left alone with my guides on that vast and bloody plain. . . . Jackals, ravens, wolves and vultures were devouring the corpses. My horses trembled with fear. All night I watched and caressed them, leaving them to the care of my companion at day-break while I went in search of grass.

Guarmani had only one of the Hutaim with him – the other had gone to find some fellow-tribesmen to help take the horses to Gufaifa. For this reason the Italian had to help to gather fodder. He explains that since the horses did not know the voices of their new owners it was impossible to let them loose to graze. He went off to cut grass with his badawin dagger, and when he had finished he climbed a large rock to call his companion to fetch a camel to carry away the bundles of fodder. At this point a strange incident befell the traveller. On the other side of the rock he found a grotto, with a pool formed by a drip from an overhang.

> The water dripped slowly from the roof and looked clear as crystal. I could not resist the temptation of quenching my thirst; I took the precaution of resting until I was certain I no longer perspired, so there could be no risk, therefore the ills I suffered undoubtedly came from another cause. The taste of the water was so bitter and nasty that I scarcely drank a drop. I spat it out and tried to rush from the grotto, when I was seized with sickness, accompanied by a violent headache and general prostration. . . . I fell back with my feet in the pool, gradually my limbs stiffened and I lost consciousness.

The story of the poisonous pool is one which has puzzled later Arabian explorers. But Carruthers (in a note to the 1938 edition) says that Philby had told him that in the area of Jabal Alam – identified as Guarmani's Jabal Tayi – badawin had spoken of such a pool, though Philby himself had not seen it. Even if the pool's existence is never verified, it could be that Guarmani and Philby had both heard the same badawin legend. The detail and generally modest tone of his narrative disposes us to believe Guarmani, but we cannot rule out the possibility that he used a story heard from the badu as the basis of an imagined first-hand experience.

True or not, the incident is vividly recounted. When he came to, it was night time, and Guarmani found himself being rubbed with butter by a group of badawin women, who were saying 'the water has affected him'. They forced him to swallow some camel's milk, continuing to rub his back, chest, and stomach. When he tried to speak he could utter no sound, and soon drifted off again into unconsciousness or sleep, experiencing a strangely pleasurable sensation.

The next time he awoke the sun was high, and he saw that he was in a tent of the Sulubba, the gypsy-like tinkers of Arabia. His two guides and other Hutaim were gathered outside with the horses. Sitting by him were three young women and a little girl – all remarkably ugly, he observes ungallantly, but all well dressed and wearing silver and gold ornaments. When he saw that the little girl held a tambourine he realised that the family must be wandering minstrels.

Guarmani learned later that when he had failed to return from gathering fodder his Hutaim guide Ali al Fidawi had followed his tracks, and finding him lying senseless had climbed to the top of the rock, from where he had seen some grazing animals indicating the presence of a camp in the far distance. Returning at once to the horses he had galloped across to get help from the Sulubba, who, in the way of the desert people, had not hesitated to return with Ali to tie the unconscious Guarmani on a camel and bring him to their tent. The Italian was deeply grateful to all of them, feeling that they had saved his life. But the day after his queer experience he felt no after-effects apart from a slight burning in his skin, which he put down to the assiduous rubbing treatment of the women.

After breakfast of camel's milk and locusts, the latter not much to Guarmani's taste, the Italian took counsel with his Hutaim companions. In spite of his earlier statement that his mission was accomplished, he decided that he would go with Ali to the Qasim, as he wished to meet Abdullah al Saud, and if possible even the great Faisal himself, now old and ailing in Riyadh, 'in order to make known to them my intention of returning every year to the Najd'. The four Hutaim were to go to Gufaifa across the *harra*, taking the horses.

Leaving the Sulubba camp at sunset, Guarmani and Ali marched for thirteen hours, passing from a landscape of granite hills into the sand-belt of Al Araij. After sleeping through the next day, 19 March, they moved off again at nightfall, heading due east in the darkness, and finally stopping an hour before dawn in a valley which was probably the Wadi Jarir, since Guarmani says it marked the edge of the Qasim.

From further down the valley they could hear sounds of men and horses, hidden from them by a rise in the ground. They guessed they were near the camp of the Amir Abdullah, but before approaching him they lay down to rest till daybreak. Next morning when Ali climbed the hill to survey the scene, he reported that the Saudi flag was flying at a large encampment of badu and villagers which lay an hour's distance away.

Ali and Guarmani discussed whether they should admit to Abdullah that they had been with the Ataiba during the recent battle, but before they had come to a decision they were surprised by forty horsemen who seized them and bore them off to the Saudi camp. When they arrived, the Amir refused to see the Italian, though he asked to see his papers, which he inspected and returned. Clearly he believed Guarmani to be a Turkish spy and wished to be rid of him as soon as possible.

In the early afternoon an Abyssinian from the Amir's camp came over to the two travellers and ordered them to prepare their camels to follow him to Anaiza. As soon as Guarmani learned their destination, any anxiety he felt about Abdullah's hostile reception disappeared. Anaiza was a place that he eagerly wished to see. He calls it the largest town in Najd, and says of it, 'its principal commerce consists in rearing horses bought by the merchants as colts from the badawin; they export them to Kuwait on the Persian Gulf, whence they are sent to Persia or India'.

Their armed escort maintained an unsociable silence during that day's journey, but at eleven o'clock in the evening an hour's halt was ordered, and the Abyssinian sent his charges some dates and a small piece of meat. The stiffness that had prevailed slowly relaxed, and some of the Abyssinian's men were allowed to sit and talk with Guarmani and Ali round the camp-fire.

When the march resumed, the Abyssinian's manner had softened noticeably, and he rode alongside the Italian's camel and carried on a lively conversation all the way to Anaiza, volunteering the information that his name was Anaibar, and that although his father had been a slave, he was a free man. While he was a subject of Faisal al Saud, he said, he considered Tallal ibn Rashid of Hail his true lord and master. He had been employed on a 'secret mission' but was now returning to Hail with a poor opinion of the Saudi amir who had been less than generous in payment for his services. Guarmani learned that the Abyssinian carried a letter concerning himself from Abdullah al Saud to Ibn Rashid, but his escort assured him that whatever it said it could do him no harm, since Ibn Rashid was a faithful servant of the Sultan of Turkey, in whose service Guarmani claimed to be.

After a total of fifteen hours' marching they reached Anaiza, one of the twin oases of the Qasim, lying almost equidistant from the Red Sea and the Persian Gulf in the heart of northern Arabia, with a population of about 10,000. Here Anaibar took his charge to the house of the Amir Zamil, protégé and friend of the family of Rashid, who had been raised from poverty to high office by Tallal's father Abdullah. It was the same Zamil of whom Palgrave heard, and who was to be described affectionately by Doughty fourteen years later. He was one of the notable personalities in Arabia in the second half of the nineteenth century, a relentless opponent of the Wahhabis and their Saudi leaders. He told Guarmani that he wished to see Najd return to the true religion 'of Abraham', and was at no pains to hide his hatred of Faisal al Saud even when speaking in open gatherings. Guarmani found Zamil intelligent and affable, and says, 'believing me to be a Musselman and a Turkish official, [he] paid me every attention'. It is perhaps more likely that Zamil, himself suspecting that Guarmani was working against the Saudis, was willing to help anyone who could harm his own enemies.

The Italian persuaded his hosts to take him to the Anaiza horse-market, but he was disappointed to find that the horses had all been sent to Kuwait a few days before, and that only a few colts were left. There was much concern among the Anaiza dealers at news of an order which threatened to stop the town's most important trade. They had heard that the export of horses by sea had been forbidden, but no one seemed to know whether the order was from Constantinople or Baghdad. Guarmani himself suspected that it was Ibn Saud who was attempting thus to hamper the traditional trade between the Qasim and the Persian Gulf. But evidently the traders' fears were ultimately groundless; when Doughty was in Anaiza the horse-trade was still flourishing.

After a night and a day in Anaiza, the traveller and his escort resumed their journey and on the following afternoon they entered Buraida, the second of the Qasim's two towns. Buraida was 'much spoilt and full of ruins', but Guarmani thought that it held richer princes and merchants than Anaiza, a judgement which is not borne out by later accounts. Its horse-market dealt in greater numbers, but the animals there seemed to be of inferior quality.

The party moved on after only a brief halt, since they were now making for the northern capital of Hail. On the morning of 24 March the travellers reached the wells of Quwara, and paused there that day and the next, reluctant to meet several hundred Mutair tribesmen who were said to be positioned across their route to the north-west. Then trekking on at night they came to Faid, an ancient village which was once the capital of the region, and went on to Taba. They were now in the generally mountainous area which forms the Jabal Shammar, whose luxuriant oases lie in the valleys between the mountain ranges. At this point Guarmani was interested to learn that Bandar, eldest son of Tallal ibn Rashid, was encamped three hours' ride to the south-west. The young shaikh was said to have 500 thoroughbred mares with him, guarded by 300 slaves who were supervising the mating of the mares with special stud-horses. On hearing this, Guarmani eagerly fell in with Anaibar's suggestion that they should make a detour to visit Bandar.

They rose two hours before daybreak, hoping with an early start to reach Bandar's camp at the time when the mares were brought to the stallions. But their unexpected arrival caused confusion in the camp, and as soon as they came in sight shots were fired to warn them off. Anaibar explained that strangers were not allowed near the mares for fear of the evil eye. The Abyssinian went ahead, while Bandar's men came forward shouting and shaking their staves until the moment when they recognised him as a friend and at once welcomed him with much pleasure and deference. As soon as Bandar heard of his arrival, Anaibar was summoned to the prince's tent, where he explained the presence of himself and his companion.

Guarmani was received by Bandar and treated with great courtesy. The young shaikh expressed the Rashids' loyalty to the Sultan of Turkey, and their esteem for anyone who travelled in his service. The meeting seems to have been both warm and jovial. Guarmani was offered tobacco, and Bandar, surprised at his refusal, asked jokingly whether the Wahhabis had invaded Constantinople. Later he chaffed Anaibar at having accepted the office of policeman over Guarmani, declaring that if the latter were a spy, the Sultan's subjects had reason to be proud of him.

Outdoing each other in good manners, Bandar and Guarmani each refused to take coffee before the other, and while a slave stood waiting with the cup held out, each of them pressed the other to drink first. The situation was finally resolved when Bandar took the *finjan* from the slave's hand and personally gave it to his guest. Later the Italian had his beard scented, but Bandar did not allow him to depart after this, insisting that he must stay three days in his tent. The prince said that he wished Guarmani to travel back to Hail with him, so that he could himself present the visitor to his father. Guarmani seems to have accepted Bandar's suggestion quite willingly, though he was now alone among strangers. They had left Ali al Fidawi at Taba, and even Anaibar was off again to Hail the same evening. Guarmani's narrative tells us no more about the three days in Bandar's camp. We can only assume that he had no opportunity to write notes, and later there was so much more to record that the earlier gaps were never filled. On 31 March they left for the capital, picking up Ali at Taba on the way. They arrived after sunset next day.

Hail, the Shammar city of northern Arabia which had so impressed Palgrave, was a centre of opposition to the extreme Wahhabi zeal, but even so it nurtured its own brand of religious fanaticism. Anyone who did not profess Islam was in danger of his life there, and Guarmani had a grim reminder of this as he passed through the gates of the city. By the gate he saw the rotting corpse of a Persian Jew who had pretended to be a Muslim but had refused, when challenged, to pronounce the familiar words of the faith. The Jew had come from Syria to buy horses for the Shah of Persia, but had been murdered by the populace when they discovered he was not a true believer. Guarmani remarks, 'If his fate was a sad one, it must be owned he had deserved it. When a man decides to risk himself in a great adventure, he must use every means in his power and be prepared to suffer all consequences of his enterprise.' It was a harsh but realistic comment, shared by Burton, Wallin, Huber,

and in our own century by Philby, who all believed in the practical
necessity of conforming outwardly to the customs of the Arabs.
Doughty stands out as the one great explorer of the Victorian age
who felt morally bound to declare himself a Christian, but even he
had no scruples about adopting badawin clothing.

News of the death of the foreigner had travelled from Hail to
Taima, and thence back along the hajj route to Syria, and had
reached the Italian's family, who not unnaturally feared that it was
Carlo himself who had been killed.

My poor family mourned me in earnest, whilst all the time I was
in excellent health, eating *pilaff* or *temmen*, and making my *rikat* to
God in my heart, but to Muhammad with my lips, in all due
reverence; and remembering Christ's Sermon on the Mount, not
to mention the stench of that Jew's rotting corpse, I was determined
not to be amongst the poor in spirit and enter Paradise with the
fools.

Guarmani's first action in Hail was to go with Bandar to the great
mosque in the town square, where he said seven *rikats* to make up
for not having prayed at all during the day. Once finished there,
he was left by Bandar in charge of a slave named Mahbub. Opposite
the mosque stood the castle, its high mud walls decorated with dog-
tooth crenellations. As darkness had fallen by now, the main gate
of the castle was shut, but Guarmani and Ali were taken through
a small wicket-gate to the coffee-hall with five columns down the
middle, which Palgrave had already described. From there the two
travellers were led out under an arcade where they were offered dates
and fresh butter. Guarmani was told that his camels were being cared
for by the amir's men, and that their baggage had been taken to
a house which had been assigned to them.

They were to lodge in one of Tallal's specially-built guest-houses,
down a street off the main square. It consisted of a walled courtyard
off which opened two rooms. When Guarmani was shown to his
quarters a fire was burning in the coffee-room, and a jar of water
had been provided. The room was comfortably furnished with mats,
rugs and cushions, and his own and Ali's belongings had been hung
up along the wall. Each room had a single pillar supporting the ceil-
ing, and the Italian, passing an idle hour, carved on one pillar the
name of his daughter Zulima, adding 1864 for the date of his visit.

On the morning of 2 April he woke early and breakfasted on
camel's milk, grapes and honey, provided by the palace. He was told
that the Amir Tallal would not be able to see him till the afternoon,
so he spent the morning looking round the market, which he found
much less interesting than that of Anaiza. Of the Hail merchants

he found that many came from Meshed Ali (Najaf), Baghdad and Basra. Guarmani's faithful Hutaimi companion, Ali, was still wearing the blue gown characteristic of his tribe, but since in Hail only women would be seen in such a colour, the Italian bought him a new white *dishdasha*, with an *abba* and a *kaffiya*. The market closed from ten o'clock till three – just as did many Italian shops, says Guarmani – during which time the traveller was given lunch in the castle. Afterwards he returned to his house to write and sleep.

As the muezzin made the call to afternoon prayer Bandar came to fetch his guest to present him to his father the Prince Tallal. They went out together to find that the amir had come out of the main mosque and was sitting against the western wall of the building with his officials, to dispense justice. The lord of the Jabal Shammar and his retinue made a fine sight. 'Twenty slaves and servants sat in a semi-circle on the ground in front of him, all well-dressed in fine black *abbas*, with red or blue cloth coats heavily embroidered with gold; in their hands they held, as did the prince and all his followers, a scimitar in a silver scabbard.' Guarmani's description of Tallal agrees with that of Palgrave, though couched in blunter terms: 'He was a man of forty: short, fat and dark.' When Bandar and Guarmani approached, the amir was hearing the complaint of a poor woman against the governor of her village. Having given judgement in her favour, Tallal received Guarmani without speaking.

He put out his hand; I touched it with mine, which I then lifted to my mouth, kissing the fingers, and then to my forehead, while he did the same with his, and at a sign from him, and without uttering a word, I seated myself on the ground at his right hand on the step of the mosque. He got rid of eight lawsuits in two hours, put on his sandals and broke up the court. He then saluted me smiling, with his hand on his heart, and I did the same, trying not to laugh, for I was not used to a dumb reception. Bandar went away with his father.

Guarmani was given his evening meal on the roof over the palace gateway. While the Italian and Ali sat eating with their hands from the dish of rice, meat and bread, they became aware that the amir's women were watching them through the lattice window of an upper room, from which an animated whispering was clearly audible. Guarmani was a little nonplussed when he thought he could distinguish among the feminine whispers the male voices of Bandar and the amir. Uncertain whether they were calling to him, he thought it politic to pretend not to hear, but when he rose and went downstairs again Bandar appeared suddenly and invited him to join Tallal in his private apartments.

The prince welcomed me with embraces and kept me talking about five hours. From time to time he had my beard perfumed and offered me both black and white coffee. He had heard that my horses were still at Mustajidda, where my Hutaim were sheltering for fear of the Mutair, who were harrying the southern frontiers. Bandar requested to be allowed to accompany me [to Mustajidda] and was given permission, it being understood that I first accepted three days of their hospitality. Anaibar was to command the escort of twenty horsemen which the amir provided, and we were permitted to travel by day.

The three days in Hail gave Guarmani all the time he needed to rest and refresh himself after the discomforts of the desert, and also to bring up to date his notes on his adventures. Every day he attended the amir's morning and afternoon sessions in the square, and heard the prince pronounce judgements in the traditional manner of the strong tribal chief. 'He ordered death for assassins, cut off the hand of those who wounded another ... ; for liars and false witnesses he ordered their beards to be burned over a fire, which often ended in their eyes being burned as well; imprisonment was the punishment for thieves; rebels had their goods confiscated.... His sentences were just and his generosity excessive.' To the foreign visitor Tallal remained the affable host, entertaining his guest every evening either in his private apartments or in the coffee-hall.

The Italian spent several hours every day sitting or strolling in the market and watching the pretty girls from the outlying villages who came to sell fodder outside the mosque. The women of Jabal Shammar, he says, 'have a bronze complexion ... with large almond-shaped eyes and flashing black pupils; ... their glossy black hair is oiled with an odourless pomade composed of finely powdered palm bark and clarified fat obtained from sheeps' tails'. The girls from the villages of Wusaita and Aqda had a special reputation for beauty and immorality, and when they sold their hay in the square their faces were covered by only the flimsiest of veils, which they were ready to drop flirtatiously if any presentable man came by. Guarmani explains that they were in fact a class of prostitutes, whose position was well understood in the social code of Hail. 'A young man stares fixedly at a girl, who lets her *shambar* drop on purpose. "Bargain for me", she says; and it is an act of prostitution and not of marriage which is settled.' It was well known that among their customers were Bandar and the other princes.

On 5 April, as arranged, the Italian, with Bandar and the armed escort left Hail and made for Mustajidda, which they reached the following afternoon. Guarmani was pleased to find his four horses in excellent condition, and was told that since the Mutair had

retreated, the way was clear for the horses to go to Gufaifa as originally arranged. Guarmani and the prince turned back towards Hail,
but at Al Qasr, the fortress at the foot of the towering rocky range
of Jabal Aja, the Italian parted company with Bandar and the Abyssinian. So that he could pay for the horses, he now had to return
to Taima where he had left his money with Muhammad and
Al Draibi. Although Bandar provided a letter to the amir of Muqaq,
the next village, Guarmani preferred to pass through without avail-
ing himself of this help; he was anxious to get on and make sure
his horses arrived safely at Gufaifa. Round this small oasis on the
plain west of Jabal Aja he was happy to find the landscape green
with spring vegetation and *nussi* grass standing about two feet high.
He found his horses enjoying these lush pastures where they grazed
with their feet hobbled in the badawin manner.

After stopping for four hours with the horses he hastened on to
buy provisions in a village named Bedan, and on 12 April started
out with Ali, his Hutaim companion, on the road to Taima. He preferred to travel without an official escort since he wanted to be free
to study the country and to map the route between Hail and Taima,
where once again as a European he was breaking new ground.

Although camps of Shammar, Walad Sulaiman and Alaidan were
everywhere, they were not hostile, and in this area, traditionally the
territory of the Bani Tayi, Guarmani felt no fear of enemy incursions,
since it was naturally protected by the Nafud to the north and the
harra to the south.

Guarmani and Ali al Fidawi took thirteen days to travel to Taima
and back to Bedan, returning on 24 April. With them came the servant Muhammad and Al Draibi, the Bani Sakhr rafiq. The next day
the horses were brought to Bedan where Guarmani paid for them
and received a declaration to that effect from the shaikhs who witnessed the transaction. 'I then paid the Hutaim who had looked after
the horses, giving them enough to make the men grateful and happy,
and without forgetting Ali's well-earned reward, I dismissed them
all.' To replace the Hutaim he engaged two Shammar horsemen,
and travelled northwards with them and the horses as far as Twaiya,
where he ordered the Shammaris, with Muhammad and Al Draibi,
to take the horses across the southern Nafud to Jubba, the oasis village lying about twenty-three miles to the north. Guarmani himself
was going to return to Hail, for there were still places he wished to
see among the settlements which nestle in the valleys of the Jabal
Shammar. He would later rejoin the men and horses at Jubba by
another route.

In Twaiya Guarmani found the village infested by a swarm of
locusts, which the inhabitants were happily catching to roast in deep
holes in the ground. He bought four sacks of them, which he had

loaded on to the camels of Muhammad and Al Draibi before they left for Jubba. Though Guarmani seems never to have appreciated locusts himself, he knew how much they were valued by the badu and the inhabitants of the villages as an additional food supply, and recognised also that they could make excellent fodder for horses. 'They fill their stomachs and increase their muscle without making them fat. If dried and made into a powder, a small amount forms abundant horse-food, and in this form it can be kept for years even if exposed to damp.'

The Italian headed back for Hail via Muqaq and Qufar, where there was a pass over the Aja mountain. Half-way up the harsh rocky slopes he observed a grotto 'formed of blocks of granite which had become detached from the mountain by an earthquake, but not enough to hurl them into the valley below'. In the grotto there was water, temptingly clear, but Guarmani did not stop to drink. He was not going to make the same mistake twice.

On 28 April he was back in his house in Hail, where the town was buzzing with the news that Prince Tallal was preparing to go on a raid against the Sherarat. Apparently he was arranging a rendezvous with some of his tribesmen at a point to the north-east called Hayaniya.

During the few days that Guarmani spent on his return to Hail he was able to visit Aqda, the group of hidden valleys in the heart of the mountains which the Bani Rashid had made into a natural fortress by closing the only access route with a fortified wall. It was used as an arsenal in times of peace, and on the occasion that Guarmani went there with Anaibar the Abyssinian's mission was to collect forty camel-loads of rifles and bring them to Hail in preparation for the impending raid.

On 3 May Guarmani was told in the evening that he was expected to accompany the Amir Tallal as far as Hayaniya on the morrow. When he rose at dawn the Rashidi standard was flying on a pole planted outside the castle, and the amir was already up distributing arms and camels to his followers.

At ten o'clock a slave seized the banner, vaulted on to his horse and began the march; all the troops, nearly a thousand men, followed him; then came the Amir, with Ali his cousin, and lastly Anaibar with myself. Anaibar distributed coins . . . to the wives and children of the slaves, who accompanied us for half an hour beyond the town yelling (or as they believed singing) in honour of their great and liberal master.

At Wajid and Leqita, villages in the Jabal Shammar, they were joined by 300 Asslam and Abdaih tribesmen and contingents from the Daghairat and Sinjara sections of the Shammar. The whole great company reached Hayaniya after sunset on the second day.

The following morning Tallal sent for Guarmani to bid him farewell and received him in a friendly manner, insisting on changing the Italian's riding camel, whose hump had grown rather thin, for his own beast. He offered Guarmani various gifts, which the Italian refused, in spite of much solicitous coaxing, and finally placed him in the care of a Shammari and a Masshur Rueli who would lead him to Jubba and Jauf. Just before he left, Guarmani recounts, he was able to buy a young grey stallion of the Kubayshan breed from an Ataiba badawi.

Leaving the great raiding army on 6 May Guarmani travelled south-west to meet his men and horses at Jubba, and arrived there the following day 'very tired indeed after a sixteen hours' march in the Nefud'. As they approached the village Guarmani inadvertently took his mount across a patch which was known as a sand-bath for camels. Once such a place has become established by usage and has a tell-tale scent, unnoticeable to man, no camel will pass it without lying down to roll. The result in this case was that the camels ridden by Guarmani and his two companions, in spite of shouts and blows, immediately lay down and prepared to wallow in the sand, while Guarmani and the two badawin were only able to scramble off in an undignified way before they did so. At this sight Al Draibi and Muhammad who had come out of the village to meet the new arrivals were overcome with laughter, as were all the other villagers who saw the incident. Guarmani laughed with them, trying to show that he did not mind, but his two companions swore in exceptionally violent terms. Badawin hate to be made to look foolish.

Guarmani and his men now faced the crossing of the great sand-desert of the Nafud, with its wind-scoured red dunes and horseshoe-shaped hills. In preparation for this last difficult stage of his journey he bought four camels with young ones. Two of the calves were for them to eat on the journey. The other two he ordered to be killed 'as a little feast for the villagers, who consequently did not make us pay the usual tariff for water, and even filled our bags with dates and butter as a gift'. The badu always respect one who is liberal with gifts and hospitality, and it is obvious that by such gestures at appropriate moments Guarmani showed himself well attuned to badawin ways, and gained the respect of his companions and of Arabs they met on the way. He understood that generosity in Arabia works as a kind of insurance, for news travels fast, and a man's reputation goes before him.

The little procession which started on 9 May consisted of Al Draibi and Muhammad mounted on two of the purchased horses, and leading the other two bay horses. They were followed by the Shammari who led the single file of camels laden with baggage and provisions; behind the camels came the Rueli with the grey stallion bought at Hayaniya. Guarmani brought up the rear on the camel Tallal had given him, 'faster but far less good-tempered' than the one he had taken away. Finally there was a white donkey which Guarmani had bought off the Sulubba for his daughter, which ran about at will, though never straying far from the caravan.

At this point of the narrative Guarmani allows himself a few reflections on the sense of achievement he felt now that his journey was nearly over. He was not the first European in Jabal Shammar, though from the way he writes he may have believed that he was. Wallin had reached Hail in 1845, and Palgrave in 1862, but Guarmani had probably not read Wallin's account, and Palgrave's book was published only in 1865. At any rate, he felt that he had added something to Europe's knowledge of Arabia, as indeed he had.

'The Jabal Shammar had at last opened its secrets to Europe, and I was leaving it without having encountered the least trouble, in fact I had received great kindnesses. ... Mussulman fanaticism is intense in these parts; the return to the old religion, after the defeat of the Wahhabites, naturally obliged the inhabitants to show themselves especially zealous to prove their sincerity.' And of the strength of Ibn Rashid he comments: 'It is on account of his immense liberality that the number of Amir Tallal's adherents increases daily and that his absolute power, although somewhat tyrannical, is yet approved of.'

It is disappointing to find that Guarmani tells us practically nothing about the crossing of the Nafud, but in a later afterthought he remarks that it rained in torrents for thirty-six hours without stopping through 11 and 12 May. Though this may have taken his thoughts off the scenery, the rain made their journey easier than normal, since the main danger of the Nafud in dry weather was the long distance between wells. They took four days to complete the crossing, and arrived at Jauf on 12 May. Guarmani says he was already familiar with this oasis, as he had visited it in 1851. (The truth of this statement has been queried, since 1851 would have been only the year after his arrival in the Levant. And yet he had no cause to lie in simply mentioning this fact in passing. Could the original printers of his book have misread a '5' for a '6' in his handwritten manuscript?)

The day after their arrival in Jauf he told Muhammad to sell the camels, 'very valuable animals, which we had milked morning and evening whilst crossing the Nefud and whose milk we had drunk ourselves, when it was not needed for the horses and the donkey'.

In Jauf Guarmani heard the news that the prince Tallal had arrived at Sakaka, about twenty-five miles away, having abandoned his expedition against the Sherarat who had moved north. It was said that he was now going to attack the Ruwala, traditional enemies of the Shammar. The Italian, showing again his Arab knack for diplomacy, decided to travel slightly off his route to Sakaka,

> to present myself again to the Amir Tallal as a mark of friendship and gratitude, especially as I was soon about to leave his country. ... This attention on my part seemed to please him exceedingly. I found him encamped beside the town; this time on seeing me, he rose and embraced me before everyone. I travelled back to Jauf at night and got there by dawn.

For Guarmani and his party the difficult part of their journey, geographically speaking, was now over. From Jauf onwards they would travel a well-worn route up the Wadi Sirhan where water was plentiful. The Italian paid off his Shammari and Rueli guides who were no longer needed, and arranged to join one of the regular camel trains which ply between Jauf and Syria. This caravan consisted of about 182 men, with many women and some children. They started on the morning of 16 May. But on the second day out they were attacked by five badawin on racing camels, and Daghairi, the leader, ordered the caravan animals to be couched in a ring, with the women and children in the centre. The men formed an outer ring round the beasts, expecting a serious attack any minute, since they believed the marauders were only the scouts of a larger party. However, though the five lone raiders held up the caravan for an hour, riding forward to fire and retiring again rapidly, no larger party appeared. The raiders were shouting the war-cries 'Akhu Josa' and 'Abid ash Shaalan' – 'a brother of Josa' and 'slaves of the Shaalan' – which indicated that they were of the Ruwala.

This tiresome harassment of the caravan stopped only when Al Draibi rebuked his comrades for their cowardice, upon which twenty men mounted their camels and rode out after the raiders, who promptly fled.

When the caravan went on, their leader sensibly changed their route from the well-known one, in case the raiders' accomplices might be waiting further on; but apart from this small skirmish, their first four days out from Jauf passed without incident and they made good headway. On the fifth day, however, they ran into trouble. They had struck camp before dawn, and as the sun rose found themselves marching through a landscape shrouded in mist. Then, as the mist lifted, a woman called out that about 200 badawin were visible on the horizon to the left of the line of march. Daghairi ordered the caravan to bear to the right, and brought it in half an hour's time to a cleft in the basalt hills which provided natural shelter. Sixty of their riflemen mounted guard on top of the flanking hills.

The party of strange badawin then approached, and on being challenged by Daghairi said they were Sherarat who had moved from their tents at the news that Ibn Rashid was about to raid them; now that he had gone into the Hamad they were returning home. 'The Sherarat were a friendly tribe,' writes Guarmani, 'and had nothing to fear from us nor we from them, so our caravan could proceed in peace. Al Draibi alone doubted their word. Ordering no one to move, including Daghairi until he should return, he took my drome-dary and descended into the valley.' On approaching the other badawin he certainly recognised some of them as Sherarat, and requested one of the leaders to come and be identified by some Sherarat in the caravan. This was satisfactorily done, and the caravan, feeling reassured, left its position in the hills and went on its way.

But their suspicions were once more aroused when the caravan noticed the odd behaviour of the group they had left. After allowing an interval of half an hour, the other party followed the caravan, always keeping out of rifle range. Daghairi re-positioned the armed men in his party, placing one group in front, one on the flank nearest the mountains and a rearguard to follow behind. The caravan con-sisted mainly of natives of Jauf who were normally on good terms with the Sherarat, though they now began to show some hostility at the way they were being followed. No one could see any reason for the Sherarat's ominous manoeuvring, but the young bloods in the caravan instinctively began to perform the ritual of the war-dance with which the desert man arouses himself and his companions in readiness for battle.

Our youths marched singing all the time. Some shawls attached to three of the lances served as flags; several of the young men in turn left the line to dance and throw their weapons in the air, catch-ing them before they touched the ground. Daghairi spoke not a word. Al Draibi, still mounted on my dromedary had assumed ... the general command.

And then the attack came.

Suddenly the badawin put their dromedaries at a trot and swept round to our left flank, which we promptly defended; then they wheeled round to the front, firing about a hundred shots and accompanying their attack with their war-cry of *Akhu Josa* and *Shaalan*, as had done our five friends on the 17th, and whom we now recognised in the forefront of their line. The mystery was explained. We were being attacked by the Shaalan (the princely

clan of the Ruwala) commanded by Hamad ibn Banaiya. The
Sherarat with him had placed themselves momentarily under his
lead to make a common cause against Tallal ibn Rashid.

The caravan was forced to halt and fight, which they did for two
hours, while prudently trying to keep out of range. The Sherarat
among them took no part, lending their arms to the men of Jauf
who had none. Guarmani says he did not himself fire a shot, not
wishing to waste ammunition. He considered the battle a farce, since
they had only 65 rifles against at least 140. Finally Daghairi ordered
a cease-fire, intending to surrender. Six of the enemy advanced to
parley. They said 'friends safe, but enemies despoiled'. By 'friends'
they meant the Sherarat families, Daghairi and his people, and
Guarmani with Muhammad and Al Draibi. The natives of Jauf were
considered the enemies. Guarmani, familiar with the badawin code
which regards travelling companions as bound together by an almost
sacred bond, knew it was impossible to accept these terms, although
the enemy threatened that the whole party would be robbed if they
did not agree. There was nothing for it but to fight it out, and the
firing began again in earnest. In ten minutes there were two dead
and ten wounded amongst the caravan party, who then lost heart
and surrendered. But Guarmani and his men had no intention of
being captured and robbed. Foremost in the Italian's mind was the
knowledge that his horses would be taken as spoils of war. Al Draibi,
quickly grasping the essentials of the situation, had lightened the load
on their one camel and removed its halter, as well as that of the donkey, to let both animals run free, and had then vaulted on to one
of the horses; Muhammad and Guarmani were already in their
saddles, Muhammad leading the free horse, and with a young
Sirhani man mounted on the grey.

The enemy rode round flashing their drawn swords, calling on
the Italian and his group to surrender. But Guarmani and his men
suddenly went off at a gallop, three of them firing on the enemy
as they rode. Their fire was returned, and Guarmani's horse was
hit and fell under him, but he was able to mount the led horse which
Al Draibi at once brought up to him, and they continued their flight.
The camel and the donkey, urged on by Al Draibi's shouts, ran with
them, keeping up at great speed. Thirty badawin were chasing them.
'Whenever we perceived them separated from each other by the inequality of the ground or the pace of their mounts, we turned to con-
front them, and they retired until joined by the others, then pursued
us again.' This continued until they got to the mountains by the
Wadi al Mukhaidhir, when their pursuers left them to go back to
loot the caravan.

It was ironical that in four months in Arabia Guarmani's life had never really been in danger until this last lap of his journey, in an area where he expected to meet no serious hazards. But Al Draibi's quick thinking and the group's determination not to surrender had allowed them to make good their escape. Guarmani must have been keenly disappointed at the loss of one of his fine stallions, but he does not express his feelings. He was a realist, and accepted misfortune philosophically.

The four men lay up in the mountains until darkness fell, then Guarmani and Al Draibi returned to the scene of the battle. There they found a pathetic sight. Their companions on the caravan had been stripped of all their belongings, the men left quite naked, and the women in nothing but their gowns, for even their head-veils had been taken. Since they could offer no practical help, Guarmani and Al Draibi returned to Mukhaidhir and rejoined Muhammad and the Sirhani. Then a march of eight or nine hours, with only one brief rest, brought them to Kaf, a village of the Wadi Sirhan due east of Qulaita where their journey had begun.

The sad remnants of the caravan reached Ithra, not far from Kaf, on 22 May in a terrible state. 'I went to meet it and distributed fifty measures of dates and assisted the so-called doctor-surgeon of the village to look after the wounded. Four of these unfortunate beings succumbed. . . .'

Having done his best for his former travelling companions, the Italian returned to Kaf and the next day pushed on to the Hauran with his friends. While he was in Kaf he felt a certain satisfaction at hearing on the badawin grapevine that while the Sherarat were helping the Ruwala to loot his caravan, a party of Anaiza had stolen all that they had left in their own tents, as well as their flocks. Because of the general preparations for a *ghazzu* against the Sherarat, the chief shaikhs of that tribe, headed by Salim al Khawi (who had given Guarmani hospitality on the outward journey), had gone to swear obedience to Ibn Rashid and to pay up the arrears of tribute that they owed.

Here Guarmani's account of his journey ends, though he mentions that he went on to Damascus, not to his home town of Jerusalem. Damascus was the centre of the horse trade in Syria, and he could make arrangements there for his newly acquired animals to be shipped out via Beirut.

Guarmani drew a map showing his route and the places he visited; a useful document, if less detailed than scholars would have wished. Among other information which he made available to Europe for the first time was an almost complete list of all the settlements of the Jabal Shammar. His narrative, though frustratingly terse in many places where one is eager for more, still holds plenty to interest a modern reader. The unpretentiousness of the style itself gains the reader's confidence, even where other scholars have cast doubts on Guarmani's story.

His knowledge of the tribes and sub-tribes of north-west Arabia was considerable, and it was this feature, perhaps more than his somewhat sketchy topographical data, which caused Guarmani's Italian book to be rescued from fifty years of oblivion and translated into English in 1916, when the Arab Bureau in Cairo was casting about for all available information which might be relevant in planning the campaigns of T. E. Lawrence.

Guarmani and his family later returned to Italy, where he became a prosperous and respected merchant in Genoa. He died in 1884.

Chapter 8

DOUGHTY

In Arabia Deserta

1876–1878

'As for me who write, I pray that nothing be looked for in this book but the seeing of an hungry man, and the telling of a most weary man; for the rest the sun made me an Arab, but never warped me to Orientalism.'

Even among his great Victorian contemporaries Charles Montagu Doughty was unique, both as traveller and as writer. He went poor to Arabia, and shared the harsh discomforts of badawin life for nearly two years. He acquired not only geographical facts but a close knowledge of the nomadic people. Among his precursors in Arabia only Guarmani had gained more than a superficial knowledge of the badu. Most of the others had moved swiftly through the desert scene, knowing the badawin's reputation for raiding and pillage. Wallin,

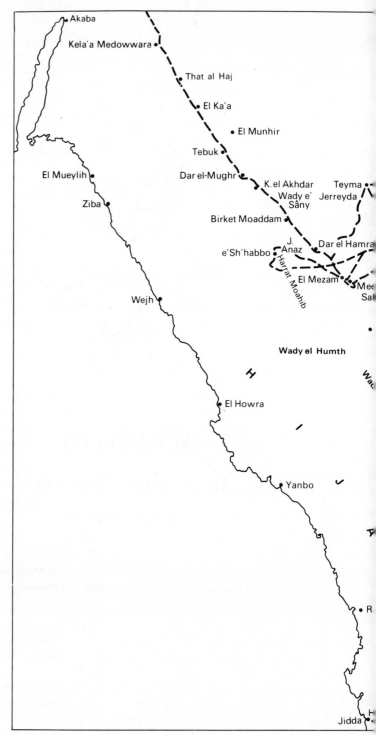

18 Doughty's routes in central and western Arabia

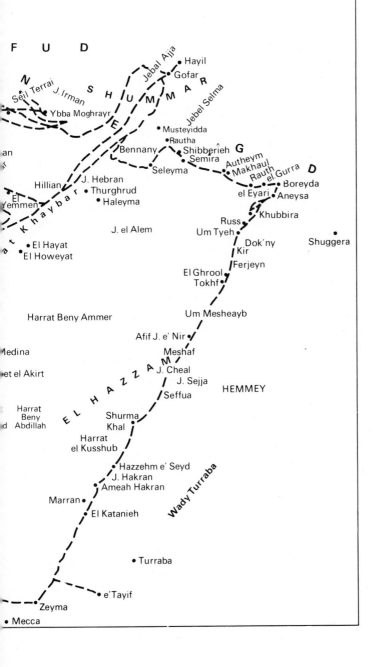

F   U   D

_N_
_S_   H   _U_   _M_   M   A   R

Sejl Terrai
J. Irman   _E_   Jebal Ajja   Hayil
Ybba Moghrayr   Gofar
Jebel Selma

Musteyidda
Rautha
Bennany   Shibberieh   G
Semira   Autheym
Seleyma   Makhaul   el Gurra   D
Rauth   Boreyda
J. Hebran   el Eyari   Aneysa
Hillian   Thurghrud
El   Haleyma   Khubbira
Yemmen

_K_ _h_ _a_ _y_ _b_ _a_ _r_   Russ
J. el Alem   Um Tyeh

_a_ _t_   Dok'ny   Shuggera
El Hayat   Kir
El Howeyat   Ferjeyn
El Ghrool
Tokhf

Harrat Beny Ammer   Um Mesheayb

Afif J. e' Nir
Medina   Meshaf
_M_
et el Akirt   J. Cheal
_A_   J. Sejja   HEMMEY
_Z_   Seffua
Harrat   _Z_
Beny   _A_   Shurma
Abdillah   _H_   Khal

_L_   Harrat   Wady Turraba
el Kusshub
_E_   Hazzehm e' Seyd
J. Hakran
Ameah Hakran
Marran
El Katanieh

Turraba

e' Tayif
Zeyma
Mecca

the Swede who reached Hail in 1845, had been intent on recording facts on such definite subjects as the geography and government of the Jabal Shammar; Palgrave had mixed little with the tribesmen; Burckhardt and Burton, both interested in the badawin, were not able to live amongst them for any length of time. For the most part, the nomads of Arabia, an elusive and amorphous community, had remained outside the reference of Western travellers, preserving their ancient, restless life, a law unto themselves.

Doughty, born in 1843, was the son of a landowning Norfolk parson. At Cambridge he had studied geology, but later at London and Oxford devoted himself to Teutonic and early English literature. In character he was grave and serious, and his fellow students found him often aloof and unsociable. As a young man he was apparently deeply religious, though in later life he called himself an agnostic. He certainly had a strong sense of man's spiritual nature, even when rejecting specific religious dogma. While he was in Arabia he made no effort to conceal his Christian belief, a matter of principle which nearly cost him his life on several occasions, but his journey of exploration went beyond mere geography to discovery about himself and his own capacities and limitations.

He was a tall and strongly-built young man with aquiline features and a reddish beard when, at the age of twenty-eight, he travelled through Europe as a poor student, reaching Palestine in 1874 and spending the summer and autumn in the Holy Land. In 1875 on a journey by camel through Sinai to Maan and Petra he met and spoke to badu who told him that at Madayin Salah there were other monuments carved in the rock face. These were unknown to Europe and Doughty decided that he must go and record them. Refused permission by the Turks, and denied official backing by the British, he decided to go anyway, at his own risk. But first he had to spend a year in Damascus perfecting his Arabic.

He intended to travel with the hajj caravan, and his Arab friends assured him that no one would object if he went only as far as Madayin Salah, since that point was not within the territory of the holy places. So, adopting the dress of a Syrian Christian – a Nasrany – and the name of Khalil, he set out with the great motley crowd of the Syrian caravan, which left Muzairib, outside Damascus, on 13 November 1876.

Madayin Salah was a watering-place on the pilgrim route, reached after three weeks on camel-back. The reservoir of water was guarded by a Turkish fort, and it was with the guards here that Doughty stayed as the caravan went on its way. Hiring a certain Zeyd, a minor shaikh of the Fejir badawin, as a guide, he spent two months exploring the monuments. Like those in Petra, they were Nabataean tombs, with elaborate façades sculptured in the sandstone cliff. Over some of them were inscriptions, of which he took careful impressions.

He had intended originally to rejoin the pilgrim caravan when it returned from the hajj, but during his time in Madayin Salah he changed his mind. He gave his records of the tomb inscriptions to one of the pilgrims for delivery to the British Consul in Damascus, and went off with Zeyd to live with him and his family in the wilderness.

Unto this new endeavour, I was but slenderly provided; yet did not greatly err, when I trusted my existence ... amongst an unlettered and reputed lawless tribesfolk, (with whom, however, I had already some more favourable acquaintance;) which amidst a life of never-ending hardship and want, continue to observe a Great Semitic Law, unwritten; namely the ancient Faith of their illimitable empty wastes.

By the word 'Faith' Doughty was referring not to Islam but to the ancient code of hospitality of the desert. For the Muslim religion he had no sympathy.

So Zeyd and Doughty, with an Ageyli companion (a camel-trooper in Turkish service), filled their water-skin at a rain-pool and headed eastwards in the direction of Taima. The Fejir shaikh, who in the hope of monetary gain was taking the Englishman to live with his people, was a man of middle age, swarthy and hollow-cheeked, with a 'hunger-bitten visage'. But 'his carriage was that haughty grace of the wild creatures', and for a badawin he was tolerant and good-humoured.

With nothing to eat except a bite of barley bread, they travelled all day across a gravelly upland plain, and towards sunset began to look for Zeyd's people. The camels came into sight first, and the herdsman welcomed Zeyd and his friends with a bowl of camel's milk. Zeyd went ahead to his tent, and shortly afterwards Doughty was surprised to be invited into the women's quarters, where Zeyd introduced their guest to his wife, Hirfa, bidding her take good care of him. In accordance with custom among the northern tribes, she was not veiled. Their black tent was a small, miserable affair, without even a carpet inside.

Now for three months without a break Doughty as Khalil lived the life of the badawin, sharing in their hardships, their adventures, and their small, infrequent joys. It was February, and the camels were eating their fill of the desert herbs and not requiring water, so there was no need for this group of badu to go near known wells or frequented routes. They moved only to find fresh pastures in the trackless wilderness.

For the men, mornings in camp were passed in coffee-drinking. Sitting round one of the camp fires, they would brew up and serve the tiny cups of coffee, and share out between them whatever small stock of tobacco they might have, till it was time for the noon prayer. After that they went to their own tents for 'the mid-day commons of their wretched country, a bowl of musty dates and another of the foul desert water', and then all retired to the women's quarters. Doughty asked one of the women one day how the men whiled away the tedious afternoon hours. 'She answered, demurely smiling, "How, sir, but in solace with the hareem!" '

Zeyd's tribe were fanatical Muslims, and at first the senior shaikh and others were angry that Zeyd had brought an outsider to live with them. But they did not deny him hospitality, and as they came to know him Doughty was welcomed with kindly words at all their coffee-fires. But these friendly badu warned him not to wander far from the camp on his own, since other tribesmen might be wild and murderous.

The Englishman was uncertain how long he could safely remain in the desert, and several times nearly decided to make for the coast and the outside world. He had little money, but the few medicines he carried were always in demand among the Arabs. In the end, trusting to badawin hospitality and the people's need for his medical help, he overcame his misgivings and stayed.

As time passed he became accepted to such an extent by Zeyd's kinsmen that he was regarded almost as one of the family. He even played a part in sorting out Zeyd's domestic troubles, and coaxed his offended wife back after she had left him. But Doughty could never come to terms with the badawin idea of marriage, in which he felt that a woman's lot was 'unequal concubinage' and 'weary servitude'. A girl could be divorced as soon as her husband tired of her, and if she remained married she often had to share her husband's affections with another.

Though the badu had come to treat Doughty as one of themselves, his presence in the desert was a constant puzzle to them. Was he a spy? they would ask. Was he banished? Was he looking for treasure? They questioned him too about his own country, wanting to know how far away it was, whether his people lived in houses or tents, and what pack animals they used. They were amazed at his answers, asking incredulously, 'Khalil, be there no Beduins at all in the land of the Nasara?'

Throughout the spring, living peacefully with Zeyd, Doughty enjoyed the simple life. 'Pleasant is the sojourn in the wandering village, in this purest earth and air, with the human fellowship, which is all day met at leisure about the cheerful coffee-fire.' This was his happiest time in Arabia.

Zeyd was only a minor shaikh in his tribe; the senior chief was a certain Motlog, a well-built man with a Jewish-looking face and thick black beard. In Motlog's majlis the badu would meet to discuss tribal affairs, in particular their relations with the dreaded Ibn Rashid of Hail. (They had fallen foul of this prince by refusing for five years to pay his taxes, until the amir had himself come and forcibly extracted the arrears.) To the majlis also was brought news of raiding parties encountered, or of fresh water and pasture, and the gathering served as a council of elders and public tribunal which settled disputes. The Englishman was impressed with the wisdom and fairness of badawin justice.

Nothing escaped Doughty's acutely observant eye. He recorded every detail of the household equipment as he made notes daily in the badu tents. They thought of him as a *hakim*, a learned man, and did not object to his writing, though in the settlements later he learned to be more cautious.

In due course, as Zeyd's camp moved from pasture to pasture, they came near Taima, the oasis visited by Guarmani, which lies between the Syrian pilgrim-route and Hail. Doughty joined Zeyd and some companions on a visit to the town to buy provisions. But, fearing Ibn Rashid, the tribe did not wish to delay near Taima and as soon as they had stocked up with supplies they decided to make a forced march eastwards into the tribal area of the Bishr, to try to keep out of the way of the Hail ruler and his tax-officials.

They rode till after sunset, and having travelled forty miles that day, halted to sleep without pitching a proper camp. At dawn they set off again, easing their pace only when they knew they had reached the safety of Bishr territory. But they continued to travel almost daily south-east till they reached the rugged heights of the Jabal Irnan group of mountains. In this region Zeyd showed Doughty some ancient rock drawings and inscriptions in a hidden gorge.

In the succeeding weeks the camp shifted frequently, settling now on the edge of the Nafud, now near the Helwan mountains. There had been rain, but locusts had ravaged the spring herbage, and with the need to find pasture the tribal group divided, Motlog going off independently with one half, while half including Zeyd and Doughty stayed with another shaikh named Rahyel. The smaller community drew more closely together, and the gatherings in Zeyd's tent were full of cheerful raillery and banter in the badawin manner. To pass the idle moments they would sometimes ask their guest to teach them English words, and Zeyd was much pleased with himself when he could say 'Girl, bring milk!' to Hirfa over the tent curtain.

Of course they asked Doughty if he had any desire to be married to one of their women, thinking it unnatural that a man should go any time without a wife. Zeyd suggested that the Englishman might like to have Hirfa if he divorced her, but Doughty declared it was contrary to his belief to take another man's wife. From time to time fathers offered him their daughters, and brothers their sisters.

Spring turned into summer, 'the drooping herb withered ... the wilderness changed colour', and in the land of the Bishr Doughty saw new scenes and facets of nomad life.

There was a dramatic moment one morning when the herdsman rode in to tell the assembly that more than sixty of their own camels had been driven off by raiders. All the shaikhs ran at once to mount their mares, and soon the camp was emptied of able-bodied men as all except Doughty went to look for the enemy. But the tribesmen who had gone out on foot returned at noon without news, and then sat all day waiting for their remaining camels to come home. It was only that evening that Rahyel led them out in pursuit of the thieves, and Doughty was critical of their feckless waste of precious time.

Four days later the party came back with a tale of failure. They had followed the enemy into the Nafud for two days until their tracks were lost in wind-blown sand. They had ridden 200 miles for nothing, but were not down-hearted; they would later learn the identity of the raiders and get their own back.

Motlog, who had been to see Ibn Rashid, came back from Hail and told the tribe that they could return without fear to their own area. The Hail rulers knew that generosity was politically expedient, and their gifts of clothing and money had won Motlog's good opinions. The tribe set off happily next morning, and a few days' marching took them back to Erudda, a great summer watering-place of the Fejir in the region of Madayin Salah.

But summer in the camp was a succession of long weary days and Doughty was feeling the debilitating effects of three months of meagre badawin food. On many occasions he again toyed with thoughts of leaving, but at other times he felt a renewed longing to be among the free Arabs of the desert. In particular he felt an urge to explore the *harra* plateau, the black lava country which was visible to the west.

Hearing of a party which was going to Wejh across the Aueyrid Harra, he took the opportunity of attaching himself to them, but he had brought neither food nor water when he joined them and was nearly fainting in the saddle as they rode through the heat of the day.

Towards sunset they reached the foot of the steep slopes which lead up to the *harra* plateau, 'a sandstone platform mountain ... over-laid, two thousand square miles, to the brink, by a general effusion of lavas'. When others dismounted to make the climb easier for the camels, Doughty was too weak to go on foot. The aching weariness of the day had been 'a long dying without death', and although even-

ing brought a respite from the heat, his life was made a misery by
the taunts and jeers of a pretty but vicious badawin girl. The rest
of the party were mostly strangers to him, rough men who would
only reluctantly pour him a little of their water to drink.

Next day, after several hours' climbing in the folds of the lower
slopes, he looked out on the sombre desolation of the plateau. 'All
about us is an iron wilderness; a bare and black shining beach of
heated vulcanic stones.' But in spite of the forbidding prospect the
air was cooler, for they were now 5,000 feet above sea level, and
though the *harra* looked as if it could not sustain life, it was the territory of the Moahib tribe who flourished in these uplands where their
flocks were safe from marauders.

When the caravan crossed the lava-field and began the descent
to the coastal plain, Doughty dropped out of the party and rested
to regain his strength in a friendly camp. But a few days later, guided
by an old man, he returned to the plateau. Now he had a changed
view of that grim landscape. 'I saw a wonderful new and horrid
world of vulcanic rusty hills and craters, – black powder, sharp lava
slag, and cinders was this soil under our camels' feet.' He counted
more than thirty small extinct volcanoes from the point where he
stood. When he startled a herd of gazelles he observed another
strange fact: these normally pale animals were here the same colour
as the basalt rocks.

They found the Moahib tribe with their shaikh, Tollog, and in
their camp Doughty was able to lodge with an itinerant trader he
had met before. It was obvious that the Moahib had mixed feelings
about his presence, but he wanted more time to explore the area.
As a geologist he was fascinated by the phenomena of the *harra*, and
in spite of Tollog's disapproval he managed to climb one of the
smaller craters, about 300 ft high. He was at pains to find out the
names of the various geographical features of this unmapped land,
and constantly questioned the badu, but like other travellers found it
hard to get reliable answers.

Tollog was anxious to get rid of him, but, says Doughty, 'as each
breath of air refreshed my spirits, I mused anew of breaking into
Arabia'. This time he was set on getting to Khaibar, that strange
oasis lying in a hidden valley of the other great *harra*. But the difficulties of travelling constantly delayed and frustrated his plans. Now
his host the trader had to go to Wejh; Doughty wanted to stay with
the Moahib, but they were moving camp and told the Nasrany
rudely that they did not want his company. For some time he
lingered disconsolately at the deserted camp, but fearing to be left
alone in that barren land, he eventually followed at some distance
behind the unfriendly nomads of the plateau. At evening, when the
tribe camped, he went and made his peace with old Tollog, who

was not so much hostile as worried by Doughty's presence, and afraid the Turkish authorities might hold him responsible if harm should befall this stranger.

One day Tollog came to Doughty's tent and asked to see his 'quaint things of the Nasara', and Doughty showed him his telescope and the pictures in his medical book. 'Shall I write thy name?' he asked, and did so to amuse the old man. But Tollog was alarmed at such magic. ' "Khalil," said he, shrinking with sudden apprehension, "I do pray thee write not my name!" Seeing him so out of countenance, I rent the paper in little pieces and buried them under the harra stones, which made him easy again.'

By 24 June all the sources of water on the *harra* were dried up, and the Moahib made for the tribe's summer camp in Wadi Thirba near Madayin Salah. In the great heat the milk from the cattle failed, and at such times the badu relied on their *mereesy* or dried milk cake, which could be crumbled and diluted with water. 'They keep a bowl standing by them and sup of it often in the long daylight.' Doughty himself had a little rice, received in payment for his doctoring, and his day's sustenance was one handful, with a little *mereesy* mixed in with it. His figure was wasted from hunger, and some of the women from neighbouring tents would pity him, and offer him some of their own scanty food. The badu were accustomed to this near-famine, suffered yearly between the drying-up of the milk supplies, and the date harvest in late summer. It was alleviated only by the occasional slaughter of a lamb, which would be shared among a man's friends.

All through the fiery weeks of July Doughty stayed among the Moahib. He was still hoping to go to Khaibar, but no one would take him, and now his strength was ebbing again.

There were always those among the badu who resented Doughty's presence, and tempers were liable to flare on the slightest provocation. An argument between the Englishman and one of the tribesmen led to an ugly and aggressive mood among some of the Moahib, and one of the shaikhs declared, 'The man is a Nasrany, I say cut his head off, and there is none that will require his blood at our hand.' But the other shaikhs supported Doughty against their kinsman and the trouble blew over. When he was aware of hostility Doughty took out the pistol which was always packed at the bottom of his saddle-bags and kept it inside his shirt. He never let the badu see it, believing that his best chance of living safely among them was to be passive and patient, but the weapon was there as a last resort, the only form of defence he had, apart from a penknife.

Shaikh Tollog and many of the Moahib moved away from the Wadi Thirba, but Doughty stayed for a few weeks longer, living with an old hunter. It was a period of almost intolerable exhaustion and low spirits, during which he began to feel that he would die of hunger if he did not manage to find hospitality again among a larger group of badu. In the end he rejoined the Moahib, and when they learned that the Fejir were back in the district, Doughty accompanied Tollog on a visit to Motlog, the Fejir shaikh. The Englishman had already been warned that even badu who had entertained him kindly would not welcome him on a return visit, and this proved to be the case when he arrived at Motlog's tent. 'The Fukara saw me again with a cold fanatical countenance.' After Motlog had provided a feast for the Moahib, which Doughty shared, he knew he was safe for a while, having partaken of their 'bread and salt', but the future seemed bleak. 'The fortune of the morrow was dark as death, all ways were shut before me.'

He had hoped to travel with the Fejir to Taima and Hail, but Motlog refused to take him. Later, relenting, he said Khalil could come as a protégé of Zeyd, his former companion. But during their earlier time together Doughty had fallen out with Zeyd; Zeyd still nursed a grudge, and now disowned his erstwhile guest. It was a bitter moment. The dispirited traveller remained somewhat uneasily in the Fejir camp. Zeyd's humour improved later, but Doughty was not disposed to resume their old association. Instead he formed a new friendship with a man named Mehsan, and a few days later moved into his tent.

They left Madayin Salah on 28 August, and Doughty's spirits rose again. 'I had Nejd before me, the free High Arabia!' With Mehsan and some other families he parted from the tribal group and made for Taima where the dates were now ripe. They arrived just as the new moon ushered in the fasting month of Ramadhan.

The Taima villagers remembered Doughty with some ill-feeling. It had chanced that just after his earlier visit the great water-pit of the town, the *Haddaj*, had fallen in, and everyone believed this to have been the result of the Nasrany's evil eye. They had rebuilt the sides of the pit three times and they had collapsed again each time.

Doughty was not unduly worried by stories that the people were ready to kill him, and went to see the water-pit with two young men of the town. He heard the comments of the bystanders: 'Look, it is the kafir! Will the sheykhs kill him? Is not this he who has overthrown the *Haddaj*? Or will they have him build it again, and give him a reward and they say it shall be better than before?' Though he had strapped his pistol inside his shirt he realised that, as so often among the Arabs, their animosity was all in talk.

Since the badu were accustomed to hunger, the month of fasting was no great hardship to them. Abstinence from water and tobacco was harder than forgoing food. During this time the cultivators gave up all but the most essential work, and the artisans worked only half-days. Mehsan and his badu passed the days sleeping under the palm-trees.

Doughty passed the whole of Ramadhan in Taima, giving medical help where he could, and being entertained in houses where the owners were well disposed. He also made excursions to see ancient sites and inscriptions outside the town. One interesting stone was shown him by the local blacksmith. Upon it was a carved scene and a script unknown to him, but he did not copy it. This was the stone with the ancient Aramaic inscription which Huber later acquired. It is now in the Louvre.

At the end of Ramadhan he shared the enjoyment of the people at the Bairam festival. The badawin women in his camp celebrated with dancing, and asked the Englishman to show them his people's 'holiday dance'. When the normally serious Doughty obliged with an obviously spirited attempt at ballroom dancing without a partner, the badu were astounded. 'Oh! what was that outlandish skipping and casting of the shanks, and this footing it to and fro!' But when he explained that it should be done 'bosom to bosom' with a woman, 'they thought of us but scorn and villainy'.

With the end of the fasting, Taima was full of tribesmen who came to stock up with the new season's dates. The rest of the Fejir arrived, bringing Doughty's old camel which had been grazing with their own. He was angered to find her back sore with galls; they had been riding and misusing her.

Among the badu in town was a group of Bishr under their shaikh Misshel, and one of them, after some reluctance, agreed to take Doughty to Hail for three riyals. With the Bishr he set out in misty rainy weather on a route which would skirt the southern edge of the Nafud and approach Jabal Shammar from the south-east. By the fifth day out they were ascending a pass which took them up to a plateau 5,400 feet high north of Jabal al Kharram.

At this point things began to go wrong. After a quarrel over Doughty's red Moroccan girdle which the Bishr shaikh coveted, Misshel threatened to send him back to Madayin Salah. But hearing next morning that an advance party was riding to Hail, Doughty arranged to go with them. It turned out to be a very unhappy ride.

The others were mounted on *theluls*, fast riding camels, and his elderly and ailing beast could not keep up. The party threatened to leave him behind; they were travelling fast for fear of hostile badu, and carried neither food nor water, counting on getting meals at tents found by the way. The first day they covered fifty miles, not stopping until they found a camp where they could have supper. The same relentless pace was kept up the next day, and even after an evening meal the party hastened on. They were ready to ride all night to reach Hail the quicker, but Doughty ached in every limb, and his camel was all in. Only when she collapsed under him did Askar the party leader agree to stop for the night.

Next day Jabal Aja, the principal mountain of the Jabal Shammar group, appeared ahead of them, and they passed Jufaifa, the village where Guarmani had collected his horses after leaving Hail. When they paused to drink from a pool of rain-water in the rock, Askar had a word of warning for Doughty.

Khalil, the people where we are going are jealous. Let them not see thee writing, for be sure they will take it amiss; but wouldst thou write, write covertly and put away these leaves of books. Thou wast hitherto with the Beduw, and the Beduw have known thee what thou art; but hearest thou? they are not like good-hearted, in yonder villages!

At the semi-derelict village of Muqaq, the Englishman at last gave up, and was left behind with his rafiq to continue at his own pace. Here he felt he 'was in the world again' when he saw Baghdad wares in the market, and observed that fire was lit no longer with flint and steel, but with Viennese matches. Like Palgrave, here in the Jabal Shammar he was struck by the purity of the classical language in central Arabia; 'it is like an Attic sweetness in the Arabian tongue'.

It was another two days before he reached Hail, for they had yet to negotiate the eighteen-mile-long pass through Jabal Aja, and another eleven miles on the bare granite plain beyond. As they approached the city, people coming out from Hail who had already heard about the Nasrany's approach, asked the rafiq, 'Why dost thou bring him?' – a query which caused some dismay to Doughty, and more to his escort.

The prince of Hail, of course, also knew of the foreigner's coming; in fact he had heard months before that a strange Christian was living among the badu. Doughty arrived dirty and in rags, but the hospitality of Ibn Rashid was available to everybody. Soon after he reached the Meshab, the town square, an official showed him where he could lodge in one of the guest-rooms opposite the palace, and then invited him into the *qasr* for breakfast – dusty old dates which he would not eat, and coffee.

From the coffee-room he was summoned to his first audience with the amir. By this time, fourteen years after Palgrave's visit, Tallal was dead, and his brother Muhammad was prince of Hail, having come to power by the murder of Tallal's two sons Bandar and Badr. When Doughty entered the prince's chamber, giving the greeting 'Peace be upon you', he received no answer; some Muslims would not give the traditional salutation to a Christian. Muhammad merely bade him be seated. The prince, who was about forty, was 'lean of flesh and hollow as the Nejders', a man of small stature with the face of a hard-living badawin. At this first meeting Muhammad started with the usual questions, whence and why had he come? When Doughty answered truthfully about his time amongst the badu, the amir, who already knew it all, seemed favourably impressed. Even more so was an elderly shaikh who sat with him, who commented '*Rajul saduk*, wellah! a man to trust', and added that this traveller was not like one who had come years before – a reference to Guarmani or Palgrave.

After the audience Muhammad Ibn Rashid led Doughty to see his pair of oryx in the palace gardens. Doughty knew of these animals from the badu, and had seen their horns used as tools at Taima, but this was the first time he had seen the creature in the flesh. (He was the first to report the existence of the oryx to scientists in England, and believed himself to have been the first European to have seen it.) Their pleasant stroll ended when the amir dismissed Doughty amicably at the garden gate.

After supper and coffee in the palace, the Englishman was confused when he was summoned by an official to go and visit 'the amir'. He had not realised that there was a second man in Hail almost equal in power to Muhammad. In a different coffee-hall he met a 'great noble figure half-lying along upon his elbow'. This was Hamud, Muhammad's cousin, the son of that same Ubaid whom Palgrave had met, and who had tried with a letter to Riyadh to make trouble for Palgrave and his companion.

Doughty found Hamud had 'a pleasant man-like countenance' and an easy, friendly manner. His conversation was more sophisticated than that of the prince, and he asked Doughty about the wonders of the Nasara's world, about the telegraph, about glass, and about a 'palace of crystal' of which he had heard. He also wanted to know about 'rock oil' – paraffin – which was being imported from the north for the lamps of Hail. Was it true that it was made from human urine? For the modern reader there is a strange, dramatic irony in Hamud's questions about oil. But the future wealth of Arabia was something that neither Doughty nor his host could have envisaged in their wildest dreams.

The arrival of an educated stranger, even under the curious circumstances of Doughty's visit to Hail, provided a nine-days' wonder for the shaikhs. On his second day Doughty was taken to sup with Hamud, and the day after, the prince Muhammad sent for him again to spend the evening in the palace, where there was another session of questions and answers.

Like other travellers, Doughty was impressed by the spectacle of Ibn Rashid's majlis in the town square, and describes it as one of the notable features of Hail life. He goes on to record all he could find out about the city and its surrounding areas. Of Ibn Rashid's government he comments: 'He rules as the hawk among buzzards, with eyes and claws in a land of ravin, yet in general not cruelly, for that would weaken him.' The people loved and feared the ruler, grateful for the security he gave them, but dreading the sharpness of his punishments. For European readers who were hungry for facts Doughty provides estimates of the number of Ibn Rashid's subjects (about 30,000), his income from taxation, the cost of his public hospitality, the number of his fighting men, and the extent of his dominions. He also tells the story of Muhammad's seizure of power and of the welter of blood through which he came to the throne.

From what Doughty saw, he could say 'Ibn Rashid is today the greatest prince in Nejd'. This was the period when the power of the Saudis was at a low ebb after the destructive rivalry of the brothers Abdullah and Saud, the two princes whom Palgrave had seen in Riyadh.

In Hail Doughty met various interesting people, among them a Baghdad Jew turned Muslim who secretly asked the Nasrany if he had any brandy; there was also Aneybar (Anaibar) an Abyssinian of the prince's household, a man of Tallal's generation and almost certainly the same who had escorted Guarmani from the Saudi camp to Hail.

In spite of the more regular meals he was receiving from the palace, and with kind hosts in Hail, Doughty was 'worn and broken in this long year of famine and fatigues', and after a week or two had 'fallen into a great languor'. He suffered particularly from being the object of everybody's curiosity in Hail, and felt this was a greater hardship than 'the daily hazards and long bodily sufferance'. But in retrospect, unhappy memories were leavened by more pleasant ones, of moments when human gratitude and kindness cut across the barriers of race and religion. Badawin who had received free medical help blessed him as they passed in the square.

A poor nomad of the Ruwella cried out simply, when he received his medicines: 'Money he had none to give the hakim, wellah! he prayed me to be content to receive his shirt.' And had I suffered it he would have stripped himself and gone away naked in his sorry open cloak ... and when I let him go, he murmured, *Jizak Ullah kheyr*, God recompense thee with good.

The weather grew colder as autumn drew on, and towards the middle of November the Englishman wished to leave Hail. He had been treating Hamud's little son for fever and dysentery, but when the child was recovered felt no more reason to stay, 'for I found little rest at all or refreshment in Hayil'.

Though Ibn Rashid had received him pleasantly enough, it was inevitable that when the novelty wore off Doughty's continued presence should rouse suspicions. The Hail rulers constantly feared spies from some hostile power. Not understanding the idea of scientific enquiry, they could believe only that travellers from distant lands had some secret and sinister purpose. We have already learned from Palgrave that it was a habit of Arab rulers, puzzled at the presence of a foreign visitor, to offer the stranger a house and render him harmless by keeping him permanently in their land. Such an offer was also made to Doughty, in the typically circuitous Arab way. Imbarak, the captain of the royal bodyguard, approached him with the suggestion that he stay in Hail in the employment of the amir – 'only become a Moslem, it is a little word and soon said'. Doughty was not prepared to accept, but he had no doubt that the message came from the prince.

At this time the Persian hajj arrived at Hail, and for a few days the capital was filled with feverish activity and thronged with badu who came to sell camels to the pilgrim camp outside the city. On the day of the caravan's departure, Doughty was watching the great procession move off, when a man dressed like a Baghdad merchant muttered something as he walked by.

I thought the hajjy would say medicines; but he answered, 'If I speak in the French language, will you understand me?'
'I shall understand it! but what countryman art thou?' I beheld a pale alien's face with a chestnut beard. . . .
He responded, 'I am an Italian, a Piedmontese of Turin'.
'And what brings you hither upon this hazardous voyage? . . . are you a Moslem?'
'Ay.'

The man said he had come to Syria eight years previously and had then gone to Baghdad, where he studied in an Islamic college, was circumcised and turned Muslim.

When I said I could never find better than a headache in the farrago of the koran, and it amazed me that one born in the Roman country . . . should become the brother of Asiatic barbarians in a fond religion! he answered. . . . 'Aha! well, a man may not always choose, but he must sometime go with the world.' . . . It was in his mind to publish his Travels when he returned to Europe.

Doughty asked the stranger his name, saying, 'Remember mine, for these are hazardous times and places.' As he left to mount his camel, the Italian answered, 'Francesco Ferrari'. It was a strange and poignant meeting, two fellow-Europeans for a moment making contact in the heart of Arabia.

Many months later, Doughty spoke to the Italian consulate in Syria about Ferrari, and even made enquiries in Italy, but never heard of him again. He feared that the Italian must have been murdered on the hajj – there were always stories of Christians in disguise being killed at Mecca.

By now Doughty had hardly any money. He had sold his camel for six or seven riyals, but some of this was stolen one day from his lodgings. After complaining to Hamud, he returned to find thirty riyals had been placed in his purse. In a typically proud gesture he sent the money back to Hamud from whom he knew it had come.

When the city was quiet again after the departure of the hajj, he appealed to Hamud to help him get to Khaibar. He said he wished to see the Jewish antiquities there, but he also wanted to explore the Khaibar *harra*, in which he expected to find the head of the Wadi Rummah which is 'the great dry waterway of all northern Arabia'. Hamud promised to help, while warning him that Khaibar was full of fever and unfriendly people.

A few days later Doughty was involved in an altercation with Imbarak, the captain of the guard, who began to insist on the foreigner's departure. Imbarak found some Hutaim, due to leave in a day or two, who would escort him to Khaibar; but an hour later, with typical capriciousness, he ordered Doughty to leave immediately. '*Ukhlus!* have done, delay not, or wellah! the Emir will send to take off thy head.' When the Englishman refused to hand over the key of his room, Imbarak's men-at-arms jostled and manhandled him, trying to push him back to his lodging. In a moment of fury, Imbarak spat in Doughty's face, but even so, when Doughty cried out '*Dakhil-ak!*' – the Arabic plea for sanctuary – he took a camel-stick and beat back his own men who had torn off their victim's outer garments.

As soon as he was left alone Doughty packed his things ready for departure, keeping his pistol inside his shirt. Angry at the indignities he had suffered he appealed to Hamud: 'Help me in this trouble, for that bread and salt which is between us.' Hamud promised to prevent Imbarak from harassing him further until the Englishman could speak to Ibn Rashid.

After the midday prayer Doughty saw the prince in the square. Latterly, he had noticed that Muhammad's manner was cold and arrogant. Now he met the haughty look that was turned on him and said, without ceremony, 'I depart.' 'So go,' answered the prince.

'Shall I come to speak with thee?' asked Doughty, and was dismissed with, 'I am too busy.'

Even so, Doughty felt that he could not leave without a guarantee of safety, and during the afternoon majlis in the square he approached the amir again, like any other suppliant citizen. He asked for safe-conduct out of Hail, and complained at the behaviour of Imbarak and his men. The prince replied, 'Fear not; but ours be the care for thy safety, and we will give thee a passport', and he ordered his secretary to provide the necessary document.

At this point the Englishman said: 'I brought thee from my country an excellent telescope', but the prince refused the gift, saying he did not require it. 'I answered the emir with a frank word of the desert, *weysh aad*, as one might say, "What odds!" Mohammed Ibn Rashid shrunk back in his seat, as if I had disparaged his dignity before the people; but recovering himself, he said, with better looks and a friendly voice, "Sit down." ' The amir then sealed the passport document, and the secretary read it out: 'That all unto whose hands this bill may come, who owe obedience to Ibn Rashid, know it is the will of the Emir that no one should do any offence to this Nasrany.'

Doughty was allowed a final supper in the palace before he left, and accepted four riyals from Muhammad and four from Hamud. When he returned to the Meshab a badawi with a camel was waiting to load his baggage, and he mounted and rode out of Hail escorted by three Hutaim men. The date of his departure was, by his reckoning, 20 November 1877. He had been in the city about a month.

They headed south-west, past Qufar, where Doughty found an example of that natural Arab courtesy which often made up for the insults he suffered. They stopped at the small hut of some date-sellers. 'These poor folk, disherited of the world, spoke to me with human kindness. . . . The women, of their own thought, took from my shoulders and mended my mantle which had been rent yesterday at Haiyl.'

On the journey to Khaibar Doughty was pushed from pillar to post, meeting generally hostile badu who wanted nothing to do with strangers. The first night he had a surly reception from a Hutaim Shaikh, who nevertheless gave him a simple meal and a night's lodging. But Doughty sensed that Salih, his guide, was anxious to be rid of him, and sure enough at the next camp they reached, the three men of his escort abandoned him. Luckily he found himself with poor but kindly people who treated him well. By these badu he was passed on to another uncooperative Hutaim leader. But among the hangers-on in the camp was a man named Ghroceyb who offered to take the stranger to Khaibar for four riyals.

The direct route to Khaibar lay over the most extensive of the north Arabian lava-fields, the great Harrat Khaibar, and Ghroceyb now led the Englishman up to the desolate black uplands. The land rose steadily to the plateau and on the first night Doughty's aneroid registered 4,300 feet. At the second night's stop he took a reading of 6,000 feet, the highest point he had yet found in Arabia, and realised he was on the watershed where the Wadi Rummah had its beginning.

During their third day on the *harra* the sky was dark with lowering clouds, and the going was abominable in an area where the lava took the form of petrified waves with sharp crests, or lay in heaps of boulders like fallen masonry, making the camel slip and stumble. The 'black horror' of the *harra* landscape was relieved only by some golden-red sandstone crags which rose incongruously out of the dark expanse of rock. Ghroceyb, armed with his matchlock, went ahead on foot, picking out a way where the ground was easiest for the camel. At one point, turning back suddenly he surprised Doughty in the act of making notes of his aneroid readings. It was an anxious moment, but the guide's only reaction was to ask the Nasrany if he could not, with his magical art of letters, write a good spell which would help them through that dreadful country. The two men began to trust one another, and when Doughty offered to carry the heavy matchlock rifle on the camel, Ghroceyb assented, so long as it hung simply where he could grab it on the instant.

The whole of the Harrat Khaibar was reputed to be four days' camel journey in length, which Doughty estimated at 100 miles. There was an easier route to Khaibar, but, as the English traveller learned later, Ghroceyb had killed a man and had not yet paid his blood debt. He had chosen to cross the *harra* because he was unlikely to meet anyone along that way. As they went on he showed a certain reluctance to enter Khaibar, which was under the Dowla, the Turkish administration, fearing he might be seized and imprisoned, but Doughty told him that he travelled under the Dowla's protection and reassured him. Because of Ghroceyb's desire to avoid other Arabs, Doughty travelled further over the *harra* than any other European before or since. Even Philby, having seen as much as he wanted of the volcanic landscape, usually took the easier routes which skirted the edges.

The weather was clearer and the going easier over a flat plain as they covered the last stretch before Khaibar. The appearance of flies told them they were nearing the oasis, and the air got warmer as they dropped to a lower altitude. Finally, leaving the basalt plateau, they descended to a valley green with cornfields, and in a bitter aside Doughty exclaims that the corn was to ripen before he got away from Khaibar. Both Ghroceyb and his charge grew edgy as they approached the oasis. Ghroceyb could not bear to dawdle on the outskirts, fearing enemies, and Doughty, reflecting that they were now in land which was considered part of the holy Hijaz, thought religious fanatics might kill him if things went badly.

Khaibar was a village of black people in a black landscape; sunk in the valleys of the *harra*, fear-ridden, gloomy and isolated, it had a strange, sinister air which Doughty sensed at once. They approached through the outlying palm-groves and fertile gardens. 'The deep ground is mire and rushes and stagnant water, and there sunk upon our spirits a sickly and fenny vapour.... How strange are these dank Kheybar valleys in the waterless Arabia! A heavy presentiment of evil lay upon my heart as we rode in this deadly drowned atmosphere.'

Coming in under the massive acropolis rock with its former Jewish citadel, which Guarmani had noted twelve years before, they reached the gate of the village on their ninth day out from Hail. They went at once to lodge with Abd el-Hady, an acquaintance of Ghroceyb. Early next morning the guide left and Doughty was later taken to call on the aga, the Ottoman commander of the garrison, who was a black man of Galla (Ethiopian) origin named Abdullah es-Siruan.

Doughty knew that his host suspected that he was not a Muslim. Back at the house he decided to be frank, and admitted he was an Englishman, pointing out that his nation was friendly with the Ottoman Dowla. But trouble was not long in coming. The garrison commander sent a domineering bully from among his soldiers to bring Doughty before him, and also demanded to inspect the stranger's baggage. The literate village head-man was ordered to come and list the contents.

Doughty watched as his precious belongings were emptied from his saddlebags into the street. His compass, wrapped in a piece of cloth, was passed over as being a piece of soap, but anything unfamiliar was suspect, and one man seized his comb, declaring it must be some trap contrived to harm Muslims. The box of medicines and a tin of tea aroused no comment, but at the sight of his books the aga became agitated, and said they would be confiscated. Doughty's passport from Ibn Rashid was ignored, and when he produced a document from the Ottoman Wali of Syria, the head-man was unable to read its flowery script.

The final item lying in the bottom of the saddlebag was the empty pistol-case. This caused the most excitement of all, and Doughty's heart sank lest they should search him for the pistol which hung on a cord round his neck under his tunic. But the sight of the empty holster seemed to confuse them, since to them it was always important to keep a pistol in its gay case. A bystander exclaimed 'It is plain that Ibn Rashid has taken it from him', and the rest repeated this, which seemed to them the most obvious answer. Abdullah es-Siruan, with some doubt, let the matter pass, and then asked the foreigner for his money. Doughty had to tell him that hidden in the tin of tea was his purse with six gold liras in it. After counting them out with obvious pleasure, Abdullah pocketed the purse, while telling his scribe, 'Write down these six liras Fransawy. I have taken them for their better keeping.' Doughty was allowed to keep his provisions and medicines but the bags and their contents were taken and locked in the aga's house.

Abd el-Hady refused to receive the Nasrany back to his house and one of the Gallas named Aman was ordered to take him to his quarters. But at this point while the general crowd pressed round with hostile scowling looks, a distinguished-looking man, tall and swarthy and dressed like a shaikh, came and sat before Doughty. Addressing the Englishman in confident and honest tones he reassured Doughty, and tried to allay his fears. This was Muhammad en-Nejumy, 'who from the morrow became to me as a father at Kheybar'. He was one of two Nejumy brothers, Madina merchants established at Khaibar.

From now on Doughty was virtually a prisoner of the black aga, who delayed three weeks before sending a message to the Turkish Pasha in Madina informing him of the stranger's presence. But while he was lodged with Aman and a fellow-soldier, Muhammad en-Nejumy (known in Khaibar as Amm Muhammad, 'Uncle Muhammad') came frequently to visit him.

As time passed official surveillance grew less strict, and Doughty made his first visit to Amm Muhammad in his own house, where a meal of girdle-cakes with butter and wild honey made a welcome change from his monotonous diet. 'I and thou are now brethren,' said Amm Muhammad, 'and sheykh Khalil, what time thou art hungry, come hither to eat, and this house is now as thine own.' He explained to the Englishman that the black Khaibar people were so taken aback when they first saw his 'red' colouring that they believed he was some supernatural being come to harm their village.

After reporting daily to the aga, Doughty liked to go up to the brow of the *harra* into the fresh air. Here, sitting alone, he could read his aneroid and make notes. One day he wished to discard a few sheets of used paper, and hid them under some stones. But eyes were watching him. News came to Abdullah that the stranger had been burying papers which were thought to be evil spells. The villagers had recovered and burnt them, but the aga warned the stranger that the people were angered, and he was told not to leave the village again.

Probably because of their origins in Africa, the Khaibar people were more superstitious than the average Arab, and believed in many forms of magic and witchcraft. They told Doughty of women who turned into witches at night, and wandered naked in the streets seeking men with whom to have intercourse. Any man who submitted to their desires went mad. The villagers also enjoyed drumming and dancing in the African manner, and during the feast of Id al Dhahia frenetic dancing crowds filled the streets all day.

The one happy feature of Doughty's time in Khaibar was the friendship which grew between him and Amm Muhammad. Doughty began to spend all the daytime with this congenial companion, and the aga made en-Nejumy answerable to him for the Nasrany's safe-keeping in detention. Often they would go together to the Hijazi's orchard where they occupied themselves in breaking through the basalt rock to make a water-pit; at other times Doughty explored the outlying areas under Amm Muhammad's protection. All around Khaibar he saw fragments of ancient walls, and blocks of dressed basalt which he thought dated from the days of the ancient Jewish settlement. Up on the *harra* there were also vaulted barrows, burial-places from the unknown past, and in one place the ruins of a dam which had once blocked a water-course from the plateau.

In spite of en-Nejumy's kindness Doughty hated Khaibar, and felt that his time there was more like dying than living. By writing of it fully he hoped to save other Europeans from suffering the physical and psychological afflictions of the place.

Weeks passed before the Turkish authorities reacted to the aga's letter, and when a dispatch finally arrived the Pasha ordered all the stranger's books and his passport to be sent to Madina. Though the aga angrily refused him permission to write personally to the Pasha, Doughty did so, telling his story, complaining of his wrongful detention, and asking to be sent on his way with reliable guides. En-Nejumy bribed the official messenger to carry the private letter also.

Passing his time round the coffee-hearths, in the endless talk of Amm Muhammad and his friends, or in his room with the Galla soldiers, Doughty learned much Hijazi lore, fables and anecdotes about the Ottomans and the holy places. He also heard Aman's account of how as a young boy in Ethiopia he had been taken by the slavers, a story which prompted the famous passage of indignation in *Arabia Deserta*: '*Jidda is now the staple town of African slavery, for the Turkish empire: – Jidda where are Frankish consuls!* But you shall find these worthies, in the pallid solitude of their palaces, affecting (great Heaven!) the simplicity of new-born babes, – they will tell you they are not aware of it!'

Through December they waited for some decision from Madina, and in all this time Doughty genuinely feared that the Turks might order his execution. Though Amm Muhammad assured him often that he would stand by him in any trouble, he was, like so many Arabs, a man of inconsistent moods. The Englishman had grown truly fond of him, but he disliked en-Nejumy's sycophancy before the aga and felt little confidence that he could help in a crisis.

Doughty had been two months in Khaibar when the aga received a brief letter from the Pasha stating that he was occupied with the hajj, but would return the books when the pilgrim season was over. He ordered that the English visitor be hospitably treated.

It was more than a week later that Doughty saw newly-arrived camels before the aga's door. Knowing this meant a new message, his first reaction was to hurry to the safety of Amm Muhammad's house. But later the aga told him the news was good and his books had been returned. He was kept in suspense till the following day, when he was given a letter addressed to himself personally from Sabri Pasha of Madina. Dated 11 January 1878, and written in execrable French, it said the Pasha understood the Englishman's purpose in travelling in Arabia to gain new knowledge, but that because of the hostile nature of so many badawin tribes it would be safer for him to return to Ibn Rashid, to whom the Pasha had written him a letter of recommendation. He requested Doughty to depart as soon as possible.

The Englishman hopefully expected his possessions to be returned to him after this, but when he asked for his six gold liras, the look on the aga's face confirmed his suspicions that Abdullah es-Siruan had spent the money. The garrison commander was in a bad humour, and when Doughty approached him again the next day to ask for his belongings, there was an angry argument, during which the aga struck Doughty brutally in the face and threatened to throw him into prison. But the Englishman had the satisfaction of knowing that he was now technically a free man, and he ignored the aga and walked off to his friend's house.

When days passed and his possessions were not restored, Doughty wrote again to the Pasha. But even if he regained his belongings he knew that leaving Khaibar presented new and peculiar problems.

Its own villagers called Khaibar an island. It lay on no main route, and only at the time of the date-harvest was there a traffic of tribesmen to and from the village. Few badawin camped on the inhospitable *harra* which totally surrounds the oasis. Doughty saw no chance of finding anyone going to Hail who might act as his guide. To attempt to travel alone was out of the question.

Guarmani, on his visit to Khaibar, had had little difficulty in finding an escort because the village had then been part of the territory of Ibn Rashid, and contact with Hail was more regular. Under the Turkish administration which had been in force for five years at the time of Doughty's visit, traffic between Khaibar and the Jabal Shammar had virtually ceased.

Another twelve days were to go by before a third and final letter from Madina ordered the aga to provide an escort of Ageyl (the camel-borne soldiers of the Ottoman army in Arabia) to take the

English traveller to Hail, and to restore immediately all his property. Fearing that he would be in trouble with his masters, Abdullah sold a cow to raise the liras he had purloined. That night he gave back the books and papers which he had been holding for a fortnight contrary to the Pasha's previous instructions. A Koran and an Arabic psalter were missing – taken by the Pasha of Madina.

Doughty started to bargain among the Ageylis for someone to escort him to Hail, but he had only about £6 sterling after the return of the stolen money, and could not offer much for a guide's services. In the end a certain Eyad agreed to do the job for five riyals and the matter was settled. Doughty was not much taken with the man, a Bishr badawi who had soldiered at Madina for some years, 'one who had drunk very nigh the dregs, of the mischiefs and vility of one and the other life', but he had no choice.

When his liras had been stolen, a few riyals had still remained to the Englishman in the pocket of his shirt, and with these he now bought Amm Muhammad a tunic and a new gun stock. He also divided his medicines with him, as a gesture of gratitude. But en-Nejumy protested that he did not need any recompense, and wished only that his friend should sometimes think of him with the pious hope, 'the Lord remember him for good'. Finally he consented to accept the gifts, but Doughty was moved by his unassuming modesty. 'Yet now I sinned ... against that charitable integrity, the human affection, which was in Amm Muhammad; and which like the waxen powder upon summer fruits, is deflowered under any rude handling. When he received my gift, it seemed to him I had taken away his good works!' In the literature of Arabian travel it would be hard to find another example of such unselfish kindness from an Arab to a European. The Arab custom of hospitality or gift-giving normally looks for requital at some distant future, but en-Nejumy expected nothing from Doughty.

It was mid-March 1878 when the 'blissful day' of departure from Khaibar arrived. Things started badly when the *rafiq*, Eyad, demanded full payment before they set out. Doughty reluctantly agreed, but he foresaw trouble from this man whose natural badawin honesty had been corrupted in Turkish service.

In spite of all that had occurred between them, the departing traveller gave the aga Abdullah 'the last word of Peace' before he moved off. On the outskirts of the village he said his final farewell to en-Nejumy. ' "Now God be with thee, my father Muhammad, and requite thee." "God speed thee Khalil," and he took my hand. Amm Muhammad went back to his own, we passed further; and the world and death, and the inhumanity of religions parted us for ever!'

He had endured the miseries of Khaibar for three months. So they set off over the *harra*. Besides Eyad they had been joined by Merjan, another young Ageyli, and Hamed a shepherd boy bound for a camp on the plateau.

In an attempt to find hospitable tents, Eyad led Doughty on a roundabout route, and after eight days' travelling they were not yet half-way to Hail. They had suffered much hunger and discomfort on the journey, but a cold, overcast morning was cheered for them by an encounter with a herdsman and his camels in a pleasant green hollow. When offered milk the hungry and thirsty travellers each drank three or four pints at a draught.

Later, coming to a tent, Doughty was surprised to recognise Salih, the unfaithful rafiq of the outward journey, who with the cheerful inconsistency of the badu gave his former charge a cordial welcome and killed a kid for supper. Afterwards a vestige of conscience prompted the host to ask Doughty if he were now 'appeased'.

After they moved on from Salih's tent there was an ugly incident between the Englishman and his guides. Merjan, tired and ill-tempered, resented a remark made by the Nasrany and levelled his gun at him. Doughty asked, 'Was there ever a Beduwy who threatened death to his rafik?' and when Merjan answered, 'With a Nasrany who need keep any law? is not this an enemy of Ullah?' Doughty was provoked to one of his rare outbursts of anger, and struck the lad with his stick. At this, Eyad seized the Englishman's arms from behind, 'and the lad, set free, came and kicked me in a villainous manner, and making a weapon of his heavy head-cord, he struck at me in the face: then he caught up a huge stone and was coming to break my head, but in this I loosed myself from Eyad'.

Leaving the north-eastern edge of the *harra* they were in dry desert, with no pasture and no badawin camps. They had eaten nothing since the night before, and now without water or food they stopped for the night in a sandy watercourse. 'The silent night in the dark khala [desert] knit again our human imbecility and misery, at the evening fire, and accorded the day's broken fellowship. Merjan forgot his spite; but showing me some swelling wheals, "Dealest thou thus, he said, with thy friend, Khalil?" ' Against the vast and inhospitable desert human quarrels shrank into insignificance.

The following evening they enjoyed a good meal with some prosperous Harb badu. Then for two days they made their way back through the foothills into the Jabal Shammar, and here they heard the news that Muhammad Ibn Rashid with his cousin Hamud was away from the capital on a raiding foray. People they met began to recognise Doughty from his previous visit, and along the valley towards Hail the passers-by were as surly as they had been at his first coming, and asked his guides, 'Why bring ye him again?'

When they reached Hail after sixteen days' journey 'the town seemed a dead and empty place'. Because of the absence of the amir the usually busy market was closed and silent, and the main square was empty. But one or two of the castle servants, including the old coffee-server, were still present, and called out to each other that the Nasrany was back: 'Now may it please Ullah he will be put to death.' They were less civil to him in the absence of Ibn Rashid.

Anaibar, the Ethiopian freed man, was acting as regent for the amir, and he invited the new arrivals into the coffee-hall. There Doughty produced a letter from the aga in Khaibar, and the Pasha's letter to Ibn Rashid. The illiterate Anaibar passed them to a secretary, who looked at the superscriptions and passed them back unopened. They were scornful of anything to do with the Dowla, whose authority carried no weight in Ibn Rashid's country.

The English traveller was given his old room for the night, but that evening Anaibar told him he must leave on the morrow. When Doughty asked 'Where to?' he could only say, 'From whence thou camest;–to Khaibar.' The traveller woke next morning in low spirits. 'There was no going forward for me nor going backward, and I was spent with fatigues.'

On going into the square he became the butt of a jeering and insolent crowd, although a former friend, the merchant Ibrahim, spoke up for him and beat back the loiterers. Then a one-eyed stranger tried to help with good advice: 'Only say thou wilt be a Moslem and quit thyself of them', and he called out to the crowd, 'Khalil is a Moslem!' At this the coarse-humoured Moorish gate-keeper called out, 'I am thinking we shall make this man a Moslem and circumcise him; go in one of you and fetch me a knife from the Kasr.' But the crowd were too much afraid of the amir to join in such horseplay. Doughty was pressed to say the formula – only a few words and they would all be his friends, and would make him rich. But he answered, 'Though ye gave me this castle ... and the sacks of hoarded silver which ye say to be therein, I could not change my faith.' They cursed him.

Anaibar was clearly worried at the responsibility the foreigner's arrival had laid upon him. In a threatening manner he forced Doughty to pay the wretch Eyad another five riyals to escort him away again. He would not permit Doughty to go north to Ibn Rashid's camp nor to Iraq, but did consent to put his seal to a safe-conduct written out by Ibrahim the merchant.

In the first week in April the Englishman left Hail for the second time. Neither he nor Eyad had any intention of going together to Khaibar. Doughty knew Eyad would abandon him and pleaded only that it should be among the badu and not in one of the settlements. Eyad no longer had to answer to anyone for the Nasrany's safety, and showed his changed mood by demanding the camel for himself and forcing Doughty to walk soon after they left town.

As they marched aimlessly south-west, there were unpleasant incidents almost daily between the guides and their charge. Once the Ageylis kindled their matchlocks with sinister mutterings, and Doughty believed they meant to shoot him, but they were unnerved by his angry reaction. That night as the Englishman lay awake he heard them planning to escape together on the camel while he was asleep, but he was ready to jump up and accuse them in front of other badawin as they attempted to get away. The next day Eyad again threatened to shoot Doughty, who responded by seizing the camel's halter ready to make the beast dislodge her rider if he attempted to raise his gun.

The effort of trying to keep up on foot with the camel caused him acute distress. Doughty turned over in his mind what he might do to free himself from his predicament, but saw no safety nearer than Syria. Even if he tried to escape on the camel himself one night he felt he would not survive in the desert. He was suffering from ophthalmia and with his poor eyesight would not be able to discern in the landscape the badu tents on whose hospitality he would depend. With the sharp stones cutting his feet cruelly, and the ground hot under the noon-day sun, he even considered threatening the two rascally rafiqs with his pistol, but felt that if he did no man would agree to escort him another time.

After five days of this protracted misery they came to the camp of Shaikh Maatuk of the Hutaim at a place named Gholfa. Next morning after much argument the Ageylis left Doughty's baggage at Maatuk's tent and departed. Doughty was not sorry to see them go.

Maatuk, and more especially his wife, turned out to be humane and charitable, though it was obvious that they feared Ibn Rashid's displeasure if they helped the stranger. The shaikh had promised to pass Doughty on to the Harb tribe further to the south-east, but tried to extricate himself from the bargain, suggesting that his guest could stay with them till the hajj season and then go north with the returning pilgrim caravan. But Doughty felt reasonably sure that Maatuk would keep his word, and his cause was helped by the wife who many times a day looked over the tent divide, quoting a badawin proverb to the effect that the stranger must be helped back to his own land.

For nearly eighteen months Doughty had carried his stock of much-loved books with him, accepting the additional burden, and risking the anger they might arouse if they were discovered, as at Khaibar. Now his future was totally uncertain; he faced new difficulties and dangers; and he was physically unfit; as he weighed up the situation he decided the time had come for him to 'carry all his worldy possessions upon one of his shoulders'. Secretly he took his books (all except *Die Alte Geographie Arabiens* and Zehme's *Arabien und die Araber seit hundert Jahren*), and 'gave them honourable burial' in the hole of a dhabb lizard, covering them well and putting a large stone on top.

The day came when Maatuk was ready to move, and he rode off with his guest in the general direction of the Qasim, the province which lies between Hail and Najd proper. After two days' trek he left his charge at the tent of a Harb tribesman named Motlog.

Because of false rumours that Ibn Saud was in the Qasim raiding the Ataiba, Doughty spent some days in Motlog's camp. During this time he was on very short commons, only a little buttermilk during the whole day, or some fresh milk when the camels came home. He grew daily more weary and anxious about his onward journey, but by a fortunate chance a Shammari arrived at the tent, and for five riyals agreed to escort Doughty to Buraida.

They set off at once on the man's camel, with Doughty in the saddle and Hamed the Shammari riding pillion. Thus they rode for three days, eating at tents on the way, and on the fourth morning came out of the area of granite grit and scattered basalt hills to a great open plain lying between Jabal Habashi and the Qasim. Though they were soaked by a rainstorm here and had to sleep in wet clothes, they were none the worse. After the troubles and fear of the previous month with Eyad, Doughty was much relieved to be in the company of a helpful and competent guide, and they were making good progress.

On the seventh day, coming down off the Jabal Sara, they entered the Qasim by the same route that Palgrave had probably followed, but Doughty does not mention a great panorama filled with oases. Four miles further on was Uyun where Palgrave saw the megaliths. Later they stopped outside Gassa, another settlement among palm-groves. Although Doughty found settled villagers often more spiteful than the badawin, their host here was a man of liberal views. In answer to a question the traveller admitted he was a Christian, adding, 'Will ye therefore drive me away and kill me?' But the Gassa man answered, 'No! and fear nothing; is not this el-Kasim? where the most part have travelled in foreign lands: they who have seen the world are not like the ignorant, they will treat thee civilly.'

The prosperous citizens of the Qasim were traditionally caravan-traders to Mecca, Kuwait, Baghdad and Riyadh, and many in youth went to the Gulf coast to seek their fortune. They had the reputation of being shrewd in business, and for this reason their hospitality was scanty. They did not give much away. The travellers pressed on and entered the sand-desert of the Qasim where Doughty for the first

time saw the great dunes typical of the Nafud type of terrain. At
sunset as they climbed to the crest of one of these high sand-dunes
they saw Buraida.

And from hence appeared a dream-like spectacle! – a great clay
town built in this waste sand with enclosing walls and towers and
streets and houses! and there beside a bluish dark wood of ethel
trees, upon high dunes! This is Boreyda! and that square minaret,
in the town, is of the great mesjid. I saw, as it were, Jerusalem in
the desert!

It was the strange contrast of the town against its unlikely surrounding wastes which inspired Doughty to such lyrical flights, and probably sunset lent the whole scene a golden glow. But the people of
Buraida had a reputation for dour puritanism and a dislike of
strangers. Doughty was to find no joy in the town of his dreamlike
vision. That evening they went to the amir's guest-house, where
Hamed left Doughty after they had finished a frugal meal. He had
offered some blunt practical advice to the Englishman, warning him
that Buraida was no place to announce his Christianity, and suggesting that he pretend to pray and be a Muslim.

As Doughty sat in the courtyard in the moonlight, he heard with
dismay the call to prayer. The amir's men invited him to pray with
them, but he asked quickly where he might sleep, and was pushed
into a small dark room, where he lay down on the hard earth floor.
His bags containing his pistol had been taken to another room; he
had only his penknife with him, and was filled with a presentiment
of trouble.

Hardly an hour passed before a voice summoned Doughty to the
coffee-hall, and in darkness he was led to where the men of the guard
were sitting round the hearth. At once they said, 'Art thou not the
Nasrany that was lately at Hail? Doughty had ceased to be amazed
at the way news travels in the desert. He was told to fetch his papers
to show Abdullah, the acting amir. (Hasan, the true ruler, was tem-
porarily absent.) As he went wearily to the store-room to rummage
in his bags, a crowd of men followed him, and one of them, shouting
angrily, struck Doughty with his fist. While one group went off with
the papers, six others now set upon the Englishman, fumbling
through his clothing searching for money, the ultimate dishonourable outrage in the Arab code of manners. Though he shouted
'Thieves!' as loudly as possible they grabbed his purse and his precious aneroid barometer, and tore the clothes from his back till he
was left standing only in his drawers. They then went to ransack
his bags, but in the darkness they did not find the pistol.

Jeyber, the amir's official, returned, and learning what had happened ordered his men to restore all that they had taken, or he would have their hands cut off. He stood and watched as one by one all the articles were grudgingly given back; but when Doughty was finally asked if he had everything he said his 'watch' was still missing. He meant the aneroid, which the thieves had thought was a watch. It needed more threats and curses from Jeyber before it was produced with much reluctance. To Doughty's relief it seemed unharmed.

Next day, after he had been taken to lodge in a different house, Doughty asked Jeyber to take him to the amir. The experience proved to be rather different from what he had expected. 'He brought me.through a street to a place before the Prince's house. A sordid fellow was sitting there...in the dust of their street:... he might be thirty-five years of age. I enquired "Where was Abdullah the Emir?" They said "He is the Emir!" – "Jeyber, I whispered, is this the Emir?" "It is he." '

Doughty's protests were fobbed off with excuses. Abdullah refused his offer of a telescope in exchange for new clothes, and requested his immediate departure, though a few minutes later he relented to the extent of granting the traveller a day's rest.

That afternoon while his host was out, a riotous mob attacked Jeyber's house where Doughty was staying. There were only two women in the house with him, and they barred the upstairs door, crying out that the Nasrany was not there. But the angry crowd attacked the door with rocks and were about to break it down when Jeyber came home and drove them off. The official reported that there was a general outcry in the town, with the people demanding the infidel's death; but after some hours the rioters dispersed, and it seemed that the amir's men had restored order. Doughty was glad to see the end of that troubled day and seal the bond of bread and salt at his supper with Jeyber that evening.

Next morning a camel-man was produced to take him to Anaiza, a day's journey away. The guide gathered up Doughty's bags and led him to a back street where a camel was couched. They mounted and left town as quietly as possible.

After his experience of the Wahhabi bigotry of Buraida, Doughty felt little trust in his rafiq, and his suspicions were justified at their first stop. They had crossed part of the sands of the Qasim Nafud and had dismounted by a palm-grove to fill their waterskin when the guide jumped on the camel and rode away. 'This was the cruellest fortune which had befallen me in Arabia! to be abandoned here without a chief town, in the midst of fanatical Najd.'

The eight riyals which were all he had were barely enough to pay someone to take him to the coast. Feeling acutely pessimistic, he forced himself to be practical. He removed his pistol from his bags, tore up his maps which might cause trouble if discovered, and then walked into the nearest orchard and approached a man for a drink of water. Explaining that his rafiq had abandoned him, he asked for an ass to carry his bags into Anaiza. The man was helpful and produced a donkey to take Doughty on his way, asking only a small fee. Even so, he would not take the foreigner right into Anaiza, and left him with some cultivators in the outlying gardens.

Next morning Doughty was taken into the town and delivered to the house of a negro who was 'beadle' to Zamil the amir. So he arrived in Anaiza, of which he has left an account which rates with Palgrave's description of Riyadh and Hail as one of the classic passages of Arabian literature. In this prosperous and comparatively sophisticated town Doughty felt reasonably optimistic. Zamil had the reputation of being just and liberal, and his hosts in the garden had told him he would find protection with their respected and popular ruler.

As soon as possible he went with the beadle to pay his respects to the amir, whom they found sitting in his customary place of audience under a shady porch off the market-square. Seeing the visitor approach, Zamil rose and took him by the hand, indicating that he should sit beside him. 'Zamil is a small-grown man with a pleasant weerish visage, and great understanding eyes.'

According to Doughty's philosophy, 'Truth may walk through the world unarmed', and in spite of occasions which might have given him cause for disillusionment he now said to Zamil, 'I am a hakim, an Engleysy, a Nasrany; I have these papers with me; and it may please thee to send me to the coast.' The amir's face was momentarily troubled as he read the papers but he replied pleasantly, 'It is well.' He told Doughty not to advertise the fact that he was a Christian; he would be safer if he gave out that he was an Ottoman deserter. They parted then but met again at Zamil's modest residence at midday. Here Doughty saw the amir's fanatical uncle, the Amir Aly, who left hastily when he appeared since he would not keep company with a Christian.

In the streets Doughty was impressed with the civil and relaxed air of the townspeople, who were not as fearful of authority as the people of Hail, and quite different from the ruffians of Buraida. Hail was basically a badawin town; Anaiza by contrast was a richer and more urbane community with broader interests and foreign contacts. The Qasim tradition of caravan-trade to the coast, both east and west, had been the basis of the great fortunes of the Anaiza merchants, who dealt as far afield as India, Egypt and Africa. The people here were originally of the Bani Tamim, an ancient tribe from whom were inherited the intelligence and industry which had made this the most prosperous town of inland Arabia.

There was no prison in Anaiza; malefactors were bound and

brought before the amir, and the common punishment was beating with green palm-sticks. (Dry sticks were not used because they might break a man's bones.) There was no amputation of hands for theft.

Anaiza had a large class of skilled artisans, smiths in copper and gold, armourers, tinkers and woodworkers. There were stone-masons who dug and lined wells, builders, and pargeters who created intricate gypsum patterns on the interior walls of fine houses. Also garment-makers, embroiderers, and leather-workers.

All this Doughty observed and recorded during the succeeding days when he formed a favourable opinion of the virtuous and moderate Anaiza people. Unfortunately, as he was to find later, moderation was by no means universal among them.

There was a demand for the Englishman's medical services, and he set himself up in an empty shop in the bazaar. But he had neither the equipment, nor the interest, nor the power of dissimulation, to make this activity a paying proposition in the way Palgrave did. Among the first visitors to his shop was a thin, gentle man who wanted Doughty to visit his sick mother. This was Abdullah el-Kenneyny, who later became a close and valued friend. At his house the Arab asked, 'And art thou an Engleysy? but wherefore tell the people so, in this wild fanatical country? I have spent many years in foreign lands, I have dwelt at Bombay, which is under government of the Engleys: thou canst say thus to me, but say it not to the ignorant and foolish people. . . .'

'Should I not speak truth, as well here as in mine own country?' asked Doughty.

'We have a tongue to further us and our friends, and to illude our enemies . . .' replied the worldly merchant. He warned Doughty that the strong Wahhabi element in the town would not tolerate his presence for long.

El-Kenneyny's home was a fine building, but sparsely furnished with barely more than the contents of a badawin tent. There were a few coffers used for storing clothes, but no beds or chairs. In an upstairs room Doughty was taken to see the old lady, who was in much pain. His medicines later gave her some relief.

That first day in the Kenneyny house Doughty enjoyed an hour or two of peace and security after the hazards and trials he had suffered. He already felt at home with his new friend, and relaxed by browsing through Abdullah's book-shelf. Among the volumes was an Arabic encyclopaedia from Beirut; when Doughty picked it up Abdullah's spectacles fell out at a place which treated of artesian wells.

The well-informed, wealthy, and broad-minded merchant class was a particular feature of Anaiza. El-Kenneyny was a *nouveau riche* in this society, but a second family who befriended Doughty were

real patricians of the community. They were the family of Abdullah
el-Bessam, a businessman with far-reaching contacts and a large
house and agency in Jidda. In the Bessam house Doughty enjoyed
refinements which were civilised luxury by comparison with the
hardships of the desert, or even by the standards of Hail. The dinner-
tray was set on a raised stool, and was surrounded by appetising and
varied side-dishes. Better still, there was intelligent conversation during the meal, a far cry from the rough badawin custom where a man
snatches up and bolts down as much food as he can in the shortest
time.

Doughty learned later that some of the Bessams were strict Wahhabis, but the head of the family set the tone among the rest of them.
Abdullah el-Bessam was 'a dove without gall in the raven's nest of
their fanaticism. . . . Large, we have seen, was the worshipful merchant's hospitality and in this also he was wise above the wisdom
of the world.'

Though he had found a new and delightful world within the
seclusion of such great men's houses the Englishman still had to
reckon with the more extremist half of the population. After one
night in his shop in the suq he was forcibly ejected by the Wahhabi
Amir Aly, Zamil's uncle, and with some difficulty found an upper
room in a household which needed his medical help. But he was
enjoying good food as the guest of kind families, and felt his strength
slowly reviving.

At first he was cordially received at Zamil's coffee-room and
believed the amir to be well disposed towards him. Though not a
dominant personality, Zamil was prudent, preferring compromise
to force, and enjoyed a high reputation for his practical wisdom and
peaceful government. But as the days passed in Anaiza Doughty
realised that Zamil's favour was not enough to protect him from Wahhabi antipathy. The religious leaders had been preaching against
him in their Friday sermons, and people who had followed Zamil's
lead in tolerating the Nasrany now began to turn against him. A
certain coolness became apparent among some of the younger
merchants, though el-Bessam and el-Kenneyny remained constant.

While many people believed that Doughty went about in tattered
clothes so as not to attract attention, el-Kenneyny suspected that
there might be another reason. He offered to lend him up to 200
riyals if he was short of money. Doughty did not accept, but was
touched by the gesture. He found much happiness in el-Kenneyny's
company, and was the more distressed that his friend was in poor
health and appeared to be consumptive. During long conversations
he learned that el-Kenneyny's commercial success had started
with slave-trading between Baghdad and Zanzibar. Later he had
shipped sugar from Mauritius, and then rice from Bombay, until he

established himself at Basra as a corn-merchant. He told Doughty that the principal merchants of Anaiza each owned capital in the region of £24,000 in the value of those days, an astronomical figure compared with the kind of trading capital the Englishman had heard about in Hail.

Doughty's regard for Abdullah el-Bessam was of a different kind from the personal sympathy and affection that he felt for el-Kenneyny. He admired Bessam's wide-ranging and well-informed mind; 'there was not such another head in Aneyza – nor very likely in all Nejd'. To Doughty's delighted surprise, Bessam questioned him about Palmerston and Disraeli, Bismarck and Tsar Alexander, and provided the latest news about the Russo-Turkish war which was going on at that time. He had his facts from a Turkish-Arabic newspaper which was widely distributed among the lettered merchants.

In the Bessam house one day a young man who had been in India said, 'Among the customs of the Engleys, he had most marvelled to see the husband giving place to the hareem', and Doughty, explaining his countrymen's respect for the opposite sex, quoted the saying 'England is the paradise of women and hell of horses' – a proverb which he felt 'came off roundly in Arabic'. Bessam repeated his words over and over, greatly amused. Other men commented, 'How strange that the Engleys have a Queen, and no man to rule over them! what Khalil is the name of the Queen?' and Doughty answered '*Mansura*, the Victorious Lady'.

Doughty felt he must move out of his lodgings when the children of the house contracted smallpox, but one of his humbler patients found him a small empty hut and provided some food, refusing to accept payment. He suspected that this generosity came indirectly from Zamil.

He did not delay in Anaiza from choice. He had made it known that he would like to join a caravan either to Kuwait or Jidda, but none was due to leave at that time.

One day with two companions he was able to ride out to the Wadi Rummah, the great valley which sweeps across central and north-east Arabia. But the more fanatical of the townspeople were suspicious of this excursion, and the general mood now turned more strongly against him. Even el-Kenneyny was being abused for showing friendship to the foreigner. 'Seeing the daily darkening and averting of the Wahaby faces', Doughty became wary, and often kept his pistol with him. Rather than face the general malevolence of the populace, he spent most days in his house, venturing out only after dark to visit his friends.

As summer drew on there were more obvious signs of the people's anger. Ordure was thrown on his threshold, and one evening his hut was besieged by women and boys screaming insults. After a second hostile crowd threatened him a few days later he protested to one of Zamil's officers, and was assured that the ruler had reprimanded the rioters. But more trouble was to come. That night he was summoned by the Amir Aly, the ruler's fanatical uncle, who ordered a badawi to take Doughty to Khubbera, a village some miles away. The unwilling traveller was forced to pay the camel-man two riyals, which left him with only the equivalent of twenty shillings in the world. Doughty was deeply disappointed that Zamil had permitted his expulsion; he had believed the amir was his friend.

Among surly and hostile villagers in Khubbera he thought of his Anaiza friends and wondered if they had forsaken him. Now he was in real need of money, and he half-hoped that el-Kenneyny would renew his offer of help. But his stay in the village lasted only three days, and then on Zamil's orders he was taken back to Anaiza and deposited in a palm-grove on the edge of town.

That afternoon Abdullah el-Kenneyny came to visit him. He explained that he and the Bessams had been greatly distressed to hear of his expulsion, and had complained to Zamil. But the ruler had answered that it was the decision of the council which he could not oppose. It was at Bessam's suggestion that the Englishman had been lodged in this outlying garden where the Wahhabis would not object.

His friend promised that he would try to arrange for Doughty to travel to Jidda, and enquired if there was anything he needed meanwhile. There was a certain finality about el-Kenneyny's manner, and Doughty feared that this might be their last meeting. He decided to request some practical help. In his bags he kept a cheque-book to use when he reached the coast, and he now asked el-Kennyeny if he would cash a cheque for a few riyals. Abdullah consented, and next day the cash was delivered by messenger. The cheque was finally returned to the drawer after he had been a year back in Europe; it had been paid through a Beirut bank. Spanish crowns were the currency of the Qasim, and fortunes in silver were carried to and from those desert towns in the well-guarded pilgrimage caravans.

Time passed slowly for Doughty in the garden, where his only shelter was a 'coffee-bower', and his bed a clay camel-manger. But he made friends with the men who tended the place, especially their foreman Ibrahim, who told the Englishman how he had spent twelve months working on the Suez Canal, from which 'moral quagmire' he had returned 'poorer in human heart, richer by a hundred or two of reals'. From another young man he heard the full story of the civil war between the two princes of Najd, and of Anaiza's struggle to keep its independence against Ibn Rashid and Ibn Saud.

Days turned into weeks, and he was disappointed that he had no word from the Bessams or el-Kenneyny, and nobody visited him any more. 'Their friendship is like the voice of a bird upon the spray: if a rumour frighten her she will return no more.' As May passed into June he wrote a note on a piece of paper: '*Katalny et-taab wa ej-jua* – I am dying of weariness and hunger', and sent it to el-Kenneyny. If nothing else, he hoped he might be able to move to one of his friends' estates on the northern side of town.

In response to the note a servant brought extra food, bread, butter, and buttermilk. From his master he also delivered a verbal message telling Doughty to keep cheerful, and saying they hoped soon to arrange his departure.

At the end of June, after six long weeks in the garden, Doughty heard from el-Kenneyny that he would be able to leave with a caravan which was soon to depart for Mecca with the Qasim's annual export of sheep's butter. He reckoned he was 450 miles from the coast, and thought longingly of the day, perhaps in six months' time, when he could board an English ship. But before that he had to face at least twenty days in the saddle travelling in midsummer heat.

He was also worried about his health. A year before he had been bitten in the knee by a greyhound, and although the wound appeared to have healed, it now broke out in an ulcer, and many other ulcers appeared on his legs and one on his wrist. His general weakness was such that he could not sit upright for long.

At last Bessam wrote to say that all was ready. He and el-Kenneyny had bought a good riding camel for Doughty to use on the journey. A certain Sleyman, one of the Kenneyny family, would travel with him and provide his water, cooking and noon shelter. Abdullah el-Bessam's son Abd er-Rahman would also be with the caravan.

At sunset the following day the camel was brought and Doughty rode to his friend's palm-garden about two miles away. He slept there, and on the morrow both el-Kenneyny and Bessam came. The latter said to him, 'Ah, Khalil, we are abashed, for the things thou hast suffered, and that it should have been here! but thou knowest we were overborne by this foolish people.' One more sympathiser came later, but no others of the many who had called themselves his friends.

When el-Kenneyny visited Doughty again that evening, riding on his donkey, he was weak and seemed to be trembling as they sat and talked. The Englishman mounted the camel with Sleyman, and they rode off while el-Kenneyny walked with them to the edge of his estate. 'I gave hearty thanks, with the Semitic blessings; and bade this gentle and beneficent son of Temin a long farewell. He stood sad and silent. . . .' Three years later Doughty was to hear from the Bessams that Abdullah el-Kenneyny had died at Basra.

The two travellers arrived at the rendezvous after dark. Sleyman had twenty-four goatskins of butter as his cargo for Mecca, together weighing about a ton. Other merchants had similar quantities. There were 170 camels in the caravan and 70 men, who divided into small parties each under a separate leader. After making enquiries Doughty could find no one in the whole party who was going to Jidda. He knew he would have to leave the caravan outside the boundaries of the holy city, and was uncertain how he could proceed from there.

At sunrise next morning they loaded and moved off. The whole train was in charge of a caravan-master who enforced the discipline necessary to set a good pace and act in co-operation. He was outwardly affable to the foreigner, but Doughty felt 'the Wahaby rust was in his soul'.

The pattern of their days on the march was to start an hour before dawn, and around noon to halt for three or four hours' rest, raising awnings to provide shade for themselves and – more important – for the butter. Even so, Doughty's thermometer registered 105°F at noon the first day. At sunset they halted again, and the camels were loosed to graze till it was dark. They did not pitch tents, but slept on the awnings laid on the ground.

The first night took them out of the Qasim sands and back into the granite and basalt terrain typical of much of western Arabia. Though the men could fill their water-skins at odd brackish and dirty wells there were only a few points along the route where good water was found in sufficient quantities to water large numbers of camels. In the heat of summer the beasts could not go much more than four or five days without drinking, and for this reason the caravan had to keep up a good pace.

They were travelling in an almost direct line south-west. For a time the heat abated somewhat as they crossed uplands 5,000 feet above sea level, but for the most part their journey was a long, dull passage across an open plain. They saw no badawin anywhere, for the tribes were gathered for the summer at known groups of wells.

Late on the sixth day they came to the wells of Afif where the camels could be watered. The master caravaneers had gone ahead and were ready when the main party rode in. They fixed a draw-reel in a forked stake over each well-mouth, and two men running backwards with the rope pulled up water in a leather bucket. A third emptied it into the drinking trough – a hollow scraped in the ground and lined with a sheet of leather. With 170 thirsty camels to be marshalled in orderly manner there was much frenzied activity, and the men drawing on the ropes chanted together like sailors.

By the tenth day they had reached country where dotted acacia trees and a changed vegetation showed they were on the edge of the monsoon belt. Once at the midday halt Doughty had no water, and in his extreme thirst stole from another man's water-skin. He was observed and threatened with a club, till Sleyman came and ordered someone to pour out for the Nasrany.

Five more monotonous days passed, and then they left the open plain. Mecca lay only two days' march away. They were now in the characteristic mountainous land of the Hijaz, and in the Wadi as-Sail the caravaneers took off their travel-stained garments, and after washing at the water-holes put on the *ihram*. From this point it was only a day's journey to Taif, and some of his companions urged Doughty to go there where the Sharif of Mecca would help him. Unsure about the Sharif's attitude, and anxious about his ulcerated legs, he refused their advice, insisting he must go to Jidda. But Abd er-Rahman el-Bessam was unsuccessful in two attempts to find Doughty a man who would conduct him to the coast.

On their seventeenth day of travelling they approached Ain az Zaima, which marked the sacred limits beyond which the Nasrany might not pass. With his pistol inside his shirt and ammunition in his pockets, Doughty entered a coffee-house where his friends were already installed, and found them trying to restrain a fierce local man who was crying 'He shall be a Moslem!' and brandishing his dagger. He knew they were talking about himself. For the last time Abd er Rahman el-Bessam tried to help his father's friend. In the coffee-house was a man from the Bessam establishment in Jidda, and Doughty was urged to mount his camel quickly with this man riding pillion, so that they might go to the coast together. But the exhausted camel refused to move with two men on her back, and the wild wretch from the coffee-house rushed out and seized the bridle, ordering them to dismount, waving his knife and threatening to kill the Nasrany.

They couched the camel, and the fanatic – a half-witted fellow named Salem – was restrained. Abd er-Rahman suggested earnestly that Doughty should confess Islam; this was always the Arabs' first advice when they foresaw trouble for the foreigner. Doughty, of course, refused. El-Bessam washed his hands of the problem and rode off to join the departing butter caravan, 'and forsook his father's friend among murderers'.

Salem now claimed Doughty's camel as booty, and it became clear that it was plunder rather than religious zeal which spurred him on. The rest of the crowd had the same idea, and they fell upon the Nasrany, grabbing his *kaffiya*, head-band and cloak, while Salem seized the bags off the camel. Finally events took an extraordinary turn when a bystander, a slave from the Sharif of Mecca's household, persuaded Salem that Doughty should be taken before the Sharif. He charged Doughty's would-be-killer with the task of escorting him to Taif. Salem hoped the Sharif would hang the Nasrany and that he himself would be given the camel. Doughty was speechless.

But with one of those quick changes of mood typical of the Arabs, Salem now took charge of Doughty and his restored belongings. The Englishman still feared he might not live to see the day out, but in spite of suffering taunts and insults he was able to start for Taif with Salem's party at sunset, riding pillion behind Fheyd the camel-master.

As they rode through the night they ate their simple supper on camel-back, and as Doughty accepted a piece of bread proffered by Salem he pointed out that there was now bread and salt between them. Later, in the darkness someone came up on foot and snatched at Doughty's girdle. Fearing it was one of the mountain-bandits, Doughty drew his pistol, and the man disappeared. When they dismounted in the early hours Salem came and demanded to see the pistol. The thief who had been warned off was one of the cameleers, and word of the incident had spread quickly among the party.

Salem drew his knife again; 'Show me all that thou hast ... or now I will kill thee.'

'Remember the bread and salt which we have eaten together, Salem!'

'Show it all to me, or now by Ullah I will slay thee with this knife.'

Some of the crowd cried, 'Let us hack him in morsels, the cursed one!'

Doughty remained calm and rose, retreating a little from them. Then drawing his pistol out of his shirt he said, 'Let none think to take away my pistol!' Thoughts raced through his head. If they attacked should he fire? Would he have time to re-load if necessary? And even if he could get away on the camel, where could he go?

The camel-men, armed only with sticks, advanced and closed round him. Finally as Fheyd came near enough to seize him he had to decide whether to shoot or yield. With his basically gentle nature and dislike of violence Doughty in the end reacted in character. He offered the revolver, butt foremost, to Fheyd, who snatched it violently, breaking the cord by which it was still attached round Doughty's neck. Salem and Fheyd proceeded to search his person and rob him of all he carried: his aneroid, his purse, his pocket thermometer – though, finding no interest in the latter, they gave it back. The two villains then sat and examined the pistol and the rest of the loot, while the bystanders awaited the signal to kill. Fheyd tried out the pistol, firing shots in the air, but after five shots Salem told him to keep the last bullet in reserve. Doughty was in no doubt as to its intended purpose. He tried to speak reasonably to them, protesting his innocence, warning them that the Sharif of Mecca would call them to account, but all to no avail. While Salem continued to reprimand him for hiding the pistol, he fell suddenly unconscious, and in the moment of falling thought that he had been mortally wounded. But when he came round there was no blood. He learned that Fheyd had struck him violently on the back of the neck with his camel-stick.

I said faintly, 'Why have you done this?'
  'Because thou didst withhold the pistol.'
  'Is the pistol mine or thine? I might have shot thee dead! but I remembered the mercy of Ullah.'

As they spoke, the caravaneer who had reported the existence of the Nasrany's pistol sat close by, eating. Doughty suddenly caught his hand with the bread, and put some in his mouth, saying, 'Enough man! there is bread and salt between us,' and the wretch said no more.

It had been the final and worst ordeal of Doughty's adventures in Arabia, but the moment of anger and violence passed, and through the next day their dreary journey to Taif continued, not happily, but without unpleasant incidents. By afternoon they were threading their way through narrow mountain gorges which had been made passable by Turkish blasting, and at evening emerged on to the plain where Taif is situated. After snatching a brief sleep, they carried on at first light past orchards of fig-trees and vines. Here they found themselves on a good made road, something Doughty had not seen since he left Damascus. A little way off, Taif lay before them, and he could see houses painted and glazed in the Turkish manner, no more the rough, mud-built walls of inner Arabia. A bugle call rang out from the barracks, reminding them that this was a garrison town.

Salem went ahead to inform the authorities of the Englishman's arrival, and returned to lead Doughty into the centre of town. Among buildings of grey volcanic stone only the Sharif's palace stood conspicuously white by the entrance gate. The soldiers' quarters were in a tall prison-like building which rose out of the centre of Taif. 'The town now before my eyes! after nigh two years' wandering in the deserts, was a wonderful vision.' Doughty was justified in feeling that he had come out of the wilds to civilisation, and that the horrors and hardships of his travels were now left behind.

Two men came to meet the traveller. The first was the servant of a Turkish officer with whom Doughty was to lodge. The second was one of the Sharif's household who had come to make sure that the new arrival had everything he needed. This man dismissed Salem – heaven be praised! exclaims Doughty – and led the tired *thelul* away to the stables.

The Englishman was to be guest of a Colonel Muhammad, and once in the friendly officer's house he became conscious of his appearance. 'The tunic was rent on my back, my mantle was old and torn; the hair was grown down under my kerchief to my shoulders, and the beard fallen and unkempt; I had bloodshot eyes, half blinded, and the scorched skin was cracked to the quick upon my face.' He was given a bath, and the services of a barber, and fitted out with a soldier's white cotton suit and fez cap. After dinner that evening a *kavass* brought a new set of Arab clothes from the Sharif, and when Doughty put them on, Colonel Muhammad took him to an audience at the palace.

The great reception hall was empty except for the Sharif Hussain Pasha and his younger brother Abdilla Pasha. 'The former is a man of pleasant face, with a sober alacrity of the eyes and humane demeanour, and he speaks with a mild and cheerful voice: his age might be forty-five years.'

For more than an hour the Sharif talked with his visitor, beginning with polite trivialities, and going on to ask him of the ill-treatment he had suffered on the journey to Taif. Hearing the full story, Hussain Pasha showed much sympathy. He assured Doughty that his troubles were now over and that he could rest in Taif until he was fit enough to travel to Jidda with an offical escort. He wanted to know all about Doughty's life among the badu, and of Ibn Rashid and Zamil, and when he heard everything he commented with understanding, 'Ay, you have suffered much.'

Later, at Colonel Muhammad's house, Salem the camel-man came by order of the Sharif to restore Doughty's stolen things. He brought the pistol, now broken, the aneroid, and four riyals. The unfortunate wretch in his turn now beseeched the Nasrany to remember the bread and salt between them. It was not in Doughty's nature to gloat at the way in which the tables were turned on his tormenter, but he asked for his purse and several other small possessions which were still missing. As they waited for these to be fetched, the Colonel told Doughty that Salem and Fheyd were to be put in irons for their misdeeds. Not surprisingly, when the two men appeared again with the last of the stolen articles, they appeared very 'chopfallen'.

Doughty had a second audience of the Sharif, this time in full majlis when the seats round the walls were all occupied by prominent citizens. Ordering a chair to be placed near him specially for the Englishman, Hussain Pasha demonstrated publicly his favour and approval.

After four days Doughty's camel was sufficiently recovered, and bidding a grateful goodbye to Colonel Muhammad he set out for Jidda with three of the Sharif's men. Everything was made easy for him on this last ride which was to take him to the coast and away from Arabia for ever. His escort had orders to travel at a comfortable speed, and provided all his needs.

They travelled down the Wadi Fatima, leaving Mecca to the south. The road was downhill almost all the way, and after a day or two they began to feel the heavy, stagnant heat of the lowlands. On the fourth day, as evening approached, the escort suggested that they should ride all night to reach Jidda, but Doughty preferred to sleep in the last village of the Wadi Fatima. Remounting before dawn, they soon joined the Darb-as-Sultani, the highway between Mecca and Jidda. Now the mountains lay behind them, and they were on the undulating coastal plain of the Tihama. Late that afternoon they topped a low hill from which they could see walls and minarets and beyond them the sea. Doughty looked his last on black nomad tents on the plain as they covered the last few miles. But before entering the town his companions insisted that he dress in the new clothes he had received from the Sharif; then they passed through the gates of Jidda, and made for the house of the Sharif's agent.

It was the first week in August, 1878; his travels were over. 'On the morrow I was called to the open hospitality of the British Consulate.'

With this sentence Doughty's narrative stops dramatically at Jidda, but it was some time before he returned to England. His health was totally undermined by his Arabian experiences, and though he broke his journey to rest at Aden on his way to India, he had to be admitted to hospital in Bombay in October. There is evidence that in addition to his general debility Doughty was suffering from bilharzia. He was able to sail home in November, but his family have recorded that even after his arrival in England he had difficulty in eating European food and spoke hesitantly and seldom, as though he had lost fluency in his native tongue after speaking only Arabic for so long.

The following spring he returned to Syria to collect his impressions of the Nabatean inscriptions from Madayin Salah, which had remained safe in the Damascus Consulate, and that summer he took a house near Naples and began work on the great story of his wanderings.

That story, of course, forms the subject of his massive work *Travels in Arabia Deserta*, a book of more than half a million words, which has an unchallenged place as the great masterpiece of travel literature. Its unique semi-archaic style reflects Doughty's love of early English poetry, but he also wished to forge a timeless form of expression to describe the nomadic life of Arabia, in which he felt as if he had been transported back to a biblical past. Four publishers rejected the manuscript. One commented that it ought to be 'practically rewritten by a literary man'.

When the book was finally published by the Cambridge University Press in 1888, Richard Burton reviewed it with mixed feelings. He disapproved of an Englishman who did not fight like a man but allowed himself to be bullied and abused by Arabs, but in his final judgement had to concede the merit of the book, 'a twice-told tale writ large ... which, despite its affectations and eccentricities, its prejudices and misjudgements, is right well told.'

Doughty's work became the inspiration of those who followed him in exploring Arabia. The stamp of his prose style may be found in most of the authors who wrote about that land in the first half of the twentieth century, but most particularly in T. E. Lawrence's *Seven Pillars of Wisdom*. Lawrence had come to know the book intimately during his desert campaign when he had used it as a military textbook and had found it of inestimable value. For him it was 'perhaps the greatest record of adventure and travel in our language'. But he was also filled with admiration for its style: 'It has no date, and can never grow old.'

Doughty himself spent the years after *Arabia Deserta* in writing poetry, but his time in Arabia had been a great formative experience, and the memory of it coloured much of his later thought and writing. In reflective moods his mind turned back to incidents and characters from those years. In particular he remembered with affection el-Kenneyny and Abdullah el-Bessam. More than thirty years after leaving Arabia he ordered two silver bowls, inscribed in Arabic and English, to be despatched to their families through the British Consul at Damascus. The men he had known were dead, but one bowl was delivered to Abdullah el-Bessam's son, Sleyman. When it was discovered that el-Kenneyny's only living descendant was a half-wit boy, the second bowl was returned to Doughty, who presented it to Caius College, Cambridge.

In England Doughty lived a secluded life. His health was never robust, but the care of a devoted wife helped him to survive to a remarkable old age. He was eighty when he died in 1926.

Chapter 9

THE BLUNTS'
Journey to Hail
1879

'The charm of the East is the absence of intellectual life there, the freedom one's mind gets from anxiety in looking forward or pain in looking back. Nobody here thinks of the past or the future, only of the present; and till the day one's death comes, I suppose the present will always be endurable.'

Lady Anne Blunt

'It is strange how gloomy thoughts vanish once one sets foot in Asia.' The opening words of Lady Anne Blunt's *A Pilgrimage to Nejd* mark her out at once as a devotee of the eastern scene.

She was the daughter of the Earl of Lovelace and granddaughter of Lord Byron, and she had the natural sense of social position which in her day might be expected of one with such an aristocratic background. In 1869 she became the wife of Wilfrid Scawen Blunt, who upon their marriage gave up a sinecure in the diplomatic service to devote himself to his private pursuits. It was Wilfrid's ill-health which first brought the couple to the Levant in 1873, and thus started a lifetime's interest in the Arabs. After this first visit they both learned Arabic, in which Anne became the more proficient scholar. Their fascination with the East was further whetted by an adventurous expedition from Syria to the Euphrates in 1878, when they had been able to buy Arab horses which they took back to Wilfrid's family

20 Blunts' route in central Arabia

estate at Crabbet Park in Sussex. After this they were, as Wilfrid wrote, 'imbued with the fancies of the desert'.

On the Euphrates expedition they had gained a useful friend, Muhammad ibn Aruk, son of the shaikh of Palmyra (Tadmor), who had been one of their companions. The fact that this young man wished to travel to Najd to find a wife gave Wilfrid and Lady Anne the chance to suggest that they should accompany him, and with this intention they returned to Damascus in December 1878 hoping to make a journey into the heart of Arabia.

Besides Anne and Wilfrid there were to be six Arabs in their party, Muhammad ibn Aruk and his cousin Abdullah; Hanna, a Christian who was to act as cook, with Ibrahim his kinsman, and two camel-men. The Blunts were to be mounted on mares and they had two riding-camels and two pack beasts. Their buying of camels and stores took them only a week, with the expert help of Muhammad who knew his way round the local suqs. It has been said that in planning their expeditions 'Wilfrid was the Commander-in-Chief, while Anne was the Quartermaster-General. In this rough way their talents were deployed in very effective harmony.'

They were preparing for 'three months' wandering and a thousand miles of desert' and the supplies they bought locally consisted of dates, flour, crushed wheat (*burghul*), carrots, onions, coffee and dried fruit. From England they had brought tea, beef tea and vegetable soup squares. For meat they were to rely on hunting hare and gazelle, and on such hospitality as they might receive. Wilfrid dressed in a fine outfit of Arab clothes, not as a disguise but with the practical intention of avoiding too much notice. Anne substituted a *kaffiya* for a hat and threw a badawin cloak over her ordinary 'travelling ulster'.

So they set out on 13 December, having asked no official permission for their journey, and taking pains to slip unobtrusively out of Damascus.

The first week of travelling took them as far as Melakh on the southern edge of the Hauran region, where they hoped to find guides from a Druse shaikh. Here they acquired a Shammari servant, Awwad, and a new camel-man, to replace two of their escort who had already proved useless, and on leaving Melakh they were accompanied by the village headman and another escort. Changing rafiqs as earlier European travellers might have changed post-horses, they went on to a camp of the Bani Sakhr, and thence headed for Kaf (the village at which Guarmani's journey had ended) at the head of the Wadi Sirhan.

Christmas Eve found them travelling in a bitter wind across the last of the Syrian *harra* – not a hard rock landscape like the *harras* Doughty had seen, but the sort where the sandy plain is strewn with large black boulders through which the animals had to pick their way. When they bivouacked that evening in a little wadi, Hanna the cook made them 'a capital curry, which with soup and burghul and a plum-pudding from a tin, makes not a bad dinner'.

After filling their water-skins at rain-pools they moved off again on Christmas morning, making better progress now over easier terrain. With their minds on Christmas dinner the Blunts rode after some gazelles, but neither the mares nor their two greyhounds could outrun the quarry. Then, quite unexpectedly, they saw a solitary young camel grazing not far off. 'Camels found astray in desert places were by acclamation declared the property of the first comers', declares Anne, and though she could not suppress a pang of compassion when the beast was despatched for their Christmas meal, she enjoyed the succulent meat as much as the rest of the party.

A sandstorm blew up in the night, and next day they struggled on through the full fury of the sand-laden blast, since their water-supplies did not allow them to delay. Visibility was almost totally blotted out, and they had difficulty in keeping the party together, but at evening they found some shelter under a clump of tamarisk bushes, where men and animals huddled together with their backs to the gale. At this stop a pack-camel they had bought on the way gave them the slip as soon as he was unloaded, disappearing in the fog of blowing sand, which at once obliterated his tracks.

By the time they reached Kaf next evening, the confident euphoria that Anne had felt a few days earlier had left her. She had been thrown off her camel and had injured her knee. Though she suffered 'indescribable' pain, she resented even more the general impairment to her physical efficiency.

In Kaf they found some of Muhammad ibn Aruk's relations, and heard that there were more in Jauf. Changing rafiqs again they found a man of the Sherarat for the next stage, and after a day's rest set off along the edge of the Wadi Sirhan, a place noted as a haunt of robbers and raiders.

Lady Anne's story is told in diary form, and its narrative style is admirably clear and easy for the modern reader. It moves forward at a brisk pace, often enlivened by astringent comments on people they meet. From it she emerges as a cool, self-assured woman, strong-willed and ready to accept all the hardships of travel. She was totally unsentimental, in strong contrast to the popular idea of the Victorian lady at home who was supposed to be incapable of facing the harsher realities of life. Her keen interest in everything seen on the way shines through her pages, and there is no undue emphasis on the risks which they ran. Above all, the reader is impressed by her sound practical common sense. She is ready to eat all the unconventional food that comes her way, the 'messes' of fly-covered dates offered in the villages, the

young camel for Christmas dinner, and the locusts which their men
collected and fried for her in the Wadi Sirhan. Her grandson has
written that 'Anne was tiny and shy, with something of the wistful
disposition of a mouse or jerboa', but this is not the impression she
gives of herself. Of course, she had the comfort and support of Wilfrid, and in their adventures the passionate interest they both shared
in Arab horses and desert travel carried them along on a wave of
enthusiasm. Towards the end of Wilfrid's life, after a period when
he had been estranged from Anne for many years, he stoutly denied
that she was a timid woman, declaring 'There was never anybody
so courageous as she was. The only thing she was afraid of was the
sea.'

For five days their passage down the wadi was uneventful. Their
Sherari guide lived up to the musical reputation of his tribe and sang
as they marched; they saw a hyena, and for the first time their greyhounds ran a hare to earth and Anne and Wilfrid enjoyed it for supper after four meatless days. But her knee injury was still troublesome, and on 2 January, in a moment of despair, she wrote, 'I sometimes think that I shall never be able to walk again'.

The next day they ran into a 'disagreeable' adventure. Anne
and Wilfrid had tied their mares to some bushes and dismounted for
their midday snack, while their escort with the camels had passed
a few hundred yards on, when they suddenly heard galloping
hooves.

Wilfrid jumped to his feet, looked round and called out, 'Get on
your mare. This is a ghazu.' As I scrambled round the bush to my
mare I saw a troop of horsemen charging down at full gallop with
their lances, not two hundred yards off. Wilfrid was up as he spoke,
and so should I have been, but for my sprained knee. . . . I fell back.
There was no time to think and I had hardly struggled to my feet,
when the enemy was upon us, and I was knocked down by a spear.
Then they all turned on Wilfrid, who had waited for me, some of
them jumping down on foot to get hold of his mare's halter. He
had my gun with him, which I had just before handed to him, but
unloaded; his own gun and his sword being on his delul. He fortunately had on very thick clothes, . . . so the lances did him no harm.
At last his assailants managed to get his gun from him and broke
it over his head, hitting him three times and smashing the stock.
Resistance seemed to me useless, and I shouted to the nearest horse-
man, '*ana dahilak*' (I am under your protection), the usual form
of surrender.

At this point the raiders paused for breath, and then enquired of
Wilfrid and Anne who they were. Together they all walked to the

Blunts' escorting party where Muhammad had formed a square inside the kneeling camels. The normal badawin enquiries established
that the raiders were Ruwala, and Muhammad declared that the
Blunts were 'Franjis, friends of Ibn Shaalan'. Ibn Shaalan, the great
chief of the Ruwala, had been their host in the desert the previous
year, and he 'was bound to protect us, even so far away in the desert,
and none of his people dared meddle with us, knowing this'. The
mares, the gun, and other things which the Blunts had lost in the
scuffle were all restored. 'The young fellows who had taken the mares
made rather wry faces, bitterly lamenting their bad fortune in finding us friends. "Ah the beautiful mares," they said, "and the beautiful gun." . . . Presently we were all on very good terms, sitting in
a circle on the sand, eating dates and passing round the pipe of
peace.' Anne's final verdict on their attackers is characteristic: 'We
liked the look of these young Ruwala. In spite of their rough behaviour, we could see that they were gentlemen. They were very much
ashamed of having used their spears against me . . . they only saw
a person wearing a cloak, and never suspected but that it belonged
to a man.'

A further day's marching, up on the northern flank of the wadi
where they hoped to be safer from raiders, brought them to Jauf.
They had covered the 190 miles from Kaf in eight days.

Jauf, which Palgrave had visited in 1862, was a small walled town,
with outlying houses and palm-gardens on the surrounding plain.
After enquiries the Blunts' party learned that Ibn Aruk's kinsman
lived in one of the outlying settlements, and at his homestead they
were given a friendly welcome. Later that evening official messengers
from the town came to invite Anne and Wilfrid to the governor's
castle, a new fortress that had been built since Palgrave's day, situated just outside the town wall. Judging it prudent to accept, they
moved to camp under the fortress walls. In the absence of the governor they were received by his deputy, Dowass. Anne comments,
'Dowass . . . is a very amiable man and all his soldiers are exceedingly
civil and obliging.' They ate a meal of various unappetising dishes –
'all nasty except the lamb' – but were better pleased later when they
were offered 'a fillet of "wild cow" from the Nafud, baked in the
ashes, one of the best meats I ever tasted'. They assumed this was
some kind of antelope. It was, in fact, oryx.

Since Dowass had told them that they must obtain permission
from the governor, Johar, before proceeding to Hail, they went on
to find him in Sakaka (Meskakeh), the neighbouring town which
he was visiting. In Sakaka they were able to stay with Nassir, the
head of another large family of Ibn Aruk cousins, and were glad
of three days' rest which they enjoyed in his house.

Now that they were among Muhammad's kinsfolk, the matter of

finding a wife for him became of immediate importance, and Anne
lost no time in sounding out the women of the family. It turned out
that their host had a fifteen-year-old niece, and after meeting her
Anne was able to report to Muhammad that the girl was pretty,
intelligent and amiable. For three days Wilfrid spoke for Muhammad in lengthy family discussions and negotiations about the bride-
price, and finally a contract was signed. It was arranged that
Muhammad would come and collect his bride in a year or two.

In between their match-making activities the Blunts had called
on Johar, Ibn Rashid's governor. After accepting a handsome
present of clothes from them he agreed to provide a guide across the
Nafud to Hail.

Anne was excited at the prospect of seeing the Nafud. Although
the established caravan route between Hail and the north lay across
this desert, which held no mysteries for the badu of the area, the
sheer size of it was intimidating, and it presented very real danger
to the unprepared traveller. The regular toll of life which it claimed
had caused the Nafud to become the subject of myths and legends,
and these the Blunts had been hearing from their friends. 'We shall
want all our strength for the next ten days', wrote Anne on the
eve of their departure.

On 12 January they took leave of the Ibn Aruks. 'Wilfrid solemnly
kissed the relations all round ... I went to the harim to say good-
bye to the rest of the family, and fortunately was not expected to
kiss them all round; and then we set out on our way.'

In mid-afternoon they saw 'a red streak on the horizon ... not
unlike a stormy sea seen from the shore, for it rose up as the sea seems
to rise, when the waves are high, above the level of the land'. It was
their first sight of the Nafud.

Anne's diary entry for the next day reflects the exhilaration and
delight which both Blunts felt under the stimulus of new experience.

We have been all day in the Nafud, which is interesting beyond
our hopes, and charming into the bargain. It is, moreover, quite
unlike the description I remember to have read of it by Mr Palgrave, which affects one as a nightmare of impossible horror. It
is true he passed it in summer, and we are now in mid-winter,
but the physical features cannot be much changed by the change
of seasons, and I cannot understand how he overlooked its main
characteristics. The thing that strikes one first about the Nafud is
its colour. It is not white like the sand dunes we passed yesterday,
nor yellow as the sand is in parts of the Egyptian desert, but a really
bright red, almost crimson in the morning when it is wet with the
dew. ... It is however a great mistake to suppose it barren. The
Nafud, on the contrary, is better wooded and richer in pasture than

any part of the desert we have passed in leaving Damascus. It is tufted all over with ghada bushes, and bushes of another kind called *yerta.* . . .

In her first flush of excitement Anne is a little unfair to Palgrave, who did not fail to comment on the desert's colour. She also under-estimated the great difference between conditions in July and in January. Before the end of the crossing she was to find that even in mid-winter the Nafud set the traveller a gruelling test of physical and emotional stamina.

Moving through the red dunes the Blunts noticed that in the apparent confusion of ridges and troughs there was 'a uniformity in the disorder'. They observed a series of huge hollows, some a quarter of a mile across, which to these two horse experts at once suggested the shape of enormous hoof-marks. 'These, though varying in size ... are all precisely alike in shape and direction. They resemble very exactly the track of an unshod horse ... the toe is sharply cut and perpendicular, while the rim of the hoof tapers gradually to nothing at the heel, the frog even being roughly ... represented by broken ground in the centre.' Today it is accepted that the uniform shape of the huge dunes which circle these horse-hoof hollows (called *falj* in Arabic) is due to wind-action. To the Blunts the answer did not seem immediately obvious. 'Wilfrid ... has not been able to decide whether they are owing to the action of wind or water or to the inequalities of the solid ground below. But at present he inclines to the theory of water.'

Two days out from Sakaka they watered and filled their skins at the ancient wells of Shakik, 225 feet deep and lined with cut stone which at the lip was worn into grooves by the rubbing of ropes since time immemorial. Here they found some Ruwala, and were pleas-antly surprised to be recognised by one man who had met them the previous year 500 miles to the north.

Now they faced the real waterless stretch. They expected to take five days at least to Jubba, the wells on the far side, and it might be six or seven. Wilfrid lectured his northern Arabs on the dangers of the great arid tract ahead, and Abdullah was put in charge of the water, which was to be doled out in strict rations.

They were pleased with Radi, the guide provided by Jofar. 'He is a curious little old man, as dry and black and withered as the dead stumps of the yerta bushes one sees here. . . . He has his delul with him, an ancient bag of bones which looks as if it would never last through the journey, and on which he sits perched hour after hour in silence, pointing now and then with his shrivelled hand towards the road we are to take.' When he chose to speak, Radi told them hair-raising tales of travellers who had perished in the desert. In nearly every hollow there were camel bones, and in one *falj* they saw the remains of both men and camels, a Ruwala party which had run out of water and failed to reach Shakik after raiding south-wards ten years before. On the bleached bones dried shreds of skin were still visible.

They could not travel in a straight line, but zigzagged slowly to avoid the steeper slopes and the deeper hollows. They managed about twenty-one miles on the first day out from Shakik, and by good fortune a thunderstorm that night hardened the sand so that the going was firmer and easier for the next day. Radi whiled away the hours by telling more 'blood and bones stories', the most lurid of which concerned a party of Turkish soldiers left to garrison Hail in the days of the first Ibn Rashid. When a long time had passed with no communication from their superiors, about 500 of them de-cided to march home. Ubaid, brother of the first amir (the 'wicked uncle' whom Palgrave met), had resolved to destroy them, and in-structed his guides to abandon the Turks in the middle of the desert. They all perished from thirst, though it was said that some of their horses managed to find their way back to Jubba.

During the morning of 16 January the Blunts sighted on the hori-zon the cheerful landmark of Aalam, the twin conical hills which reassure travellers that they are on the right line for Jubba. When Anne felt some anxiety or doubt she usually refrained from expressing it till her fears were proved groundless. Thus, at the sight of the black sandstone peaks she wrote, 'It was an immense relief to see them, for we had begun to distrust the sagacity of our guide on account of the tortuous line we followed. . . .' Her entry for the day ends, 'I have filled a little bottle with sand to make an hour-glass with at home.'

On their sixth day in the Nafud most of the men dismounted and walked to spare the camels. The party was in good heart, with the Syrians running ahead and playing pranks to keep up their spirits. Abdullah ibn Aruk was especially jovial. 'When there is any particu-larly hard piece of climbing to do and the rest seem fagged [he] generally runs on and stands on his head till they come up. We en-courage this mirth as it makes the work lighter.'

But graver matters could not be pushed out of their minds. Three of the camels were showing signs of distress and there was little fresh pasture which might have provided them with moisture. The next day the camels were weaker and one was incapable of carrying his load. The ebullience of the day before had ebbed, and all of them were in a serious mood towards evening.

The 19th was 'a terrible day for camels and men'. Two of the beasts were too thirsty to eat, and could not stand under their loads; a third was too exhausted to keep up. Wilfrid and Anne were the only ones who rode, though at times Wilfrid persuaded Hanna, the old cook, to mount his mare for a while.

But the end of the waterless crossing was at hand. That afternoon they reached the rocky hills outside Jubba, and with relief left the sand for hard ground. Just after sunset they arrived at the oasis itself. At the end of that day Anne admitted in her diary that she had feared they would never make the crossing, 'adding a new chapter to old Radi's tales of horror'.

Jubba was 'a great bare space in the ocean of sand', with a village of eighty houses, and palm-gardens. Here they stayed two nights, and though the headman treated them hospitably the other villagers were surly, and the word Nasrany (Christian) was bandied about with some show of rudeness.

The Blunts thought they would be the first self-confessed English Christians to reach the Jabal Shammar, and were worried at the unfriendliness of the Jubba people, which seemed a possible foretaste of things to come. They did not know that Doughty had preceded them to Hail. He had left Arabia only six months before they started out, and the story of his travels had not yet reached the world. Accepting as inevitable some hostility from the ordinary people, the Blunts felt that all would depend on the attitude of Ibn Rashid. 'Without his countenance and protection, we should be running considerable risk in entering Hail.' But Anne's brisk common sense soon reasserted itself. 'Still, the die was cast. We had crossed our Rubicon, the Red Desert. . . . There was nothing to be done but to put a good face on things and proceed on our way.' So they set out once more, and took the opportunity as they rode to learn from Radi all they could about Ibn Rashid and affairs at Hail. They heard the full story of Muhammad's blood-stained rise to power, how he killed his four nephews and several cousins, and how the people attributed his childless state to God's anger at his crimes. 'All this', says Anne, 'was anything but agreeable intelligence to us as we travelled on to Hail. We felt as though we were going towards a wild beast's den.' They also heard about Ubaid, the late uncle of the amir, who, though he had never been ruler, had gained a legendary reputation. It was said that Ubaid had given away all his property in his lifetime, and on his death nine years before had left only his sword, his mare, and his young wife. 'These he left to his nephew Muhammad ibn Rashid, the reigning Amir, with the request that his sword should remain undrawn, his mare unridden, and his wife unmarried for ever afterwards. Ibn Rashid had respected his uncle's first two wishes, but he has taken the wife into his own harim.'

Meanwhile they were determined to enjoy the four days' ride which still lay before them. 'There is something in the air of Najd which would exhilarate even a condemned man, and we were far from being condemned.' The high spirits of their companions returned, and in the evenings as they sat round great bonfires of *yerta* their men competed in feats of skill.

During this time they discussed with Muhammad ibn Aruk the way in which they should introduce themselves to the amir of Hail. 'Muhammad will have it that Wilfrid ought to represent himself as a merchant travelling to Basra to recover a debt, but this we will not listen to. ... We intend to tell Ibn Rashid that we are persons of distinction in search of other persons of distinction.' It was a superb example of aristocratic self-confidence, an approach that no other traveller of their time had dared to adopt in Arabia. In words reminiscent of the Queen of Sheba's visit to Solomon, Anne says they will tell Ibn Rashid that they have met all the great shaikhs of the north, and 'each time we have been told that these were nothing in point of splendour to Hail, and that hearing this, and being on our way to Basra, we have crossed the Nafud to visit him. ...' And so it was settled.

Radi fully approved of the dignified attitude they had decided upon, and promised that he would sing the Blunts' praises 'below stairs' in the palace. Now, for the first time, he mentioned that a Franji had already been to Hail, and had gone away with money and clothes from Ibn Rashid. The Blunts were puzzled. 'Who this can be, we cannot imagine, for Mr Palgrave was not known there as a European.'

They reached the Jabal Shammar on 23 January. 'All our journey today has been a romance,' wrote Anne.

> The view in front of us was beautiful beyond description, a perfectly even plain sloping gradually upwards, out of which these rocks and tells cropped up like islands, and beyond it the violet-coloured mountains ... with a precipitous cliff which has been our landmark for several days towering over all. The outline of Jabal Shammar is strangely fantastic, running up into spires and domes and pinnacles, with here and there a loop-hole through which you can see the sky, or a wonderful boulder perched like a rocking-stone. ...

She was quite carried away with delight.

> It is like a dream to be sitting here, writing a journal on a rock in Jabal Shammar. When I remember how, years ago, I read that romantic account by Mr Palgrave, which nobody believed, of an ideal state in the heart of Arabia ... and how impossibly remote and unreal it all appeared; and how, later during our travels, we heard of Najd and Hail and this very Jabal Shammar, spoken of with a kind of awe by all who knew the name, ... I feel that we have achieved something which it is not given to everyone to do.

Wilfrid declares that he shall die happy now, even if we have our heads cut off at Hail.

Early next morning they sent Radi ahead with letters to Ibn Rashid, for they were only a few miles from the capital. While feeling a certain nervousness, they sensibly prepared to create the right impression by putting on their best clothes and making their mares look smart. Soon they met Radi coming back, with a message that the amir would be delighted to receive them and that a guest-house would be prepared for them. 'Nothing more remained for us to do, than to present ourselves at the qasr.' Which they did.

Wilfrid and Anne understood the Arabs well enough to know that an air of authority commands respect. Their letters to Ibn Rashid had evidently struck the right note, for their reception in the square outside the castle was 'everything we could have wished'. They were met by twenty handsomely-dressed palace guards in whose midst stood a venerable old man. He was the chamberlain, but for a moment they thought it might be Ibn Rashid himself. Wilfrid's 'Salaam alaikum' was cordially returned by a chorus of voices, and the Blunts, with Muhammad ibn Aruk, were led to the great pillared coffee-room where Palgrave, Guarmani, and Doughty had been received before them.

After coffee there was a whispering and stirring, and then the assembly rose as Muhammad ibn Rashid arrived. He held out his hand to the three visitors in turn, exchanging the usual salutations with them in the most friendly way. We may imagine that Anne secretly felt some relief when this first encounter went off so well. 'It was plain that we now had nothing to fear.'

In features the famous and much-feared amir recalled to Anne the portraits of Richard III, a parallel inspired by the history of past ruthlessness which the two had in common. Muhammad ibn Rashid's face was lean and sallow, with sunken cheeks, and lips which 'bore an expression of pain except when smiling'. His deep-sunk eyes moved restlessly over the faces of the visitors, and his long, claw-like hands played incessantly with his beads or with his *abba*. 'With all this . . . clothed as he was in purple and fine linen, he looked every inch a king.' The weapons he carried were of a quality to match his status; 'he wore several golden-hilted daggers and a handsome golden-hilted sword, ornamented with turquoises and rubies'. Anne was amazed at the general splendour of apparel to be seen at the court.

This first meeting with Ibn Rashid lasted only a quarter of an hour, and for the rest of the day the visitors were ushered hither and thither about the palace. When the time came for the morning majlis in the square, they were taken down to sit with the amir as he dis-

pensed justice. Of all the Europeans who have described this colourful occasion none was more impressed than the Blunts. 'We were
quite dazzled by the spectacle which met our eyes.' Anne counted
800 of the amir's soldiers lining the square. Behind them there
pressed a great throng of citizens and pilgrims, for the returning Persian hajj had just arrived at Hail.

At one o'clock, when the majlis was over, they were shown to the
house where they were to stay. It was spacious enough for the whole
party, with a courtyard where they could keep their mares. But they
had only an hour in which to relax in privacy before a messenger
summoned them again to an audience with the amir. They found
him alone with his cousin Hamud in an upper room. Muhammad
ibn Aruk had been asked to present the gifts which the Blunts had
brought, but 'we were a little ashamed of their insignificance, for
we had no conception of Ibn Rashid's true position when we left
Damascus, and the scarlet cloth jibbeh we had considered the *ne plus
ultra* of splendour for him looked shabby among the gorgeous dresses
worn at Hail'. They offered in addition a revolver, a good telescope,
and a Winchester rifle, but were left with the feeling that the amir
was not specially impressed. 'Even the rifle was no novelty for he
had an exactly similar one in his armoury,' remarked Anne ruefully.

Muhammad ibn Aruk practically monopolised the conversation
which followed, for Ibn Rashid knew his relations in Jauf, and the
Syrian recounted the legend of his family's migration from Najd in
the distant past. This story had begun to pall a little for Anne, who
had heard it repeatedly on the journey. In fact the Blunts considered
that Ibn Aruk was getting a little above himself and exaggerating
his own importance, and were not sorry when the conversation was
interrupted by the call to afternoon prayer.

After the amir and Hamud had performed their devotions Wilfrid
and Anne were delighted by an invitation to see the palace gardens.
In a walled palm-grove they were shown gazelles, ibexes, and three
oryxes, so that their curiosity about the 'wild cows' was now satisfied.
Passing through an orchard of orange and lemon trees, they came
finally to a third enclosure which was a stable-yard full of mares,
tethered in rows, each to a manger. 'I was almost too excited to look,'
writes Anne, 'for it was principally to see these that we had come
so far.' With a deprecatory wave Ibn Rashid said, 'The horses of
my slaves'. Altogether the Blunts saw about forty mares, eight stallions, and thirty or forty foals, but on this occasion they were allowed
only a brief look, and there was little time to ask questions. 'We had
seen enough, however, to make us very happy. . . . There was no
doubt whatever that, in spite of the Amir's disclaimer, these were
Ibn Rashid's celebrated mares. . . .' From this first hurried view the
Blunts gained the opinion that the Hail animals 'were not comparable

for beauty of form or for quality' with the horses of the Syrian tribes, but they modified this judgement later.

Their tour ended with an anticlimax – an inspection of the royal kitchens, which Ibn Rashid showed off with some pride, for here was prepared the large quantity of food which the palace distributed daily to hundreds of guests and strangers. Back in their lodgings at last, the Blunts were served with dinner brought from these same kitchens. Anne's verdict on their first day in Hail: 'a day of wonderful interest, but not a little fatiguing'.

During the following days Wilfrid and Ibn Aruk paid courtesy calls on the notables of the city, escorted always by a soldier from the palace. Anne wisely did not venture into the streets alone, and spent her days indoors except when they were both invited to the castle. Later comments show how much she hated these days of cloistered idleness.

When the Blunts had met Hamud they had both found this cousin of the amir the more *sympathique* of the two strong men of Hail. In this they agreed with Doughty. Anne comments that 'his manners are certainly as distinguished as can be found anywhere in the world, and he is besides intelligent and well-informed'. She was also much taken with Hamud's eldest son Majid, the boy who appears also in Doughty's story. He had 'the attraction of perfectly candid youth, and quite ideal beauty'.

A unique passage in Anne's book tells of her visit to the women's quarters in the castle. Ibn Rashid seemed gratified at her request to meet his family, and all the women put on their gayest clothes and jewellery when they heard they were to receive the foreign lady. Led by a slave down many tortuous alleys in the palace, Anne came finally to the ladies' reception room, where she was received by Amusheh, the principal wife.

All the persons present rose to their feet when I arrived. Amusheh could easily be singled out from among the crowd, even before she advanced to do the honours.... But she, the daughter of Ubaid and sister of Hamud, has every right to outshine friends, relatives and fellow-wives. Her face ... is sufficiently good-looking, with a well-cut nose and mouth, and something singularly sparkling and brilliant. Hedusheh and Lulya, the next two wives ... had gold brocade as rich as hers, and lips and cheeks smeared as red as hers with carmine, and eyes with borders kohled as black as hers, but lacked her charm.

Of the women's clothing, Anne remarks:

The rich clothes worn by Amusheh and her companion wives are somewhat difficult to describe, presenting as they did an appearance of splendid shapelessness. . . . Amusheh wore crimson and gold, and round her neck a mass of gold chains studded with turquoises and pearls. Her hair hung down in four long plaits, plastered smooth with some reddish stuff, and on top of her head stuck a gold and turquoise ornament like a small plate, about four inches in diameter.

Every woman also wore a nose-ring, an inch and a half to two inches across, attached by a chain to the side lappet of the gold cap. 'It is worn in the left nostril, but taken out and left dangling while the wearer eats and drinks. . . . A most inconvenient ornament, I thought and said. . . . But fashion rules the ladies at Hail as in other places, and my new acquaintances only laughed at such criticisms.'

Amusheh was very chatty, and volunteered much information about the various relationships within the Rashid family, facts which Anne received without showing any curiosity. Later, Amusheh insisted that Anne go upstairs to see her bedroom. 'This apartment was well carpeted, and contained . . . a large bed, or couch, composed of a pile of mattresses, with a velvet and gold counterpane spread over it; also a kind of press or cupboard, a box rather clumsily made of dark wood, ornamented by coarse, thin plaques of silver stuck on it here and there.' On the floor in front of this cupboard were 'three or four rows of china and crockery of a common sort, and a few Indian bowls, all arranged on the floor like articles for sale in the streets'. Amusheh was childishly eager for the visitor's approval, and Anne's reaction was suitably diplomatic.

Next Anne went to the quarters of Hamud's wife, Beneyeh. Here, much to her surprise, three armchairs were produced. 'On these I and Beneyeh and the second-class wife sat, drinking tea out of tea-cups, with saucers and teaspoons.' When Beneyeh too wished to take Anne to see her bedchamber, Anne found a quite different and rather more interesting room. It contained several European articles of furniture, an iron bedstead, some looking-glasses, and a clock with weights. But the most surprising feature of the room was that the walls were decorated with weapons.

There were eighteen or twenty swords, and several guns and daggers, arranged with some care and taste as ornaments. The guns were all very old-fashioned things, with long barrels, but most of them beautifully inlaid with silver. . . . The swords, or sword-hilts, were of various degrees of richness. . . . Unfortunately at the moment I did not think of Ubaid and his three wishes, and so forgot to ask Beneyeh whether Ubaid's sword was among these; it would not have done to inquire about the widow, but there would have been no impropriety in asking about the sword.

After a third visit to another of Hamud's wives, Anne was summoned away by a slave who said that the Beg – the respectful title by which Wilfrid was known – wished her to join him in the *kahwa*.

She had one more chance to see inside a harem when a few days later she called on the wife of Hamud's uncle Sulaiman. 'Ghut, his wife, was the stupidest person I had seen at Hail, but very talkative, and hospitable, with dates, fresh butter floating in its own butter-milk, and sugar-plums.' Anne was introduced to a married daughter named Zehowa, and gives a sample of the conversation she held with this young lady. The active and adventurous English-woman found it hard to understand how these women could be con-tent with a life of total idleness.

'Then you never ride as we do?' she asked Zehowa.

'No, we have no mares to ride.'

'What a pity! and don't you ever go into the country outside Hail . . .?'

'Oh no, of course not.'

'But to pass the time, what do you do?'

'We do nothing.'

'I should die if I did nothing,' said Anne emphatically. 'When I am at home I always walk round the first thing in the morning to look at my horses.'

The pleasantest part of Anne's day was the evening when the amir regularly invited them to visit him, though Anne admits that she never felt quite at ease in his presence, remembering 'the horrible story of his usurpation'. Of the great Ibn Rashid she comments: 'He has something of the spoiled child in his way of wandering on from one subject to another; and ... of asking questions which he does not always wait to hear answered.' But at these meetings she enjoyed hearing desert news of the Ruwala and the Shammar whom they had known in the north. Far from sitting back and letting the men talk she took an active part in the discussions. For Ibn Rashid this must have been a novel experience, for he had never met a European woman, let alone one so spirited and intelligent as Anne. On one occasion the amir produced 'one of those toys called telephones, which were the fashion last year in Europe. This the Amir caused two of his slaves to perform with, one going into the courtyard out-side, and the other listening. ... We expressed great surprise, as in duty bound; indeed it was the first time we had actually seen the toy, and it is singular to find so very modern an invention already at Hail.'

When the opportunity arose, they talked about horses, 'and our knowledge on this head caused general astonishment'. Since horses were the Blunts' major interest it is natural that Anne devotes a whole chapter of her book to the subject, giving detailed descriptions of some of the finer animals in Ibn Rashid's stables. With the rise of Ibn Rashid's power his horses had become the most celebrated in Arabia, taking pride of place from the Saudi stud at Riyadh which was dispersed after the death of Faisal the Great. Though the horses in the palace yard were ungroomed and practically never exercised, Anne realised on a closer look that under the slovenly appearance were some very fine animals: 'mounted and in motion, these at once became transfigured'.

From their discussions with the amir they learned that in the drier areas of central Arabia the camel was the more practical beast for everyday use, and that horses were kept only for prestige and for raiding, 'and looked upon as far too precious to run unnecessary risks'.

All seemed to be going well on their visit to Hail, but then, after four days, the amir's cordiality towards the Blunts suddenly cooled. On the fifth day they were not invited to the evening party, and on the sixth Wilfrid was refused admission when he called at the palace. They were filled with anxiety, and feared that this change of mood indicated imminent danger. But Mubarak, the chief slave at the palace, solved the mystery; he told Wilfrid that Muhammad ibn Aruk was the cause of the trouble. His vanity had 'led him to aggrandise his own position in the eyes of Ibn Rashid's court, by representing us as persons whom he had taken under his protection and who were in some way dependent upon him'. Wilfrid reproved Ibn Aruk severely, and explained the true position to the palace chamberlain. The same evening they were invited once more to the palace and good relations were restored. 'Still the incident was a lesson and warning ... that Hail was a lion's den, though fortunately we were friends with the lion. We began to make our plans for moving on.'

Before they left they enjoyed an occasion which remained one of their most vivid memories of Hail. Anne and Wilfrid rode out with Ibn Rashid to the plain where the Persian pilgrim caravan was camped, and where the amir's soldiers and mares were preparing to give a display of horsemanship. 'We saw what we would have come the whole journey to see ... all the best of the Amir's horses out and galloping about.' After tedious days in town Anne felt alive once again. 'It was one of those mornings one only finds in Najd. The air brilliant and sparkling to a degree one cannot imagine in Europe, ... The sky of an intense blue, and the hills in front of us carved out of sapphire.'

Hamud and the other horsemen galloped over the plain and indulged in sham fights, charging and doubling back, yelling with badawin zest.

At last the Amir could resist it no longer, and seizing a ... palm-stick from one of the slaves, went off himself among the others. In a moment his dignity was forgotten, and he became the Bedouin again which he and his family really are, ... bare-headed with his long Bedouin plaits streaming in the wind and bare-legged and bare-armed, he galloped hither and thither.

While they were out on the plain, Wilfrid met the chief personage of the Persian hajj, and decided that it would be a good idea for himself and Anne, with their party, to travel to Najaf in Iraq with the pilgrim caravan. Ibn Rashid later approved the plan when they consulted him. They bought two new camels, and supplies of rice and dates for the journey, and the amir gave them some excellent coffee. On 1 February they took formal leave of Muhammad ibn Rashid, and paid a farewell visit to Hamud which was one 'of friendly regard more than of ceremony'; then they mounted and rode out of town.

With the city behind them Wilfrid and Anne each drew a long sigh of relief, 'for Hail with all the charm of its strangeness, and its interesting inhabitants, had come to be like a prison to us, and at one time when we had that quarrel with Muhammad, had seemed very like a tomb'.

Part of the Persian hajj was already on its way, but large numbers of pilgrims still lingered in the city. Wilfrid and Anne wanted to travel close enough to the caravan for security, but not close enough to mingle with the throng. They did not consider themselves under the discipline of the Amir al Hajj, the caravan marshal, and when the caravan camped ten miles out of Hail and waited three days for the stragglers to catch up, the Blunts moved on ahead, but not too far. They amused themselves with a hawk they had bought in Hail, which they hoped would catch hare and bustard.

On 5 February, waiting on a hilltop as the hajj moved forward again, they enjoyed the spectacle of the whole vast caravan coming towards them across the plain, 4,000 camels in a procession three miles long, with hundreds of men on foot. Out in front were a group of dervishes and others who walked out of piety, but the real head of the procession was the mounted troop of caparisoned camels, in the midst of which was the bearer of Ibn Rashid's standard, a great purple flag with a green border and a white inscription in the middle. Ambar, the negro Amir al Hajj, was usually with this group. Many of the richer Persian pilgrims rode in various forms of litter, including one elaborate type which required two camels or mules to carry it.

Although Ibn Aruk and their servants would have preferred to stay with the hajj, the Blunts were finding the pace of the caravan too slow, and by the sixth day out they decided to make their own

way at a faster speed. This became possible when they met a Shammari lad who was ready to act as their guide. It was about 400 miles
to Najaf, and they had laid in provisions for what they estimated
would be twenty days' journey. A week had now passed and they
were still only twenty miles from Hail; they could not afford to loiter
any longer.

Led by Izzar the Shammari, they skirted the southern edge of the
Nafud for three days, then turned north after Shaybeh wells. They
were now on the well-trodden track of the old hajj road from Iraq
to Buraida. Here the Blunts sighted an animal in the distance and
gave chase. It turned out to be a hyena, which the dogs held at bay
while Wilfrid shot it. The servants prepared it for supper. 'Wilfrid
pronounces it eatable, but I, though I have just tasted a morsel, could
not bring myself to make a meal off it', says Anne. This was the only
time she decided she could not stomach one of the dishes of their
improvised desert fare.

Though they wasted time on a detour to Torba, where Ibn
Rashid's guards would not allow them to draw water, they made good
progress in the next four days. In the evenings they could see the
zodiacal light. 'It is a very remarkable and beautiful phenomenon,
seen only, I believe in Arabia. It is a cone of light extending from
the horizon half-way to the zenith, and is rather brighter than the
Milky Way.' She was, of course, wrong in this; the 'light' varies in
brightness and can be seen elsewhere. By now they had come
to the series of cisterns built along the pilgrim-route by Zubaida,
queen of Caliph Harun al Rashid. Many were ruinous, but a few
still held some water.

On 14 February they ran into a group of badawin who were from
the camp of Muttlak ibn Aruk, head of yet another branch of that
widely-scattered family, and they made a diversion of two days' journey to meet him. After they had been entertained by him for a day,
the hajj procession, now at its full strength, double its former size,
caught up with them and swept past. From now on they travelled
with the caravan.

A drum-beat in the early morning was the signal for the procession
to move off daily, and a brisk pace was set, about three miles an
hour, with no stopping. But on 20 February the Blunts were puzzled
when the hajj did not move off at the usual time. They found that
Ambar, the official leader, had ordered the delay 'so that he may
send the hat round for a private contribution to his own benefit'.
The following day the caravan was hurried forward to make up for
lost time and did over thirty miles. Two of the Blunts' camels now
showed signs of exhaustion. The flour they had brought to feed them
was finished and there was little pasture. When their route took them
up a steep escarpment the next day, one of their beasts collapsed

and they had to abandon him. 'We left him, I am glad to say, in a bit of a wady, where there was some grass, but I fear his chance is a small one.' Many of the camels in the caravan were terribly thin after several days of forced marching when their riders would not stop to let them graze. Among the pilgrims, too, all but the richest were short of food. But everyone recognised the need to proceed as fast as possible.

After four hard days, averaging about twenty-eight miles a day, the caravan reached Qasr Ruhaim, a Turkish outpost on the edge of the Euphrates district. The last day had been a terrible one, ten hours of marching against a bitterly cold north wind which blew sand constantly into their faces. The Blunts had lost no more camels, but 'many of the pilgrims' camels, sixty, or some say seventy, lay down and died on the road. . . . In the last six days we have marched a hundred and seventy miles, the greater part of the Haj on foot and almost fasting.' It was a marvellous relief at Ruhaim to camp amid green grass on the bank of a running stream.

On the morning of 27 February they were cheered by the sight of the golden dome of the mosque of Ali rising above the town of Najaf, which topped a line of cliffs on the far side of a lake. But they still had a tedious twenty-mile march round the lake. 'It was a beautiful sight as far as nature was concerned, but made horrible by the sufferings of the poor dying camels, which now lay thick upon the road, with their unfortunate owners, poor Bedouins perhaps with nothing else in the world, standing beside them. . . .' Many camels went into the lake to drink, and lay down there never to rise again. The pilgrims complained that it was the Amir al Hajj's delay outside Hail which had made the journey so hard.

When they had to climb the cliff below Najaf, 'the camels lay down by scores, among the rest our beautiful camel Amud. . . . Between five and six hundred must have perished thus today.' But once at the top, the pilgrim caravan had reached its destination. Wilfrid had estimated it would take twenty days; in the event it had been twenty-seven, with the last few a real test of endurance.

After resting and buying supplies in Najaf, Anne and Wilfrid moved on to Baghdad in a more leisurely fashion, and there they were welcomed at the British Residency. 'On the 6th of March we slept once more in beds, having been without that luxury for almost three months.' Their Arabian journey was over.

In 1881 the Blunts bought the estate of Shaikh Obeyd in Egypt, and divided their time between this home and Crabbet Park. Wilfrid became more and more involved in political interests, and Anne did her best to support him financially and morally. But in 1906 they parted, and he stayed in Sussex while she returned to Shaikh Obeyd, where she died in 1917. Their daughter, Lady Wentworth, embittered against her father, was later to write of Lady Anne that Wilfrid 'played havoc with her heart, wrecked her life and, jealous of her intellectual gifts, appropriated the credit of her brains to himself with shameless arrogance'. But in Arabia they had been happy together. She was the first European woman to penetrate the heart of the peninsula, and remains one of the most attractive and sympathetic figures among the great travellers of her age.

Glossary of Arabic Words and Phrases

abba Arab cloak
Allah akbar! God is great!
burqhul crushed wheat
dakhilak binding plea for sanctuary
dira area of particular tribe
dishdasha man's white gown
dowla authority or official
falj hollow between sand dunes
fatihah opening verses of Koran, recited in prayer
Galla black man, Abyssinian
ghazzu badawin raid, foray
hajj pilgrimage to Mecca
hakim doctor or wise man
haramieh thieves
Haram holy precincts of Mecca
harem women's quarter
harra rough terrain of volcanic rock
Hegira 'flight' of Prophet, marks beginning of Muslim era
ihram special pilgrim garb, consisting of two pieces of seamless cloth
imam religious leader
jabal mountain (often used for hill)
jambiyah dagger
kadhi local magistrate
kaffiya Arab head-cloth
kahwa coffee or coffee room
kavass (Turkish) armed servant or guide
khatib preacher
kiswa black-and-gold covering of Kaaba at Mecca
labbai, labbaik 'Here am I', at thy service. Devotional cry at Mecca
lisam, litham badu face mask made by tying ends of *kaffiya* across nose, mouth and chin
mahmal camel litter of ceremonial type
majilis assembly or council
mashab camel stick
mereesy dried milk cake
mizrak weapon, primitive incendiary device
moghreby, moghrib Occidental
muhallil special guide at Mecca who contracts formal marriage to enable divorced or widowed women to perform pilgrimage
muharramat acts forbidden by Islamic law
mutowwaf pilgrim guide or escort at Mecca

muzowwar   pilgrim guide or escort at Madina

nafud   sand dunes

nasrany   Christian

qasr, kasra   a fort or palace

rafiq, rafik   traveller's escort who vouches for him in specific tribal territory

raju, saduk   truthful or honest man

Raudha   section of mosque at Madina, literally 'garden'

rikat, ruka'at   symbolic movements associated with each of the salah, the five obligatory daily prayers of the Muslim

sai   'the running', ceremony at Mecca

samn   sheep's butter

sharif   noble, also used as titles of rulers of *Hijaz*

shugduf   camel litter

tawaf, towaf   ritual circumambulation of the Kaaba at Mecca

takbir   symbolic gesture at beginning of Muslim prayer

tahlil   completion of first movement of prayer, derived with above from *Allah akbar!*

ta kruri   hajji, usually from Africa

thelul, dhalul   fast female riding camel

ukhlus!   finish! have done!

umra   the 'little pilgrimage', consisting of visit to certain holy places at Mecca

wadi   valley, depression

zair   pilgrim visitor to holy places at Madina

ziyara   excursion to holy places around Madina

zemzem   holy watering well at Mecca, associated with legend of Hagar and Ishmael

Bibliographical Notes

GENERAL SECTION

Ali Bey, *Travels of Ali al Abbassi, alias Domingo Badia y Lieblich of Cadiz between 1803 and 1807*, London, 1816.

Avril, Adolphe D., *L'Arabie contemporaine, avec la description du pèlerinage à la Mecque*, Paris, 1868.

Blunt, Lady Anne, *Bedouin Tribes of the Euphrates*, London, 1879.

Brydges, Sir H. Jones, *A Brief History of the Wahauby* (Vol. II of *An Account of the Transactions of His Majesty's Mission to the Court of Persia*), London, 1834.

Burckhardt, J. L., *Notes on the Bedouins and Wahabys*, 2 vols, London, 1831.

Carruthers, A. D. M., *Arabian Adventure to the Great Nafud*, London, 1935.

De Boncheman, A., *Matériel de la vie Bedouine*, Institut Francais, Damascus, 1934.

De Gaury, Gerald, *Rulers of Mecca*, Harrap, London, 1951.

Euting, J., *Tagbuch einer Reise in Inner-Arabien*, Leyden, 1914.

Gibb, H. A. R., *Travels of Ibn Battuta*, 1325–54, an abbreviated translation, London, 1929.

Heyd, W., *Histoire du commerce du Levant au moyen age*, Leipzig, 1885.

Halevy, J., *Rapport sur une mission archaeologie dans le Yemen*, Paris, 1872.

Hitti, P. K., *The History of the Arabs*, Macmillan, London, 1940.

Hurgronje, C. Snouck, *Mekka*, The Hague, 1888.

Jomard, Edmé F., *Études géographiques et historiques sur l'Arabie*, Paris, 1839.

Kiernan, R. H., *The Unveiling of Arabia*, Harrap, London, 1937.

Lane Poole, S., *The Mohammadan Dynasties*, Constable, 1893.

Laemmens, H., *Le berceau de l'Islam, l'Arabie occidentale à la veille de l'hégire*, Rome, 1914.

Muir, Sir William, *The Caliphate, Its Rise, Decline and Fall* (Ed. T. W. Weir), Grant, London, 1924.
—— *The Mameluke or Slave Dynasty of Egypt, AD 1260–1517*, Smith, Elder, 1896.

Musil, A., *Arabia Petraea*, 4 vols, Vienna 1907–8.
—— *Arabia Deserta: A Topographical Itinerary*, New York, 1927.
—— *The Manners and Customs of the Rwala Bedouins*, New York, 1928.
—— *Northern Nejd: A Topographical Itinerary*, New York, 1928.

O'Leary, de Lacy, *Arabia before Muhammad*, Kegan Paul, London, 1923.

Rutter, E., *The Holy Cities of Arabia*, Putnam, New York & London, 1928.

Wallin, G. A., 'Report on a Journey to Hail and in Nejd', *Journal of the Royal Geographical Society*, Vol. XXIV, 1854.

Wollaston, A. N., *The Pilgrimage to Mecca*, Leyden, 1880.

Wuestenfeld, F., *Chroniken der Stadt Mekka*, Leipzig, 1857.

LODOVICO VARTHEMA

Varthema, Lodovico, *Itinerario de Lodovico Varthema Bolognese nello Egypto nella Persia nella India e nella Ethiopia*. First published by S. G. Loreno and H. de Nani for L. de Henricis da Carneto, Rome, 1510. Latin edition: *Ludovico Patrii Romani novum Itinerarium Ethiopiae, Egypti, etc.*, Milan, 1511.

Alboquerque, Alfonso d', *Commentaries*, Hakluyt Series, London, 1875.

Burton, Sir Richard, Appendix to *Pilgrimage to Al-Medinah and Meccah*, Memorial edition, London, 1893. An abridged account of Varthema's *Itinerary* taken from Hakluyt. Burton states that the first English translation appeared in Richard Eden's *Decades*, AD 1555. This is incorrect. Eden's translation from the Latin was included in *The History of Travel in the West and East Indies*, 'Navigation and Voyages of Lewes Wertomannus', edited by Richard Willes in 1577.

Casamassima, Emanuele, *Itinerario del Varthema*, Rome, 1962.

Hakluyt's *Voyages, Navigation and Voyages of Lewes Wertomannus*, from the translation of Richard Eden, Vol. IV, 1811.

Hakluyt Society, John Winter Jones' translation edited by G. P. Badger, London, 1863.

Hogarth, D. G., *The Penetration of Arabia*, London, 1904; Clarendon Press, 1922.

Penzer, N. M., Introduction to J. Winter Jones' translation, Argonaut Press, London, 1928. With a discourse by Sir Richard Carnac Temple.

Purchas, Samuel the Elder, *Hakluytus Posthumus or Purchas His Pilgrimes*, 1625, Eden's translation corrected according to Ramusio. Re-issued by the University Press, Glasgow, 1905.

Ramusio, G. B., *Raccolta di Navigationi e Viaggi*, Vol. I, Rome, 1554.

Recueil de Voyages, Les Voyages de Ludovico di Varthema, Vol. IX, Paris, 1888. Translated from the Italian by J. de Raconis Balarin. Quotes San Filippo as suggesting that Varthema may have been of German origin, since families with the Germanic names Wartmann and Wertheim were well known in the Bologna district.

San Filippo, Pietro Amato di, *Bibliografia dei Viaggiatori Italiana*, Rome, 1874. Lists seven editions of Varthema's work in Italian and Latin. The British Library lists many more prior to that date.

JOSEPH PITTS

Pitts, Joseph, *A true and faithful Account of the religion and manners of the Muhammadans*, etc. Printed by S. Forley for Philip Bishop and Edward Score in High Street, Exeter, 1704. Second edition printed and published in Exeter, 1717. Third edition, dedicated to Baron Ockham, the Lord Chancellor, corrected, and published in London by Osborn, Longman and Hett at the Ship in Paternoster Row and the Bible and Crown in the Poultry, 1731, with Pitts' drawing of the Great Mosque at Mecca. In his preface to the third edition the author complained bitterly that the second edition was published without his permission and that it contained many inaccuracies.

Burton, Sir Richard, Appendices to *Pilgrimage to Al-Medinah and Meccah*, Memorial edition. A précis of Pitts' account.

Foster, Sir William, *The Red Sea and Adjacent Countries*, Hakluyt Society Transactions Series II, Vol. C; Oxford University Press, 1949.

World Displayed, The: Pitts' Journey Described, Vol. 17, 1774.

Pitts was living in Exeter in May 1731, aged 68. Place and date of death are not known. (According to Exeter City Librarian, letter to authors, 1973, relevant records were destroyed by enemy action in the Second World War.) When he came to write his book, Pitts had the advantage of being able to refer to the works of some Arab and European historians. The first geography of Arabia was published at the Medici Press in 1592, containing material from the *Book of Climates*, a Ptolemaic account of the known world compiled by Idrisi in Sicily in the twelfth century. That geography was subsequently published in Paris, 1619, as *Geographia Nubiensis*. In 1650 Dr Pococke rendered its description of Mecca into English. Jean de Thevenot had also brought some of the major Arabic authorities to notice in his *Journeaux*, the Arabic parts of which came out between 1674 and 1684. Lovell produced an English translation in 1687. Pitts had certainly read de Thevenot, for in correcting one of the Frenchman's references to Mecca he observed: 'M. de Thevenot ... is very exact in almost everything of Turkish matters; and I pay much deference to that great author.' D'Herbelot's *Bibliotheque Orientale* was published in 1697, though Pitts may not have had access to the work since no English version was available at the time he wrote.

CARSTEN NIEBUHR

Niebuhr, Carsten, *Reisebeschreibung nach Arabien und andern umliegenden Laendern*, Copenhagen, 1772. First English edition, *Travels in Arabia*, London, 1792.

Forsskal, Dr Peter, *Descriptiones Animalium, etc, et Flora Aegyptiaco-Arabica*, Copenhagen, 1775 (posthumous).

Arabien: Dokumente zur Entdeckungsgeschichte, Niebuhr's Reise in den Yemen, p. 72, Stuttgart, 1965.

Hansen, Thorkild, *Arabia Felix*, Gregg International, London, 1964.

Hogarth, D. G., op. cit.

Stern, H. A., *Journal of a Missionary Journey into Arabia Felix*, London, 1858.

JEAN LOUIS BURCKHARDT

Burckhardt, J. L., *Travels in Arabia*, London, 1829. Also *Travels in Nubia*, with biographical sketch, 1819; *Travels in Syria and the Holy Land*, 1822; *Arabic Proverbs, or the Manners and Customs of the Modern Egyptians*, 1830; *Notes on the Bedouins and Wahabys*, 1831.

Arabien, op. cit., *Burckhardt's Reise nach Mekka und Medina*, p. 101.

Hogarth, D. G., op. cit.

Sim, Katherine, *Desert Traveller*, Gollancz, London, 1969.

RICHARD BURTON

Burton, Sir Richard, *Pilgrimage to Al-Medinah and Meccah*, London, 1855. Memorial edition, with preface by Lady Isabel Burton, 1893.

Burton, Lady, *Life of Sir Richard Burton*, London, 1893. Second edition with preface by W. H. Wilkins, 1895.

Brodie, Fawn, *The Devil Drives*, Eyre & Spottiswoode, London, 1967.

Hogarth, D. G., op. cit.

Penzer, N. M., *Selected Papers*, an edited version of Burton's views on anthropology, travel and exploration, London, 1924.

Sadleir, G., *Diary of a Journey Across Arabia*, etc., Bombay, 1866.

Wright, Thomas, *Life of Sir Richard Burton*, London, 1906.

W. G. PALGRAVE

Palgrave, W. G., *Personal Narrative of a Year's Journey Through Central and Eastern Arabia*, London, 1865; Gregg International, 1969.

Allen, Mea, *Palgrave of Arabia*, Macmillan, London, 1972.

Philby, H. St J., *The Heart of Arabia*, Constable, London, 1922; *Arabia of the Wahhabis*, Constable, London 1928, *et al.*

CARLO GUARMANI

Guarmani, Carlo, *Northern Nejd: Journey from Jerusalem to Anaiza in Kasim*, Press of the Franciscan Fathers, Jerusalem, 1866. Edited version prepared by Douglas Carruthers for Arab Bureau, Cairo, 1917. Translated by Lady Capel-Cure and introduced by Douglas Carruthers, London, 1938.

Guarmani, Carlo, *El Kamsa*, Rome, 1864.

Hogarth, D. G., op. cit.

Visit to Khaibar, p. 202. Neither Guarmani nor Doughty appears to have known that Varthema had been there.

C. M. DOUGHTY

Doughty, C. M., *Travels in Arabia Deserta*, Cambridge University Press, Cambridge, 1888. New edition published by Philip Lee Warner and Jonathan Cape, London, 1921, with introduction by T. E. Lawrence. Definitive edition in two volumes, Cape, 1936; paperback edition, Cape, 1964.

Arabien, op. cit., *Doughty's Reise durch Innerarabien*, p. 180.

Hogarth, D. G., *The Life of Charles M. Doughty*, London, 1928.

WILFRID AND LADY ANNE BLUNT

Blunt, Lady Anne, *A Pilgrimage to Nejd*, London, 1881; Frank Cass, 1968.

Assad, Thomas J., *Three Victorian Travellers*, Routledge, London, 1964 (studies of Burton, Blunt, Doughty).

Hogarth, D. G., *The Penetration of Arabia*, op. cit.

Lytton, Earl of, *W. S. Bunt*, London, 1961.

Diary of Major Journeys of Exploration in Arabia, from AD 1500

1503–08   Lodovico Varthema: Damascus, Hijaz, Yemen
1607   Johann Wild: Cairo, Hijaz, Mocha
1687c   Joseph Pitts: Hijaz, Cairo
1762–7   Carsten Niebuhr: Yemen, Aleppo
1806–15   Ulrich Seetzen: Petra, Sinai, Cairo, Hijaz, Yemen
1807   Ali Bey al-Abbasi (Domingo Badia y Lieblich): Hijaz
1814–15   J. L. Burckhardt: Petra, Hijaz
1818–19   Capt. George F. Sadlier: Hasa, Najd, Madina
1830   J. R. Wellsted: Suez, Red Sea Coast (with 'Palinurus' expedition led by Captain Moresby)
1835   J. R. Wellstead and Charles Cruttenden: South Arabian coast (Palinurus expedition)
1835–6   J. R. Wellstead: Oman
1836   Charles Cruttenden: Yemen
1843   Th. J. Arnaud: Yemen
1843   A. von Wrede: Hadramaut
1845–8   Dr G. A. Wallin: Wadi Sirhan, Hail, Tabuk, Taima
1853   Lt. R. F. Burton: Hijaz
1860   H. von Maltzan: Hijaz
1862   W. G. Palgrave: Syria, Nafud, Najd to Riyadh, Hasa
1864   Carlo Guarmani: Jerusalem, Taima, Khaibar, Hail, Sirhan
1865   Col. Lewis Pelly: Kuwait to Najd (Riyadh)
1870   J. Halevy: Yemen
1870   S. B. Miles and W. Munzinger: hinterland, Aden to Hadramaut
1876   C. M. Doughty: northern and central Arabia
1878–84   Charles Huber: northern and central Arabia (three journeys)
1878–9   W. S. and Lady Anne Blunt: Najd, Hail
1882–4   E. Glaser: northern Yemen
1883–4   J. Euting: northern Arabia, inscriptions of Dedan
1885   C. Snouck Hurgronje: Hijaz (definitive record of Mecca)
1885–6   E. Glaser: southern Yemen (ruins of Zafar)
1892–4   E. Glaser: Yemen (inscriptions of Sana)
1893   Baron Nolde: northern Arabia, Nafud, Hail
1901–06   Major Percy Cox: Oman
1906–08   Col. S. G. Knox: Kuwait hinterland, Al Hasa
1907–10   A. Jaussen and R. Savignac: Hijaz, Taima, Dedan (ruins)
1909   Capt. D. Carruthers: northern and west-central deserts
1908–10   A. Musil: Hijaz and northern Arabia
1910–17   Capt. G. Leachman: northern, central and eastern Arabia
1911–13   Capt. W. H. I. Shakespear: north-eastern Arabia, Kuwait hinterland (south Arabian inscriptions)

1912	Barclay Raunkiaer: eastern and central Arabia
1913–14	Gertrude Bell: Damascus, Hail, Baghdad
1913–14	Capt. W. H. I. Shakespear: central Arabia, east–west crossing
1915	A. Musil: Nafud and Jabal Shammar
1917	H. St J. Philby: Persian Gulf to Red Sea through Najd
1918	H. St J. Philby: central Arabia to northern part of Empty Quarter
1924	Capt. R. E. Cheesman: northern region of Empty Quarter
1927–8	C. Rathjens and H. von Wissman: Yemen (al-Huqqa)
1928	B. Thomas: Muskat, Oman, Dofar
1930	B. Thomas: Dofar and southern hinterland of Empty Quarter
1930–1	B. Thomas: crossing of Empty Quarter from south to north
1932	H. St J. Philby: Empty Quarter, Hufuf, Yabrin, Sulayil
1934	W. H. Ingrams: Hadramaut
1934	Freya Stark: Hadramaut
1936	H. St J. Philby: Jidda, Nejran, ruins of Sabwa, Hadramaut, Asir
1938	Freya Stark: Hadramaut
1939	D. van der Meulen and H. von Wissman: Aden to Hadramaut
1945–8	W. Thesiger: Hadramaut, Empty Quarter, eastern Arabia

INDEX

Index